THE POLITICS OF EDUCATION
AT THE LOCAL, STATE AND FEDERAL LEVELS

edited by
Michael W. Kirst
Stanford University

70197

McCutchan Publishing Corporation
2526 Grove Street
Berkeley, California 94704

Standard Book Number: 8211-1009-8
Library of Congress Catalog Card Number: 75-100956

TABLE OF CONTENTS

Introduction to the Selections v
Contributors xii

Part I
Political Influence in Local Education Policy Making 1

Editor's Introduction to Part I 3

A. Politics of Education in Large Cities
Schools and Politics in the Big City 17
    Robert H. Salisbury
Fiscal Status and School Policy Making in Six Large School Districts 33
    Marilyn Gittell, T. Edward Hollander, and William S. Vincent
The School Budget Process in Large Cities 74
    H. Thomas James, James A. Kelly, and Walter Garms
Administrator-Teacher Relations: Harmony or Conflict 90
    Alan Rosenthal
New Voices in Public Education 101
    Alan Rosenthal
Political Issues in School Decentralization 111
    Robert F. Lyke
Politics of School Desegregation 133
    Robert L. Crain

B. Politics of Education in Suburbs
School Government 146
    Roscoe Martin
Educational Decision-Making in Suburban Politics 167
    David Minar
Politics Without Power 183
    Robert L. Stout and Gerald E. Sroufe
A Suburban School Superintendent Plays Politics 191
    Lesley H. Browder

Part II
Politics of Education at the State Level

Editor's Introduction to Part II 215

Schoolmen and Politics:
A Study of State Aid to Education in the Northeast 220
    Stephen Bailey, Robert T. Frost, Paul E. Marsh and Robert C. Wood
Michigan: The Lack of Consensus 251
    Nicholas Masters, Robert H. Salisbury, and Thomas H. Eliot
State Politics of Education 284
    Laurence Iannaccone
The Socio-Economic, Political and Fiscal Environment
of Educational Policy-Making in Large Cities 300
    Alan K. Campbell

Part III
Politics of Education at the Federal Level

Editor's Introduction to Part III 321

For the Young, Schools 326
    James L. Sundquist
The Office of Education and the Education Act of 1965 357
    Stephen K. Bailey
ESEA–The Office of Education Administers a Law 384
    Edith K. Mosher and Stephen K. Bailey
The Case for General Aid 399
    Albert H. Quie
The Case for Categorical Aid 403
    John Brademas

INTRODUCTION TO THE SELECTIONS

Objectives of the Volume

In recent years there has been a new interest in conducting research on the politics of education. We have just begun to explore political behavior in education policy making and as yet no general operational theories have emerged. Nevertheless, there have been a substantial number of comparative case studies and surveys that focus on the same policy outputs (curriculum, facilities, budget, etc.), and these studies have disclosed surprisingly uniform findings about who wields influence in American school politics. For instance, the political influence of the superintendent (and/or the bureaucracy) appears to dominate most spheres of urban and suburban school policy. The formal institutional description of powers and prerogatives would lead one to believe that the school board plays a more decisive role in school policy making. Indeed, research has shattered the myth of lay control of schools.

The objective of this volume is to present political studies at all levels of the government of education. The editor will generalize from these and other studies about the political aspects of education policy—who gets what, when, and how. The goal is to study who has political influence and how this influence is aggregated to reach policy objectives. There is no attempt to evaluate in a normative sense the policy objectives or outcomes.

Generalizations on political influence at the state and local level must be regarded as tentative hypotheses based on hard data to date. We do have an increasing number of political case studies and surveys. But the case studies do not comprise a representative sample. Nor has the methodology of the various survey efforts been uniform in some design components. There is, however, a great deal of documented research from cities, suburbs, and state governments all over the nation.

The selections are based on the premise that the structure and process of political influence is different at the several levels of education, 1) local, 2) state, 3) national. The local section is divided between big cities and suburbs.

v

Surprisingly, the empirical research to date shows little difference between cities and suburbs in terms of the locus of political power. Many trends in political influence seem to transcend community social-economic differences.

At the state level the editor found the greatest lack of recent empirical data. Moreover, even the few recent studies may be outdated by the rapid changes in state political coalitions. Indeed, the entire field of politics of education is in great transition as new political actors from student bodies, black inner cities, and teachers' unions exert stronger political influence than in the early 1960's.

We have the most solid research base at the federal level for generalizing about education policy making. There is only one federal government (as contrasted to 50 states and 19,000 local districts), and there has been a great deal of research on the federal domestic policy making process in areas similar to education.[1] This does not mean, of course, that we have all the answers at the federal level, but it does highlight the complexities of generalizing about state and local education government.

Intergovernmental Influence on Education Policy

The government of education reflects the structural characteristics of our federal system. Federalism presumes that each level of government must retain inviolate its own sphere of responsibility and activity. Each of the three levels has maintained autonomy in some areas of educational policy, and this autonomy cannot be obliterated by higher central authorities.[2] Autonomy against encroachments is embodied in federal and state laws.

But in practice these autonomous levels of educational government (federal, state, and local) interact and have a system of mutual obligation and dependence. Congress has authorized some educational programs for purposes found to be particularly relevant to national, as opposed to sectional, interests. The Constitution grants the states responsibility for the provision of public education. The states have delegated most of their powers to local school districts but continue a number of regulations over fiscal and program matters.

Although the local educational agencies depend on the support of state and Federal levels, they normally exert decisive influence over the selection of teachers, operation and building of school facilities, and curriculum. While local government does not have legal autonomy from the state, its prerogatives are preserved by public support for the value of "local control of schools." This value of local control is usually written into state statutes.[3]

The federal and state governments are dependent on local governments to operate the schools—a function it would be undesirable to centralize. When the costs of operation exceed local capacity, grants-in-aid from higher levels subsidize their local agents. But with these funds come policy controls through the establishment of objectives and priorities, and requirements for eligibility and accountability. On the other hand, states and localities try to get federal funds with as few requirements as possible. Congress supports local control verbally, but shies away from unrestricted grants advocated by the school administrators and boards.

While this volume is organized so that each level is considered separately, the reader should keep in mind how various educational agencies relate to each other at each level of government. No selection was included on intergovernmental relations in education simply because no appropriate article or book has been published. Patterns of potential interaction are exceedingly complex. Bailey and Mosher have produced a simplified grid that indicates the dimensions of the problem.

Influences on Educational Policy-Making in the United States*

	NATIONAL	STATE	LOCAL
General Legislative	(1) Congress	(2) State Legislature	(3) Common Council
Educational Legislative	(4) President	(5) State School Board	(6) Local School Board
Executive	(7) President	(8) Governor	(9) Mayor
Administrative	(10) HEW-USOE	(11) State Dept. of Education	(12) School Superintendent
Judicial	(13) Supreme Court	(14) State Supreme Court	(15) Federal or State District Court
Professional Interests	(16) NEA	(17) State Teachers' Association	(18) Local PTA
Other Private Interests	(19) U.S. Catholic Conference	(20) State Chamber of Commerce	(21) John Birch Society Chapter

*From Stephen K. Bailey and Edith K. Mosher, *ESEA: The Office of Education Administers A Law* (Syracuse: Syracuse University Press, 1968) p. 222.

They stress that cutting across their grid are the "pervasive influences of various ideologues and journalists, and of the producers of textbooks and educational hardware." The fear of federal domination is diminished if the reader notes that only 6 of the 24 boxes include national influence. Moreover, in any locality boxes 2, 5, 6, 12, and 21 are likely to be more influential in the making of educational policy than boxes 1, 7, 10, 16, and 19.

Recent trends indicate that local schools will become increasingly reliant on the federal and state revenue base. One result from an increasing state proportion of local school finance would be further yielding to pressures for centralization at the state level of decisions on curriculum, materials, and even teachers' salaries. Bailey and Mosher correctly conclude that educational policy "increasingly is bound to reflect the extended interaction of all levels and types of government and of a wide variety of private and professional forces."

The Process and Structure of Political Influence in Education

Carl Friedrich defines theory, as distinguished from philosophy and opinion, "as the more or less systematized body of demonstrable or at least coherently arguable generalizations based upon rigorous analysis of ascertainable facts."[4] One type of theory is an operational theory such as the Newtonian law that claimed bodies fall in a certain way, and constructed an explanation for it. This section will present Edward Banfield's conceptual framework of political influence as a tool for the reader to compare political systems in education. This is not an operational theory in the scientific sense that *explains* the structure or process of political influence in education.

Before one can attempt to generalize there must be clear definitions. This is especially true in politics where such words as "power," "authority" and "influence" have different connotations for different people. In this regard, the writer must be rather arbitrary in denoting a political phenomenon or experience with the term most suitable for the context of politics in education.

A definition that may assist the reader is Banfield's concept of political influence.[5] By "influence" he means the ability to get others to act, think, or feel as one intends. A school superintendent that persuades his board to approve a new school facility exercises influence. Enough total influence, however, must be aggregated to induce, coerce, deceive, or otherwise persuade someone to do what is required of him. Politics from this standpoint consists of acts of influence— to study patterns of influence so that proposals are adopted is to study education policy making.

The selections in this volume help illuminate five general conceptual questions.[6]
1) *Who has influence in school policy making and who is subject to it?* The head of the State Department of Education may have influence with respect to general school aid allocation formulas but not on state desegregation policies. Thus the relevant questions are: Who has influence with whom and with regard to what?
2) *How does influence in the education context work?* What means does (or could) the influencer employ to affect the behavior of the influencee, and how

do these means act upon the motivations and expectations of the influencee? Actual or potential influence can rest upon a sense of obligation or rational persuasion. In an education setting the school superintendent's influence on the school board frequently rests on his expertise in educational matters and his access to detailed information. The superintendent can use the persuasion of partisan analysis to show the school board that its objectionable policy does not actually serve the board's *own interests.*

3) *What are the terms upon which influence is expended?* The President of the United States may have ample influence to secure the passage of federal aid to private schools, but the costs and depletion of his influence for future bills may be greater than the advantage of private school aid.

4) *How is action concerted by influence?* A political situation may often be viewed as one in which an educational proposal is to be adopted or not adopted. The conceptual issue is: on what terms will the actors who have it within their ability to give or withhold these acts be influenced to give or withhold them? On what terms will the Chamber of Commerce support an increase in property taxes to pay for special reading teachers for disadvantaged children? Will a cost analysis demonstrating savings from a new building persuade a school board?

5) A related issue is: *Who aggregates enough "pieces of influence" so that the total is sufficient to adopt the proposal?* This concept relates to the influence "broker" who perhaps trades some future influence for someone else's present influence. Political influence in the American system of separation of power comes in bits and pieces. Someone must aggregate enough bits and pieces to have a proposal adopted. To get someone else's influence, however, the broker often must pay a price or persuade someone with partisan policy analysis.[7] Through partisan analysis the "broker" can persuade influence holders "that what he wants of them is what their own appraisal of their own responsibilities requires them to do in their interest, not his."[8]

This conceptual framework for analyzing the research in this volume (or in new studies) has several advantages. With respect to general theories the methodological problems for education are similar to a comparative study of the political systems of our large cities. Each state and local educational-political system has peculiarities and differences based on such things as tradition, values, and formal structural arrangements. One of the purposes of the concepts presented above is to provide a partial framework for comparative analysis among 50 states and 18,000 local school districts.

This framework also helps the researcher to focus on the way policy is really made in school systems instead of the legal-formal arrangements that describe the way educational policy is supposed to be made.[9]

The selections do not concentrate exclusively on cases of intense conflict or controversy. Many of the studies attempt to document the "normal" process or low conflict situation of school policy making at the local level where the majority of the important decisions on budget, curriculum, and personnel are made. Several selections on school desegregation highlight the radical changes in political influence when intense conflict is generated. In the federal government section the legislative process highlights the conflict element, but after the bills are passed many key program decisions are made by administrators in an environment of relatively low conflict. Consequently, there is a selection from Bailey and Mosher's *ESEA—The Office of Education Administers A Law.*

Systems Analysis and Political Influence

In using the framework of political influence to interpret the readings one should supplement this concept with the insights of political systems analysis. Political influence as outlined in this volume does not address itself explicitly to how the present system for government of education has been able to persist over a long period of time or how it is changing through time. As David Easton pointed out,[10]

> a systems approach draws us away from a discussion of the way in which the political pie is cut up and how it happens to get cut up in one way rather than another. There is a status quo bias built into allocative research [such as political influence] ... To escape this bias, we need a theoretical framework that helps us understand how the very pie itself comes into existence and changes in its basic content or structure... If we know how [political] systems manage to cope with stress, how they manage to persist in the face of either stable or changing environments, other theories or sets of ideas aspiring to theoretical status that deal with various aspects of political life—decision making, coalition strategies, game theories, power, and group analysis all fit into place. They are no longer alternative or competing modes of analysis; they represent partial theories of allocation, referring to and explaining some special part or aspect of a political system.

Political influence as used here concentrates on the fundamental political questions of who gets what, when, and how *for a particular era in time.* The reader should note in each selection how the influence pattern and allocation of political power is changing over a period of time, and why it is changing. For instance, what is there that would stand as a possible threat to the continued dominance of professional educators in many internal policies? Clearly, the increasing demands for community and student involvement in decision making have implications for the government of education. A related question is how the existing system of educational government copes with stress. This is highlighted in the analysis of desegregation crises in the selection by David Crain.

Laurence Iannaccone's work is an application of political systems analysis to educational government. He contends that the government of education at the local level is a closed system that is not open on a continuous basis to influence from its environment; e.g., educators and board members have the predominant influence and they frequently reject new policy inputs from the community.[11] Iannaccone contends that there is no institutionalized opposition to people who hold official positions in education government, and consequently alternatives are often not presented. A two party system is designed to create such a loyal opposition but the party system does not operate in local education policy decisions. Consequently, the government of education is characterized by (1) long periods of stability under the dominance of education officials with little influence from the community, (2) shorter periods of abrupt change that often destroy professional careers when the concerns of society finally penetrate the education influence structure.

FOOTNOTES

[1] Robert L. Peabody and Nelson Polsby, *New Perspectives on the House of Representatives* (Chicago: Rand-McNally, 1963); Douglass Cater, *Power in Washington* (New York: Random House, 1964); Francis E. Rourke, *Bureaucratic Power in National Politics* (Boston: Little Brown, 1965); See especially James L. Sundquist, *Politics and Policy* (Washington: Brookings, 1968).

[2] For an analysis of federalism see Carl Friedrich, *Man and His Government* (New York: McGraw-Hill; 1963) pp. 584-613.

[3] The writer is indebted to Edith Mosher for supplying her unpublished dissertation, *The Origin, Enactment and Implementation of the Elementary and Secondary Education Act of 1965* (Berkeley: University of California, 1967).

[4] Carl J. Friedrich, *op. cit.,* p. 1.

[5] Edward C. Banfield, *Political Influence* (New York: Free Press, 1961), p. 3.

[6] *Ibid.,* pp. 4-11.

[7] See Charles Lindblom, *The Policy Making Process* (Englewood: Prentice Hall, 1968).

[8] See Richard E. Neustadt, *Presidential Power* (New York: John Wiley and Sons, 1960), p. 46.

[9] See Banfield, *op. cit.,* p. 8, for a critique of the reputational technique.

[10] David Easton, *A Systems Analysis of Political Life* (New York: John Wiley and Sons, 1965), pp. 474-478. For a critique of such concepts as political influence for building empirical political theory see James G. March, "The Power of Power," in David Easton, editor, *Varieties of Political Theory* (Englewood: Prentice-Hall, 1966).

[11] Laurence Iannaccone, *Politics in Education* (New York: The Center for Applied Research in Education, 1967).

Contributors

(In order of their Contributions)

Robert H. Salisbury is on the faculty of Political Science at Washington University in St. Louis.

Marilyn Gittell is Professor of Political Science and Director of the Institute for Community Studies at Queens College.

T. Edward Hollander is on the faculty of the Baruch School of Business and Public Administration at the City College of New York.

H. Thomas James is Dean of the School of Education at Stanford University.

William S. Vincent is with the Institute of Administrative Research, Teachers College, Columbia University.

H. Thomas James is Dean of the School of Education at Stanford University.

James A. Kelly is an Associate Professor at Columbia Teachers College and the education consultant for the Urban Coalition.

Walter I. Garms is on the faculty of Columbia Teachers College.

Alan Rosenthal is Professor of Political Science and Director of the Center for State Legislative Research and Service of the Eagleton Institute of Politics at Rutgers University.

Robert F. Lyke is an Assistant Professor at the Woodrow Wilson School of Public and International Affairs at Princeton University.

Robert L. Crain is an Assistant Professor of Sociology at the University of Chicago and Senior Study Director of the National Opinion Research Center.

Roscoe C. Martin is Professor of Political Science at Syracuse University.

David Minar is the Chairman of the Department of Political Science at the University of Washington.

Gerald E. Sroufe is the Executive Director of the National Committee for the Support of Public Schools, Washington, D. C.

Robert T. Stout is on the faculty in education and sociology at Claremont Graduate School.

Lesley H. Browder is a Lecturer in Education at Stanford University and a former Superintendent of Schools in New Jersey.

Stephen Bailey is a Professor at the Maxwell School of Public Affairs, Syracuse University and Chairman of the Policy Institute of the Syracuse University Research Corporation.

Nicholas Masters is a Professor of Political Science at Southern Illinois University. University.

Thomas H. Eliot has served as Chancellor of Washington University at St. Louis, where he was Professor of Political Science.

Lawrence Iannaccone is a Professor of Education at New York University.

Alan K. Campbell is Dean of the Maxwell School of Public Affairs at Syracuse University.

James L. Sundquist is a senior staff member of the Brookings Institution and formerly a legislative assistant to Senator Joseph S. Clark.

Edith K. Mosher is on the staff of the Bureau of Educational Research at the University of Virginia.

Albert H. Quie is a United States Congressman from Minnesota and member of the House Education Subcommittee.

John Brademas is a United States Congressman from Indiana and member of the House Education Subcommittee.

PART I
POLITICAL INFLUENCE IN LOCAL EDUCATION
POLICY MAKING

INTRODUCTION TO PART I

Political Influence in Education at the Local
Level — Cities and Suburbs:

This introduction will advance some empirically based generalizations on the structure, pattern, and process of political influence in local education policy making. There will be no attempt to explore whether a particular form and style of education government results in particular education policies. The writer will summarize characteristics of political influence that most local educational policy-making systems have in common. These generalizations are based on only a partial sample of states and localities. Moreover, as research in political science often is, these generalizations are not substantiated by all cases. They do pertain to the vast majority of the existing case studies. In short, the generalizations hold for the research we have completed, and they could be negated as we gather data on a larger and more recent sample.

Monopolistic vs. Plural Structure of Political Influence

In the early 1950's, perhaps the leading research controversy concerned monopolistic vs. pluralistic influence in education policy making.[1] Using the reputational technique of asking a sample of informants who had power, leadership and influence, Floyd Hunter found in Regional City that a monolithic power structure of "economic dominants" monopolized influence over all local policy issues *including education.* Influence over education policy was exercised by a small, wealthy atypical proportion of the citizenry. Little could be initiated that affected large numbers of school children without the approval and guidance of these economic dominants whose influence was felt in every area of civic life. This finding was derived by nominations of *reputedly* influential community figures from individuals who were at the center of the communication and institutional structure of a community. Other studies of community power tended to confirm the Hunter monopolistic influence theses.[2]

A comparative study of four *rural southern* school districts by Ralph Kimbrough discovered behind-the-scenes informal power groupings who had crucial influence over educational policy along with most other areas of local government. Kimbrough's findings can be summarized as:

Decisive power is exercised in most local school districts by relatively few persons who hold top positions of influence in the informal power structure of the school district. The success of significant educational projects and proposals is often heavily dependent upon the support or lack of support of the men of power.[3]

Kimbrough's conclusions are contrary to the studies included in this volume that focus exclusively on *urban or suburban areas*. Moreover, other reviewers of the existing literature assert Kimbrough's findings are *not* supported by numerous case studies in the metropolitan areas where the majority of the pupils live.[4] Kimbrough's study is jeopardized by methodological procedures that use anecdotes arising out of experiences as empirically derived data upon which generalizations are constructed. Keith Goldhammer has pointed out, "the empirical researcher will find that the lack of systematic theory and the disregard both of scholarly criteria for analysis of data and standards for reporting research are limitations upon the utility of the book."[5] It is quite possible, however, that Kimbrough's economic dominants still exist in the rural South where his study was based.

The opposite of Hunter's economic dominants is confirmed by study after study; e.g., the ability to exert crucial influence and concert action on proposals in the area of budget, personnel, curriculum, facilities, etc. rests with persons who are involved in educational affairs because *they hold* (now or in the past) *official positions* in educational institutions or public affairs. For instance, the studies listed below confirm this view.

Marilyn Gittell (5 cities)—Philadelphia, Detroit, St. Louis, New York, Chicago, Baltimore

H. Thomas James (14 cities)—Boston, Buffalo, New York, Cleveland, Philadelphia, Pittsburgh, Baltimore, St. Louis, Chicago, Milwaukee, Houston, San Francisco, Los Angeles, Detroit

Alan Rosenthal (5 cities)—Atlanta, Boston, Chicago, New York, San Francisco

Joseph Pois—Chicago

Alan K. Campbell (5 cities)—New York, Boston, Chicago, Atlanta, San Francisco

David Minar (4 suburban Chicago communities)

Robert Dahl—New Haven

Roscoe Martin (200 suburban systems in 28 states and 34 metropolitan areas; 12 in depth—4 in Syracuse suburbs, 4 in Detroit suburbs, 4 in Portland suburbs)

Louis Massotti—New Trier[6]

None of these studies found substantial evidence of an informal "power elite" (economic or otherwise) in school politics.[7]

Political Influence Within the School System

The base and range of case studies listed above is quite broad and includes local districts in all geographical sections of the nation.[8] Even though there are significant differences in methodology, one must be impressed by how *uniform* the main conclusions are. *On the basis of these data* the following tentative hypotheses are advanced with respect to:

> *Who has Influence in Local School Policy and Who is Subject to It.*
> *How is Influence Concerted and Aggregated so that Proposals are Adopted.*

The most productive way to analyze these questions is to start with the concept of who has influence *with whom* and with regard to *what*. The "what" in terms of education can be defined as:

— Budget (including program priorities, teacher salaries, etc.)

— Curriculum content (course outlines, books, instructional equipment, etc.)

— Personnel policy (tenure, hiring, decentralization and deployment of personnel, etc.)

— Facilities (including remodeling)

— Integration (including local school boundaries)

The studies in this volume indicate the superintendent and top school system line and staff officials usually have the political influence—the ability to get others to act, think or feel as they intend—on *internal issues*. Internal issues do not require extensive negotiations with elements in the political stratrum not primarily concerned with the public schools. Moreover, with the exception of some large cities it is usually the superintendent and the central staff *that concerts and aggregates influence* so that specific proposals relating to *external issues* are adopted. An important distinction is that the superintendent cannot always use his hierarchical position to issue commands, but he is the chief negotiator and political bargainer. Another important qualification is that the research often fails to differentiate the influence of the bureaucracy from the frequently limited influence of the superintendent over his own line and staff officers. Curriculum, personnel, promotions, and building policy are usually internal. Integration is an external issue. Budget is both an internal and external issue.

Such general statements on influence, however, must be considered within the outside constraints on local policy makers. Most of a typical local budget is determined by mandated salary increases and fixed costs. State education codes may specify textbooks and curriculum that all local schools in the state must use.

The Budget

The school budget determines the educational program for the future and establishes priorities and levels of instructional activity. H. Thomas James researched the budget process in 14 large cities. He documented that the superintendent initiates the budget and maintains control of the detailed information needed by the board and the community to make informed decisions on alternatives. This statement from his study could apply to curriculum or personnel policies as well as the budget.

> To prepare this vast array of information requires time and technical knowledge, both of which are available in the school staff; the complexity of a big city budget increases the importance of technical knowledge and therefore places substantial power for budget preparation in the school staff. Later, we will discuss the degree to which the power of the board of education to shape the budget is limited by the concentration of budgetary expertise in the professional staff.[9]

Although James stresses the limited role of the school board in budget *preparation,* he does recognize that other actors exert influence on the superintendent's recommendation. Indeed, the superintendent must play a "balancing" role between the key participants in the budget process (taxpayers associations, teachers' organizations, etc.)[10] Since the superintendent controls the technical information upon which the budget is based, however, he can choose not to inform these participants. For example, in one city the superintendent presents only a two page summary.[11] James concludes there are substantial external constraints on the superintendent's flexibility, but these constraints often immobilize the board.

> The typical board of education finds itself hemmed in by a growing body of state regulations, levy limitations, state-mandated services, salary schedules, tenure provisions, and other staff benefits, which place a large part of expenditures beyond their control. In the vortex of these pressures a board of education may become immobilized, and this tendency may be more difficult to resist as systems grow and age. Thus, the typical big city board of education attempts only relatively minor adjustments in the school budget during the brief time it considers it.[12]

Typically the mayor in fiscally dependent or independent cities does not become involved in the *program* decisions of the budget. The mayor restricts the area of his influence to the *overall budget ceiling* the tax base can stand, and in some cities the amount of the salary increase for teachers. Often teachers initially present their salary demands to superintendents but in many large cities carry their case directly to the board and local government officials.[13] In New York the mayor now plays the critical role in settling teacher salary disputes.

David Minar's and Roscoe Martin's studies of a large number of suburban districts reach the same general conclusions. Martin concludes the superintendent's influence is derived from:

> he [the superintendent] is as much a policy maker as he is a manager in the narrow sense; for he enjoys an expertise, a professional reputation, and a community position which combine to give him an almost irresistible voice in school affairs.[14]

On public issues with a community audience appeal the superintendent's influence is less overt but usually equally effective.[15] The superintendent exercises influence in public issues by defining them, proposing acceptable alternatives, providing ammunition for his supporters, and in the end implementing (or not implementing) the decisions.[16]

Most of the selections discuss the restricted influence of the school board. School boards usually have no expert or even part time staff. Board members are also part-time officials who meet at night once or twice a week after a full day in a responsible position.[17] These busy laymen are usually not presented with performance criteria or objective output data upon which to question the judgment of the superintendent and his staff.[18] For instance, budgets are not related to identifiable programs, nor are curriculum proposals based on student attainment measures.

The school board's lack of political influence also stems from its method of selection.[19] Issues are usually not presented to the voters. Consequently, rarely does a board member have a policy mandate from his election campaign. Moreover, almost all school boards are chosen at large. A board member will not hold specific policy views derived from a ward or subcommunity electoral base. As Robert Salisbury's paper stresses, the board has the same viewpoint as the superintendent as far as representation is concerned: regardless of ethnic, racial, religious, economic, or political differences in other areas of urban life, education should not legitimize those differences. Education is a process that must not be differentiated according to section or class, and the city is a *unity* for purposes of the school program.

These characteristics weaken the board's potential influence. The lack of staff and time cause boards to concentrate on routine details, required by law or custom, which have little impact on general policy.[20] At most the board is a mediating agency among the most influential actors. The board, however, plays the crucial role of concerting and aggregating influence in order to adopt proposals on *integration.* The selections by Robert Crain and Stout-Sroufe cite the superintendent's lack of influence and understanding of this issue as the cause of his inability to resolve it. Crain stresses that the superintendent is unable to deal with the issue because he regards it as a social (not educational) controversy. Consequently, the problem is left for the school board to negotiate with the community.

The selection by Rosenthal illuminates the increasing influence of teachers' organizations over salary, promotions, and working conditions. But Rosenthal's comparative study of 5 cities reveals the political pressure of teachers is relegated to "bread and butter issues" (including relief from non-instructional duties). To date, their influence rarely extends to curriculum, facilities, and the program areas of the budget.[21] Rosenthal finds, however, AFT locals desire a much wider range of concern than NEA affiliates. Despite this AFT desire, James found demands from teacher organizations in 14 cities relate to staff benefits and not to the expansion of educational services. Rosenthal also finds the mayor in some cities has influence over budget ceilings and teacher salaries, but on other educational matters his involvement is typically "insignificant."

Some studies do contain conclusions on the centralization of power *within* the central office administrative structure. Large city school systems have a number of decentralized district administrators serving smaller areas of the city. Gittell's study of 6 cities, for example, points out:

> The general policy role of the district superintendent is most difficult to rate. From the information available, such powers appear to be small. It is true that they may sit on various councils but their voices do not seem to carry much authority. Their role seems to consist almost entirely of making curriculum recommendations and assuring that policies set down by central headquarters are followed in their districts.[22]

Gittell's views were confirmed by James' study of the budget process in 14 cities. In only 7 cities did building principals participate in the budget process, and their role was restricted to such tasks as supplying neighborhood enrollment projections for use in applying central office formulas, plus special requests for building or equipment alterations.[23]

While influence *within the school bureaucracy* is concentrated at the central office level, there is considerable variation among cities as to the superintendent's influence over his top line and staff officers. Top staff is traditionally chosen from within the system by the superintendent or a committee chosen by the superintendent.[24] But a *new* superintendent cannot always bring in a new team of top line administrators. Few incumbents have ever been removed.[25] Consequently, the political influence of the superintendent may be greater with respect to the school board than it is with regard to certain areas of policy where he disagrees with incumbent top central staff. Indeed, studies that probe more deeply into the bureaucracy may find the superintendent is powerless in many policy areas, and no one in the school system can aggregate enough influence to bring about educational change.[26]

According to Gittell, Calvin Gross in New York was "unable to penetrate the huge bureaucratic system because he could not hire top personnel that would be loyal to him."[27] By contrast, new Philadelphia and Detroit superintendents were able to bring in new central staff who were in some cases from outside the city school system.

There is an influence structure on curriculum and personnel policy that is external to the school system and limits greatly the superintendent's initiative. Outside bodies such as professional associations, accrediting agencies, and institutions of higher education exert unofficial and often unseen influence. For instance, a plan to drastically reduce the number of courses in a curriculum area such as vocational education, music, or art will usually lead to an investigation by a regional accrediting agency, an NEA affiliate, or the relevant state department unit. This investigation can recommend the reduced courses be restored in order to maintain accreditation or to avoid critical publicity by one of these organizations. Even more frequent is the use of accreditation and certification requirements to thwart a superintendent's attempt to bring in new personnel without a public education background. Unfortunately, most research has failed to analyze the political interrelationships and interactions between the local school system and exogenous influences such as professional associations and state government.

In sum, the empirical studies to date have stressed: the predominant influence of the superintendent and/or the central line officers on internal issues of curriculum, personnel, and facilities; the superintendent's influence broker role in external issues; the passive role of the board that allows the superintendent to expend his stock of influence without high costs in terms of loss of future influence with the board; the specialized influence of teachers' organizations on salary and fringe benefit issues that are very costly, but not program or curriculum oriented; and the restricted influence of the mayor to at most overall budget ceilings and teacher salary increases. The studies in this volume are based on a large range of cases from all over the nation. An important finding is that structures and processes of influence do not differ greatly from city to suburb.[28]

The Influence of the Community

So far the analysis has focused on the structure of influence *within* the school system. But what about the community and municipal officials? If empirical research does not support the Hunter-Kimbrough thesis of an *informal* power elite of economic dominants, how and to what extent does the external community exercise influence school policy?

From a political science viewpoint school policy making is distinctive because of its *lack* of regular formal procedures for generating alternative proposals to those advanced by school officials. A likely area for community influence would be the general program or salary aspects of the school budget. The study by James of 14 cities, however, concluded:

> By contrast we should note that generally during the budget preparation stage there is no similar channel open for formal communication from those who seek additional educational services.

> Community associations interested in extending educational services are rarely consulted by administrators. It is true that some groups (e.g. civil rights) press for policies and services on a year-round basis, but the board's public hearing is still the first available opportunity for those groups to express their views directly to the board. By that time, however, the budget is already prepared. Major changes may be difficult at a later stage, because of revenue limitations, and because the changes would probably require a corresponding decrease in another expenditure category, such as teachers' salaries.[29]

The influence of the mayor and taxpayers' associations is usually limited to the overall amount of money the schools have to work with and not the educational program.[30] But the superintendent in most cities gauges what tax rate the community will tolerate in his recommendations to the board.

A consistent theme of the urban selections is that education is an isolated policy making system—isolated from significant influence by other community officers or citizens. Again, the uniformity of conclusions on this isolation phenomenon is striking. And once again we also find suburban school politics is just as isolated as urban education. Martin's findings from 200 suburban systems could have just as easily been written by an urban based researcher:

> ... general government, the principal agency through which democracy is achieved and safeguarded is a rough and tumble affair of the market place. As an organism primarily, directly, and continuously connected with the realization of the aspirations and welfare of the people, the city in particular is deeply involved in general politics, which by doctrine is an anathema to the schoolmen. Public education therefore shuns urban government, its institutions and its works, preferring to go it alone as a public program entirely separate from the local government with which in principle, and as a matter of tradition and doctrine, the public schools are identified.

Thus is the circle closed and the paradox completed. Thus does the public school heralded by its champions as the cornerstone of democracy reject the political world in which democratic institutions operate.[31]

This doctrine is the operational procedure in an overwhelming majority of urban and suburban school districts. A notable exception is the Schrag study of schools in Appalachia. Local government officials use the schools as a patronage operation and source of contracts for local businessmen who can help keep county politicians in office.[32]

Can the public influence school policy so that actions it desires are taken? Community organizations and leaders react to school policy but there is little evidence to indicate they have enough influence or allies to frequently shape or change it. There is considerable evidence that boards of education do *not* fashion public policy to the demands of community organizations. Nor do they view themselves as representatives of the popular viewpoint.[33] Indeed, the nonpartisan, at-large, 3-year staggered terms of many board elections are deliberately designed to impede *representation* in the sense that political scientists use the term.[34] Certainly the professional ethic of the educationist does not give much weight to the community's view of sound educational curriculum.

The nature of community political influence seems to be most often a *negative action* such as the defeat of a bond issue-tax increase, some board members, or the termination of controversial curriculum offerings like sex education. Roscoe Martin surveyed a large sample of suburban citizens, mayors, presidents of local Leagues of Women Voters, and officials of local Chambers of Commerce and concluded:

> The respondents indicated no particular interest in curriculum, textbooks, subversive activities, personalities, athletics, race relations...
> This suggests that these areas provide a reservoir for what we have called episodic issues—issues which emerge under unusual or special conditions and shortly subside. Thus, it is not textbooks which cause concern, but a particular textbook under a special set of circumstances. (p. 55)

The public is not a continuous or annual participant, nor does it have the influence to enact *positive* alternatives to school system policy.[35] There are exceptions such as Philadelphia where the Greater Philadelphia Movement of local civic groups initiated changes in the leadership and content of public education. But other cases do not fit the Philadelphia model. Nor do they fit the New Haven study by Dahl where an aggressive mayor could exert decisive influence on external and internal school issues.

Suburban conflict may be caused by rapid school population growth. Such growth brings newcomers with different educational values and a need for a college oriented curriculum.[36] In the city, public concern may stem from a voter revolt against steadily rising taxes, integration, or a racial minority that desires special programs. But these interludes of sharp conflict and public awareness are followed by long periods of unchecked influence by school officials. The case study by Lesley Browder indicates how unprepared school officials are for leadership of a persuasive political campaign that must sway voters.[37] The PTA and many older community organizations are usually supportive of school officials. But these groups do not have experienced political campaign skills either, nor can they conduct as effective a canvass as a strong party organization.[38]

Policy Outcomes and The Structure of Political Influence

Several selections conclude that the structure of local influence over education results in a lack of innovation and a lack of budgetary support. But these studies also demonstrate that a superintendent who wants to devise new curriculum for minority groups, for instance, will usually have enough political influence to persuade the board and the community to adopt it. However, none of the studies have focused on the implementation of curriculum change. We do not know whether a superintendent has enough influence over his bureaucracy to insure that curriculum innovations are carried out in the classroom.

The theme in the selection by Robert Salisbury is that the costs of political isolation from the community are greater than the benefits because schoolmen lack allies such as city officials and state legislators who can help the school raise more money through local or state taxes. Schoolmen have no network of support from groups and interests for whom the educators have done favors in the past and who will subsequently reciprocate.

Superintendents and school boards alone do not have enough political influence to provide for continuous large increases in educational expenditures by any level of government. A way to accumulate more influence for increased taxes may be to surrender some influence over curriculum, personnel, or facilities to non-school groups that will support higher taxes. In effect, a superintendent can *invest* his limited stock of influence with outside allies to gain more budget, instead of consuming all his influence in internal policy making. For instance, Mayor Daley of Chicago maintains control of the city council only by continual outlays of patronage to ward leaders.[39]

In making his choice of alternative investments of his influence the superintendent should carefully calculate the uncertainty of return as well as its probable value. Is it more valuable to allow the mayor to formulate the educational component of a model cities program if this will increase the mayor's support for increased school expenditures? On the other hand, how certain is it that the mayor's support will sway many voters or state legislators opposed to increased school taxes?

The superintendent has a great many sources of influence over school policy that rest on his authority, respect, control of information, ability to sell his views, etc. The empirical studies indicate that he has consumed this influence on controlling internal policy in areas such as curriculum and personnel. He has not chosen to invest substantial influence in "favors" for outside groups—the mayor, the state legislature, the black community—in return for support for overall budget increases. If a larger education budget is the primary need for American education, then superintendents have not been maximizing their marginal investments of *influence* in order to gain a larger budget.[40]

A hypotheses advanced by Martin is that this isolation of school government from the community and other local government functions is a result of what political scientists call "political culture." Political culture in the education context is the bundle of values, attitudes, customs, habits, and shared subjective outlooks on the character of the governmental or education political system. The hypothesis that political separatism is a traditional and universal value of the vast majority of schoolmen is supported by documentation that actors outside of school systems exercise only slight influence *regardless* of the social-economic nature or location of the community. School officials have tried in both cities and suburbs to separate themselves from outside political forces.

New Actors and New Patterns of Influence

Very recently new actors from the community have been gaining influence. The empirical studies in this volume were completed before a number of experiments in community (particularly black community) "control" were under way. A major objective of community control is to diminish the political influence of the incumbent central office educators and the largely passive school boards. Robert Lyke questions whether a new community selected superintendent would eventually exert as much influence over the board as his predecessor.

At this point there are not enough "community controlled schools" to make statements based on case studies. Most school districts are proceeding cautiously and studying the issue with the New York City experience as a reference point.[41] It is safe to state that as of now substantial community control is not widespread, nor has the concept changed the influence structure of school policy making process in a significant number of localities.

The selection by Robert Lyke addresses some of the crucial political issues of "community control." Who has influence over personnel, budget, and curriculum? Is this influence advisory or decisive—e.g. can the elected local board overrule the professional educator? Does the community board have the time and expertise to critically review the professional educators' recommendations? How does the community use its new political influence to alter the substance of budget or curriculum? Does the community board concert and aggregate influence so that proposals are adopted, or is this the role of the district superintendent? Does the professional educator pay a high price (in terms of his stock of potential influence) to have his proposals ratified by the local board?

Protest as a Political Resource

There is a growing use of the tactic of *protest* to exert increased community influence on the school policy making process dominated by school (including board) officials.[42] The school has been the focus of student-parent strikes, pickets, and sit-ins. Such protest can be viewed as a problem of bargaining in which the basic problem is that the community groups (often black) lack political resources to exchange. James Q. Wilson has correctly called this "the problem of the powerless."[43]

In the early 1960's the objective of the powerless in school protest activity often was to activate *"third parties"* to exert political influence in the school policy making area in ways favorable to the protesters. With or without third parties, however, protest is one of the few ways that community groups can create a stock of political influence for negotiating with *school officials.*

The parents and students who picket the board of education do not have enough total influence to enact proposals. Frequently, their objective is to appeal to a wider public to which the school superintendent and board is sensitive.[44] This activation of "reference publics" is different from alliance formation where third parties join the conflict because their value orientations are similar to those of the protesting groups and concerted action is possible.

The school protestors rely on conveying information on their goals through our public communications network. Often the type of presentation of the school protest by the communications media determines whether third parties will exert their influence on the school policy makers. For example, parent strikes may encourage news coverage but alienate target groups who could add their political influence to the protesters.

Wilson stresses that the civic groups most likely to be sympathetic to such protests are devoted to service in the public welfare or "liberally oriented" groups (such as reform political clubs.)[45] Recent demonstrations by the black community, however, do not appear to be designed to appeal to these third parties. In many ways black protest organizations lack the resources of staff and expertise that permit established civic groups to *enter* the school policy making process. The demand for "community control" can be viewed as an attempt to acquire stable political resources—resources that do not rely on the *goodwill* of third parties. These political resources will be most stable if the community has the assured influence base now held by a central board of education.

FOOTNOTES

[1] For a complete discussion of this issue see Chapter 14, R. F. Campbell *et al.*, *The Organization and Control of American Schools*, (Columbus: Charles E. Merrill, 1965) and Stephen Hencley and Robert Cahill's *The Politics of Education in the Local Community*, (Danville: Interstate, 1964), pp. 5-27. Also see Floyd Hunter, *Community Power Structure* (Chapel Hill: University of North Carolina Press, 1953).

[2] See Robert O. Schulze and Leonard V. Blumberg, "The Determination of Local Power Elites," *American Journal of Sociology*, LXIII (Nov. 1957), pp. 290-296; William II. Form and William V. D'Antonio, "Integration and Cleavage Among Community Influentials in Two Border Cities," *American Sociological Review*, XXIV (Dec. 1959), pp. 804-814.

[3] Ralph Kimbrough, *Political Power and Educational Decision Making* (Chicago: Rand McNally and Company, 1964), p. 200.

[4] See Alan K. Campbell, "Who Governs the Schools," *Saturday Review*, (Dec. 21, 1968); Robert H. Salisbury, "Schools and Politics in the Big City," *Harvard Education Review*, Summer 1967, pp. 408-424, and Laurence Iannaccone, *Politics in Education* (New York: N.Y.U. Press, 1967), pp. 19-29 and 82-89.

[5] See book review by Keith Goldhammer in *Educational Administration Quarterly*, Volume 1, (Spring 1965), p. 55.

[6] See also Roland Pellegra's *Community Power Structure and Educational Decision -Making in the Local Community* (Univ. of Oregon: 1965) for his study of 3 Oregon communities.

[7] An exception to this statement is Peter Schrag's analysis of the politics of education in Appalachia. See his "Schools of Appalachia," *Saturday Review* (May 15, 1965).

[8] For integration policy see Robert L. Crain, *Politics of School Desegregation* (Chicago: Aldine, 1968). Crain studied 15 cities through an in-depth case analysis.

[9] H. Thomas James *et al.*, *Determinants of Educational Expenditures in Large Cities in the United States* (Stanford, 1966), p. 56.

[10] *Ibid.*, p. 70.

[11] *Ibid.*, p. 71.

[12] *Ibid.*, p. 80.

[13] H. Thomas James *et al.*, *Determinants of Educational Expenditures in Large Cities in the United States* p. 69 and p. 61.

[14] Roscoe Martin, *Government and the Suburban School* (Syracuse: Syracuse University Press, 1962), p. 61.

[15] See Alan Rosenthal, "Community Leadership and Public School Politics, Two Case Studies" (Princeton Univ., unpublished Ph. D. dissertation, 1960), p. 498.

[16] See Keith Goldhammer, *et al.*, *Issues and Problems in Contemporary Educational Administration*, (Center for the Advanced Study of Educational Administration: University of Oregon, 1967), pp. 3-4.

[17] For a confirmation of this statement in suburban districts see David Minar, *Educational Decision Making in Suburban Communities* (Office of Education-Cooperative Research Project No. 2440), p. 53. Indeed, suburban commuters may have even less time for board matters than city dwellers.

[18] See James, *op. cit.*, p. 89.

[19] Robert Lyke, "Representation and Urban Schools," presented at Brookings Institution Conference on Community Schools (1968) in Washington, D.C.

[20] See Minar, *op. cit.*, pp. 57-89, and H. Thomas James, School Board Bibliography (Stanford University: 1967), pp. 5-6 and 61 ff. Also see Keith Goldhammer, *The School Board* (New York: Center for Applied Research, 1964). Goldhammer found Board members

spent 84% of their time on managerial details (p. 76). His study concluded, "experience in working with boards indicates that they spend a considerable amount of time working on technical details...they leave the major policy decisions concerning educational program to the professional staff."

[21] See also a questionnaire sent to 16,000 California teachers, "Let Us Teach: Final Report on the Helpfulness of Certain Aspects of the School Program to Classroom Teaching." (Sacramento: California Senate Factfinding Committee on Governmental Administration, 1965).

[22] Marilyn Gittell et al., Investigation of Fiscally Independent and Dependent City School Districts (Washington: Office of Education, Cooperative Research Project No. 3,237; 1967) p. 83 ff.

[23] James, Determinants of Educational Expenditures, p. 58.

[24] See Gittell, op. cit., pp. 69-72.

[25] Ibid., p. 72. This study, however, covered only five large cities.

[26] See David Rogers, New York City and the Politics of School Desegregation (New York: Center for Urban Education, 1968). Also see David Rogers, 110 Livingston Street (New York: Random House, 1968).

[27] Gittell et al., op. cit., p. 86.

[28] Minar's selection found the style of superintendent-board relations depended on the social-economic status of the district.

[29] James, et al., Determinants of Educational Expenditures in Large Cities, p. 63.

[30] See Gittell, op. cit., pp. 119-121.

[31] Martin, op. cit., p. 89.

[32] Peter Schrag, op. cit., p. 71.

[33] See Lyke, op. cit., pp. 7-20.

[34] See for example Hanna Pitkin, The Concept of Representation (Berkeley: The University of California Press, 1967).

[35] See Gittell et al., op. cit., pp. 103-108, for voter turnout studies. The average turnout for a board or bond election seems to be 25% to 35% of the registered voters. Financial issues elicit the most public interest and voter turnout—only small proportions of the public are interested in curriculum.

[36] See Frank E. Seely, Consideration In Administrator Contract Terminations (Unpublished doctoral dissertation, Stanford, 1964).

[37] See also Louis H. Masotti, Education and Politics in Suburbia (Cleveland: Western Reserve, 1967).

[38] School officials may have to adopt political campaign techniques used by major candidates including the use of advertising agencies and a carefully planned multi-media campaign stressing TV and radio.

[39] See Banfield, op. cit., p. 313 ff. for application of his political influence theory to the mayor.

[40] The isolation of the school political system makes it difficult to mount comprehensive urban programs (like model cities) with an integrated school component.

[41] See the Wall Street Journal, Dec. 13, 1968.

[42] Often this protest concerns "community control" of schools.

[43] James Q. Wilson, "The Strategy of Protest: Problems of Negro Civic Action," Journal of Conflict Resolution, 3 (Sept. 1961), pp. 291-303.

[44] For an analysis of protest as a political resource, see Michael Lipsky, "Protest as a Political Resource," American Political Science Review, No. 4 (Dec. 1968).

[45] See James Q. Wilson, The Amateur Democrat (Chicago: University of Chicago, 1962).

A. POLITICS OF EDUCATION IN BIG CITIES

SCHOOLS AND POLITICS IN
THE BIG CITY*

Robert H. Salisbury

After decades of silence, both social scientists and educators are at last explicitly examining and re-examining all the options regarding the relationship between the political system and the schools. Descriptive analysis has greatly enriched our understanding of how alternative structures operate. A full menu of recipes for changing the structures has been developed and here and there implemented. And while we are far from realizing closure on our uncertainties, the art of social engineering with respect to school-community relations is finally getting an underpinning of evidence and systematic analysis.[1]

Broadly, there seem to be three themes running through this new wave of literature. One is primarily descriptive: How are educational decisions made, and what variables are relevant for explaining alternative outcomes? A second theme merges this descriptive task with a special concern: What accounts for variations in the money available to the schools, and implicitly, how might more money be made available? The third theme is a bit different. It raises a more complex question, and answers depend not only upon careful descriptive analysis but also upon performance criteria that are very difficult to work out: How may the school system do a more effective job in the total context of community life?

It is apparent that the "context of community life" is a concept fraught with snares and difficulties. I propose to look at it mainly with reference to the problems of the core city; there, it encompasses major facets of the problems of race, of poverty, of physical decay and renewal, of perennial fiscal trauma, indeed most of those troubles we label "urban problems" in contemporary American society. The issue I wish to ruminate about here is whether one type of political system-school system relationship might be more effective than another in attacking these dilemmas of urban life. Specifically, I propose to consider the thesis that direct political-system control of the schools (historically anathema to educators) might have significant virtues in making the schools more effective instruments of social change and development.[2]

We know that many big-city school systems operate with substantial formal autonomy. They are not run by the political or administrative leaders of the city,

*Robert H. Salisbury, "Schools and Politics in the Big City," *Harvard Educational Review,* 37, Summer 1967, 408-424. Copyright ©1967 by President and Fellows of Harvard College.

but are insulated from those leaders and the interests they represent. In part this autonomy is a consequence of various formal features of local government which give to the schools the authority to run their affairs with little or no reference to the demands of other city officials. Perhaps in larger part, however, the insulation of the schools may be a function of the ideology, propagated by schoolmen but widely shared by the larger public, that schools should be free from "politics," i.e., the influence of nonschool officials. Insofar as this view is shared, it has made formal independence a less relevant variable, and most of what evidence we have suggests that the formal structure of school-city relations does not matter very much: the schools are largely autonomous anyway.

It has been argued that autonomy for the schools means that professional educators would be free to carry out educational policies which they, as professionals, deem most effective without the intrusion of conflicting and educationally deleterious demands from nonprofessionals. But autonomy and insulation may also result in other things. Autonomous schools may be unresponsive to important groups in the community whose interests are not effectively served by the dominant values of professional schoolmen. Autonomy may mean a fragmenting of efforts aimed at solving community problems because of inadequate coordination and planning. And autonomy may also bring vulnerability as well as insulation. If the schools are separated from the rest of the community's political system, they may be more easily exposed to the protests or demands of groups which are disaffected from that system, unable to work their will within its often labyrinthine structures, but able to organize direct popular support. And if they attempt direct protest action, they can make life most difficult for schoolmen who are unable to retreat into positions of mutual support among city officials with many programs and agencies and client groups. Unable to trade off one group against another, the schools may be and often are the targets of protest which may well have its roots in other facets of the city's life, but are directed against the schools precisely because they are autonomous and vulnerable.

The argument that the costs of "political control" far exceed the costs of autonomy needs re-examination. I have been struck by the frequent reference in that argument to the allegedly baleful effects of Big Bill Thompson's 1927 campaign for election as mayor of Chicago in which he concentrated much of his flamboyant oratory on the issue of control of the public schools. Big Bill promised to sack the superintendent who was, said Thompson, a lackey of King George and the British. Educators have ever since been agreed that a mayoral campaign subjecting the schools to this kind of educationally irrelevant attack was ample evidence of the need for protection from big city politics. Thompson's rhetoric was, of course, so blatantly demagogic that he makes an easy object lesson, but behind the rhetoric the issue has other features which make its moral much less clear.

In a most interesting book, called *School and Society in Chicago*,[3] George S. Counts examined the 1927 election soon after it happened. Counts' assessment is one of considerable ambivalence. On the one hand, he has no sympathy for Thompson's tactics of catering to his anti-British constituents by threatening to "punch King George in the snoot." Yet Thompson, in denouncing Superintendent McAndrew, was exploiting a very real conflict within the schools which had already engaged major socio-economic sectors in the community.

William McAndrew had come to Chicago in 1924 in the wake of a series of political scandals and convictions affecting members of the school board. McAndrew was looked to as a reformer who would use his office more vigorously than had his predecessors. Particularly, he was expected, apparently by all the most interested parties, to establish the superintendency as the center from which the schools would thereafter be run. Professional educational criteria were to prevail. No more politics!

McAndrew interpreted this mandate to mean that *he* would select the criteria; the classroom teachers would not. He believed that *professional* educators should embrace teachers and administrators in the same organizational units, so he effectively discouraged the previously vigorous teachers councils in the Chicago schools. Chicago had a strong and long-standing set of teacher organizations including units of the American Federation of Teachers, and McAndrew's unsympathetic view of their status led to abiding tension. Counts reports that the teachers' groups provided effective support for Thompson's election.

In addition, McAndrew had alienated organized labor in general. Not only had he rejected the propriety of the teachers' unions. He had introduced the junior high school. Chicago labor spokesmen construed this to be a step toward separate vocational training for working-class children. They viewed the junior high as an early breakaway from an equalitarian curriculum and this, they feared, was aimed at producing a docile, cheap labor force. Finally, McAndrew was a champion of the platoon system, or, as it was generally referred to, the Gary Plan. He favored the alleged efficiencies of the Plan and justified them quite frankly in a business-oriented way. Moreover, he actively and often consulted with representatives of the Chicago Association of Commerce; never with spokesmen of labor.

The result was a fairly considerable class conflict over McAndrew and his policies, both inside the school system and in the community. William Hale Thompson exploited these tensions and, in a way, helped resolve them. At least, after Thompson won, McAndrew was fired.

The important morals of this story seem to me to be the following: First, McAndrew provoked a severe conflict among the schoolmen themselves. The alleged intrusion of "politics" into the schools was really more the widening of a breach that already existed. Breaches among the schoolmen have been rather exceptional, from McAndrew's time until very nearly the present. Educators have proclaimed their fundamental unity of purpose and interest; and to a remarkable degree, they have lived up to it. But as teachers' unions grow strong and make demands and, occasionally, strike, and as community-wide controversies develop over the location, programs, and financing of the schools, the myths and practices which lead educators to maintain a united front in facing the outside, nonprofessional, world cannot survive. And, if there are conflicts, they will be exploited. The only question is, "By whom?"

The second lesson of the Chicago case of 1927 relates to the ultimate problem-solving machinery. McAndrew and the schools became a central issue in a partisan political race. Was this an appropriate mechanism for resolving a virtual class conflict involving the largest category of public expenditure? If it was not, then what is the regular political process for? Why are educational issues not properly determined in this arena? Why not indeed, except, perhaps, that Big Bill made the final determination. This dramatic fact has been enough to cinch the argument whenever some hardy soul could be found to play devil's advocate.

Later in this paper I shall explore further the two features I have drawn from the Chicago case; the political significance of unity among the schoolmen, and the possible consequences of determining school questions within the regular political processes of the community. Before I do, however, I would like to consider further what seems to me an important element of the context of school politics, in Chicago and every other city, then and now. This is what I shall call *the myth of the unitary community.*

George Counts concludes his analysis of the McAndrew affair by calling for "the frank recognition of the pluralistic quality of the modern city. Such recognition would involve the extension of a direct voice in the control of education to the more powerful interests and the more significant points of view."[4] The recommendation troubled Counts. He believed that it would really only "regularize practices already in existence," since these groups were already actively engaged in the struggle for influence over the schools. Still Counts recognized that he was making a "radical" proposal. It went directly counter to an historic perspective which has long pervaded the thinking of educators: namely, that the city is a unity for purposes of the school program. That is, regardless of ethnic, racial, religious, economic, or political differences and group conflicts in other arenas of urban life, education need not, and should not if it could, recognize or legitimize those differences. Education is a process that must not be differentiated according to section or class. Learning is the same phenomenon, or should be, in every neighborhood. Physical facilities and personnel should be allocated without regard to whatever group conflicts might exist in the community.

Schools have not always been run this way in reality. In the nineteenth century, some concessions were made to such prominent ethnic groups as the Germans by providing special classes in the German language; but in St. Louis, these were discontinued in 1888, or just about the time that ethnic heterogeneity really blossomed in the city. In recent years, a good many departures from the norm can be observed. In many cities, ethnic representation on the school board has been accepted as a hostage to the times, though the tendency is generally to deplore the necessity of special group recognition. Representatives of labor, of Negroes, and of Catholics hold big-city board memberships today and their constituents would complain if they did not. But the prevailing doctrines have not altered as much as the practice, I suspect, and the perspective which denies the legitimacy of group conflicts over school policy is certainly still widely held.

Surely an important element of this view of the city was the egalitarian democracy espoused by a large portion of professional education's intellectuals. The common school, later the high school, and now the community college have been urged and supported as mechanisms for equalizing the life chances of everyone in the community. To introduce programs for one group that were not available to another, or to build different kinds of school buildings for different neighborhoods, would cultivate group and class differences in the twig-bending stage which would lead to deeper socio-economic cleavages in the adult community. Most people, it seemed, never considered the possibility that the have-not groups might receive *more* and *better* education than the middle class.

It looked like the poor child could only get short-changed in a system of differentiated education and a caste system would result. This was the position not only of educators but probably of most actively concerned lay citizens too. It was an operative theory to guide education policy, and it was linked to a view of the community beyond the school system. For a consensual, integrated, organic community was and is an abiding standard for many American intellectuals. A proper city should manifest no deep-seated social or economic cleavages. Groups and classes with opposing interests are considered dangerous to the continued tranquillity of the polity. When they exist, as they increasingly did in the industrial city of turn-of-the-century America, it becomes necessary to adopt programs, such as universal education, and institutions, such as nonpartisan local government or at-large elections, that overcome the threatening heterogeneity.

But burgeoning immigration, the rise of the urban political machine, the emergence of corporate economic interests, and the enormous increases in scale of the urban community were parallel and closely connected phenomena of the 1880-1910 era. The metropolis which emerged threatened to erupt in group conflicts that would engulf the schools unless defenses could be found. The unitary-community perspective, more or less accurate as description a generation before and still serviceable for many smaller communities outside the metropolis, from that time on has been primarily a myth for the big city.

Still, it is a useful myth, and its uses were and are many. First, it served as a sharp contrast to the "political" world. Urban politics in the muckraker era was plainly a politics of group conflict and accommodation. The boss was a broker of social and economic tensions, and part of his brokerage fee to the community was the heightening of group consciousness. Ethnic identity for many Europeans was first achieved through the processes of American ward politics. Irish, Italian, or Czech nationalisms, for example, were much promoted in the cities of this era, as candidates and parties sought ways to secure the loyalties of the urban electorate.

With the political arena patently corrupt and marked by the conflicts of a myriad of "special" interests, the unitary-community perspective of education could justify the institutional separation of the schools from the rest of the political community. Independence from "politics" would keep out the selfish aims and corrupt tactics of the politician.

Independent school systems were not new of course. Institutional separation had always been a prevailing pattern. But in the larger cities, until the end of the nineteenth century, the structure of the independent school systems had been highly political.[5] Many school boards were chosen by wards. Some were selected by the city council, some by direct and frequent election. Ward representation was not originally viewed as a way of representing diverse group interests in the city as much as it was a means of keeping the board in close touch with the electorate. It resulted, however, in highly "politicized" school boards, sensitive to neighborhood pressures, particularly in the area of school-building. The ward system promoted log-rolling among sections of the city over many components of the school program. Neighborhoods sometimes traded off advantages, thereby probably facilitating rapid construction in many cities. Wards might also block one another, however, and thus retard the whole system.

The development of the professional educator to fill the newly created position of superintendent of schools inaugurated a different approach to education in which lay control would operate in increasing tension with the professional expert. With ward representation, this tension might well have been unbearable, at least to the professional educator. But parallel to the rise of the superintendency came the elimination of the ward system, and at-large election systems were rapidly adopted for the selection of school-board members.

The unitary myth was and is of great use in justifying an at-large school board. If the community is an organic whole with a single public interest in education, the board member should be protected against local, "selfish," interests by giving him a city-wide constituency. Moreover, since there are no legitimate "special" group interests in education, any responsible citizen can serve on the board, and there is no reason to give particular groups in the community a seat. To give a seat to labor, for example, would be wrong because it would constitute recognition of a special-group perspective on educational policy. Indeed, in a unitary community, there is really no such thing as representation on the school board, since there are no interests to represent. If, as George Counts and others found, urban school-board members were drawn predominantly from middle class, WASP, business-oriented strata of the community, it was a fact without significance in a unitary community.[6] In a recent study of school desegregation in eight northern cities, Robert Crain found that business and professional persons who serve on the school board, do so as individuals, not as class or elite spokesmen, and that such "nonrepresentative" individuals have been more acquiescent to integration than Board members elected by party or ethnic constituencies.[7]

The myth has thus been important in underwriting equalitarian educational programs, in separating the school systems from the main political process of the city, and in validating middle-class control of the schools. In addition, it was a useful adjunct to the emergence of professional expertise in education and school administration. Expertise rested on the assumption that valid ways and means to run the schools existed and were independent of the particular interests and values of particular groups. A good school system is good for everyone, not just a portion of the community. Experts, those people with professional training in the field, are qualified by their specialized training to tell good from bad, and laymen, if they are sensible, should defer to this expertise. If the unitary assumption is undermined, however, then no one, however well trained, can identify or administer a "good" school system. One may then ask only, "Good for whom? For which groups?"

Apart from a social scientist's perverse interest in exploring the myths we live by, is there any point to this discussion of the unitary-community myth? I believe the answer is "Emphatically, yes!" When educators treat the community as a unitary phenomenon, they are less able to offer programs and facilities which are differentiated to serve the diverse needs and values of particular subgroups in the city. It is an indictment of educational political theory that head-start projects for the urban poor only began on a large scale in 1965. Not that schoolmen did not often recognize the differential needs of slum children and sometimes tailor programs to fit those special needs. Rather, they had to do it in an inarticulate, often *sub rosa,* fashion since such programs went counter to the main stream of schoolmen's thinking. And so the programs were generally ineffective in meeting a problem of such magnitude.

The unitary-community idea was not simply for the guidance of educators. As we have seen, it helped protect the independence of the schools from the community's political processes. Or did it? Raymond E. Callahan has argued that the independent urban schoolmen were, in the period from about 1910 to 1930, extremely vulnerable; not, perhaps, to partisan political pressure, but to the dominant socio-economic interests of the community.[8] In this period, business was pretty generally dominant, and Callahan attributes the rise of the "cult of efficiency" in educational administration to the desire of vulnerable schoolmen to please the influential businessmen. In a way, Counts's story of Chicago confirms this point; during the relatively "nonpolitical" period when McAndrew was exercising full authority, the Association of Commerce occupied a very influential place while labor was excluded from school affairs. The "intrusion of politics" under Thompson meant the return of the teachers and other nonbusiness interests to active and influential positions.

Independent schools, operating according to the myth of the unitary community, were and are rather feeble instruments for seeking public support, and this weakness is one key to the business domination Callahan has described. School-tax rates and bond issues and, in some states, the annual school budget, may require specific voter approval in a referendum. How are the schoolmen to persuade the electorate to say yes? They have relatively little of what in urban politics is sometimes called "clout." They have no network of support from groups and interests for whom the educators have done favors in the past and who now can be asked to reciprocate. They may sometimes get the teachers and the parents and the children to ring doorbells, but such efforts are often ineffectual compared to the canvassing a strong party organization might do. Since approval of a school referendum invariably costs the taxpayers money immediately—there is no intervening lapse of time as there is between the election of a candidate to a city office and the possible future increase in taxes—a sizable negative vote may normally be assumed. Where is the positive vote coming from? Educators have gone on the assumption, quite probably correct, that the benevolent patronage of the business leadership was necessary if they were to have a chance of referendum success.

Today, in the big city, the structure of the situation has not changed. Only the interests which effectively make demands upon the schools have changed. Negroes, the poor, middle-class intellectuals, and teachers have partially, perhaps largely, displaced the businessmen. The unitary-community myth is still used as a defense of the schools. In order to persuade predominantly Catholic, lower-middle-class voters of Irish or Polish descent to support higher taxes for public schools, it is very important to emphasize the undivided benefits which all residents receive from an undifferentiated educational program. The difficulty is that today the pitch is no longer believed. It is evident, for example, that Negroes do not buy the myth that the community is unitary. They know better. Moreover, even though a school board with a unitary-community perspective may permit integration, Negroes demand a differentiated school program with compensatory facilities to help them fight prejudice and poverty, to help them reach a high enough level so that equal educational programs will no longer leave them behind. Meanwhile, those ethnic groups whom Wilson and Banfield have shown to be comparatively unwilling to vote for public expenditures for *any* purpose are especially unenthusiastic about putting high-cost programs into Negro slum schools.[9] Unions are anxious about job competition from the products of improved vocational programs. And although property taxes for schools may be only a minor problem for large corporate business, they are often severe in their effect on smaller business and on small householders. The latter groups, especially, are potential city dropouts; that is, they may move to suburbia if taxes go up, and the result may be to depreciate further the city's tax base while its educational needs increase. The unitary-community myth no longer serves to quiet the demonstrations or to pass the tax increase. It has largely outlived its usefulness. Yet it is still frequently articulated by schoolmen and lay supporters of the schools, perhaps because, as the inveterate gambler said in explaining his continued patronage of the crooked card game, "It's the only one in town."

There is another dimension in which unity has been emphasized with respect to schools. Educators have tried very hard to achieve and maintain consensus among all those engaged in the educational enterprise. Unity is a prerequisite to a reputation for expertise, and it thus adds to the bargaining power of schoolmen as they seek public support. Unity inside the school helps justify independence from "politics." In the Chicago case of 1927 and again today, in Chicago and elsewhere, the vulnerability of the schools to group pressures from the community depends heavily on the extent to which the board, the superintendent and his administrative associates, and the teaching staff remain as professional allies rather than splitting into conflicting camps.

The consensus among school interests is equally sought after at the state level, and as my colleagues and I have suggested in our study of state politics and the schools,[10] a number of devices have been developed to help achieve and preserve unity, even at some cost in terms of goal achievements—dollar volume of state aid, or teacher tenure law protection, for example. The point I wish to make here, however, is that unity among schoolmen is frequently a considerable handicap for big-city school interests, particularly in their efforts to get increased state aid.

Let me illustrate my point with a discussion that leans heavily on experience in Missouri. There, a moderately malapportioned legislature for many years exhibited great fiscal prudence. They spend more than they used to, but the state still ranks much lower in comparison to other states in expenditures than in income. Education is no exception, but, thanks largely to the skillful efforts of the Missouri State Teachers Association, both district consolidation and equalization grants under a foundation program have steadily improved the financial condition of most *rural* schools. But these programs are of much less benefit to schools in the large cities.

St. Louis and Kansas City schools receive state aid, to be sure, but on a somewhat different basis from other districts. State aid is legally less assured in the large cities, and it gets a smaller portion of the job done. The city of today has high-cost educational needs as compared to noncity areas. The core-city wealth, which is effectively taxable by local action, is comparatively less great than it used to be. State-aid programs which aim at providing minimum per-pupil expenditure do not solve big-city needs, and the states have not been receptive to extra demands of urban educators any more than they have responded to other urban interests.

When the city-school interests go to the state capital to press their special claims, they carry with them the norms of their professional colleagues everywhere, the norms of unity. All educators are united in favor of education, one and indivisible, to be provided equally for all. Yet this same delegation comes to ask special treatment from the state, either in the form of additional state money or additional authority to act for themselves. Moreover, the statewide education interests normally take no stand on the requests of the city-school interests. The statewide groups are interested in equalization, not special programs for the cities. They might even oppose urban-oriented school legislation since it would either compete for monies desired for equalization or, at the least, serve the needs of "the city," a symbol which noncity school leaders look on with suspicion. And these school leaders occupy the state department of education and dominate the state teachers association. From the point of view of the city schools, the best thing, and the usual thing, is to have the state groups stay out.

The urban school forces, assuming they have at least the neutrality of the state educational groups, confront another unity norm when they arrive at the state capital. This is the unwritten rule of the state legislature for dealing with all "local" issues, and the school needs of a city like St. Louis are treated within the same system of legislative practice as a proposed salary increase for the sheriff. They are all local issues. The rule provides that the legislators will approve a request from a local community provided that the state representatives from that community are substantially united in their support of the request.

One might suppose that, since the school groups all strive for internal unity, the legislators' prerequisite would be easy to fulfill. Such is not the case, and much of the reason lies in the separation of the schools from the political system of the city. The problem lies in the relationship, or rather the lack thereof, between the spokesmen for the schools and the city delegation in the legislature. City legislators are not interested in the schools. They avoid service on education committees, take little part in debate on school issues, and generally are thought by other legislators who are concerned about state school policy to contribute very little. Urban legislators are likely indeed to be profoundly uninterested in the concerns of *any* groups which successfully keep themselves apart from the political system of the city. They, after all, are products of that system and their points of reference are mainly contained within it. The school representatives cannot eschew politics and still make meaningful contact with the legislature.

Although most state legislators would be merely indifferent to the schools' plea for state help, some may actively, though covertly, oppose the requests. In the St. Louis case, a number of influential city legislators identify themselves with the "state" as a fiscal entity apart from the "city," and resist increased state expenditures of any kind for the city. Others may reflect a Catholic constituency and say, for instance, that unless money is provided for transportation to parochial schools they will oppose extra funds for public education in the city. Still others have been known to be engaged in various kinds of alliances, for instance with school-building and maintenance crews, and hope to gain benefits for their allies by helping to block the school board's requests in the legislature. Most of the city-based legislative opposition will be behind the scenes. In a roll call vote it would seldom show up. Nevertheless it may effectively block passage of the program.

The key to the problem is in the fact that the schoolmen have no way to reach the pivotal legislators where it counts. There is no network of mutual obligation and support connecting the two groupings. The school board can cash no influence checks in payment for past or future favors done for legislators. There are a few favors the school can do for a highly political legislator, but every element in professional education training and ideology contributes to the refusal to think in these terms. Parenthetically, it might be noted here that lay board members seem to get more righteously indignant than professional superintendents at the suggestion that they do a little trading if they want their program passed. Political naiveté, especially at the level of articulated ideology, helps reinforce the incapacity of urban school interests (though not necessarily in rural areas where schoolmen are often highly skilled in the arts of "forks of the creek" politics) to get what they want from the state. Not only the congenital opposition of educators to these elemental political tactics, but the widespread misconception of the source of their opposition further confounds them. Newspapers and other "spectator elites" such as academics have assumed that it was the rural interests that were doing in the urban claims. The inability to understand that urban legislators were often unresponsive, not only regarding school problems but on many other desires of some city-based interests, has led to invalid inferences about what to do next. One of these has been simply to reassert the evils of politics and the importance of insulating the schools against their bitter breath. The second is to await with confidence the coming of reapportionment. "Give us an urban majority and our urban programs will pass," is the assumption underlying this optimism. But an urban state legislative majority may still not care much about the schools; and, without more political savvy than they have displayed in the past, the spokesmen for city school interests will continue to get unsatisfactory treatment.

There is, obviously, the now genuinely optimistic prospect of federal funding, especially rich for urban schools serving slum populations. I shall not explore this dimension in detail, but I want to note an important point: urban interests have for years done much better at the federal level than in the state capitol. The reasons are complex and not very well understood, but among them is the strong, warm, and skillfully administered relationship between city political leaders and federal officials. Federal officials in all the relevant branches and agencies have come to be responsive to political leaders and politically skillful administrators in the cities. Mayors, urban-renewal directors, and local poverty-program administrators are especially skilled, individually and through their national associations, at bringing their points of view to the sympathetic attention of Washington. The newspaper accounts of the federal treatment of the Chicago schools in 1965 suggest to me that, as Mayor Daley salvaged Superintendent Willis's federal school money from the fire, so the help of political leaders in other cities may be necessary to maintain satisfactory relationships with this newly opened source of major financial assistance to big-city schools. Indeed, the requirement, which Washington officials seem to be taking seriously, that poverty programs and the new educational programs be closely coordinated may, in turn, force the schools into closer relationship with many other agencies of city government and thus, inevitably, into the mainstream of urban politics.

Earlier I raised the question of the significance of deciding the McAndrew affair within a partisan electoral process. Let us return to that dimension of our general problem. I have suggested that autonomy and isolation have serious disadvantages for urban schools. What is to be said on the other side? What would it be like if the schools were a more integral part of the urban political system; if, for example, they were made a regular line department of the city government with a director appointed by the mayor to serve at his pleasure? How would such a process work? What would be the substantive effects on educational policy and on the city generally?

To examine this issue directly, we need to be clear about how city political systems actually function. No single formulation will do justice to the complexities of the question but at least three points seem especially pertinent. First, political scientists generally have found that in large cities, and some of the smaller ones too, influence is rather widely dispersed, specialized, and exercised in a discontinuous fashion. That is, one person or group will be active and influential on one set of issues while quite a different array dominates the next set. This tendency is perhaps accentuated when a specialized set of issues, such as education, is determined within a specialized institutional framework. But the institutional framework is primarily reinforcing, not by itself determining. A second, related, finding of political scientists' examinations of the urban community is that great pressure is generally exercised in questions of substantive policy program (though not so much on elections or top level personnel appointments or tax rates) by the program's professional and administrative experts. In urban renewal or public health and hospitals, to take two examples from regular city government, the professional personnel run the programs about as completely as schoolmen run the schools; perhaps, more so.

A third finding is rather different from the first two, however. In many cities, though by no means in all of them, a critical and continuing role of substantial import is played by the mayor. He is the chief organizer of the dominant coalition of interests and the chief broker among them. He is the chief negotiator in balancing not only the disparate and often conflicting groups in the city but also in representing city needs to state and especially to federal agencies. More than that the mayor is the single most important problem-solver. He is committed, out of sheer re-election necessity if for no other reason, to rebuilding the slums, attracting new business, renovating downtown, implementing equal rights and opportunity and, as federal money is at last making it possible, improving the life chances of the urban poor. Not all mayors face the same circumstances, of course. Some are weak in formal authority to control even their governmental environment; many are lacking in the fiscal and human resources to get the necessary leverage on the social and economic environment. Nevertheless, there is a substantial similarity in the orientation and role of big-city mayors, and this convergence has been especially pronounced during the past decade. In style or substance, mayors of today have little in common with Big Bill Thompson. Actually, mayors might not relish taking more direct responsibility for the schools. Why should they take on another large problem area when they too can fall back on the argument that the schools should be nonpolitical? If they were to accept a more active role, it might be because they really want to resolve the complicated difficulties of urban life, and solutions *must* include effective use of the schools.

These three generalizations are all relevant to my question but in somewhat different ways. They suggest that if the schools were integrated with the urban governmental system, the educators would continue to make most of the technical and administrative decisions but the mayor and his coalition of community support would play a major role in giving over-all program and fiscal direction. The schools would compete more directly than now with other city programs for available money. Their programs might be more differentiated among different segments of the community, as the mayor tried at once to solve problems and ease tensions and to please the major elements of the coalition that elected him. Their top administrative personnel might be more vulnerable to the vicissitudes of electoral fortune, though mayors might be only slightly more effective in breaking through the defenses of the educators' bureaucracy to choose (or fire) their own men than are independent school boards now. Educators might find themselves and their programs more often subordinated to other agencies and programs than is presently the case, but this subordination might be more a difference in perception than reality; an independent school system already must compete for money and support, but in an indirect and segmented manner. It is not clear that mayor-directed schools would be more generously financed from the local community but neither is it inevitable that they would be poorer.

In my judgement, the principal difference between the existing arrangements for the government of urban public education and this hypothetical control by the mayor would be in the schools' relationship with the increasingly pluralistic and tension-filled community. An independent school system asks for community support directly, unprotected by any of the confusions of mandate that attend the election of political officials. The schools are naked against community pressures except as their unitary-community ideology and whatever rational citizen demand there may be for their services may shield them. I have argued, and so do the protest demonstrations and the negative votes in referenda, that these are not sufficient protection if the urban schools are to perform the extraordinarily difficult, high cost, tasks of educating the urban poor. It is not coincidence, I think, that recently the schools have been so often the target of the alienated and disaffected elements of society. Whether protesting against *de facto* segregation, double taxation of Catholics, or alleged Communist infiltration, the pickets know that the schools are vulnerable to direct assault. No other programs or interests get in the way. No other issues or loyalties intrude.

But the processes involved in electing a mayor and a council, especially on a partisan ticket, but also in a large, heterogeneous city with nonpartisan government, do mute these kinds of pressures. Mandates *are* vague; constraints on the specific policy choices which the officials will subsequntly make are loose. And the protection afforded to the professionals is considerable. They may administer their programs while someone else takes the heat, and diffuses it.

There is evidence that in the controversies over fluoridation those communities in which the voters decided the question in a referendum were often in the process racked by deep social conflict. In those cities where a mayor played a strong role, on the other hand, fluoridating the city water supply by administrative order, there was little untoward excitement.[11] The schools have far more substantive impact on urban life than fluoridation, of course; the latter seems to be mainly symbolic. But educational issues are laden with affect, and they may come more and more to resemble fluoridation as a focus for the manifold discontents of the city. The broader political process might help to protect the schools against becoming the urban community's battlefield.

In all that I have said thus far, my principal points appear to be as follows: (1) more direct and effective political (mayoral) control of the schools will be difficult to engineer becuase of the resistance of schoolmen, regardless of formal governmental structure, to "nonprofessional" direction; and (2) big-city school interests might get a more receptive hearing in state and national capitals and be partially screened from local direct action protests if they merge their interests more fully with the over-all city administration. But would this type of result lead to more effective education? This, in my judgement, is precisely the *wrong* question. In the urban center, there is no education which is separate from the issues of race, poverty, housing, crime, and the other human problems of the metropolis. The issue we need to face is whether greater mayoral control would lead to changes in school policy (e.g., better coordination and cooperation with urban renewal, recreation, and poverty programs) which would make the educational program more effective in solving the larger complex of community problems. In a simpler era, one could argue that Big Bill Thompson may well have done just this in Chicago. And, forty years later, one might well feel that, in the same city, Mayor Daley might have achieved more effective integration than Superintendent Willis seemed disposed to provide had the mayor chosen to violate the educators' code of independence and exert more direct control of the situation.

At the same time, there should be no mistake about the fact that greater administrative integration of schools with city would, in many cases, mean subordination of the schools to the city government. Moreover, such subordination might often mean that the schools were being used as instruments to achieve policy goals which extended well beyond more narrowly defined educational objectives. To some extent, of course, this is happening anyway, and indeed it has always been so. But the issue of political control forces us to be explicit about the question of how the many goals we wish to achieve in the city can best be approached. If it turned out that education was not at the head of the list, educators would be compelled to acknowledge that fact in a situation where they had to bargain for their share of the local resources against the direct competition of other programs as well as against the fiscal prudence of the electorate.

Direct competition for local money; subordination of educators to other public officials with other interests and programs; the self-conscious use of the schools as instruments to fight poverty, improve housing conditions, or fight city-suburb separation: these have been virtually unthinkable heresies to devoted schoolmen. Yet, are they much more than an explicit statement of steps and tendencies already being taken or implicit in present practices? I think not; we are already moving this way, to some extent we always have been doing so, and the real question to be faced is: How might we do these things better? A greater measure of local political leadership in education and coordination of the schools with other portions of the community might well contribute to this end.

FOOTNOTES

[1] I have chosen not to try to provide a full array of bibliographical citation to the relevant literature. Partly, this decision is based on my desire to present an argument which raises questions for public examination and debate rather than to assert that some things are so and others not. Partly, however, this particular body of literature is growing so rapidly that reference footnotes would be incomplete virtually as soon as they were written.

[2] I have explored some facets of this question in briefer compass in my essay, "Urban Politics and Education," in Sam Bass Warner, Jr., *Planning for a Nation of Cities* (Cambridge, Mass.: MIT Press, 1966), pp. 268-84.

[3] New York: Harcourt, Brace and Co., 1928.

[4] *Ibid.,* p. 357.

[5] See the discussion in Thomas McDowell Gilland, *The Origin and Development of the*

Power and Duties of the City School Superintendent (Chicago: University of Chicago Press, 1935), esp. Ch. vi.

[6]George S. Counts, "The Social Composition of Boards of Education: A Study in the Social Control of Public Education," *Supplementary Educational Monographs,* Vol. XXX, July 1927, p. 83. See also the more recent findings of Roy Coughran, "The School Board Member Today," *The American School Board Journal,* No. 6 (December, 1956), pp. 25-6, reprinted in August Kerber and Wilfred R. Smith, eds., *Educational Issues in a Changing Society,* rev. ed. (Detroit: Wayne State University Press, 1964), pp. 284-7. W. W. Charters argues cogently that whatever the political significance of middle-class membership on school boards may have been, there is little empirical basis for concluding that membership really has meant policy control anyway. See his "Social Class Analysis and the Control of Public Education," *Harvard Educational Review,* Vol. XXIII (Fall, 1953), pp. 268-83.

[7]Reported in "Educational Decision-Making and the Distribution of Influence in Cities," (paper presented to the American Political Science Association, September 7, 1966).

[8]*Education and the Cult of Efficiency* (Chicago: University of Chicago Press, 1962).

[9]James Q. Wilson and Edward C. Banfield, "Public-Regardingness as a Value Premise in Voting Behavior," *American Political Science Review,* Vol. LVIII (December, 1964), pp. 876-88.

[10]Nicholas A. Masters, Robert H. Salisbury, and Thomas H. Eliot, *State Politics and the Public Schools* (New York: Alfred Knopf, 1964).

[11]See Elihu Katz, Robert Crain, Donald Rosenthal, and Aaron J. Spector, *The Fluoridation Decision: Community Structure and Innovation* (Mss, March, 1965). The processes by which an affect-laden issue like education may ignite previously latent community tensions have been inadequately explored. James S. Coleman's highly suggestive synthesis of the then existing materials, *Community Conflict* (Glencoe, Illinois: The Free Press, 1957), has not been followed by much further empirical work.

FISCAL STATUS AND SCHOOL POLICY MAKING
IN SIX LARGE SCHOOL DISTRICTS *

Marilyn Gittell, T. Edward Hollander, William S. Vincent

Inputs are classified under three major functions: 1) administrative organization, 2) participation, and 3) allocation of financial resources. Each of these functions is influenced by a series of conditions which have been developed for analytic purposes and are described under each function.

These inputs were tested to try to establish relationships between characteristics of school systems and the output of innovation. Since so little difference was demonstrated in outputs one could anticipate great similarity in the inputs.

As Chapter 2 concluded, Detroit and Philadelphia were the two cities which seemed to show greater flexibility and receptivity to change. Part of the objective of the study was to explain the reason for that distinction. St. Louis and Chicago were the most static systems while Baltimore and New York City fell somewhere in-between but closer to the static model. It should be repeated, however, that the six school systems were generally not innovative and differences, particularly between the latter four, were small.

Of the three functions the most direct and clear cut cause and effect relationship with innovation appears to be public participation. The only apparent difference in any of the seven conditions or functions among the cities was in that area. The Detroit school system is a more open participatory system encouraging wider public participation than any of the other systems. More alternative choices are presented for policy making because of the proliferation of influence wielders and reactors and supporters. This circumstance can explain the greater flexibility and innovativeness of the Detroit school system. Similarly, the process of change and reform in Philadelphia further supports the relevance of broader public participation to change in the school system.

On the other end of the scale Chicago, St. Louis, Baltimore and New York

*From Cooperative Research Project No. 3237 published by the United States Office of Education, 1967, pp. 60-63, 66, 69-108, 115-117, 123-130.
Note: this article appears in an abridged form. Several tables are omitted.

City proved to be more closed systems with very limited outside participation. The cities did not differ appreciably in the area of school expenditures, nor did any of them show significant changes in the level and kind of expenditures made. In administrative organization some minor differences again distinguishing Detroit and Philadelphia were apparent but those differences were largely feedback and had been cited as outputs because they were of so recent vintage. The broader distribution of power in Detroit in the administrative structure and change in recruiting in Philadelphia were not influential factors as inputs. It did seem likely, however, that administrative reorganization in both cities would produce or had already produced other innovations in their respective school systems.

Some of the conditions which were originally hypothesized as relevant to innovation, and accepted by many to be significant, proved tentatively invalid. Such factors as selection of a superintendent from outside the system, fiscal status, and method of selection of the school board did not vary to any appreciable extent with output. In most other areas similarity was the predominant finding. The detailed discussion of the findings in each of the functions and conditions which follows provides further evidence for the conclusions.

Analysis of the administrative organization of the six districts identified the following problem areas:

1. Size of the bureaucracy.
2. Insularity of the staff resulting from promotion procedures that limited the opportunity for recruitment of outsiders and non-education administrative professionals.
3. Overcentralization of power in implementing policies.
4. Weaknesses inherent in the superintendent's office because of his lack of full power in selecting the top administrative staff.

These weaknesses in administration were identified in the pilot test of the City of New York school system. Thus, our analysis of other school systems emphasized these measures of the administrative structure.

Size and Role of the Bureaucracy

The development of ratios of bureaucratization did not suggest any significant relationships in the sample of six cities. No conclusions could reasonably be drawn to show that the level of bureaucratization influenced the adaptability of the system. Nor did fiscal independence and size of bureaucracy prove to be related.

Administrative staff was defined to include all professional supervisors ranging from bureau chief to superintendent. The number of persons holding such positions were identified and comparisons were made on the basis of staffing rate per 1000 pupils. Detroit had the smallest administrative staff of .32 per 1000 pupils in average daily attendance.

It had fewer professional administrators than Baltimore and Philadephia which were smaller districts. Philadelphia and St. Louis both had administrative staffing ratios of .80 and Baltimore had a ratio of .64. Chicago and New York had smaller ratios of .43 and .57 respectively, reflecting in part the size of the districts.

Two districts are differentiated by these ratios. New York has more administrative personnel on a per pupil basis than Chicago despite its dependent status and its large relative size. Further analysis showed that the ratio for New York more than doubled during the ten-year period rising from .24 in 1955 to .57 in 1965. Ratios for the other cities except Detroit remained approximately the same. In Detroit, the ratio rose by less than one-third. During the same period, administrative costs rose by 233.4% in New York, more than double the increase in Baltimore and St. Louis and slightly less than three times the increase in the other districts. The data suggest that the administrative staff in New York City is high and rising more rapidly than in the five other cities.

Detroit, on the other hand, shows a relatively low administrative staff ratio, though its fiscal status would suggest that it would have to provide services that municipal government provides in the dependent districts. Detroit's administrative costs rose by only 81.5% in the ten years ending 1965.

Viewed another way, administrative staff was analyzed in relation to classroom teachers. Detroit again showed the lowest ratio of less than one administrator per 100 teachers, New York and Chicago were 1.2, Philadelphia was 1.9, and Baltimore was the highest at 3.1. (Data was not available for St. Louis.) The ratios in 1965 were almost identical with 1955 except for New York City where the ratio doubled between 1955 and 1965.

Several factors interfere with the usefulness of the data—the title descriptions for administrators vary from city to city making it difficult to determine accurately the number of administrators on a comparable basis. Comparable data has been assembled to the extent that the persons in classifications specified by the school district are engaged in such work. For example, we have determined that in New York City almost 1000 teachers are assigned to central headquarters, performing administrative functions. Further, size is a factor, the larger the district, the greater economics of scale we would expect. Size explains New York City and Chicago's low ratios. Finally, we would expect that fiscally independent districts would require larger administrative staffs but the data do not bear this out. In summarizing, the only conclusions we can draw are that Detroit seems to have smaller bureaucracies than the other cities, and New York seems to have grown very rapidly during the last ten years.

The power of the top administrative staffs were examined in relation to three categories: powerful, limited power, and little power.

Detroit and New York are the only cities which could be categorized as having powerful administrative staffs. Staffs in the other cities are strong but would be categorized as limited in power.

The strength of administrative staffs in New York City and Detroit is in part reflected in their organization. The Detroit Organization of School Administrators and Supervisors has a collective bargaining agreement with the board of education. The New York City Council of Supervisory Associations successfully established a salary ratio in state legislation which provides for automatic adjustment of salaries to meet increases in teachers' salaries. In both cities these groups make policy statements. The New York City group is more vocal in expressing opposition to change and often will disagree with adopted board policy.

Only in New York City does the supervisory staff have tenure in office. In all of the other cities, however, no supervisor was ever removed from office. Interviews verified that informal tenure in the other cities was as strong as formal tenure in New York City. In all of the cities the supervisory staff was most influential in budgeting and curriculum policy-making. In several of the cities, particularly New York City and Chicago, the supervisory staff was consulted in the appointment of the superintendent. (See Table 4-5.)

Insularity of the Staff

Top staff was chosen from within the system in every city but Philadelphia and, to a minor degree, Detroit. Educationists monopolized top administrative positions in the school systems regardless of the character of their tasks.

Table 4-6 indicates the wide acceptance of insiders as administrators in the large city school systems. The promotion process reinforced by regulations requires every administrator to have come up through the ranks starting as teachers. In all of the cities requirements for examination and review in the appointment of administrators gave incumbent administrators the strongest role in the process.

In all the cities written and oral testing is used to establish eligibility for principal. In Detroit, Baltimore, New York and Philadelphia candidates for principal also are interviewed or approved in one way or another by a committee, usually composed of assistant, district or area superintendents, principals and members of a personnel committee. Appointments are generally made by the immediate supervisor and approved by the superintendent.

Assistant or district superintendents or their equivalents are appointed in Philadelphia and Baltimore by a committee with the approval of the superintendent. In Philadelphia the board of education must also approve. In other cities the superintendent appoints with board of education approval. In all instances, board of education approval is automatic.

Although, technically, most administrators are appointed for specific terms of office, few have ever been removed. The only possible break in this procedure is in Detroit where a one year review has been established for all supervisory appointments.

Table 4–5: Role of Administrative Organizations; Six School Districts; 1967

	Independent			Dependent		
	Chicago	Detroit	St. Louis	Baltimore	New York	Philadelphia*...
Professional Organization	CPC	MAESP OSAS^a	ESPA HSPA	BPA	CSA	PPA
Size	400	130 900		300	4,000	
Meet with School Officials	X	X	X	X	X	
Activities:						
Shape Policy:						
Curriculum		X	X X		X	
Budget		X	X		X	
Salary Negotiations	X	X			b	X
Prepare Proposals, Make Policy Statements	X	X	X		X	X

*Independent until 1966. ^a Recognized bargaining agent. ^b Ratio agreement on salaries. Source: Field interviews.
Key: CPC–Chicago Principals Club MAESP–Michigan Association of Elementary School Principals OSAS–Organization of School Administrators and Supervisors ESPA–Elementary School Principals Association HSPA–High School Principals Association BPA–Baltimore Principals Association CSA–Council of Supervisory Associations (Federation) PPA–Philadelphia Principals Association

Table 4–6: Non-School Professionals and Outsiders in
Top Administrative Staff; Six School Districts; 1967

Independent			Dependent		
Chicago	Detroit	St. Louis	Baltimore	New York	Philadelphia*
None	Deputy Super-intendent in charge of school-community relations[a] (1) School-Community Agents[a] (40)	None	Superinten-dent of Schools[b] (1) Director of Music[b] (1) Director of Art[b] (1) Director of Physical Educa-tion[b] (1) Director of Special Educa-tion[b] (1)	None	Superintendent of Schools[b] (1) Administrative Assistant to President[a] (1) Assistant to Superinten-dent[a] (1) Business Mana-ger[a] (1) Director of Data Process-ing[a] (1) Director of Financial Plan-ning[a] (1) Assistant Direc-tor of Financial Planning[a] (1) Controller[a] (1) Director of Devel-opment[a] (1) Director of Inte-gration and Inter-group Educa-tion[a] (1) Director of Plan-ning and research[a] (1) Assistant Super-intendent of School Facili-ties[b] (1) Director of Informational Services[a] (1)

*Independent until 1966.
[a]Non-school professionals
[b]From outside of school system

Source: Field interviews.

Much of the change in staff in the Philadelphia school district is on the top level where, for the first time, a concerted effort has been made to recruit professionals from outside the school system. There is already evidence that these "new" professionals are planning a greater degree of innovation.

In all the cities there is a stated preference for local talent. Only Philadelphia (under Shed) and Detroit (under Brownell) have made an effort to recruit out of the city. Even when superintendents are chosen from outside the city they are reluctant to recruit non-local people for staff.

Decentralization

Each of the six school systems has some form of decentralization. The district superintendents (Chicago, St. Louis, New York and Philadelphia), region superintendents (Detroit) and area directors (Baltimore) are administrative officers concerned with school activities in a part of each of the school systems.

In order to identify the extent of decentralization in each of the cities, certain key powers of the district superintendents were examined.

The first was budgetary power. Some degree of budgetary power is necessary for the assistant superintendent to function independently. The power potential can vary from no powers at one extreme to full control over the formulation and administration of the budget within the district, on the other hand. All district superintendents played some role limited largely to coordination of budget requests for supplies and equipment from the schools and formulation of staff requirements from enrollment estimates and predetermined staffing ratios. But the presence of real budgetary power requires either that an assistant superintendent play a major role in formulating the budget for his district based on his assessment of educational needs, or, alternatively, be given a specific amount to spend, and have the discretion to allocate the available funds according to his assessment of school needs.

Personnel power is also believed to be significant. Superintendents could have no power, evaluation powers only, power of transfer of principals and teachers, appointive powers in addition to the above and complete power over appointment, transfer evaluation and removal of staff.

Participation in general policy formulation may range from no participation to complete independence over policy formulation at the district level. He may play some role in central policy-making as a reactor to policies under consideration or he may participate with the superintendent in an administrative policy-making council. The district superintendent may also be examined in terms of the discretion he exercises in implementing policy. Does he have the power to adopt general policies, formulated centrally, to the needs of his district or is he compelled to administer instructional programs in his district in accordance with specific policies formulated centrally?

Salary may also be indicative of the power of the assistant superintendents and is considered in assessing his powers.

Finally, the nature and size of the assistant superintendent's staff may be indicative of the overall role he plays in the school district.

Short summaries concerning the role of the district superintendent in each of the systems follow. Heavy emphasis is placed upon the real powers of the district superintendents rather than their formal powers.

Chicago. There are twenty-seven district superintendents in Chicago. The local school districts in Chicago have local school boards which exercise very little power. The boards possess no appointment or budgetary powers and have no staffs. They do not appoint district superintendents. District superintendents are appointed by the general superintendent who has never seen fit to fire one.

The district superintendents have small staffs. Their offices include two persons performing duties of a clerical nature in addition to a supervisor and a psychologist. The supervisors, however, are responsible to the central office and not to the district superintendent.

In an interview, the controller of the Chicago Board of Education pointed out that principals and district superintendents play a small role in the budgetary process. Principals make requests for supplies and equipment which are invariably cut by the district superintendent who coordinates the budget requests of the schools in his district. New funds, according to the controller, are under the control of the general superintendent.[1]

A professor at Northwestern University noted that the superintendent (Benjamin C. Willis) ostensibly increased the power of district superintendents in 1959. He suggested, however, that the district superintendents were unwilling to take on the increased responsibility and the general superintendent was unwilling to delegate authority. Recommendations which were made by the district superintendents were generally ignored. The general superintendent, however, was hesitant to appoint principals or vice-principals who were opposed by the superintendent of the district in which the school was located.[2] The new general superintendent, James F. Redmond, has said that he will improve the low calibre district superintendents and give them more power.

Detroit. On March 14, 1967, Superintendent Norman Drachler submitted a reorganization plan to the Detroit Board of Education; part of the reorganization plan dealt with the decentralization of the school system.

The title of the nine field executives was changed to region superintendent. Each of the region superintendents was given a region assistant and a maintenance and operations assistant. These two officials are directly responsible to the region superintendent. Prior to the change, any staff assistance for the field executives had come from the central office.

The region superintendent's functions include school-community relations, supervision of staff, approval of major requisitions and reorganization plans within his region. They are responsible to the assistant superintendent for elementary education and to the deputy superintendent (administration). Each of the regions has between 30,000 and 35,000 pupils. Along with the reorganization plan went salary increases to $21,800.[3]

In an interview, Superintendent Drachler said that the region superintendents were not really aware of what was going on in the system as a whole. He said that a greater degree of decentralization was needed including further budgeting and personnel powers for the region superintendents.[4] If official statements can be taken as an indication of projected policy, more decentralization will be forthcoming in Detroit. In a statement made at the time he submitted his reorganization plan, Drachler said: "Eventually, it is hoped that a designation shall be made for each school and region in order to permit for flexibility within the overall policies of the board of education while at the same time holding the field executives and the principals accountable for efficient and adequate use of textbooks, supplies, repairs, etc."[5]

St. Louis. The six district superintendents in the St. Louis school system are appointed by the board of education upon the nomination of the superintendent.

The budgetary powers of the district superintendents are minor. They make estimates of the amount of supplies and equipment and the number of teachers needed in their districts. These latter estimates, however, involve no discretion since they must be made according to predetermined formulas (e.g., there is a set pupil-teacher ratio). Further, the secretary-treasurer makes independent enrollment estimates which are invariably lower and are usually adopted.

The personnel powers of the district superintendents seem to be much more important. They can appoint principals for schools within their districts. They may choose any person on the eligible list (regardless of position on that list) and from any part of the school system. Appointments are subject to the approval of the superintendent and the board. Such approval is ordinarily granted.

The district superintendents also supervise the work of principals and teachers. To aid them in this task there are three subject area supervisors assigned to the office. Each superintendent also has one secretary to perform clerical tasks.

The district superintendents are responsible primarily for the instructional aspects of the entire school program. Prior to this year the district superintendents were concerned only with the elementary schools. High schools are now coming under the jurisdiction of the district superintendents.

One of the district superintendents is engaged in a special program in his district, financed by the federal government. Significantly, none of the money involved in his program is being provided from the St. Louis school system. It is notable, however, that this enterprise, known as the Banneker District Community Project, is highly innovative.

Baltimore. Baltimore has no district superintendents as such. In 1954, however, the post of area director for elementary education was created. There are, at present, seven area directors for elementary education and two area directors for secondary education.

The area directors seem to be without an appreciable amount of power. They maintain offices in the central headquarters building and the impression gathered from an official explanation of their function is that they serve chiefly as funnels for communication between schools and the central headquarters. They lack any sort of budgetary or personnel powers. Principals remain responsible to the assistant superintendent for elementary education. They are described as working as a team with the assistant superintendent and the director of elementary education. In this teamwork they presumably bring to light the special concerns and problems of their district; they have no power to operate independently.[6]

These impressions are borne out by an assistant superintendent who stated that the area directors have no budgetary powers. The superintendent has the power to appoint the area directors but according to the assistant superintendent, all the present area directors were appointed through the personnel office.[7] The present superintendent admitted in an interview that despite the existence of the area directors the system is not really decentralized.[8]

An area resource team consisting of a supervisor of elementary education and specialists in elementary education, art education, music education and physical education is assigned to each area. This team (located at headquarters) is responsible both to the area director and the elementary supervisors.[9]

New York. New York City has thirty district superintendents who are appointed by the superintendent of schools with the approval of the board of education. The present superintendent has announced increased powers for district superintendents in personnel and budgeting. The district superintendent may now allocate financial resources and personnel among the schools of his district. He may choose principals from among the top three on a list provided by central headquarters. Teachers are assigned to schools by the central staff and district superintendents may transfer them within the district but only with the teacher's consent.

In 1967, local school boards were given the power to recommend names of candidates for the position to the superintendent. This was to allow for the expression of local opinion in the selection process. In the first attempt by a local board to use the power the superintendent refused to appoint the nominee of the local board. This seems to indicate that local opinion and preferences will not be allowed to interfere with the determination of the central administration.

The district superintendents in New York City are severely limited in the amount of budgetary discretion they can exercise and their personnel powers are similarly restricted. The strength of the central headquarters bureaucracy seems to be the chief inhibiting factor. Although the district superintendents are the chief avenues of possible decentralization of the system they are virtually powerless in the formulation of school policy. They feel that they cannot pinpoint problems and that even if they could they would not be able to do anything about them. They are hampered by small staffs which are largely clerical. Their main function seems to be to serve as a buffer to protect the central bureaucracy from dissatisfied parents.

In a series of interviews conducted by the study staff we found that the district superintendents are generally unwilling to exercise the little power that they do possess. The efforts to achieve a degree of decentralization by the board and the last two superintendents have met with two major obstacles, the vested interests of the central decision-making core at headquarters and the unwillingness of the district superintendents to take on the added responsibility. Many studies of the New York City school system have repeated the call for decentralization, but little has been accomplished.[10]

Philadelphia. There are, at present, nine district superintendents for eight districts within the Philadelphia school system. The size of the districts varies from 20,000 to 40,000 pupils. Two districts are predominantly white, two predominantly Negro and four are termed mixed.[11] The Odell study suggests that the optimum size for a school district is 20,000, and he recommends the immediate creation of two new districts in order to reduce the size of the two largest districts.[12]

The district superintendents are chosen by the superintendent. They are appointed on a year-to-year basis but they always have been reappointed.

According to the Deputy Superintendent, Robert L. Poindexter, the district superintendents have negligible power. They possess no budgetary powers and their personnel powers are severely limited. They have no authority to appoint principals (although Odell says they play an informal role in their selection) or to transfer teachers within their districts. They do rate principals and teachers. Neither teachers nor principals, however, are ever rated unsatisfactory. District superintendents do make curriculum recommendations to principals and implement guidelines set at central headquarters.[13]

The district superintendents in Philadelphia are plagued by the problem of insufficient office space (they are located in schools within their districts) and inadequate clerical staff. They are supplied with five clerks from headquarters. The size of the staff does not vary with the size of the district or with the special problems a district may have. No professional staff is directly responsible to the district superintendents.

According to Odell, the district superintendents are mainly concerned with the elementary schools. Attention given to the high schools depends upon the background and the concerns of the individual superintendent.

The Odell survey advocated more responsibility for district superintendents. However, it recognized that district superintendents were not ready to receive new responsibilities. Several other groups in Philadelphia and the new school superintendent have also supported greater decentralization and there is now a movement developing in that general direction.

Rankings of the Six Districts. The district superintendents have been ranked in each of the four categories of comparison outlined above—budgeting, personnel, general policy, and staff—and a composite ranking was developed. (See Table 4-7.)

Table 4—7
Composite Ranking of Six Districts
According to Power of District Superintendent
1965

District	Budgeting	Personnel	General Policy	Staff	Composite
Independent					
Chicago	2	3	4.5	3.5	3.25
Detroit	1	4	1	1	1.75
St. Louis	4	1	2	6	3.25
Dependent					
Baltimore	5.5	6	4.5	2	4.50
New York	3	2	4.5	3.5	3.25
Philadelphia*	5.5	5	4.5	3.5	5.00

*Independent until 1966.

The rank given to each system in each area may well be argued with. Since the focus of interest is real power and not the legal or formal power, judgment of the authors enters into the ranking. Differences in rank may often be attributed to the general impression of the system that has been conveyed. This is particularly true when the differences between the systems seem imperceptible from the information that was available.

In the area of budgeting, Detroit has been ranked first. The region superintendents may now approve major requisitions made by schools in their districts, thus playing a role in the formulation of the budget. This in itself is not a great deal of power, but in comparison to the other systems it is relevant.

Baltimore and Philadelphia have been ranked last because the area directors in Baltimore and the district superintendents in Philadelphia have no budgetary powers.

In Chicago the district superintendents play a minor role in budget formulation; St. Louis is ranked fourth because budgetary power does exist even though it is minimal; New York is ranked third because of the board's stated policy to extend budgetary power to the associate superintendents.

St. Louis has been ranked first in regard to the district superintendents' personnel powers. This ranking has been based on the district superintendents' power to appoint principals from anywhere on the eligibility list. The superintendent plays a role in the selection of principals and this power is considerable in comparison with the other systems. Baltimore ranks last because the area directors have no personnel powers.

New York was ranked second because the district superintendents may select a principal from among the top three names on the eligible list. But they have limited teacher transfer and rating powers. This placement may well be argued with because so few district superintendents have exercised this power.

Chicago has been ranked third (district superintendents apparently give their informal consent to the appointment of principals), Detroit fourth (supervision of staff), and Philadelphia fifth. Philadelphia's district superintendents do have the power to rate teachers and principals; however, this power can be considered perfunctory because all ratings are satisfactory.

The general policy role of the district superintendent is most difficult to rate. From the information available, such powers appear to be small. It is true that they may sit on various councils but their voices do not seem to carry much authority. Their role seems to consist almost entirely of making curriculum recommendations and assuring that policies set down by central headquarters are followed in their districts.

The only exceptions to these generalizations are Detroit and St. Louis and these exceptions may well be minor. In Detroit the region superintendent may make reorganization plans for his district. In St. Louis the superintendent of the Banneker district is being allowed to carry on an innovative program with federal funds.

Detroit and St. Louis were therefore ranked first and second, respectively. The other four systems, because no differences could be found at this time, were classed together and given a ranking of 4.5.

Staffing provided a further basis for ranking. Detroit was ranked first for providing the region superintendent with a good staff. The region superintendent is the only one of the local superintendents in any of the systems with a professional staff directly responsible to him. Despite location at the central headquarters the area director of Baltimore is ranked second because a professional staff is at least partially responsible to the area director. In none of the other cities is a professional staff responsible to the district superintendent.

The table shows that Detroit's region superintendent is the strongest of any of the district superintendents. His budgetary and general policy powers are greater than those of the other district superintendents, and he has a professional staff directly responsible to him.

New York, Chicago and St. Louis rank second, their district superintendents being very close in powers and staff, although in St. Louis staff aid is insufficient.[14] Baltimore is fifth and Philadelphia sixth. Both have district superintendents with almost a complete absence of power, and Philadelphia has poor staff facilities.

Conclusions. The emphasis placed upon differences in the school systems may have led to the conclusion that there are great differences between the systems. In reality, the differences are minor and the similarities striking. Detroit might be the only exception to this generalization. The difference between Detroit, on the one hand, and New York and Chicago, on the other, is greater than the difference between New York, Chicago and Baltimore. (See Table 4-7.)

Certain general conclusions are notable:

1. The district superintendents, almost without exception, are nearly totally powerless. They have not served as an innovative force in their school systems. Their potential for doing so is very sharply limited because they do not have the power necessary to initiate programs on their own.

2. The district superintendents' chief function seems to be to serve as a liaison between the central administration on the one hand and the schools, parents and other community groups on the other. They tend to act as a buffer protecting the central staff from parental dissatisfaction.

3. Secure tenure is a relevant factor characteristic of district superintendents. Even in Philadelphia, where there is an annual appointment, they are always reappointed. None of the cities, except Detroit, provide for review of the district superintendents.

4. In nearly all the cities recommendations have been made to increase the power and responsibility of the district superintendents. The delegation of power at this point, however, might be extremely difficult. James W. Fesler has pointed out that if authority is not delegated soon after the creation of an agency the agency will not be able to attract good men to its field service. This lack of good men in the field makes later decentralization even more difficult because mediocre men are not likely to be trusted enough to have authority delegated to them.[15]

This very problem was cited by Odell in Philadelphia. While favoring decentralization he was reluctant to recommend anything more than a gradual start, beginning with two districts.[16] It seemed quite clear that he was not altogether satisfied that the present district superintendents had the competence to make decentralization work. The same problem has arisen in New York City.

The Superintendent

The superintendent as the chief executive officer of the school system was a subject of primary concern.

The power of the superintendent is a function of tenure, salary, control of budget, power of appointment, relations with the board and extent of municipal and state involvement. On the basis of these criteria, the status of large city superintendents can be categorized as limited or strong. Relatively strong superintendencies were found in Detroit, Chicago and Philadelphia; weaker ones in St. Louis, Baltimore and New York. (See Table 4-8.)

Table 4–8
School Superintendents
Six School Districts
1900–1967

	Independent			Dependent		
	Chicago	Detroit	St. Louis	Baltimore	New York	Philadelphia*
Beginning of present Superintendent's term	1966	1967	1965	1965	1965	1967
Tenure of Superintendent (years)	4	3	4	b	6	3
Average term of Office (years)a	7	12.8	9	8	9	7
Age of Present Superintendent	50	55	n/a	50	54	40
Salary of present Superintendent	$48,500	$33,000	$25,000	$35,000	$40,000	$32,000
Number of Superintendents appointed from inside system	5	4	7	4	7	5
Number of Superintendents appointed from outside system	6	2	1	5	2	6
Powers of Superintendents:						
a) budget coordinator	X	X				
b) chief executive	X	X		X	X	
c) review of top supervisory staff		X	X	X	X	
d) top administrative staff appointed from outside system		X				X
e) overall power S = strong L = limited	S	S	L	L	L	S

n/a = not available
a 1900–1964.
bServes at pleasure of Board of Education.

*Independent until 1966.
Source: Statistical data from boards of education of the six school districts and interviews conducted in each district.

Control of the Budget. In all of the cities the superintendents prepare and control their own budgets. Only in St. Louis does the superintendent of instruction legally share power with four other executives—the building commissioner, the auditor, the secretary-treasurer and an attorney. In the past his power was limited to instructional programs, but at present, at the board's discretion, he functions as chief executive officer as well as executive budget officer of the system.[17] A bill is now pending to further strengthen his office by giving him the power to appoint his own budget director and staff. In Philadelphia, the business function was not centralized under the superintendent until 1963; in New York unit control was established as early as 1903.

Power of Appointment. The power of appointment strengthens the superintendencies in Detroit and Philadelphia. In Detroit, the new superintendent (Norman Drachler) can review appointments after one year. In Philadelphia, the new superintendent (Mark Shed) has been given added strength by the board to recruit personnel from outside the city. In addition, new directors have been recruited from outside the education field.

In contrast, tenured assistant superintendents in New York City severely limit the power of the superintendent. The previous superintendent (Calvin Gross), was unable to penetrate the huge bureaucratic system because he could not hire top personnel who would be loyal to him. In Baltimore, the superintendent has no contract but works on a day-to-day basis.

Superintendent's Role in State Relations

Because education is a state function, the percent of state aid may reflect the superintendent's power. In Detroit, during the administration of the former superintendent (Samuel Brownell, 1956-66) the percent of operating expenditures covered by state aid was the highest of any city.[18] Recent increases have been in effect in Chicago, Baltimore and Philadelphia. Despite increases, however, Chicago ranks lowest with St. Louis in the proportion of state aid to total revenues. State aid in St. Louis has remained at about twenty percent for the past ten years, while the percent in New York City has remained constant for six years.[19]

The importance of the role of the superintendent in securing state aid is evidenced in the success of Brownell in developing two special programs for Detroit.[20]

In Baltimore, under William Lemmel (1946-1953), the percent of state aid doubled enabling new programs and new building to get underway. Two other superintendents in Baltimore, Brain and Fisher, were skittish about involvement in politics and state aid was relatively low under their administrations.

In St. Louis, the new superintendent (William Kottmeyer) is a lobbyist for the board in Jefferson City and he has succeeded (with board members assistance) in obtaining the governor's support for greater state aid.

Tenure. The argument for long tenure for an executive is based on the notion that it takes from three to five years to initiate a program and even longer to build it into the system. But tenure, alone, does not insure innovation or strength. Phillip Hickey of St. Louis enjoyed long tenure (twenty-three years) but the limited powers of the superintendent in St. Louis confined his role to maintaining the status quo. Benjamin Willis of Chicago had the second highest tenure (thirteen years). Although he is credited with increased school construction, few innovations were adopted during that period. In Detroit, Brownell's ten years in office were marked by innovation. There were many complaints, however, that he did not delegate responsibility. In Philadelphia, Allen Wetter had a tenure of nine years, from 1955-1964. He was dominated by the business manager, and educational needs were subservient.

All of the superintendents have contracts except the superintendent in Baltimore. The superintendent's contract in New York City is the longest (6 years), Philadelphia and Detroit's are the shortest (3 years). In average term of office Detroit's superintendent was the longest. It would seem, therefore, that long tenure in itself does not insure innovation in the school system nor is it directly related to the strength of the superintendent.

Relations with Board. There was no evidence in the cities to suggest that any of the superintendents now influence directly the appointment of board members. Prior to 1961, the business manager in Philadelphia was said to play a major role in board appointments.[21] None have tenure of office under contracts longer than the board's term of office. All in practice, serve at discretion of the board.

In Chicago, school board-superintendent relations have frequently been uncertain. In the 1930's, an NEA investigation revealed the president of the school board was, in effect, the chief administrator of the school system. In the postwar era the two superintendents (Harold Hunt and Benjamin Willis) dominated the school environment. Both seemed to have worked successfully with their boards for most of their careers. At the end of his tenure Willis had divided support on the board because of his opposition to a survey of the Chicago schools and his failure to cooperate with the board's integration plans. The latter issue finally led to an open rupture.

In Philadelphia, Detroit, and St. Louis, boards have strengthened the superintendency. By contrast, in New York City, superintendents have conflicted in competition for power.

Salary. Some indication of the importance given to the superintendent's position may be seen from salary level, particularly as compared with that of the mayor's or other city officials. In Chicago, the superintendent's salary is highest at $48,500. The mayor of Chicago receives $35,000. The next highest superintendent's salary is in New York City at $40,000. The mayor receives $50,000. In Baltimore, the superintendent receives $35,000 as compared to $25,000 for the mayor. In Philadelphia, the superintendent receives $32,000 as compared to $30,000 for the mayor. In Detroit, the superintendent's salary is $32,000, $2,000 less than the mayor's. In St. Louis both the superintendent and the mayor receive $25,000. In Chicago, Baltimore and Philadelphia, the superintendent of schools is the highest paid city official. Of the superintendents ranked strong only in Detroit is the superintendent paid less than the mayor. (See Table 4-9.)

Table 4–9
Salary and Term of Office of
Mayor, Superintendent, and City Council
Six School Districts
1967

	Independent			Dependent		
	Chicago	Detroit	St. Louis	Baltimore	New York	Philadelphia*
SALARY (per year):						
Mayor	$35,000	$35,000	$25,000	$25,000	$50,000	$30,000
Superintendent	48,500	33,000	25,000	35,000	40,000	32,000
City Council[a]	8,000	17,500	5,000[b]	6,500[c]	10,000	15,000[d]
TERM OF OFFICE (in years)						
Board of Education	5	6	6	6	7	6
Mayor	4	4	4	4	4	4
Superintendent	4	3	4	e	6	3
City Council[a]	4	4	4	4	4	4

*Independent until 1966.
[a] St. Louis = Board of Aldermen
[b] President gets $7,500
[c] President gets $10,000
[d] President gets $20,000
[e] At pleasure of board

Sources: Field interviews.
Information Please Almanac and Year-book
(New York: Simon and Schuster, 1967), p. 624.

Insider-Outsider. In analyzing the board's selection of a superintendent, insider vs. outsider is the most frequently mentioned criterion. We did not find this by itself to be predictive of a superintendent's power.

According to Carlson,[22] when boards are dissatisfied, they choose outsiders and tend to pay them higher salaries and give them greater support. Yet, in New York City, the relations between the board and outsider, Calvin Gross, were marked by conflict. It would seem that in New York City the problem of an outsider establishing his authority is further complicated by the strength and competition for power with the top administrative staff. Reviewing the history of the New York City superintendency, we find that it was an insider (Harold Campbell) who achieved the greatest measure of innovation.

Outsiders can bring new ideas into a system as evidenced by former Superintendent Samuel Brownell in Detroit. Yet, it should be noted that it was Brownell's successor, Norman Drachler, an insider, who initiated review of appointments and is directing a reorganization of the staff.

In Baltimore, outsider George Brain did not cultivate close municipal and state ties, whereas, his successor Superintendent Paquin, an outsider, is actively doing this.[23]

In Chicago, outsider, Benjamin Willis, was innovative in curriculum but failed over a larger period of time to satisfy other pressing demands for integration and compensatory education.

In general, it can be tentatively said that in cities with a strong affinity for insiders, such as New York and St. Louis, such affinity may be a sign of inflexibility. However, wide acceptance of outsiders will not necessarily result in greater innovation, but it does suggest a more open system.

Participation

The Participants

Within any school system, the potential participants in the policy-making process are essentially the same. Legal power is usually divided between a board of education and the superintendent. The bureaucracy breaks down into the central administrative bureaucracy, field administrators, top supervisory staff, and middle management. Organizations representing each of these groups are common in the larger school districts, and the activities of each can be significant. Teachers and teacher organizations, parents and parents organizations are also potential participants. Specialized education interest groups (*ad hoc* and permanent) have been active in many communities, and their role can be a vital one. In the general community, there are other potential participants—local, state, and federal officials, civic groups, the press, business organizations, and individual entrepreneurs seeking the rewards of the school system. Interrelationships between these potential participants, the relative power of each, and their role in particular decisions, differs with the nature of the issues and the political environment of the school system.

Participation in school policy formulation can take three forms: (1) *closed* —only the professionals in the system participate; (2) *limited*—the board of education and/or the mayor and specialized educational interest groups participate; and (3) *wide*—groups not wholly concerned with school policy participate.

The participants analyzed for the study are school boards, teachers' organizations, community participants and government officials. Community participation includes direct participation (voting) and indirect (through interest groups). The latter are divided into special education groups, civic organizations, civil rights groups and *ad hoc* agencies. In classifying the six cities the most open systems were Detroit and Philadelphia. These cities had a larger number of influence wielders, reactors, and supporters. In both cities participation was encouraged as was opposition. In the four other cities participation was limited to the school establishment. It is notable that those cities with the strongest boards also were the most closed systems.

School Boards

The study compared the relative strength of the boards in each city as well as the responsiveness of the board to the community. On the basis of these findings city school boards were classified strong or weak. Those boards which had a term of office longer than the superintendent and/or longer than the mayor, participated effectively in budgeting (raised or lowered the budget), had active standing committees and staff are classified as strong.

In all of the cities the board members had longer terms of office than the superintendent and the mayor. (See Table 4-10.)

In four of the six cities, the board presidents complained about their inability to make budget policy. In Detroit, the board had to face the reality of voter control which limited new funds that could be raised through taxation. Chicago and Philadelphia through most of this period, had to rely upon the state legislature to raise the tax limit. New York and Baltimore were dependent upon the city government for funds.

Philadelphia (under the new board) and St. Louis were the only cities in which the board chairman felt they exercised adequate budgeting discretion. The board in St. Louis was concerned about the lack of funds and the difficulty of obtaining voter approval in tax elections, but the board chairman believed that the board budget was a "needs" budget and they were able to raise the funds they required. The new board chairman in Philadelphia has been able to obtain whatever taxing power he has needed from the Philadelphia City Council that sets the tax rate for schools.

With respect to staff, none of the boards have built independent staffs of any size. All depend on the superintendent and administrative staff for information

Table 4–10

Board of Education:
Size, Term of Office, and Method of Selection
Six School Districts
1967

		Independent		Independent		Dependent		
		Chicago	Detroit	St. Louis	Baltimore	New York	Philadelphia*
Size		11	7	12	9	9	9
Term of Office (years)		5	6	6	6	7	6
Method of Selection[a]		M–C–SP[b]	E	E	M–C	M–SP	M–SP

*Independent until 1966
[a] E = Elected
M = Appointed by Mayor
C = Council Approval Required
SP = Nomination by Selection Panel
[b] Selection panel is extra-legal

Source: Field interviews.

and assistance. The Chicago board has an influential and independent legal staff of eight, a secretary and one other staff member. New York City also has a legal staff, a research staff of three and an executive assistant. In St. Louis, five separate officers report to the board, but the board has no separate staff of its own. Baltimore also has no staff at all.

As regards standing committees, New York City and Philadelphia have no standing committees. Chicago has two, St. Louis and Baltimore have three and Detroit has five. (See Table 4-11.)

Frequent executive sessions of a board of education can be interpreted as reflecting a strong board which exercises power independently. In Chicago, Baltimore, St. Louis and Philadelphia the board holds frequent closed executive sessions as compared to the other cities. It should be noted that executive sessions might also reflect greater removal from public review and a more closed system.

The school boards in Chicago, Baltimore and St. Louis appear to be the strongest. Philadelphia and Detroit follow close behind and then New York City. Cities otherwise classified as the least open in the study are those with the strongest boards of education.

A comparison of the composition of the boards suggests great similarity and only minor differences. All of the boards' memberships take into account the need to represent ethnic and religious groups. All but St. Louis have two Negroes serving on the board; St. Louis has three. All the Negroes on the city school boards are professionals not intimately identified with civil rights causes. New York City and Philadelphia each have one woman and Baltimore has two serving on the board. Chicago, Detroit, and St. Louis have three women. In each case the women are representatives of established local women's civic groups. Each board includes representation of the three religious groups although not necessarily in strict proportion to the population of the city. The religious balance appeared to be a more sensitive issue in New York City than in any of the other cities. The panel selection device in Philadelphia, New York and Chicago has made little difference in the composition of the board as compared to other cities or as compared to memberships on earlier boards in their own cities.

The most common advanced degree for board members is the law degree. In each of the cities at least one and usually more of the board members are lawyers. In St. Louis four of the twelve members are lawyers, in New York and Philadelphia three members of the board are lawyers. Approximately two-thirds of the board members have some college degree, generally a Bachelor of Arts. Chicago, New York City and Detroit have labor represented on the board indicating the importance of unions in those cities. In St. Louis labor has been excluded from the board.

Approximately two-thirds of the board members in every city are over fifty years of age. Only one board member in any of the cities is under forty years of age.

Table 4-11

Board of Education: Operating Procedures
Six School Districts
1967

	Independent			Dependent		
	Chicago	Detroit	St. Louis	Baltimore	New York	Philadelphia*
Standing Committees	X	X	X	X		
Committee Meetings Closed		a	X	X		
Number of Monthly Open Meetings of Board	2	2	1	2	1	2
Holds Executive Sessions	X	X	X	X	X	X
Board Members Hold Informal Meetings with Outside Groups	X	X	X	X	X	X
Board Has Own Staff	X				X	X
Contract Negotiations With Union	X	X	n/a	X	X	X

n/a = not applicable
*Independent until 1966.
aMeetings of Personnel Committee are closed, others are open.

Source: Field interviews and data provided by the boards of education.

Detroit, Philadelphia and St. Louis have religious leaders on the board. The business community is represented on all of the boards except New York. St. Louis has the largest representation of the business community. New York City has six board members with a background in professional education, St. Louis and Baltimore have three members with an education background and Philadelphia has one. Teachers are not represented on any of the boards. (See Tables 4-12 and 13.)

Although no attempt was made to systematically collect data on the number of board members with children in the public school system it seemed evident that few of the board members in any of the cities had children in the public schools. The age factor alone would limit such a possibility.

Teachers' Organizations

The ever increasing role of the teachers' union and/or associations, particularly in salary negotiations, is of particular interest to analysis of the shifting roles of participants and their relative commitment to change in the school system. (Table 4-14.) The teachers union is recognized in Baltimore (1967), New York City (1963), Philadelphia (1965), Chicago (1966), and Detroit (1964). The union in each of those cities has been primarily concerned with salaries and conditions of employment, at least these are the issues that they have bargained on most strongly. Recognized unions are, of course, stronger and tend to be more influential as participants in the school policy process, especially in policies that relate to teaching loads and teacher assignments. In Detroit, Philadelphia and Chicago, the union conducts its negotiations largely with the superintendent and seldom meets with the board. The union in Chicago and New York City and the PSTA in Baltimore have used their political leverage to by-pass school officials and negotiate directly with the mayor to secure salary increases. In New York City and Philadelphia the union contract tends to contribute to a lack of flexibility in educational policy. Efforts to secure decentralization in New York City have run up against the restrictions in the present contract which limit personnel transfer, salaries and review procedures.

In Baltimore, the PSTA and the BTU have been competing with each other for recognition and as a consequence, the PSTA has become more militant and critical of the school system. Its direct influence, however, is not appreciable. In June, 1967, the BTU achieved recognition in a closely contested election.

There are two competing groups of teachers organizations in St. Louis (the AFT and NEA groups), neither of which are recognized bargaining agents. In Missouri collective bargaining for teachers is prohibited by state law. The teachers organizations in St. Louis are the weakest as compared to organizations in the other cities.

The unions have generally been uninterested in areas outside of the salary issue except in New York City where the UFT was instrumental in the creation of "More Effective Schools" and regularly voices public views on particular

Table 4–12: Board of Education; Age, and Educational and Professional Background; Six School Districts; 1967

	Independent				Dependent	
	Chicago	Detroit	St. Louis	Baltimore	New York	Philadelphia*
Size of Board	11	7	12	9	9	9
Age:a						
30 – 39		3	1	2	2	1
40 – 49		3	2	4	4	2
50 – 59		1	8	3	3	3
60 – over			1			
Educational Background by highest degree:b						
High School Diploma		3	2	2	1	5
Bachelor's		2	6	1		
Masters				2	2	3
Law		1	4	2	3	3
Ph. D.				1	3	
M. D.		1		1		1
Professional Background:c						
Educator		1	2	3	6	1
Labor Leader	2	1			2	
Accountant		1			1	
Attorney	1	1	3	2	3	3
Civic Organizations	2	3	3	2	1	1
Medical Doctor		1		1		
Religious Leader		1	2			2
Politician						1
Engineer						1
Business Administrator	2	2	4	2		1

*Independent until 1966. aData not available for Chicago. Data available for only six members in Philadelphia. bData not available for Chicago. cData available for 7 members only for Chicago. Source: Biographical data furnished by boards of education.

Table 4-13

Board of Education:
Religious and Racial Composition and Sex
Six School Districts
1967

	Independent			Dependent		
	Chicago	Detroit	St. Louis	Baltimore	New York	Philadelphia*
Religious Ratio[a]	4-2-5	0-1-3[c]	4-1-4[c]	1-2-6	3-3-3	2-2-5
Racial Composition[b]	9-2	5-2	9-3	7-2	7-2	7-2
Number of Women	3	3	3	2	1	1

*Independent until 1966.
[a]Catholic—Jewish—Protestant.
[b]White—Nonwhite.
[c]Incomplete data.
Source: Biographical data of board members.

Table 4–14
Role of Teacher Organizations–Six School Districts–1967

	Independent				Dependent			
	Chicago	Detroit	St. Louis		Baltimore		New York	Philadelphia*
Professional Organization	CTUa (AFT)	DFTa (AFT)	SLTU (AFT)	SLTA (NEA)	BTUa P (AFT)	PSTA (NEA)	UFTa (AFT)	FTa
Size	1400+	6000	1200	1800	1800	5000b	40,000	6700
Meet with School Officials	X	X	X	X	X		X	X
Activities:								
Shape Policy-Curriculum Budget	X	X			X	X	X	X
Prepare Proposals, Studies, Make Policy Statements								
Salary Negotiations	X	X	X		X		X	X
Collective Bargaining	X	X	c	c	X		X	X
Strike	X			X	X		X	
Strike Threat	X	X			X	X	X	X
Sanctions	X				X	X	X	X
Grievance Procedure	X	X			X	X	X	X
Support Tax Program	X				X	X	X	X
Meet with City Officials	X	X			X		X	X

*Independent until 1966.
aRecognized bargaining agent
bMembership includes administrative staff.
cCollective bargaining prohibited state law.
Source: Field interviews.

CTU = Chicago Teachers Union
DFT = Detroit Federation of Teachers
SLTU = St. Louis Teachers Union
BTU = Baltimore Teachers Union
PSTA = Public School Teachers Association

UFT = United Federation of Teachers
FT = Federation of Teachers
AFT = American Federation of Teachers
NEA = National Education Association

school issues. The New York City union has the strongest role of any of the unions in the various cities.

In several of the other cities the unions have issued reports and studies with recommendations for school improvement. Generally, these recommendations are not particularly influential in the determination of school policy.

The ever increasing strength and gradual recognition of teachers unions in large cities reflects the emergence of a significant new participant in the school policy process. The New York City experience serves as an example of the trend. Thus far, the role of the unions is one of limiting flexibility and stifling innovation—as contracts become more extensive this trend will probably be intensified. It is notable that teachers as a group have had almost no role in determining local school needs or curriculum.

Community Participants

Any definitive measure of community participation is most difficult to achieve. The role of outside participants in school policy making is continually shifting depending upon the issue. Yet it is the presence of the variety of participants that may determine the responsiveness of the system to public demands.

School Voting and Elections. Direct public participation includes the presence or absence of opportunity for direct participation as well as the degree of actual participation. Direct voting on school issues takes place only in the independent districts, and in those districts such public votes are limited to tax and debt questions and in two districts to school board elections.

In Detroit, St. Louis and Chicago the voters are required to vote on increases in school taxes and on school debt. The level of participation in voting, however, indicates the minimal role of direct elections as a means of stimulating community interest. In St. Louis in April, 1967, for instance, 27.2 percent of those eligible to vote voted in the school tax election. (Table 4-15.) The tax increase was approved by 76 percent of those voting. In the last twenty years fourteen votes have been held; twice the voters have failed to approve increases. In both instances the question was returned to the voters for approval and was dutifully approved. In only one year (1953) did more than 50 percent of the registered voters turn out for the elections—the usual response is between 20 and 30 percent of the electorate voting.[24] (Table 4-16.)

In Chicago from 1957-1967 there were three school bond and one school tax election. All were approved with well over 60 percent of the vote. The tax election in 1967 was the first to be held by the board under state legislation passed in 1965.[25] Taxes levied by the board are subject to statutory limitations by the state. The current law provides for a maximum of $1.71 on the education fund which may be increased by referendum to a $2.01 maximum. In any one referendum the levy may not be increased by more than 14¢. Currently, because

Table 4–15: Vote on School Tax Elections; Chicago, Detroit, and St. Louis; 1955–1967

City and Date of vote	Registration	Votes Cast		Affirmative Vote	
		Number	% of Votes Cast	Number	% of Votes Cast
Chicago:a					
Special Millage Election—2/67	725,056	453,905			62.1
Detroit:b					
Millage Election — 1959	848,738	303,558	44	194,557	64
Millage Election — 4/63	855,974	346,545	48.4	135,141	39
Regular Election—11/63	853,990	285,506	32.4	180,860	63
Millage Election—5/66	768,711	147,561	19.2	67,815	46
Regular Election—11/66	785,226	357,137	45.5	192,240	54
St. Louis:c					
Primary Election—3/55	331,910	111,493	33.6	90,309	81
Special Election—4/56	346,161	62,019	17.9	42,173	68
Special Election—3/58	357,387	94,562	26.5	59,574	63
Special Election—4/59	305,903	79,419	24.3	34,944	44
Special Election—3/60	319,695	102,878	32.2	65,842	64
Special Election—1/62	330,778	96,141	29.1	64,414	67
Alderman Election—3/63	292,039	98,932	33.9	49,565	50.1
Special Election—5/65	299,025	64,462	21.6	29,653	46
Special Election—6/65	299,025	122,273	40.9	83,146	68
General Election—4/67	259,623	70,675	27.2	53,713	76

aState Statute provides for referendum to increase taxes; tax may not be raised more than 15 cents in any one election.   bTotal millage for city and school district combined cannot exceed 50 mills.   cCan raise millage up to 3 times base with simple majority; after, a 2/3 majority is needed. If no election is held for two years, then voters must reaffirm base.   Sources: Statistical data provided by Board of Education, City of Chicago; Board of Education, City of St. Louis; and Report of Vote, November, 1963 and May, 1966, Citizens for Schools, Detroit.

TABLE 4 - 16

Vote on School Bond Referenda
Chicago and St. Louis[a]
1955 - 1967

City and Date of Vote	Registration	Votes Cast		Affirmative Vote	
		Number	% of Registration	Number	% of Votes Cast
Chicago:[b]					
Special Election - 6/57		790,813		684,240	86.5
Special Election - 4/59		705,113		539,802	76.6
General Election - 11/66		557,024		405,405	72.8
St. Louis:[c]					
Special Election - 3/60	319,695	98,008	30.7	62,236	63.5
Special Election - 3/60	319,695	96,322	30.1	63,493	65.9
Special Election - 5/60	319,695	57,297	17.9	35,826	62.5
General Election - 11/60		165,722		99,657	60.1
Special Election - 1/62	330,778	95,477	28.9	63,585	66.59
City Election - 3/62	330,778	133,560	40.4	98,301	73.6

[a]Data for Detroit not available; bond referenda held in 1959, 1963, and 1964. 1959 passed, but subsequent referenda were defeated.

[b]State Constitution sets debt limit of 5% of taxable property.

[c]School bond issues are passed by a 2/3 majority of those voting in bond referendum.

Sources: Statistical data provided by the Board of Education, City of Chicago; and Board of Education, City of St. Louis.

of the integration problem, the board does not want to go to the public on any issue and is trying to have the referendum provision deleted from the state law.[26]

In Detroit, the defeat of increased millage in May, 1966 led to a resubmission of the issue in November. In the May election, 20 percent of the registered voters participated.[27] After a well organized campaign supported by all of the local labor, business and civic groups in the city and with mayoral support, 61.9 percent of the voters turned out to approve the increase. In May there had been 129,646 blank votes cast; in November blank votes had been reduced to 9,118.

School board elections in Detroit and St. Louis are non-partisan; these are the only cities of the six included in the study which hold such elections. In Detroit, the UAW and the Democratic party are influential in nominations and elections. Board elections in both cities are held at the same time as general local elections. In St. Louis a reform group was organized in the early 1960's to promote reform candidates for the board. CAPS (Citizens Association for the Public Schools) (the reform group) functioned during two board elections. In 1961, they elected five board members and in 1963, four without opposition. Mr. Daniel Schlafly, chairman of the board, was the major influence in CAPS and internal disagreement with his position is believed to have led to its dissolution. A new group organized and Mr. Schlafly has since supported that group and its candidates for election.

School board elections in St. Louis have been under the control of the school board since 1963 and as such do not provide the kind of mechanism for participation that could be considered especially significant. Several groups and individuals in St. Louis indicated their impression that the board ignores the community once elected to office.

Hearings. More indirect forms of public participation are common to all of the other cities in varying degrees. School board hearings on budget matters are held in Chicago, New York and Philadelphia for one day in each city. The hearings in each city are generally attended by the most well organized groups in the city and present only a very limited sounding board for other dissenters. Open board meetings in the other cities allow for discussion of the budget but again the lack of public information limits the usefulness of these sessions. In some instances, other limitations, such as space, further restrict the value of hearings. The Baltimore hearings take place in a room which holds less than 30 people. In New York City in 1967, speakers at the hearings sat-in to protest the limited time available to present their points of view.

Public hearings are seldom held on issues other than the budget although several of the cities have held hearings on integration in recent years.

Interest Groups. The role of interest groups in the various cities is vital to the issue of participation. Such groups can be divided into those which are concerned only with education and those which are general but active in education. The effectiveness of these groups is related to their organization, size of staff, character of membership and leadership. Their influence is measured by their *entre* to the system and the extent to which their proposals are translated into policy. We have attempted to determine the extent to which these groups are innovative, supportive of innovation, supportive of budget increases, supportive of school officials and critical of school officials.

Education Groups. All of the cities have special educational interest groups. These include parent groups and citizen organizations. The parent groups in all of the cities play generally the same role. They are not strongly organized centrally nor do they have any professional staff except in New York City.[28] Their concerns are, therefore, largely with local and individual school problems. They are generally supportive of school officials especially in the areas of budget and special services. Parent groups tend to be less organized and active in the ghetto areas of each city. Exceptions are notable. In Detroit the Mothers Clubs have been active in achieving special services. In St. Louis, the parents groups have emerged as participants in school affairs in the Banneker District with the encouragement of the local superintendent.

Citizens' committees for schools function in all of the cities; their character and power varies from city to city.

In Philadelphia, New York and Chicago, these organizations are standing committees coordinating the work of affiliated groups in the area of education. They do not have their own memberships. In Philadelphia and Chicago, they have no professional staff, only an executive director. The New York City group, in contrast, has a sizable professional staff. As a group, these organizations cannot be classified as innovative; they tend to be more supportive than critical of the school system and its policies. They have good relations with school officials and are called on for support regularly.

On the other hand, citizens' committees have been organized in Detroit and to a lesser extent in Philadelphia on an *ad hoc* basis with the cooperation or participation of the board. They are given specific assignments by the board and are furnished with staff. They include influential members of the community including the business leadership of the cities. They usually conduct studies and make recommendations which are seriously considered and often adopted by the board. Though convened on an *ad hoc* basis, the committees replace old ones, so that one or another is in operation.

In St. Louis, a citizens' committee was convened by the board to examine integration policies and some of its recommendations were adopted.

Civic Organizations. General civic groups are not particularly active in school affairs in most of the cities. The Leagues of Women Voters spend a small percentage of their time and energies on education and are generally observers of the scene supplying information to their membership rather than participating in the development of policy.

Only in Philadelphia and Detroit and to a very limited extent, in St. Louis, have business groups and prominent economic notables become involved directly in school affairs. As noted in the description of school reform in Philadelphia, the Greater Philadelphia Movement was a prime element in the achievement of change and continues to be an active participant. In Detroit, the UAW encourages its membership to become involved through citizens' committees and provides guidance for participation through its education section. The union also supports candidates for board offices and has encouraged new school programs. Business leaders from the three automobile makers and Hudsons Department Store have also been significantly involved in school matters. The lack of involvement by business groups and unions in other cities is in sharp contrast to Philadelphia and Detroit. Business participation explains in part the greater openness in these two systems and perhaps also their greater receptivity to change and innovation.

Civil Rights Groups. Civil rights groups have only recently entered the school scene. As a result of the 1954 Supreme Court decision they were instrumental in every city in exposing school policy to public view. Although their emphasis has been largely in the area of school and staff integration, their impact was primarily in the area of demonstrating the closed character of school politics.

Civil rights groups are reactors to the school establishment. They serve as opposition groups, and their influence is negligible in terms of policy responses. The lack of adoption of integration programs and also the lack of general improvement in ghetto schools in all of the city school systems studied indicates their powerlessness. City school officials are, however, concerned with what their reaction will be to programs and policies.

Urban League, NAACP, and CORE function in all of the cities. CORE is the most militant and the least well organized in all the cities and it has been the group least involved with education. Although the NAACP generally sports large memberships in each city, it is the Urban League which provides organization, professional staff and education departments and financing for the most comprehensive programs. However, the Urban League is generally the most supportive of the system. The civil rights groups appear to be better organized and more active in education matters in Detroit and New York. In New York City local *ad hoc* groups have carried a large part of the civil rights protests in the schools. The recent emphasis in New York City is for local control of the schools. This kind of local initiative does not seem to be as prevalent in the other cities and may indicate a disenchantment with city-wide civil rights groups activity in New York.

In Detroit, TULC (Trade Union Leadership Council), an organization of Negro trade union leaders, has actively worked toward job training of Negro youth in the public schools. They enlisted the support of the board of education and the superintendent in their fight to change union policy which discriminated against Negroes, particularly in their apprenticeship programs.

Other. In several of the cities, religious groups and organizations concerned with special programs, i.e., the handicapped and retarded, tend to function as supporters of school policy. Their educational role is, however, limited to a narrow area of interest and they are more often supportive than innovative.

It is evident from the survey of community participation that the six city school systems display different degrees of openness and receptivity to such groups. In Detroit, the system appears to encourage outside participation and involvement which is not necesarily supportive of the establishment. Although the Detroit school system organizes the citizens' committees, it does not attempt to control or even direct them. This reflects a corollary willingness to view the school system in the broadest social role. It is not surprising, therefore, that Detroit proved to be the most innovative of the school systems studied.

In contrast, in St. Louis and Chicago, the systems are virtually closed to public participation although both are independent school districts. In both cities the school establishment controls all aspects of school policy. The number of influence wielders and reactors and supporters is negligible.

In New York City, although organizations proliferate, they are supportive or non-influential.

In a study of the politics of education in three states[29] the authors suggest, however, that large city delegations to the state legislatures, if they are unified, can get more school legislation advantageous to them. Perhaps more important than political conflicts is the lack of unified city education interests operating on the state level. This failure reduces the pressure for state education programs for cities. In Baltimore, city officials complained that school officials politicking on the state level conflicted with the efforts of other city officials.[30] The Usdan study of educational power in New York State also concluded that New York City's influence was minimal on the state level.[31] Similar conclusions have been made regarding Detroit's role.[32]

In some instances, state governments tend to be more conservative, thus limiting their own role. One can project, however, that the state, if it chose to be, could become a strong influence for change in local school systems. In New York State for instance in 1961, after pressure had mounted locally, the state commissioner of education was instrumental in having the state legislature remove the entire board of education in New York City. The commissioner also subsequently recommended the change in procedure for selection of school board members. However, his constant pressure and condemnation of *de facto* segregation in New York City have been completely ignored.

In Illinois and Michigan elected state superintendents of education are more influential with the legislature and the governor on school policy than are the appointed state officials in the other states,[33] yet this has not worked to the advantage of either Detroit or Chicago in terms of state aid programs.

State aid has come to be an increasingly significant source of funds for financing educational expenditures in the six cities studied. This increase does not reflect increasing state concern with big-city school problems, but rather the growing pressure on the state to assume a larger share of financing of all school systems within the state.

A comparison of the 1955 with the 1965 data shows that the districts that are dependent directly upon local officials for financial support have received larger increases in state aid in proportion to total revenues than the independent districts, perhaps reflecting the greater political bargaining power of municipal officials in the state legislature. In New York and Baltimore, the mayor, who has had to raise revenues for schools, represents the school district before the state in appealing for state aid. In Philadelphia, during this period, the school district has had to obtain increased taxing power from the state directly and/or additional aid, and the battle has been fought for the school system by local party leaders. On the other hand, the independent school systems had to rely to a greater extent on their own political influence in the state and their school officials appear to have had less influence in obtaining increased financing.

Data available for the period 1962/63 for eighteen (18) independent and dependent large city districts confirm that the dependent districts received larger amounts of state aid per pupil than their independent counterparts, with state aid for dependent districts growing at a faster rate.[34] (See Table 4-24.)

State aid has had minimal impact on innovation in the six districts studied. Because the preponderant amount of aid is allocated on a formula basis rather than on a program-by-program basis, state aid has substituted for local taxes in support of traditional programs. With the exception of New York City all of the state aid in the cities goes for support of regular school programs, special programs for the handicapped, and to a minor extent, for vocational training. In New York City, $200,000 out of $320 million went for experimental programs. This is in contrast to federal aid which is allocated largely on a program basis requiring the school system to adopt the program in order to qualify for the federal funds. (See Table 4-25.)

Federal Participation

The federal government is a relatively new but extremely important participant in large city school policy. As noted above in Chapter 3 the innovation output of all of these cities was largely conditioned by federal aid programs. Theodore Lowi in his study of New York City, *At the Pleasure of the Mayor,* concluded that external forces were the primary causes of innovation. It is clear that the emerging role of the federal government through the office of education is as an external force promoting the greatest change in the large city school districts that have been witnessed in the course of their history. Although the comprehensive federal aid programs in education are relatively new, their impact

Table 4—24

Comparison of State Aid to Total School Revenues
City and State-Wide Data
Six School Districts
1955 and 1965

	Percent of Total Revenues				Differences Between City and State Percentage	
	1955		1965			
Independent	City	State	City	State	1955	1965
Chicago	18%	16%	23%	23%	2[a]	—
Detroit	40	38	35	45	2[a]	10
St. Louis	23	30	23	32	7	9
Dependent						
Baltimore	18	25	31	33	7	2
New York	26	25	37	44	1[a]	7
Philadelphia*	24	41	34	43	17	9

*Independent until 1966.

[a]Percentage of current expenditures covered by state aid in city exceeds state-wide share.

Sources: City data from annual reports of the boards of education. State data for 1955: *Biennial Survey of Education Statistics, 1954/56* (Washington, D. C.: U. S. Office of Education, 1959), p. 72. State data for 1965: National Education Association, *Estimates of School Statistics*, 1966—1967 (Washington, D. C.: National Education Association, 1966), p. 31.

Table 4–25

Distribution of State Aid Among Programs
Six School Districts
1965[a]
(millions of dollars)

	Independent			Dependent		
	Chicago	Detroit	St. Louis	Baltimore	New York	Phila-delphia*
Support of Regular School Programs	58.7	57.9	13.7	21.9	321.0	38.3
Special Education	9.1	1.0	.8	.3	–	8.3
Teacher Training			.1			
Experimental Programs					.2	
	67.8	58.9	14.6	22.2	321.2	46.6

*Independent until 1966.
[a]1964/65 for Baltimore, Calendar year 1965 for Chicago and Philadelphia, 1965/66 for other districts.

Source: Annual reports and budgets of the boards of education.

can be witnessed in each of the cities. Compensatory education was virtually non-existent prior to federal aid. The proliferation of experimental programs can be traced directly to the influence of federal aid policies. Pre-school education is now widely accepted under "Headstart" auspices.

The only major compensatory program in the city of St. Louis is in the Banneker project which is completely federally funded. St. Louis also began a summer program in 30 schools with federal funding. Philadelphia has many programs begun with federal funding in the areas of work training, community action counseling services, teacher training and retraining, reading clinics and summer schools. Detroit has similar programs, including one for continuing education of pregnant girls. Baltimore began a compensatory program called Upward Bound with federal funds. New York City has programs similar to those in the other cities.

Federal project directors in each of the cities strain to come up with acceptable programs to be eligible for federal assistance. Appendix A, Tables I through VI indicate that federal aid now represents a sizable proportion of city school district expenditures. In Philadelphia federal aid is now 19.6%. New York has the lowest ratio of federal aid at 5.2%. Per capita federal aid to the cities per average daily attendance on a four-year average strongly suggests that political pressure is no small factor in securing large amounts of federal aid. Philadelphia has the highest per capita at $245.35. Chicago is next highest with $200.16. New York and Baltimore are the lowest with respectively $81.41 and $87.84.

Federal aid is significant not only in the amounts of money but in terms of the kinds of programs which are stimulated by it. The routine and status quo thinking of educational bureaucrats in normal budgeting processes is no longer acceptable under the federal aid programs. Younger and more vigorous administrators have been engaged in the development of federal programs. One of the most important requirements under Titles I and III of the Elementary and Secondary Education Acts of 1965 and 1966 is for the education establishment to cooperate with the local community groups. Although many of the cities have ignored the provision, in some it has assured participation of groups which have heretofore been removed from school affairs. Detroit is the only city in which a viable relationship has been established among the mayor, the school system and local community groups. The federal aid programs in Detroit reinforced the community-school concept and the open participatory quality of the school system. In contrast, in New York City the education committee of the Anti-Poverty Operations Board has repeatedly criticized the board of education and the superintendent for proceeding with federal programs without consultation.[35]

Federal aid has also encouraged greater cooperation between religious schools and the public school system. Although in several of the cities, primarily New York, there has been a public reaction to increased aid to religious institutions,

Table 4–26

Distribution of Federal Aid Among Programs
Six School Districts
1965[a]
(millions of dollars)

	Independent			Dependent		
	Chicago	Detroit	St. Louis	Balti-more	New York	Phila-delphia*
Compensatory Education	1.8	4.9	7.0	6.2	83.6	6.3
Pre-School	4.5	1.7		.2		6.0
Work Study	9.3	2.2	.9	1.6	4.6	.7
Adult Education	.5	.3		.3	1.9	.3
Educational T. V.		2.2				.2
Teacher Training		1.5	.1		1.3	4.1
Community Relations						.9
Curriculum and Guidance	1.1	5.9	.1	1.1	3.5	2.7
	17.2	18.7	8.1	9.4	94.9	21.2

*Independent until 1966.
[a]1966/67 for Baltimore and New York.

Source: Data furnished by boards of education.

competition between the systems and pressure for limiting support to public education has been undermined.

There is no question but that federal aid has to some degree disrupted the school systems. There are those people who will be critical of its influence and suggest as Willis did in Chicago that they will not adjust the school system to obtain federal funds which are wasteful. Some of the systems have also channeled funds into existing programs by relabeling them. The intrinsic value of federal aid, however, is in the degree to which change can be affected as a result of the scramble for federal funds. As long as federal guidelines require experimentation and innovation and encourage broader participation they can accomplish what no other element in the city school structure has been able to achieve over the last thirty years—a more flexible and responsive school policy process. (See Table 4-26.)

Foundation Support

Private foundations have also contributed to the innovativeness of some of the school systems. They generally award their grants for experimental programs, thus encouraging change in the system.

Detroit, Philadelphia and Chicago received funds from the Ford Foundation for their Great Cities Projects. Philadelphia also received Carnegie Foundation funds to begin its Magnet Schools Program. Baltimore began its pre-school classes and its Project Mission with Ford Foundation funding. Although the St. Louis public school system did not directly receive the funding, it participated in a Carnegie Foundation supported study conducted by Washington University on Child Motivation to Achieve. New York City is currently negotiating with Ford Foundation for three local school demonstration projects which will include wider control and community participation. In each case experimentation in the foundation sponsored effort was far greater than in the regular school program.

FOOTNOTES

[1] Interview with Robert W. Stickles, controller, Chicago Board of Education, April, 1967.

[2] Interview with Professor Lester Schloerb, former Chicago school officer, April, 1967.

[3] Norman Drachler, *The Superintendent's Pipeline*, "A report on the Board of Education Meeting of March 14, 1967." "Statement by Superintendent Norman Drachler on the Reorganization of the Executive Administrative Staff" (March 14, 1967.)

[4] Interview with Norman Drachler, Superintendent, Detroit Public Schools, March, 1967.

[5] "Statement by Superintendent Norman Drachler on the Reorganization of the Executive Administrative Staff," March 17, 1967.

[6] *One Hundred Twenty-Third Report of the Board of School Commissioners of Baltimore to the Mayor and City Council*, July 1, 1956 to June 30, 1958 and the Fiscal Years 1956 and 1957, pp. 22-4.

[7] Interview with Edith Walker, Assistant Superintendent of Elementary Education, Baltimore City Public Schools, February, 1967.

[8] Interview with Laurence G. Paquin, Superintendent, Baltimore City Public Schools, February, 1967.

[9]*One Hundred Twenty-Third Report*, pp. 134-5.

[10]Marilyn Gittell, *Participants and Participation: A Study of School Policy in New York City* (New York: Center for Urban Education, 1967), pp. 11, 13-4, 82-7, 89 (n. 13.)

[11]William R. Odell, *Educational Survey Report for the Philadelphia Board of Public Education* (Philadelphia: The Board of Public Education, 1965), p. 20.

[12]*Ibid.*, p. 373.

[13]Interview with Robert L. Poindexter, Deputy Superintendent of Schools for General Administration, Philadelphia, Public Schools, January, 1967. Odell, *op. cit.*, p. 27.

[14]Salaries were not considered in the ranking because in this area relative size of the school system would need to be considered. Detroit and Philadelphia gave their district superintendents a fixed salary, $21,800 in Detroit and $21,000 in Philadelphia. The average salary of New York's district superintendents was $23,485. In Chicago the salary varies from $17,700 to $22,400 per year. The weighted average salary is $21,619. The directors in Baltimore get either $16,000 or $15,700. The salaries of assistant superintendents in St. Louis range from $12,000 to $18,662.

[15]James W. Fesler, *Area and Administration* (University, Alabama: University of Alabama Press, 1949), p. 65.

[16]Odell, *op. cit.*, pp. 373ff.

[17]Interview with board member, St. Louis, May, 1967.

[18]See Table 4-24 and Appendix A, Table XII.

[19]See Table 4-24 and Appendix A, Table XII.

[20]Detroit Board of Education, *Project I and Project II for Integration* (1965.)

[21]Interviews with Philadelphia educators, January, 1967. For a more detailed discussion, see Chapter 3.

[22]Richard O. Carlson, *Executive Succession and Organizational Change* (Chicago: Midwest Administration Center, The University of Chicago, 1962), as cited in Joseph Marr Cronin, *The Board of Education in the Great Cities*, Unpublished E. Ed. dissertation (Stanford University, June 1965), pp. 281-2.

[23]Interviews with Baltimore educators, February, 1967.

[24]Statistical data provided by the Board of Education, St. Louis.

[25]Statistical data provided by the Board of Education, Chicago.

[26]Interview with official of Chicago Board of Education, March, 1967.

[27]Citizens for Schools, *Report of the Vote, November, 1963* (Detroit.)

[28]United Parents Associations, a centrally organized federation of over 400 parent and parent-teacher associations in New York City, has a sizeable professional staff.

[29]Nicholas A. Masters, Robert H. Salisbury and Thomas H. Eliot, *State Politics and the Public Schools: An Exploratory Analysis* (New York: Alfred A. Knopf, 1964), pp. 26-7.

[30]Interview with official of Baltimore City Council, February, 1967.

[31]Michael D. Usdan, *The Political Power of Education in New York State* (New York: The Institute of Administrative Research, Teachers College, Columbia University, 1963.)

[32]Masters, Salisbury and Eliot, *op. cit.*, p. 199.

[33]*Ibid.*, p. 277.

[34]See Part I, p. 81, *supra*.

[35]Interview with Poverty Program official, April-May, 1967.

THE SCHOOL BUDGET PROCESS
IN LARGE CITIES *

H. Thomas James, James A. Kelly, Walter I. Garms

Preparing the Budget

A great deal of preliminary work must be done by the administrative staff of a school district before the superintendent of schools (or in some cases, a co-equal business manager) makes a firm decision about the budget he will recommend to the board of education. Information must be collected about past expenditures and projected enrollments, about teachers' salaries in other districts, about state aid and the prospects for increasing it, about the demands for wage increases likely to come from employee groups and the demands from community groups for additional educational services. Organizing this information for decision-making and (in fiscally independent districts) screening it through the reality-test of probable revenue levels are the principal activities of school budget officials during the preparation stage.

To prepare this vast array of information requires time and technical knowledge, both of which are available in the school staff; the complexity of a big city budget increases the importance of technical knowledge and therefore places substantial power for budget preparation in the school staff. Later, we will discuss the degree to which the power of the board of education to shape the budget is limited by the concentration of budgetary expertise in the professional staff.

Formality in the Budget Process

Our field staff noted marked variations in the degree of formality with which the budget preparation process is carried on and in the extent to which individual staff members are involved in the process.[1]

In one city that typifies a pattern of wide formal involvement, the preparation of the budget starts with the system's principals, who fill in budget request forms in prescribed ways. The forms flow upward through channels of authority on a strict schedule, pausing at various review and approval stations along the way. When all requests as modified by the various approving authorities

*From *Determinants of Educational Expenditures in Large Cities of the United States,* by H. Thomas James, James A. Kelly and Walter I. Garms. Published by the School of Education, Stanford University, 1966, pp. 55-80.

have been compiled, the superintendent and his staff develop a budget proposal for presentation to the board.

In another city a pattern of centralized informal participation by a few key staff members is observed. Budget preparation is delegated by the superintendent to a staff assistant, who adjusts last year's budget by adding amounts reflecting increased price levels, salary changes, and increased enrollments. Beyond this, he relies on occasional phone calls from supervisors and principals, who may make special requests for changes in programs. The superintendent reviews the budget draft and passes it, relatively unchanged, to the school board for approval.

Formulas

While school superintendents and their budget directors are deciding upon salary levels of certificated and non-certificated personnel to recommend in their budget proposals, a separate budget process is under way in the area of supplies and equipment. To budget for supplies, materials, and even personnel, the typical procedure is to utilize a formula based upon the enrollment in a school or district, the number of teachers in a school or district, or a similar quantitative index. For example, a school district may decide through experience that a certain amount of money per pupil is required for art supplies in the elementary schools. This amount is used as a formula during the budget preparation period to determine how much will be required for elementary school art supplies, and is also used during the execution phase of the budget to determine the exact appropriations to be made to each school or district. Cities differ in the extent to which they require itemized lists to support budget requests for equipment, but the use of formulas is widespread both among cities and across a variety of budget categories within a city.

Formulas are also frequently used to determine the allocation of personnel. A city may determine from experience that a school with under 500 pupils needs a half-time clerk, a school with between 500 and 1,000 pupils needs a full-time clerk, etc. The allocation of teachers to a district or building is often made on the same basis. Suburban or rural schoolmen, accustomed to less bureaucratic budget procedures, may feel that this use of formulas is mechanical and inflexible. When a school system has hundreds of schools, however, it is not surprising that the search for equitable patterns for the distribution of materials and personnel leads to the use of universalistic formulas applied throughout the system.

One consequence of the use of formulas is the centralization of budgetary decision-making. Participation in the budget process by individual principals was observed in only 7 of the 14 big city school systems studied, and then not in roles of central importance. For instance, where principals are involved in the budget process, their activities include such tasks as supplying neighborhood enrollment projections used in the central office for applying formulas, and preparing requests for special building alterations and special items of equipment.

Generally speaking, it is difficult to change or adjust the formulas, even from one year to the next. Further evidence of the stability of these formulas over time is found in expenditures data (13 of the 14 cities reporting). Between 1959-60 and 1965-66, for instance, there was little change in the percentage distribution of total expenditures among various categories of expenditures. The only exception to this pattern was in expenditures for transportation; despite a rapid rise (57 percent) during the past six years, perhaps attributable to the civil rights demands for integration, transportation still accounted for only 1.1 percent of the total current expenditures for 1965-66 in the 13 cities. (See Table 6.)

Table 6

Total Percentage Distribution of Current Expenditures of
13 Cities, 1959-60 and 1965-66[a]

Category	1959-60 (Actual)	1965-66 (Budgeted)
Administration	2.6%	2.7%
Instruction	72.3	72.3
Operation and Maintenance	14.9	14.0
Fixed Charges	7.8	7.3
Attendance and Health	1.7	1.6
Transportation	.7	1.1
Other	—	1.0

[a]Sources: U. S. Office of Education, 1959-60 data; National Education Association, 1965-66 data.

Despite the traditional inflexibility of formulas, however, examples could be cited of their having been adjusted to meet local needs. In Chicago, a selected district was provided with extra remedial teachers; in Los Angeles, technological progress made possible a change in maintenance formulas; in New York, the "More Effective School" plan substituted a "saturation" for a "normal" staffing pattern; in St. Louis, a slum district was given an increased allotment of teachers. Similar instances could be cited in almost every city, but generally they occurred only as a result of severe political pressures.

Teachers and Salaries

The largest single item in any school district budget is teachers' salaries. During the preparation stage of the budget process, teachers' salaries and other benefits are a major item of concern, both to the representatives of teacher organizations and to the administrative staff of the school district. In virtually every city we studied, some form of salary demands were received from teacher organizations during the preparation stage of the budget process. Teacher organizations, including those affiliated with the American Federation of Teachers and with the National Education Association, prepared specific salary demands and submitted them either to the superintendent or to the board of education. In some instances, these demands were received in the form of a letter or brief memorandum, with little follow-up negotiations. In other instances, though, substantial communication was observed between representatives of teacher organizations and the administrative staff responsible for preparing the budget. In either circumstance, teachers' salaries were uppermost in the minds of budget directors as they were preparing the budget.

In Chapter II we distinguished between demands related to staff benefits and demands related to the extension of educational services, and commented that the two were not necessarily the same. With few exceptions, the demands from teacher organizations tend to relate to staff benefits, such as salary increases or released time, and not to the extension of educational services.[2]

The timing of collective bargaining with teachers, in relation to the legal schedule of events during a budget process, is an important consideration in the preparation of a big city school budget. In the few cities in which teachers' unions have succeeded in establishing a collective bargaining agreement with the board of education, negotiations over salaries are usually continued into late stages of the budget process. When a union negotiation will not be concluded by the end of the budget process, budget officials have only two realistic alternatives. They can ignore the fact that costs will obviously be incurred as a result of later negotiations; if they do, then supplementary funds must be obtained from whatever sources are available (such as from the Mayor in fiscally dependent New York City).

An alternative more consistent with the conception of a board of education as an independent policy-making group is to estimate in the original budget the minimal costs of the future collective bargaining settlement. In New York City, where the strength of the teachers' union is greater than in other cities,[3] the superintendent and board included $20 million in their budget to cover teachers' demands. This action, of course, notifies the union as to the amount the board has available to meet its demands, thus operationally becoming a minimum beneath which the union will refuse to settle. Far from accepting that amount, however, the United Federation of Teachers in New York City pressed for funds over and above the $20 million estimate, and eventually obtained a settlement of $65 million, agreed upon through mediation (and a supplementary appropriation) from the Mayor of New York City.

The success of a teachers' union in pressing its demands upon either the board of education or the city official responsible for the school budget is a function of many factors, including the solidarity of its support among rank-and-file teachers, the militancy of union leadership in threatening a strike, the revenue flexibility of the board of education, the political importance of unions, and the local attitude toward union membership for public employees. For instance, a teacher's strike threat would probably be perceived less favorably in some cities than in New York City owing to the different ways in which unionism as a general phenomenon is viewed in various cities. Where teachers' organizations do not have power to bargain collectively, the factor of contract timing is not yet a problem. Although cities that do not now have a collective bargaining agreement are witnessing a steady increase in the participation of teachers in matters related to their own welfare, teacher organizations are not yet the paramount influence on budget decisions in a majority of these cities.

Whether or not the increased participation of teachers in the management of urban schools is desirable is a matter of opinion. On the other hand, the nationwide struggle of teachers to promote their interests directly with boards of education has been viewed with some alarm by those who label it a dangerous intrusion of labor-management concepts into a professional realm. Wildman and Perry identify two assumptions underlying the theory and practice of collective bargaining, and question whether they are appropriate to a professional situation:

> the assumption of significant and continuing conflict between the managers and the managed in any enterprise, and . . . the corollary assumption that there will be a strong, identifiable community of interest and consensus within the employee group with regard to large numbers of items and areas of judgment on which there will be conflict with the managing authority.[4]

On the other hand, the traditional role of the beneficent but essentially authoritarian superintendent of schools, who himself represents the staff's best interests in negotiations with a board of education, does not apply in many large cities today. Two observations can be cited in support of this conclusion. First, teachers do not necessarily perceive the big city superintendent as their spokesman, despite his widely accepted status as the titular head of the hierarchy. Rather, they increasingly view him as the board's man, as management, whether the superintendent is an "insider" or an "outsider." More often, the real spokesmen for the instructional staff are found at the level of deputy, associate, or assistant superintendent, except in areas in which teachers' unions refuse or discourage membership by administrators. Second, attempts by teachers' unions to negotiate labor-management contracts can be viewed as the substitution of written law and due process for informal agreements and even human caprice. Such a substitution, after its accomplishment, is generally regarded as progress.

We conclude then that teachers' salaries and working conditions are the paramount issues facing decision-makers in big city budget processes, but that there is considerable variation in the arrangements through which teachers express, or bargain for, their interests. In most instances, however, demands for teachers' salaries are presented to the superintendent of schools or his budget director at an early date in the budget process so that changes in teachers' salaries can be reflected in early stages of budget preparation. Teachers also carry their demands directly to boards of education and municipal officials later in the budget process.

By contrast, we should note that generally during the preparation stage there is no similar channel open for formal communication from those who seek additional educational services. Community associations interested in extending educational services are rarely consulted by administrators. It is true that some groups (e.g., civil rights) press for policies and services on a year-round basis, but the board's public hearing is still the first available opportunity for these groups to express their views directly to the board. By that time, however, the budget is already prepared. Major changes may be difficult at a later stage, because of revenue limitations, and because the changes would probably require a corresponding decrease in another expenditure category, such as teachers' salaries.

Of course, demands from teacher organizations are not the only influence on school budget directors as they consider their recommendations for teachers' salaries. State laws may establish minimum levels of teacher's pay. Another factor is competition, primarily in the particular city's labor market but also with respect to other large cities across the country. The Research Council of the Great Cities Program for School Improvement regularly provides data to its members on salary levels in other cities. One school budget director commented, for instance, that in deciding upon the level of teachers' salaries to recommend to the board of education, he attempted to keep his district's minimum teacher's salary equal to that of the highest paying suburb in his metropolitan area, and to keep increments and maximums at the median of the cities in the Research Council. We conclude that demands from teachers themselves, competition for teachers in the labor market, and of course, the revenue situation are the principal factors in the issue of teachers' salaries.

Service Personnel

In most cities, non-certificated service personnel are organized into a number of unions and employee associations that negotiate their salaries and working conditions with senior administrative officials and boards of education. Sometimes closely linked with partisan political power or organized labor, the non-certificated employees exercise significant influence during the preparation stage of the budget process in most cities.

The channel for communication between this group, the superintendent of schools, and the board of education is frequently through an assistant superintendent of schools for business (called a secretary of the board or business manager in some districts), who functions as the spokesman for service personnel. He is usually, but not always, more responsive to local political norms than to the type of national professional norms with which other school administrators identify. The business manager may, in fact, possess a very substantial degree of influence over fiscal decisions in city and state government, and may serve over a period of decades as the principal liaison between the educational and political worlds.

The power of service personnel in several of the great cities achieved such importance during the nineteenth century and the early twentieth century that their spokesman reported directly to the board of education and not to the superintendent of schools. In several cities, this pattern has persisted.[5] Where this occurs, two or more separate budgets may be presented to the board, or the business manager may prepare the budget for all school departments and submit it directly to the board. This arrangement usually represents a bifurcation of power, where educational policies are the domain of the superintendent of schools and fiscal policies are the concern of the business manager, but frequently the division of power is not even, particularly where a strong business manager uses fiscal power to determine educational policy.

According to traditional school administration doctrine, this so-called "two-headed monster" is an ineffective administrative arrangement. Whether this is a fair evaluation is conjectural, but it is a matter of record that some big city systems have been governed with apparent harmony by two or more co-equal administrators for many years. In other cities, however, the harmony may be more apparent than real. Instances were reported to our research team of internal disputes over such things as whether a financial surplus existed. The finance man denied the existence of surplus funds, but his co-equal, the superintendent, claimed there were monies available for spending. Since financial reports showing account balances were not prepared for system-wide distribution, the superintendent was forced to rely upon information supplied from unofficial accounts kept by one of his men. In another instance, an administrative co-equal of a superintendent reportedly "leaked" a confidential "minimum budget" memorandum to powerful community taxpayer groups, thereby setting the stage for a storm of controversy at budget-hearing time.

Typically, service personnel have been the last school employee group to be placed under civil service (or tenure laws) and thus be removed from the influence of municipal patronage. In some big cities today, custodial and maintenance personnel have not been fully placed on civil service status; "temporary" or "pending" appointments are sometimes used to employ service personnel without full civil service status. During the 1960s there have been damaging scandals attracting widespread public and legislative attention in at least two cities (St. Louis and New York) where misconduct by non-civil-service personnel was noted.

A close relationship between the city government and the school government in some big cities, particularly in fiscally dependent school districts, has led to many attempts on the part of city administrators to have identical school and city salaries for similar grades of personnel. School administrators in such districts typically resist these efforts. This dispute is a symptom of the continuing ambiguity, discussed later in this chapter, with respect to whether a fiscally dependent school district is a municipal or a state agency. Courts have consistently held that the schools are a state agency, but fiscally dependent districts are usually regarded by city officials as a municipal department.

Boards of Education

The extent to which a board of education becomes involved in the budget process during its preparation stage apparently depends on the superintendent of schools. In districts where the superintendent wishes to involve the board intensively at this stage, board members, and perhaps a board budget committee, will informally exchange viewpoints with budget officials. In other districts, however, the first knowledge the board has of the school budget is the superintendent's formal presentation to them.[6]

While school officials or board of education members may consult municipal officials regarding the fiscal outlook for the city as a whole, it is unusual for municipal officials to become involved in the details of preparing the school budget even in fiscally dependent school districts. The budgets prepared by superintendents and boards in fiscally dependent cities are usually reduced in size when subjected to the lenses of political reality by municipal officials, who alone have the authority to levy taxes and who must then answer to the public for their actions. We will comment later on the relationship between fiscal independence and actual expenditures.

Budget preparations by school administrators in fiscally dependent cities tend to show greater increases in proposed expenditures (when compared to the previous year's level of actual expenditures) than budgets prepared by school administrators in fiscally independent school districts. In fiscally independent districts, the superintendent's immediate reference group—the board of education—is itself responsible for levying taxes and will usually tend to treat school budget requests more conservatively than the board in a fiscally dependent city. This difference is consistent with the behavior of school administrators as they formulate a budget; administrators in fiscally dependent districts tend to permit a more generous level of requested expenditures in the budget than in the dependent districts.

Although some boards of education as well as municipal officials in fiscally dependent districts do not play an active part in budget preparation, it is evident in some cities that quite early in the budget process the superintendent and his budget director have discussed the revenue and expenditures outlook for the coming budget with members of the board (and with municipal officials, where appropriate).[7] In many cases, the administrative staff has in mind a definite dollar amount, or percentage figure, which they believe the board will accept.

In one fiscally dependent city, not subject to state imposed maximum levy limitations, a consensus between city and school officials was apparently sustained for several years that the total property tax rate for school and city purposes would not exceed a certain amount. School administrators requested that school personnel "hold the line" in their budget requests, and balance any necessary increases by corresponding decreases in other areas. In another school district, fiscally independent of city government, it is customary for a member or two from the board of education to communicate quietly with the local Chamber of Commerce leaders to reach an agreement about what the school property tax rate ought to be for the following year. The amount of revenue that such a rate would produce then becomes the *de facto* ceiling below which budget requests must be fitted.

Thus, although boards of education, city officials, and community organizations do not ordinarily play an important role in the preparation stage of a big city school budget process, their influence at that stage may be present through an informal budget ceiling known to top administrators. Such predetermined ceilings, approximate though they may be, reflect existing political and economic realities and obviously affect many detailed decisions that must be made during the budget preparation stage.

The presence of predetermined budget ceilings, hammered out on the anvil of local political and fiscal realities, challenges the decision-making model that characterizes the discussion of the budget process in some school finance texts. These texts assume that educational need and policy largely determine expenditures; but the budget process of big city school districts, and perhaps most of the other school districts as well, simply is not primarily characterized by a "rational" determination of the educational needs of children. For too many years, big city school systems have had the quality of their services determined by the revenues available, and not by the needs they served. As we have observed earlier, this would appear to be a poor public policy that needs reversing if we would reverse the troublesome trend in urban education.

Determining the Budget

The Superintendent

The decision by the superintendent and top school staff members about the budget to be recommended to the board of education is the first major event in the determination stage of a big city school budget process.[8]

Nowhere is the "balancing" role of the school superintendent more evident than in his budget function. Here, he must be aware of the needs and pressures existing in his school system, including those from all of the other six classes of participants in the budget process. For example, he must attempt to construct his recommendations in such a way that civil rights groups, teachers' organizations, and taxpayers' associations all will accept them, even when they are not elated over the final budget.

Superintendents vary in two important ways with respect to the strategies they follow in presenting a budget to a board of education. First, they vary in the extent to which they press for higher educational expenditures; some superintendents pride themselves on "moving" a school system toward increased services for children and higher levels of teacher pay, while others place greater priority on frugality and efficiency in operation. Apart from these abstractions, however, superintendents (if they are to last long in their position) must be realistic about the revenue situation of the board of education, particularly in fiscally independent districts.

Second, superintendents vary both in the amount of information they provide to boards of education with their budget and in the timing of their presentation. In one large city, the superintendent did not discuss budget matters specifically with the board prior to the time he formally presented his published budget to them. The board promptly held a public hearing and an executive session on the budget. As a result, the board made only minor changes in the superintendent's budget. Yet it is difficult to stereotype the situation even in a given city, because in the situation just cited, the superintendent in the succeeding year increased substantially his communication with the board about budget matters during the budget preparation stage. As a consequence, during the second year, the board prepared a priority list of programs it wished to implement and used these priorities in evaluating the superintendent's formal budget recommendations.

The range in the amount of information provided by superintendents is extraordinary. In most cities the budget and supporting documents form an imposing pile of materials. In a few cities, though, important budget recommendations from the superintendent are accompanied by little or no detailed supporting data. In one city the superintendent's preliminary budget estimate for the board in a recent year was only two pages long; in another, the board for many years did not receive a detailed expenditures breakdown at any time during the budget process. Of course, these variations are partially a function of what a particular board wants and what it will accept, but on the whole the superintendent himself shapes the format of his budget presentation to the board of education.

Of the 14 cities, the greatest flow of information from the administrative staff to the board was observed in Los Angeles. There the board receives with the superintendent's budget a packet of 30 or 40 memoranda, showing revenue and expenditure trends over a period of years, with projections of these trends into future years. Detailed trends are shown for such areas as textbooks, teachers' salaries, revenues, and ADA. The Los Angeles Board, and particularly its

Budget and Finance Committee, analyze these materials thoroughly in a solid week of all-day public meetings before adopting the budget.

In most big cities, it is fair to say that the superintendent provides a substantial amount of supporting information when presenting his budget to the board. Budget specialists may argue over whether this information is presented in the most usable form or not; later we will discuss questions related to the utility of program budgeting as one alternative for increasing the usefulness of budget information to top decision-making. But when current budget documents are compared to those of a half-century ago, it is evident that budgeting today has become far more responsible and informative.

The Board of Education

A crucial use of power of a big city board of education is exemplified in the development of its annual budget, specifying the amount of tax money to be made available, and establishing rules as to how the money shall be distributed within the system.

To understand the role of big city boards of education in budget determination, it may be useful to review briefly the functions of boards of education in general. The classic view of the local board of education in the literature of school administration is that of policy-maker. The power of local boards of education is derived from state legislatures, which establish them by virtue of the state's plenary power over education. The legislature specifies the forms, powers, duties, and limitations of local boards of education.

It is only realistic to view local boards of education as political bodies, in as much as they are required by law to make policy for the local school system, and to see that policies made by the legislature are enforced. Boards thus represent a direct extension of the plenary power of the state. Some boards have direct access to renewable resources through the power to tax, while others have a state-mandated claim on taxes that are formally levied by the city government. In addition, when boards exercise the rule-making authority delegated to them by the State, their rules have the force of law within the school system.

In practice, however, increasingly detailed rules for schools are being written in state legislatures, thus in effect abrogating the rule-making power of local boards in any area affected, and returning to the legislature the authority once delegated to local boards. In addition, legislatures in many states have created separate bodies of law for regulating different classes of school systems; thus frequently legislatures enact laws applying only to "cities over 500,000 in population," which in most states means one or a few cities. These separate bodies of law for large districts tend to erode rather than increase the powers of their boards, reducing the alternatives for decision available to them. For instance, in 7 of the 14 cities, the fiscal discretion of local boards of education is more restricted than in smaller school districts in the same states.[9]

These laws reflect the suspicion with which rural-dominated state legislatures have historically viewed large cities. They also reflect the corollary view that big cities are better able to finance education than other cities and therefore require less fiscal discretion to meet their own interests through state restrictions on local taxing authority, thus further contributing to the fiscal difficulties of urban schools. As we noted in Chapter I, it is difficult to reconcile these views with our appraisals of the conditions and needs in our cities today.[10]

Some boards and superintendents in the 14 cities were observed to have close communication with political leaders in the state legislature, but other big city school systems seemed virtually isolated from the centers of political power at the state and sometimes even at the municipal level. Carefully planned and comprehensive attempts by educators to establish close liaison between school officials and partisan political leaders are the exception rather than the rule in cities today.

Lobbying is usually assigned to a member of the superintendent's staff, although in most cities with dual control it traditionally is a responsibility of the business manager. City school districts vary in the degree to which they appear to value lobbying;[11] some maintain a full-time staff in the state capital, while others restrict their attempts to influence the legislature to occasional trips to the capital to testify at hearings. Board members in most cities are not active lobbyists and participate only when critical measures are before the legislature. Superintendents themselves rarely carry the routine tasks of lobbying, but invariably become involved as important legislation is being considered.

Similarly, school staffs and board members typically do not enjoy close or friendly relationships with the local assessor; in some instances, these relationships are hostile. Few city school administrators and board members perceive themselves as part of the same political world as assessors and city councilmen. The general view of educators appears to be that they would rather be isolated than risk municipal control. It is by no means certain that the choices are in fact dichotomized. In one city, an exception to the general practice, the superintendent and board members are cultivating closer informal relationships with city and state political leaders, so that the schools can be better "represented" in the chambers of city and state government; neither the educators nor the politicians view these new relationships as leading to municipal control of this fiscally independent school district.

If the contention is correct that legislatures are increasing their body of policy for schools, then we should expect to see boards of education increasingly engaged in mediating the terms under which state or national policy is applied in the local system, and less involved with the formulation of policy in the traditional sense.

The control of big city boards of education by partisan political leaders has been observed at times in the past, but this phenomenon is far less frequently observed today. The traditional separation of schools and partisan politics, while not as uniformly upheld in cities as elsewhere, has been maintained in many cities. Thus, persons elected or appointed to boards of education in big cities today have rarely occupied other political office. Board positions are not typically regarded as a political stepping-stone, and ex-board members usually do not run for other political offices. In some cities, particularly where boards are appointive, the role of school board member is one of the last remaining opportunities for "gentlemen in public office." In many of the very large school systems, periods of relative peace and quiet in the management of the district's affairs have in the past been characterized by high incidence of "gentlemen" on the board, who frequently prefer to avoid controversy rather than to extend it. Therefore, some of the most consequential educational issues of our time, because they have been the most violently controversial, have often been sidestepped by big city boards of education, rather than being met "head on," and so have had to be resolved in the less squeamish but more realistic arenas of partisan politics. Public concern about school policies, particularly in the area of civil rights, is so serious today that it may no longer be possible for boards to do anything but face these concerns squarely. (Indeed, as we shall see, raising a controversial issue is one way to put pressure on the board.)

The Board and the Budget

As school districts become larger and more complicated, budget-making also becomes more complex, requiring extensive study of a wide-range of information, usually much more information than can ever be examined during a few meetings of a board of education. Throughout the budget preparation process, expert attention must be brought to bear on the budget, and the time and expertise required for budget preparation is within the school bureaucracy. Consequently, a substantial part of the control of the budget process passes into the hands of the bureaucracy itself, simply because of the size and complexity of the system's operations.

The power of the school bureaucracy during the budget preparation stage, substantial though it is, is countered in some large cities by unions, taxpayers' groups, and others who develop their own professional research staffs to present their point of view at budget hearings. In most cities, economy-oriented taxpayer associations are active during the school budget process, thus sustaining the influence held by many private "municipal research bureaus" for decades. Of course, voluntary associations demanding additional services will also attempt to influence the board, but in many cities these associations are not as influential as taxpayer associations or teachers' organizations.

The influence of economy-oriented taxpayers is substantial in some cases. For example, in one city the Chamber of Commerce represents the interests of the business community in keeping school budgets "in line." The Chamber leads a publicity campaign each time a tax election is held. It has supported the proposed school levy in all but two of the tax elections during the past several decades. However, in return for this support, the Chamber reserves the right to approve or disapprove the proposed levy before it is made public. It claims this right because Chamber members pay about 70 percent of the city's real estate taxes. Reportedly, Chamber of Commerce staff members confer with individual members of the school board, discussing the proposed levy. The board members generally face reality and hesitate to exceed the figure that the Chamber will support. In the two elections in which the Chamber of Commerce did not support the proposed school tax levy, the proposed levy was defeated. The Chamber of Commerce in this city views itself as a mediator of demands by some businessmen for low taxes and demands by school officials for increased expenditures.

Of course, not all members of the school clientele support higher expenditures and not all economy-oriented groups necessarily favor lower expenditures. In metropolitan areas, increasing attention is being given to the importance of education for economic activity. In one city, leaders of the Junior Chamber of Commerce in 1964 organized a group supporting the school budget increases proposed by the superintendent. This can be seen as part of the larger realization on the part of economists, educators, and national political leaders that education is an investment paying high and predictable dividends to the economy. In some cities employees and industrial promotion groups are offering increased support, or less vocal opposition, to increases in school budgets. Pressures on boards of education from business groups are thus divided between on the one hand those who favor reduced taxes, viewing educational expenditures as short-term demands from the public sector that are to be resisted, and on the other hand those who are willing to accept and even support higher educational expenditures as investments necessary for the long-term economic health of the community. But the primary orientation of most business and industry groups in large cities today is still skeptical toward increases in school expenditures.

The result of all this is that the principal function of a big city board in the budget process is to balance the conflicting pressures placed upon it. We have noted three kinds of pressures which appear to dominate the budget process. One is generated by the clientele of the school, the parents seeking improvement and extension of educational services. Their pressure tends to increase expenditures. The second kind of pressure is generated by the personnel of the school seeking to improve the conditions of work and staff benefits. This pressure also tends to increase expenditures, but it should be noted once again that increases in staff benefits do not necessarily increase the services to the clientele of the school. The third variety of pressure, which tends to reduce expenditures or minimize necessary increases, is generated by those citizens most interested in minimizing or at least stabilizing their tax load. A distinction should be made between groups primarily interested in efficiency and not necessarily opposed to budget increases (e.g., The Citizens Union in New York City), and groups definitely working to reduce budgets or at least minimize any required increases.

Face-to-face communication between these three major reference groups and the board of education becomes more and more difficult as the size of local systems increases. Associations begin to take over the task of expressing demands of special interest groups, and in some cities, the communication between the governing board and one or more of these three major reference groups periodically breaks down.

These three major reference groups have two avenues available to them for influencing the budget determination of boards of education. One is through direct pressure during the budget process itself, in the form of public statements, news releases, support or lack of it during tax election campaigns, appearances at public hearings, and strike threats. Of the three reference groups, personnel groups alone seem able to insert their demands into the budget during its early preparation stage.

School employees and citizens also can influence the budget determination of a board by affecting the selection of the board's members. Where the board is elected by popular vote, or where the tax levy must be approved by voters, all associational groups can seek to accomplish their purposes by increasing the votes favorable to their purposes. Where the board is appointed, these groups may attempt to influence the appointment itself. In New York, presidents of prominent voluntary associations and universities serve on a screening panel which provides a list of potential board members to the Mayor. The Mayor is required by law to appoint only from this list (although a bill has recently passed one house of the New York State Legislature revoking the mandatory provision). In Chicago, where a panel is also used to present names to the Mayor, the Mayor is not legally required to restrict his appointments to the list submitted by the screening panel, but the custom has been continued through several municipal administrations.

A possible alternative strategy for influencing school policy is by deliberately creating controversy; as noted above, boards of education generally seem disposed to move toward reducing controversy. Civil rights groups have employed this strategy with success in many cities, although not in all; in at least two cities, civil rights pressures have not yet had observable direct influence on the total budget. Other associations may move through state-wide organizations for legislation to require a local board to render a particular service or stay within a particular tax limit. The taxpayers' group can work through political channels to reduce the exposure of their property to taxation through underassessment.[12] The personnel group can organize and bargain with boards and legislatures with the ultimate threat implicit in this bargaining that they will withhold their services. If greatly aggrieved, citizens may withdraw from the field by moving to another district, or they may support schools in the private sector.

The typical board of education, in determining its budget, finds itself hemmed in by a growing body of state regulations, levy limitations, state-mandated services, salary schedules, tenure provisions, and other staff benefits, which place a large part of expenditures beyond their control. In the vortex of these pressures a board of education may become immobilized, and this tendency may be more difficult to resist as systems grow and age. Thus, the typical big city board of education attempts only relatively minor adjustments in the school budget during the brief time it considers it.

FOOTNOTES

[1]The descriptions of the budget process for New York and Los Angeles (contained in Appendixes B and C) illustrate the complexities of organizing and screening information during the budget preparation process.

[2]An exception to this general observation is the More Effective Schools Program, supported by the United Federation of Teachers in New York. Proposed increases in this program were a part of the U.F.T. demands during 1965 contract negotiations, but the cost of these increases was quite small compared with the cost of salary and working condition demands being negotiated at the same time. See Appendix B.

[3]Approximately 75 percent of New York City's 45,000 teachers are members of the United Federation of Teachers.

[4]Wesley A. Wildman and Charles R. Perry, "Group Conflict and School Organization," *Phi Delta Kappan*, XLVII, No. 5 (January 1966), p. 245.

[5]In 1960 St. Louis had five executive officers who reported to the Board (the Superintendent of Instruction, the Secretary-Treasurer, the Attorney, the Auditor, and the Director of School Buildings), but St. Louis has since designated the Superintendent of Instruction as the chief executive of the system. In Milwaukee the Superintendent of Schools and the Business Manager report to the Board. In Detroit it is the Superintendent of Schools and the Business Manager; in Cleveland, the Superintendent, the Clerk-Treasurer of the Board, and the Business Manager; in Philadelphia, the Superintendent and the Secretary-Business Manager (at present one man holds both positions). In Cleveland the Board of Education has moved to strengthen the Superintendent *vis-a-vis* the Business Manager and Clerk-Treasurer.

[6]See, for instance, Joseph Pois, *The School Board Crisis: A Chicago Case Study* (Chicago: Educational Methods, Inc., 1964).

[7]Some cities, such as St. Louis, are on a two-year budget cycle, because of bi-annual tax elections; during the second year, available revenues are known quite accurately before the budget process begins.

[8]We have noted earlier that in some districts part or all of the budget may be presented directly to the board by a business manager or other school official.

[9]Buffalo, Chicago, Milwaukee, New York City, Philadelphia, Pittsburgh, and St. Louis.

[10]See Chapter I.

[11]Excellent analyses of school-state relationships are found in: N. A. Masters, R. H. Salisbury, and T. H. Eliot, *State Politics and the Public Schools* (New York: Alfred A. Knopf, 1964) and in Stephen K. Bailey, *et al., Schoolmen in Politics,* The Economics and Politics of Public Education (Syracuse: Syracuse University Press, 1962).

[12]For other comments on assessment practices see Chapters I and IV.

ADMINISTRATOR-TEACHER RELATIONS:
HARMONY OR CONFLICT? *

Alan Rosenthal

Relations between school administrators and teachers have always evidenced strains arising from the clash between the professional norm of individual autonomy for the classroom teacher and the bureaucratic requirement of hierarchical authority in a school system. In the past, internal squabbles generally remained muted, as American schoolmen stood shoulder to shoulder pleading the cause of better education. The show of professional unity was remarkable indeed. Such unity, however, rested on sand.

Now school administrators are being harried by more, and more compelling, pressures from outside their professional ranks. Proposed changes in curriculum and instruction, problems of disadvantaged pupils, and dilemmas of *de facto* segregation, among others, pose new threats to administrative equanimity.

At the same time, they are being challenged from within. Even their "friends" seem to be conspiring to complicate further their already complicated lives. As the president of the National Education Association (NEA) said: "It is understandable that a superintendent faced with such problems might be disappointed when teachers whom he has looked upon as supporters make a public issue of their desire for a more responsible role in the decision-making process for the school system."[1]

One thing is clear. Public school teachers are no longer quiescent. Spearheaded by resolute organizations and stimulated by the furious competition between NEA and the American Federation of Teachers (AFT), a teachers movement is fast becoming a factor in many school systems, particularly in large cities. The former widespread, if passive, agreement on the operating rules of the educational game has undergone erosion. Teachers, or at least their leaders, are talking about full partnership in the educational enterprise, and they seem to mean what they are saying, as perhaps never before.

One approach to understanding emerging patterns in administrator-teacher relations is to examine certain dimensions of power in local education. Among the most important are: (1) the extent and nature of participation by teachers in educational policy making; (2) the character of organizational involvement; and (3) the manner in which differences are resolved. What roles should teachers play, what

*Alan Rosenthal, "Administrator-Teacher Relations: Harmony or Conflict?" in the *Public Administration Review,* June 1967. Reprinted by permission.

roles do they play, in deciding policy? Should they, or do they, participate by virtue of organizational membership or in their individual capacities as faculty members? Is harmony or conflict between teachers and administrators the norm? Should differences, if and when they exist, be settled in friendly fashion, or by resort to combat? How in fact are they settled?

It is more difficult to determine actual relationships than those the participants in public education think ought to exist. In some degree, the wants and beliefs of participants affect what they themselves do, what others do, and what results. The principal aim here is to explore the doctrines and attitudes of administrators and teachers with special regard for their views on the questions noted above. To ascertain administrative doctrine, a number of leading textbooks in the field of educational administration have been surveyed. To determine the doctrines and attitudes of teacher leaders, the pronouncements of national teacher organizations and opinions expressed by members of executive boards of local teacher groups in five large cities have been examined.[2]

Admittedly, the methodology lacks precision. Specification of administrative doctrine is of necessity indirect. Rather than analyzing attitudinal data directly, as was done in the case of local teacher leaders, the writer has deduced the views of administrators from the textual writings of professors of educational administration. It is assumed that the beliefs of school superintendents and the prescriptive statements in the training literature bear close resemblance. Most likely, the two are inextricably linked. Texts influence the ideas of practicing administrators and, in turn, the views and behavior of administrators help shape the textual lessons.

**Teacher Participation In
Educational Policy Making**

The Doctrine of Administrators

There was a time, decades ago, when few people thought that teachers might play a role in determining school policies. The doctrine of educational administration stressed the "authority" of the superintendent, not "democracy" and "participation" as it does today. With regard to teachers and their spokesmen, except for the hardy souls promoting the cause of unionization, scarcely any addressed themselves to this question.

Until the mid-1930's school administration was heavily influenced by concepts and practices associated with scientific management and efficiency. In the works of men like Franklin Bobbitt and Ellwood Cubberly the school administrator was pictured as the dominant education figure—the man who knew all the answers and who could and should tell others what to do and how to do it. Cubberly, for instance, described the superintendency as the office "up to which and down from which authority, direction, and inspiration flow." Insofar as he had to deal with workers on the line, the superintendent was "the supervisor of

instruction ... and also the leader, adviser, inspirer, and friend of teachers."
While administrators were obliged to manage their staffs in humane and
understanding fashion, teachers were obligated to perform faithfully their productive functions. As loyal workers in the vineyards of education, they might be
trusted to advise and counsel their administrative leaders, but anything smacking
of policy decision was beyond both their rightful purview and their professional
competence.[3]

Thanks to the human relations movement, an entirely different strain
dominates current literature on educational administration. Sophisticated methods of content analysis are not required to discern the pervasiveness of
democracy in contemporary doctrine. Commenting on this recent development,
W. W. Charters has observed that "hardly a textbook on school administration
fails to invoke the distinction between autocratic and democratic leadership ...,"
the former disavowed and the latter enthusiastically applauded.[4] Internal democracy brings with it teacher participation. Therefore, administrators now are
taught to engage their staffs in the formulation of policy, especially on matters
which immediately affect teachers and their work.[5]

Although seldom clearly stated, the rationale for teacher involvement can
readily be pieced together. It is, in fact, quite obvious. Teacher participation
improves staff performance and facilitates administration. Techniques such as
two-way communication, teacher committees, and cooperatively planned policies
promote staff morale, an ingredient believed vital to the success of instructional
programs.[6] In addition, the understanding and sense of joint responsibility
engendered by participation helps to improve the execution of policy. That is to
say, if teachers have worked on a problem, shared in developing alternatives, and
been in on making a choice, they will undoubtedly be more willing to implement
policy and adapt to promulgated change. A final reason, one usually not made
explicit, is that the cooperative approach to decision making promotes more
effective administrative control of the educational enterprise. It permits administrators' artful influence upon the behavior of their employees and it enables
them, by methods resembling cooptation, to discourage tendencies toward an
anti-managerial orientation.[7]

Since staff involvement is justified not only because of what it does for
teachers but, more importantly, in terms of how it aids administration, we might
guess that a line setting limits would be drawn somewhere. Indeed, it is.
Implicitly noted in the literature is the following argument: responsibility for
decisions is delegated by boards of education to school superintendents; it cannot
satisfactorily be shared; thus, superintendents are obligated to make final
decisions. One authority states the limitation in a rather backhanded way.
Teachers should be made aware, he writes, that they are being consulted on vital
educational matters and that "their ideas or proposals for action make a
difference to *those who have the power to make final decisions.*"[8] Or as another

puts it, the staff must recognize its own subordinate role in the cooperative enterprise and "develop understanding and appreciation of the limits within which it has power of *final* decision."[9] No doubt, the objectives of educational administration require that democratic leaders reduce master-servant feelings by treating teachers justly, consulting with them as much as possible, and even seeking their approval for administration proposals. Nevertheless, it must be understood, nothing should be done to dislodge authority from the hands of school administrators.

The Teachers' Doctrine

The views of teacher spokesmen regarding the staff's rightful role in policy making could be expected to differ substantially from those of administrators. Until recently, however, differences were slight. A national organization like NEA took little cognizance of the local school scene. Its platforms repeatedly referred to local teacher participation, but its energies were almost entirely devoted to other matters. Standards and ethics, tasks of lobbying for Federal funds, the conduct and dissemination of research, and the support of State affiliates commanded major attention.

AFT has long waved the banner of participation, and more vigorously. The union has shown little reluctance to express its dissatisfaction with the participatory rights actually accorded teachers. If administrators had surrendered some doctrinal ground, this meant little, for teachers were only permitted to take part in policy making on the most inconsequential matters. Yet, and in spite of its firm opposition to hierarchy in the schools, the Federation's positive program appeared modest or ambiguous. AFT seemed to call not for equal power in making decisions but rather for some system of consultation which would ensure that administrators took seriously the views of their staffs.

Because of the impetus of events and changing conditions, both national groups are more vociferous today in demanding an increased share of authority. AFT's current president, Charles Cogen, misses few occasions to mention that teachers can settle for no less than equality. Richard Batchelder, NEA's president, told the 1966 convention of school administrators that teachers "have been taking seriously the things that superintendents have been saying to each other . . . about the right of teachers to participate in the formulation of policies which affect them."[10] Since 1962, when its convention at Denver adopted a resolution on professional negotiations, NEA has vehemently insisted on the right of local associations to participate in the formulation of school policies, not only on "welfare" or "working conditions," but also on the conditions under which teachers teach and children learn. As one staff member of NEA interpreted the scope: "The subject matter of negotiations, then, should be as broadly defined as the educational program itself."[11]

Leaders of teacher organizations in New York City, Chicago, Boston, San

Francisco, and Atlanta are increasingly concerned about staff participation in decision making. With regard to policy making in general, leaders divide about equally between those who think their groups should have either more to say or a voice equal to that of the board and/or administration and those who feel they should be consulted and have their advice given weighty consideration. Union leaders are likely to prescribe at least an equal share, while non-union leaders overwhelmingly advocate a consultative role for their own groups.

What policy areas should be open to teacher influence is another question. The opinions of large-city teacher leaders vary, but not significantly, as to whether policy includes salary, personnel, curriculum and instruction, or in addition the organization of the school system. More representatives of both union and non-union groups desire at least an equal voice on salary policies; fewer desire the same say on issues related to the organization of the school system. Nevertheless, nearly all local leaders want greater power for their groups in the several domains of educational policy.

The Character of Organizational Involvement

Few community based teacher groups have realized or tapped the power potential which they possess. This is hardly surprising, since the ascendency of local organizations appears to be a recent phenomenon. Some years back, local education associations were kept busy parcelling out their limited resources among social functions, salary campaigns, and activities in alliance with other schoolmen to benefit public schools. In certain places, such as New York City, teachers were so organizationally fragmented that often effective intervention in educational affairs was practically impossible. Today, individualistic participation by teachers continues, but collective action is fast becoming a new norm in the educational game.

School administrators used to deal with individual teachers, not teacher organizations. As a consequence, the doctrines of educational administration which are expressed in the texts pay little attention to formal, organized groups of teachers but, incidentally, great attention to organized—i.e. "pressure"—groups in the community. Teachers are simply individuals in the system's employ. Their participation derives from their status as faculty members and not from their status as representatives of an organization. When groups themselves are accorded recognition in administrative doctrine, their prescribed role in decision-making is severely circumscribed.[12] Often their primary function is considered to be that of working within a coalition and demanding of a community additional monies for higher salaries and other public school needs.[13]

Both NEA and AFT naturally regard local teacher organizations and collective action as necessary in order to achieve the professional rights which teachers claim. The former group had in the past given scant attention to the tasks of energizing local associations, but instead allowed teachers to go it alone in their respective communities. Now NEA talks more and more about group representation and professional negotiations as the best avenues for teacher involvement in local decision making. In contrast, the Federation since earliest days put great stress on local organization as the only effective means of staff participation. "Teachers organize," AFT's Commission on Educational Reconstruction wrote, "because acting individually in matters of urgent immediacy, they have no opportunity to participate in decisions that directly affect them."[14] Local teachers and their leaders agree completely. A nationwide survey by NEA's research division reveals that nine out of ten rank-and-file teachers favor some type of group action, with many more opting for professional negotiations than for collective bargaining.[15] Surveys in five cities predictably show that leaders think their own groups ought to take an active role. No longer can teachers influence educational affairs through individual or committee action. Nine in ten union leaders and about half of the leaders of other groups believe that organizations must intervene if issues between administrators and teachers are to be equitably resolved. Even higher proportions agree that groups such as their own should not be content with obtaining benefits for their members, but should strive to increase their power to share in determining policies for the school system.

The Resolution of Differences

Commonality of Interests

The danger of group activity, according to tenets of educational administration, is that it may foster unnecessary and harmful conflict. True to human relations precepts, administrative doctrine emphasizes the harmony of interests and the agreement on goals that are supposed to exist among administrators and teachers. Start with these vital ingredients, add a pinch or two of consultation, and stir well with humane administration. Then, few genuine misunderstandings need arise. If disagreement should occur, it may often be attributable not to the inadequacy of the recipe but to willful intent on the parts of some to spoil the broth. Specifically, once employee organizations become viable political entities, their leaderships may develop a vested interest in seeking out and maintaining conflict situations. Little of positive value, however, can be accomplished by means of conflict. When people think separately, make demands upon each other, and wage battle, public schools stand to lose. Satisfaction and justice within the system depend upon real cooperation; consequently, rationality, not power, is the road to educational progress. In short, administration counsels: why fight when we all are bound together by ties of professionalism, common ends, and the mutual ability to settle minor differences sensibly?[16]

Along similar lines, NEA speaks of shared interests and close cooperation. Into one inclusive organization NEA recruits administrators and teachers alike, all of whom are colleagues rather than adversaries. One Association official, arguing the case for administrator membership, acknowledged some problems, but reiterated that "the primary premise underlying the concept of education as a profession is that all of its practitioners, regardless of their individual role in the overall process, have a common interest and objective."[17] Gradually, NEA has begun to recognize that the very nature of the superintendency forces administrators to respond not only to professional norms but also to nonprofessional pressures. Thus, differences of opinion on the means of achieving common ends may occasionally arise. However, this does not mean that professional solidarity need be sacrificed. Even with formal negotiating, no breach with administration is necessary. The superintendent should play the role of educational statesman, aligning himself with neither the school board nor the teachers association. Given good faith in negotiations, the resolution of differences does not depend on power but rather on orderly methods of reaching mutually satisfactory agreements without resorting to channels outside of education. In fact, where professional negotiations have been instituted, the employment of pressure and sanctions has been unnecessary. An occasional battle may have to be waged with school boards and politicians, but the major battle today finds all true professionals united in resisting "Those forces which would pit one segment of the teaching profession against another."[18]

The Uses of Conflict

Perhaps the sharpest ideological differences between AFT and NEA are over questions concerning the commonality of interests, the need for combat, and the uses of power. The Federation has long called attention to the contrasting positions of teachers and administrators. It excludes school superintendents from membership, not because it sees them as inherently hostile to teachers' interests but because they are believed to have different ideas and responsibilities as a result of their dissimilar roles in the school organization.[19] Nevertheless, much of the literature distributed by AFT is critical of school administration and portrays administrators as servants of the boards which employ them.

A confidential document written by the union's chief organizational strategist, David Selden, provides a good example. In suggesting tactics for local collective bargaining campaigns, Selden points out that if union representatives meet with the superintendent they will inevitably find him doing the school board's bidding and stalling on their carefully formulated proposals.[20] For AFT, conflict rather than harmony characterizes school relationships. If teachers are to attain their rightful role in decision making and deserved personal benefits, they must resort to mass action and seek collective power through a labor-affiliated organization. The educational business, like democratic politics generally, is often rough and ready, involving of necessity the push and pull of conflicting power groups.[21] Power counts heavily and the best means of gaining power are those furnished by militant, hard-hitting organizations.

Among teacher leaders in several large cities the union's viewpoint prevails. Substantial numbers of executive board members are critical of administration, indeed more critical than of many other aspects of urban education. The idea that the interests of teachers and administrators diverge definitely holds sway. Large majorities in both union and other organizations see the need for collective action, by means of mobilizing members, organizing petition campaigns, and sponsoring rallies, in order to advance their programs. Even more interesting, over four-fifths of the union leaders and about two-thirds of those heading other organizations feel that, if they are to get anywhere with school authorities, teachers usually have to fight. Nearly as many unionists, go so far as to endorse strikes, boycotts, work stoppages, and the like, if their organizations disagree strongly with board and/or administration policy proposals. Only one-quarter of the NEA and independent group officials will go this far. This new tendency toward conflict is strikingly illustrated by responses to one item in the survey. As many as one-third of non-union and well over half of the union leaders think that personal diplomacy—quietly working things out with the board and administration—no longer serves as an effective means of resolving most differences on issues of public school policy.

Emerging Patterns

The distribution and exercise of influence depend upon a variety of factors in addition to the attitudes of administrators and teachers. Just as prescriptive views differ from place to place and time to time, so relationships involving power vary according to a number of personal, structural, and situational factors. In New York City, Chicago, Boston, San Francisco, and Atlanta, for instance, relationships are the same in some respects but dissimilar in others. And patterns of interaction in large cities probably differ substantially from those in smaller communities. Our task here is not to examine behavior in detail. More modestly, we hope only to point out very general patterns of administrator-teacher relations which seem to be emerging.

One basic trend is the increasing strength and vitality of local teacher groups. For several years AFT has been extremely active in large cities and in other locales too. Even more significant, NEA has shifted its organizational emphasis from nation and State to localities. The national office today makes special provision for urban services and some sixty-five urban associations now have executive secretaries. It does not appear that the tide will soon be stemmed, and administrators have begun to realize this. As they see it, the problem is not how to prevent some form of negotiation or bargaining but rather how best to cope with it. Most of them, faced with a Hobson's choice, now encourage the development of local associations, which they much prefer to unions. One of the resolutions adopted by their 1966 convention clearly demonstrated where administrators stood. Declaring that "efforts to superimpose a pattern of staff relations borrowed from another segment of society" should be resisted vigorously, it went on to support local education associations as suitable to preserve unity, promote harmony, and serve the cause of education.[22]

As matters now stand, there is little systematic evidence concerning the policy-making roles teachers do play. A decade ago observers of the educational scene were likely to describe teachers as having little or no say in the formulation of school policies.[23] Recently one expert, Wesley A. Wildman, assessed things differently. He maintained that, given high professional autonomy and the low visibility of classroom activities, individual teachers acting alone are far from powerless. Moreover, in concert with their colleagues, their power is further increased. Finally, a formal framework of collective bargaining or professional negotiation enhances still more the power position of individual teachers and teacher organizations in the school system.[24] At least in some communities, teachers themselves think that they are accorded some say in formulating policy and that their recommendations carry weight in final decisions. In the five cities we have surveyed, where teacher groups are comparatively strong in terms of both membership and institutionalized arrangements, their power is still limited. According to leaders, only on a policy relating to salaries and working conditions do they play a major role. On other issues administrators dominate, not solely by virtue of their formal authority or claims to superior professional competence but also because of the unwillingness or inability of teacher organizations thus far to successfully challenge them.

Teacher organizations, however, appear to be showing expanded interest in acquiring power and increasing willingness to challenge patterns of authority in public school systems. Adversary relationships and strenuous combat are becoming more and more frequent, as teachers attempt first to establish collective bargaining or professional negotiations and then broaden the scope of issues subject to genuine joint decision making. Especially in large cities, but elsewhere as well, teacher organizations may be counted on to press for substantive benefits, such as higher salaries and improved working conditions, and also seek procedural reforms designed to enlarge their shares in educational policy making broadly defined. At the same time, school boards and administrators may be expected to resist as best they can erosion of their own prerogatives. The incidence of teacher militancy has been rising. In the future there is the likelihood of more extensive, and perhaps intensive, conflict, accompanying a widening cleavage between teachers and administrators. All this will probably result in still less effective control by lay school boards and the whittling away of the discretionary authority of school administrators.[25] It is even possible that the state of public education will prosper, if conflict succeeds in promoting a necessary adjustment of norms and power relations in accordance with new conditions and new needs.

FOOTNOTES

[1]Remarks of Richard D. Batchelder before the 98th annual meeting of the American Association of School Administrators (AASA), Atlantic City, N.J., February 15, 1966. (NEA press release.)

[2]The cities are New York, Chicago, Boston, San Francisco, and Atlanta. Questionnaires were mailed out in late 1965 and early 1966. Responses have been received from 185 executive board members of nine teacher organizations in the five cities.

[3]Quoted and discussed in Raymond E. Callahan and H. Warren Button, "Historial Change of the Role of the Man in the Organization: 1865-1950," in Daniel F. Griffiths, ed., *Behavioral Science and Educational Administration,* 63rd Yearbook of the National Society for the Study of Education (The Society, 1964), pp. 73-92. See also Russell T. Gregg, "The Administrative Process," in Roald F. Campbell and Russell T. Gregg, eds., *Administrative Behavior in Education* (Harper 1957), p. 307.

[4]W. W. Charters, Jr., "The Social Background of Teaching," in N.L. Gage, ed., *Handbook of Research on Teaching* (Rand McNally, 1963), p. 781.

[5]There is some evidence available on the attitudes of administrators. Neal Gross and his associates, in their study of the superintendency role, indicate that of 105 Massachusetts superintendents interviewed all but three thought it highly desirable or desirable for teachers to participate in policy formation. *Explorations in Role Analysis* (Wiley, 1958), p. 362.

[6]Empirical research, however, has cast some doubt on the simplicity of the linkage between participation, morale, and performance. See the review by Charters, *op. cit.,* pp. 783-784.

[7]Gregg, *loc. cit.;* also Edwin A. Fensch and Robert E. Wilson, *The Superintendency Team* (Merrill, 1964), p. 39.

[8]Roald F. Campbell *et al., Introduction to Educational Administration* (Allyn & Bacon, 1958), p. 214. Emphasis added.

[9]Gregg, *op. cit.,* p. 280; see also Edgar L. Morphet *et al., Educational Administration* (Prentice-Hall, 1959), pp. 98-99.

[10]Batchelder, *loc. cit.*

[11]Jack H. Kleinmann, "Guidelines for Professional Negotiation," paper delivered before discussion group, AASA meetings, (February 15, 1966). In addition, see Office of Professional Development and Welfare, NEA, *Guidelines for Professional Negotiation* (The Association, 1965) and Allan M. West, "What's Bugging Teachers," *Saturday Review* (October 16, 1965), p. 88.

[12]Calvin Gross, former superintendent of New York City, learned to live with an extremely powerful teachers group. Nevertheless, he believed that teacher participation, on matters other than salaries and working conditions, should not be channeled through the organization which bargained collectively. "Ways to Deal with the New Teacher Militancy," *Phi Delta Kappan,* XLVI (December, 1964), p. 149.

[13]The textual literature contains exceptions. Daniel Griffiths, for instance, recommends that administrators recognize the role of teacher groups in "the power structure of a school and learn to work with them." *Human Relations in School Administration* (Appleton-Century Crofts, 1956), pp. 117-118.

[14]The Commission on Educational Reconstruction, *Organizing the Teaching Profession* (Free Press, 1955), p. 103, also pp. 90, 138. Wesley A. Wildman suggests that increasing organization is due in part to the fact that teachers are actually playing a larger participatory role under the new ground rules of consultive administration. "It appears at least conceivable," he writes, "that in some situations democratic administration of any enterprise may actually hasten the process of organization and power accumulation." "Implications of Teacher Bargaining for School Administration," *Phi Delta Kappan,* XLVI (December, 1964), p. 154.

[15]"Teacher Opinion Poll," *NEA Journal,* LIV (September 1965), pp. 23-24.

[16]See the following: Campbell, *Introduction to Educational Administration,* p. 213; Wesley A. Wildman and Charles R. Perry, "Group Conflict and School Organization," *Phi Delta Kappan,* XLVII (January 1966), pp. 245-246; and especially AASA's 1966 resolution on the subject of administrator-teacher relations.

[17]Robbins Barstow, Jr., "Which Way New York City—Which Way the Profession?" *Phi Delta Kappan,* XLIII (December 1961), p. 124.

[18]Quoted from Batchelder's address before school administrators, *loc. cit.*

[19]Commission on Educational Reconstruction, *op. cit.,* p. 140; Wildman and Perry, *op. cit.,* p. 248; and Roald F. Campbell *et al., The Organization and Control of American Schools* (Merrill, 1965), p. 274.

[20]"Winning Collective Bargaining," AFT (Chicago, 1963). Calvin Gross seems to agree noting that as teachers become better organized and more demanding "the superintendent will gravitate closer to the school board." *op. cit.,* p. 151.

[21]Commission on Educational Reconstruction, *op. cit.,* p. 12.

[22] Reprinted in *The American Teacher* (March 1966), p. 14.

[23]For example, Griffiths, *op. cit.,* p. 106.

[24]*Op. cit.,* p. 155.

[25]But see *ibid.* Wildman maintains that the leadership of administrators need not be diminished. He points out that, even with mechanisms for negotiations, the status and functional potential of administrators may be enhanced rather than eroded.

NEW VOICES IN PUBLIC EDUCATION[*]

Alan Rosenthal

In what was described by the *New York Times* as "one of the most militant talks delivered by an NEA president," Richard D. Batchelder told the 1966 convention of the American Association of School Administrators that teachers wanted to become "full partners in the school enterprise." Only a few weeks before, the Kentucky Education Association had called a one-day walkout to press its demand for higher salaries and greater support for education by the state. At about the same time, another NEA affiliate, the Massachusetts Teachers Association, imposed professional sanctions against the public school system of Nantucket. And then, in defiance of New Jersey's constitution, a court order, and the canons of professionalism long subscribed to by NEA, came a two-day strike by the Newark Teachers Association. Within the short span of two months, the National Education Association had joined its rival, the American Federation of Teachers, in sponsoring revolutionary change in the rules of the educational game. Apparently teachers, and more particularly the leaders of teacher organizations, are no longer content with arrangements under which school boards and administrators decide educational matters among themselves. Teacher groups now are seeking, in the words of one expert on labor relations, "some sort of guarantee that teachers will not only be listened to on matters concerning school policy but that they shall be given an active part in determining this policy."[1]

Their demand for a real voice in making policies that affect local education is not startlingly new. Its origins can be traced back several years. Among the fundamental causes of this developing interest in greater participation, it has been noted, are the increased size and accompanying bureaucratization of school systems and the growing number of men teachers in the nation's classrooms. More immediately, just as the major impetus of the civil rights revolution seems to have been the Birmingham demonstrations of 1963, so the upsurge in teacher militancy appears to be an outgrowth from events involved in the collective bargaining victory by the United Federation of Teachers in New York City. Since the referenda of 1961 in which teachers voted overwhelmingly for collective bargaining and for UFT in preference to an NEA coalition, teachers throughout

*Alan Rosenthal, "New Voices in Public Education," from *Teachers College Record*, Volume 68, October 1966, pp. 13-20. Reprinted by permission.

the nation, especially those in large cities, have been showing their collective muscle. During the period from 1962 through early 1966, there had been almost forty instances of strikes, sitdowns, extended picketing or impositions of professional sanctions by teacher organizations.

These happenings, as well as the less dramatic stirrings by teachers, have been sparked in large part by the rivalry between NEA and AFT. Again, an appropriate analogy may be drawn to the civil rights movement. The initial effect of newly emergent and comparatively militant civil rights groups such as the Student Non-Violent Coordinating Committee and the Southern Christian Leadership Conference was to impel established and moderate groups like the National Association for the Advancement of Colored People and the National Urban League toward more aggressive positions. With teacher organizations likewise competing for followings, the apparent success of AFT's combativeness has generated increased militancy on the parts of national, state, and local NEA groups. A graphic example, the recent strike led by the Newark Teachers Association, shows how close competition for rank-and-file allegiance impels one group to match or outdo the other in terms of militancy.

According to a perceptive observer of the civil rights scene, the protest movement will never be the same again, for "it is bound to become more militant. . . ."[2] One student of the educational scene puts things in a rather similar way: "The contest that is developing for teacher loyalty between the NEA and the AFT will serve to drive both organizations into more militant postures."[3] In the immediate future, at any rate, there are no convincing indications that this latter trend will be reserved.

Teacher Militancy

In light of late developments, it is not at all surprising that the public has turned its attention to the substantive demands and prominent activities of teacher groups. National newspapers, for instance, increasingly refer to the new militancy in headlines and copy like the following:

A resurgence of militancy among the nation's public school teachers marked the year 1963 (New York Times, Jan. 16, 1964); Teachers Union Plans L.I. Drive—Militant Campaign Promised to Organize All Districts (New York Times, Jan. 23, 1966); The opening shots of what may be a 'militant union fight to create a good educational system' in Washington were fired by leaders of a national teachers' union yesterday (Washington Post, Feb. 12, 1966); Teachers Viewed as More Militant (New York Times, Feb. 16, 1966).

Popular conceptions of militancy, along with dictionary definitions, stress behavioral features—aggressive activity, hard conflict, open warfare. But a number of attitudinal factors also seem to be extremely relevant to the concept of militancy. Properly to appreciate its dimensions, we should assess not only what teachers actually do but what objectives they have in mind and what strategies they pursue. It is helpful, therefore, to distinguish between militant behavior and militant attitudes.

Engaging in this task, we shall examine the attitudes of the UFT leadership regarding its organization's role in shaping educational policies in New York City. Of interest here are leaders' views of organizational goals and strategies as well as their willingness to resort to combat. Our reported findings are based primarily on responses by 39 of 47 members of the Federation's Executive Board to a questionnaire mailed out in December, 1965.[4] For a variety of reasons the United Federation of Teachers provides a valuable focus for examination of the concept of militancy. First, and most obvious, is the fact that the New York union was the first major teachers group to engage in vigorous action and achieve status as a recognized bargaining agent. Second, despite the passage of years, its significant growth in membership, and its manifest gains in influence, UFT has evidenced no visible decline in aggressiveness. Third, it may plausibly be regarded as a prototype, which by exemplary accomplishment and direct and indirect proselytism, has helped to shape the course of quite a few teacher groups.

Leadership Goals

Sensational news stories, inevitably concentrating on organizational drives to win salary increases, have undoubtedly distorted the public's image of the contemporary teachers movement. It is true, of course, that from the very beginning the Federation campaigned hard for higher teacher salaries and other benefits. Yet, simultaneously, the union had as its objective, in the words of its current president, Albert Shanker, the formation of "a movement which would give the teacher a voice—which would give him some decision making power in his area of competence."[5] Status and dignity, the rights of teachers, the introduction of democracy in the schools, the extension of teacher control, participation rather than consultation, an equal voice in the shaping of policies which determine our professional lives—these are typical of the phrases which since 1961 have been liberally sprinkled through the editorials of the UFT newspaper, *The United Teacher*.

That this amounts to more than mere rhetoric is evident, by way of illustration, from the views and activities of participants in collective bargaining negotiations of 1963. Neither management nor labor was oblivious to perhaps the main issue in the struggle. A union newsletter posed the problem succinctly: "Will the Board agree to give teachers a real stake in the school system by letting them share in the decisions which so vitally affect everything we do?"[6] On their parts, the board and administration conceived of collective bargaining as being narrowly limited to the terms and conditions of employment, with neither bargaining procedures nor union representatives legitimately having anything to do with policy matters. Nevertheless, the Federation made stringent demands for increased teacher influence, continuing the fight even after salary raises were no longer in contest. It is clear that UFT's leadership, if not its membership, conceived of collective bargaining and teacher participation both as a means and an end. It was naturally a means to gain improvements in salaries and personal benefits. The end toward which the union was striving might well be labeled "democratic professionalism," a new system of rules and arrangements permitting professional educators, at whatever levels in the hierarchy, to share in formulating citywide and school policies.

A Voice in Policy-Making

Present leaders of the United Federation of Teachers feel just about the same. All but one of the 39 Executive Board respondents in the leadership survey agreed that UFT should not be content with obtaining benefits for teachers, but should endeavor to win a share in the determination of educational policy. At the very least, this means, according to Shanker, that ". . . teachers have the right, through their Union, to make their voices heard in educational matters at the school level, at the district level, and city-wide."[7] In the opinions of Executive Board members, UFT is entitled to considerably more than advisory status. It should play a decisive role in shaping educational policy. Responding to one item on the questionnaire, seven members stated that teacher organizations generally should have more to say than the board and/or administration and another twenty-three said that they should have a voice equal to that of the board and/or administration. Only nine chose essentially a consultative role as the recommended one for a teachers group.

Educational policy-making covers a wide range of matters. Among the highly significant domains in which policies are made we find salaries, personnel, curriculum and instruction, and the organization of the school system. These domains include respectively issues such as the establishment of new salary schedules, recruitment and placement, the formulation of instructional programs and the adoption of textual materials, and decentralization and the assignment of grade levels to various types of schools. Table 1 reports responses of Executive Board members to several prescribed organizational roles in the different areas of educational policy.

Leadership Strategies

Leadership aims to participate equally in policy-making and leadership strategies to achieve greater organizational power do not necessarily go hand in hand. We can imagine circumstances in which group leaders value equal rights, but at the same time feel satisfied with the share in decision-making their organization is already allotted. They might really have or only think they have what is earnestly desired. There can be little doubt, however, that in earlier years UFT leaders were extremely discontented. The distribution of power in the New York City school system was not at all to their liking. To attain democracy

TABLE 1: Leadership attitudes regarding prescriptive organizational roles in educational policy-making

Role of teacher organizations	Educational policy generally	Salaries	Personnel	Curriculum and instruction	School system organization
They should have more to say than the board and/or administration	18%	18%	11%	21%	16%
They should have a voice equal to that of the board and/or administration	59%	63%	63%	45%	55%
They should be consulted, and the board and/or administration should weigh heavily their advice	23%	18%	26%	32%	29%
They should be kept informed by the board and/or administration, but should not necessarily be called on for advice	00	00	00	00	00
They should not be involved	00	00	00	03%	00
Totals	100%	99%*	100%	101%*	100%
Numbers	(39)	(38)	(38)	(38)	(38)

*Errors in totals due to rounding

within the ranks of professionals, their strategy included attracting a large teacher following, bargaining strenuously, and increasing the Federation's influence in educational affairs. Some time ago, the first president, Charles Cogen, pointed out that the Board of Education was obliged to cede managerial prerogatives and accord the union its inevitable "role in the Board's policy-making procedures."[8] Only a short time later, during feverish collective bargaining, Superintendent Calvin Gross showed that he had few illusions about the stakes being contested. In a television address he stated candidly: "...I think what the United Federation of Teachers wants basically is more control of the school system." What this meant, Gross continued, was that the union wanted "...to have more say in every school and in every phase of the administration of the school system, a little more say-so in what goes on."[9]

Few people would deny that since then UFT has obtained at least "a little more say-so" in matters which previously had been considered the prerogatives of the mayor, board, superintendent, or administrative staff. Both the 1963 and 1965 contracts, and their implementation, evidence substantial gains in influence by the union. Even after several milestones, however, Federation leaders persist in their dissatisfaction. Generally speaking, they perceive UFT power to be meager compared to power wielded by other individuals and groups who participate in educational affairs.[10] One important strategy of the Executive Board continues to be the building of influence. This is indicated by the

TABLE 2: Leadership perceptions and prescriptions regarding organizational power in educational policy-making

		Educational policy generally	Salaries	Personnel	Curriculum and instruc- tion	School system or- ganization
Actual UFT power	Much	05%	63%	08%	00%	00%
	Some	54%	29%	58%	11%	47%
	Little	41%	08%	34%	89%	53%
	Totals	100%	100%	100%	100%	100%
	Numbers	(39)	(38)	(38)	(38)	(38)
Prescribed UFT power	More	97%	77%	92%	92%	92%
	Same	03%	23%	08%	08%	08%
	Less	00%	00%	00%	00%	00%
	Totals	100%	100%	100%	100%	100%
	Numbers	(38)	(39)	(37)	(38)	(38)

collective belief that the union should have more power than presently over educational policy while others should have either the same amount or less. The perceptions and prescriptive views of leaders regarding power to determine policy in general and to shape particular kinds of policies are summarized in Table 2.

Whether or not their perceptions are accurate, leaders believe the union plays a decisive role only on salary matters. On curriculum and instruction especially, but also in the domains of personnel and school system organization, most of them think UFT plays a minor role at best. Consequently, it is understandable that in every domain, with the exception of salaries, nine of ten leaders desire greater power for their organization. Interestingly, with regard to salary policy, although Executive Board members attribute a great deal of actual power to UFT (more, in fact, than to any group except the mayor and municipal officials), three-quarters of them want still more power. Right or wrong, leaders feel that the Federation has some distance to travel and much to win before their objectives of equal participation for teachers are realized.

Leadership Tactics

Adequate description of the tactics available to and employed by UFT to accomplish its ends would take us far afield. But aggressive tactics comprise important elements in any realistic conception of group militancy. Goals and strategies alone are insufficient unless some attempt is made to further them. However ambitious the aim of participation and however great the appetite for influence, the militancy of a teachers organization depends upon its willingness to engage in combat, use novel techniques, take unpopular action, and run recognizable risks. Using these criteria as a rough standard, the history of the Federation leaves no question as to the authenticity of its militancy. Since 1959 intermittent but harsh conflict between the teachers and the school managers has become almost a normal phase of public business in New York City.

The Federation's combative disposition is best illustrated by the leadership's reliance on the strike tactic. At the time when the first UFT walkout was called in November 1960 to pressure the school board into holding a collective bargaining election, the strike was widely regarded as a very unusual method for a teachers group to employ. Nor was the second strike, waged in April 1962 to push salary and other demands, generally deemed an appropriate measure for professional people engaged in collective bargaining. Both strikes, unpopular with everyone but the city's teachers and perhaps organized labor, were condemned by public officials, civic groups, and most heartily by editorial writers of the influential *New York Times.* Referring to 1962, Joseph P. Lyford, former staff director of the Public Education Association, stated: "When they struck, I don't think they were sure that they had public support, but they felt strongly enough to do it, public or no public."[11] On both occasions the union, in order to impress its adversaries and build a reputation as ". . . a hard-hitting, militant organization, which is not afraid to act," took considerable risks.[12] There was the possibility, however remote during the latter demonstration, that too few teachers would participate for an impressive showing to be made. Even if strike turnout was large, there was a chance that school authorities, backled up and bolstered by civic support, would adamantly oppose the Federation. In 1962 a state court had issued an injunction prohibiting UFT leaders from urging teachers to stop work and the Commissioner of Education had implied that he might annul the teaching certificates of strikers. Furthermore, the potential sanctions of the Condon-Wadlin Act in those days could not be taken too lightly. All in all, there are numerous reasons why UFT's tactics might have proved abortive and might have severely damaged the young organization. That things worked out to the union's advantage does not detract from the seriousness of the risks taken in these early years and what might conceivably have happened.

By now, of course, the strike is no longer unconventional in New York. This tactic, in fact, ranks as the most conventional megaton weapon in the UFT arsenal. The bargaining scenario currently is such that participants and public alike expect, if not an actual walkout or work stoppage, at least a strike threat, retracted only at the last minute when school managers make substantial concessions to their employees. As Albert Shanker said at a 1964 budget hearing before the Board of Education: "We can't help wondering whether the only way to bring about progress in the school system is to have a teachers' strike pending."[13] More recently, in their responses to the leadership questionnaire, members of the Executive Board indicated a high degree of consensus on the necessity for an aggressive stance and strong action. Of 39 leaders replying, 85%

agreed that teachers organizations usually have to fight in order to get what they want from educational authorities. Only a few felt that on most issues optimum results could be obtained by personal diplomacy at discussions and private conferences between managerial and union leaders. Nine of ten endorsed demonstrations, such as petition campaigns and rallies, as worthwhile and legitimate tactics. Somewhat fewer—eight of ten—also advocated more extreme measures, such as boycotts, work stoppages, and strikes, if there were strong union disagreement with the policy proposals of the board and/or administration.

Given the brief history of UFT and the increasing forcefulness of the teachers movement, what was radical and risky some years ago is becoming more commonplace and acceptable today. Still, the New York City union has not moderated its goals or become too affluent to brawl. Even in its age of respectability, UFT can be characterized as an organization predisposed to combat and willing to use militant tactics in pursuit of greater influence in educational policy-making.

Results of Organizational Militancy

Thus far strategies and tactics have not proven entirely adequate in winning for the United Federation of Teachers its goal of a decisive voice in policy. In light of the concern of so many of the city's teachers with personal benefits rather than collective power, this partial failure is quite understandable. It can also be explained by the disinclination of board and administration to surrender willingly or easily their long-held prerogatives. The enduring effects of organizational militancy, however, cannot be dismissed. The first UFT strike, in addition to ensuring collective bargaining, heightened teachers' estimates of the union's ability to promote their interests and thereby reduced the appeal of rival groups. The second one not only led to an attractive salary settlement but also resulted in tremendous growth in the membership strength of the organization. Both strikes, but especially the second in which about half the teachers in the system participated, served as outlets for indignation, relievers of anxiety, and manifestations of strength. Teachers in New York developed a new image and, even more important, a new self image. No longer did they provoke only sympathy, but they began to engender respect and, according to Shanker, "perhaps a little bit of fear."[14] No longer did they see themselves and their colleagues as docile and unable to improve things, but they began to feel some confidence and potency. Undeniably, teacher morale, reputedly at a low ebb before UFT, started to rise.

The three agreements negotiated by the union certainly have whittled away the bilateral authority of board and administration. The first contract legally established the Federation as a serious contender on behalf of teachers. One of the more militant union officers, George Altomare, described the outcome this way: "We have set down, in writing, the fact that we are to be consulted on all changes; the days when we hear about changes only after they are made are gone."[15] The following year, the leadership's principal bargaining aim—the recognition of union rights in policy matters—went much further. After lengthy and arduous negotiations, a settlement of landmark proportions was finally reached. Most gratifying to UFT leaders was the agreement's preamble, which provided for monthly meetings between the superintendent and representatives of the union on matters of educational policy, such as recruiting of qualified teachers, the improvement of difficult schools, the reduction of class size, and the development of a more effective curriculum. By way of compromise, the conclusion of the contract noted that the board of education retained complete authority over the policies and administration of the school system, a responsibility it had by virtue of law. While there has been some dispute over the meaning of these two provisions, the Federation saw little contradiction. It regarded the contract as a giant step toward teacher participation in the making of school policy. Nor have subsequent events shown the union to be wrong.

Before the ascendancy of UFT, teachers in New York City, despite organizational fragmentation and divisiveness, exercised some control over their own personnel system and their career opportunities. As pressure groups, teacher organizations were not powerless. They were capable of pressing for what they wanted and of preventing educational authorities from moving in directions they found repugnant.[16] In the years since 1962, teachers through their union have become an even weightier factor in the reckoning of the municipal managers of public education. As in the past, the city's teachers are able to immobilize policies which they strongly oppose. But now, they have an opportunity, as never before, to advance proposals of their own with realistic expectation of success. Today, the United Federation of Teachers and a growing number of other teacher groups as well aspire to full partnership in educational policy-making. Whether they actually achieve it is conjectural, but they are moving, and moving rapidly, in their chosen direction.

FOOTNOTES

[1]Doherty, Robert E. Teacher participation in the determination of school policy. N.Y. State School Boards Assn., Feb. 1966, *8*, 1-5.

[2]Silberman, Charles E. *Crisis in black and white.* N.Y.: Random House, 1964.

[3]Adams, Floyd. Teacher organizations and community power structure, in August Kerber and Barbara Bommarito, Eds., *The Schools and the urban crisis.* N.Y.: Holt, Rinehart and Winston, 1965.

[4]Similar questionnaires were also sent to leaders of teacher groups in several other cities. These surveys and the author's investigation of teacher organizations are one phase of a Carnegie sponsored study of policies and policy-making in large city educational systems being conducted by the Metropolitan Studies Program of Syracuse University. In my own work I have received material support from the Urban Research Center of Hunter College, the City University of New York, and research assistance from Miss Renee Glattstein.

[5]*United Teacher,* Apr. 13, 1965.

[6]*United Action,* June, 1963.

[7] *United Teacher,* Oct. 8, 1965.

[8] *United Teacher,* Oct. 1962.

[9] *N.Y. Times,* July 7, 1963.

[10] While it is not our intention to discuss how union leaders perceive the distribution of power among individuals and groups, their overall assessment should be mentioned. The ranking, based on their perceptions, is as follows: (1) superintendent; (2) board of education; (3) deputy, associate, and assistant superintendents at headquarters; (4) mayor and municipal officials; (5) school principals; and (6) UFT.

[11] *United Teacher,* Apr.-May, 1962.

[12] *United Teacher, Sept., 1960.*

[13] *United Teacher,* May 7, 1964.

[14] *N.Y. Times,* Jan. 23, 1966.

[15] *United Teacher*, Oct. 1962.

[16] Sayre, Wallace S. and Kaufman, Herbert, *Governing New York City.* N. Y.: Russell Sage, 1960.

POLITICAL ISSUES IN SCHOOL DECENTRALIZATION

Robert F. Lyke

American public education has long been characterized by political decentralization. Until the passage of the Elementary and Secondary Education Act of 1965 the Federal government's involvement in educational policy-formation was generally minimal.[1] Even state governments, which legally bear the primary responsibility for public education, have customarily granted wide discretion in policy-formation to boards of education appointed or elected in over 20,000 separate local school districts.[2] It is true that increasingly state legislatures and state departments of education have established requirements and promulgated regulations that restrict local autonomy, but still most observers would agree with Roscoe Martin that "the public school is the nation's principal hostage to its ancient tradition of grassroots control over local government."[3]

So pervasive is the ideology of localism in American public education that there has customarily been areal decentralization within individual school districts as well. Although there are exceptions, districts commonly have comprehensive schools serving local attendance areas, so that all public school children, regardless of their ability or interests, attend a school near their home. Elementary schools in particular reflect neighborhood identity by promoting meetings of parents and teachers and encouraging use of school facilities for social events. While the ideology of the neighborhood school generously overestimates the actual extent of community participation, let alone influence, in school affairs, education does have more citizen involvement than do other governmental services.

Areal decentralization in American education is symbolized in the power of the principal. While the board of education and the superintendent set some district-wide policies and maintain a cursory review over school programs, much administrative decision-making is decentralized to the local school. There the principal oversees all programs: there are few personnel in his school who are primarily responsible to someone else. Principals' recommendations about personnel policy and budget allocations help shape the general district policy, and their decisions about hiring and promoting teachers are often automatically approved. Principals have considerable discretion for settling disputes and disciplining students, judging whether the district policy should be applied to particular controversies. Moreover, they generally direct curriculum development within their schools, approving course content and teaching methods.

That the structure of American school systems is generally decentralized does not mean that there are no strong centralizing forces as well.[4] Members of the board of education, the superintendent, and other central staff officials attempt to control the policies and actions of principals and teachers in the individual schools. Using budgetary and personnel powers, they have in places reduced the autonomy of principals and teachers, at times even putting tight controls on the curriculum and teaching methods. Forces of decentralization and centralization are thus set against each other in an uneasy balance, sometimes tipping one way and sometimes the other.

To a great extent public interest in decentralization is due to the bitter dispute in New York City over three demonstration school districts and the proposals of a panel headed by McGeorge Bundy to restructure the City's school system. While the events in that dispute are interesting, they have been adequately described by other writers and will not be dwelled upon here.[5] Instead, this paper will discuss basic political issues underlying school decentralization movements in large cities in general. These movements are a reaction to strong centralizing forces which have come to dominate large urban school systems since the late nineteenth century. It is important to recognize, however, that current disputes are not merely between advocates of centralization and advocates of decentralization. The latter, in fact, are sharply split into two groups, one advocating administrative decentralization and the other community control. By comparing these two types of decentralization with centralization one can understand both the underlying political issues and the strategies of the affected interests.

Centralization in Urban Education

In the middle of the nineteenth century large cities frequently were divided into small, separate school districts or had community boards with extensive control over the local schools. For example, both New York City and Pittsburgh are now composed of cities which were once legally autonomous and maintained their own school systems; as population expanded and problems of intercity cooperation arose, annexation or consolidation occurred, thus creating one common school district.[6] Even those cities which underwent little or no geographical expansion and had but one school district frequently had a weak central board of education and strong local boards. In Philadelphia, for example, the present boundaries of the school district were established in 1854 but the district was divided into twenty-four wards, each with a board of twelve directors. One director from each ward was then selected to sit on the central board of education.[7] Although the central board of education exercised general supervision over the school system, the local boards retained the important powers to erect schools, appoint teachers, and provide supplies.[8] New York City's school district was also decentralized with twenty-four boards of trustees who had similar authority. In Brooklyn there was such a committee for each school building.[9] The local boards in Philadelphia were elected, while those in New York and Brooklyn were, at least after 1871, appointed. The impact in either case was the same: strong, central direction of the schools was discouraged while local influences were strengthened.

During the late nineteenth and early twentieth centuries, however, the structure of large urban school districts became more centralized: local community boards were weakened and then abolished; uniform personnel, purchasing, and curriculum standards were adopted; and a single superintendent, responsible only to the central board of education, was appointed to administer the growing system. In 1905, for instance, the Pennsylvania legislature reduced the size of the central Philadelphia Board of Public Education, gave it most powers formerly held by the local boards, and created three superintendency positions: one for buildings, one for supplies, and one for instruction. The local boards retained only the power to appoint elementary school janitors and to make recommendations to the central board.[10]

Supporters of this centralization made three main arguments. The most prominent one, and the one which may have had the greatest impact on state legislators, was that local school boards were often corrupt. Board members often had connections with local political machines, and they used their influence for personal or partisan ends. A critic in New York City charged that:

> some—perhaps many—of the Trustees were illiterate men, who secured their places through political influence; that they considered the appointment of teachers as so much "patronage," which they dealt out in turn; that they displayed marked favoritism in the promotion of teachers, and "pulled wires" in the interest of their favorites; and that in the matter of repairs to school buildings, etc., they assigned the work to favored mechanics, for the purpose of strengthening their position with an eye to political preferment, and the like.[11]

The reformers realized that in the short run political machines would still attempt to place people in school jobs, but they hoped that with centralization higher nonpartisan standards would at least weed out those who were incompetent. In the long run, the reformers thought, removing the schools from the influence of political parties would speed the collapse of the machines themselves.

The reformers' second argument was that good administrative practice required centralization. When small, semi-rural areas were annexed to larger cities it was thought less confusing and more equitable to abolish the legally autonomous boards that controlled scattered elementary schools. Similar arguments were made, though with perhaps less merit, when separate cities were consolidated. If city councils and municipal administrations were going to be unified, why should boards of education not be included? But the reformers were as much concerned about reducing or even abolishing the power of local community boards as they were about areal consolidation. By strengthening the central board of education they thought it possible to reduce inequities among the various communities, introduce rational revenue policies and uniform budget practices, plan modern curricula, and, most important in their eyes, adopt higher, nonpartisan personnel standards. Instead of corruption there would be apolitical, rational standards; instead of political patronage there would be professional competence.[12]

The reformers' third argument was that centralization would modernize urban public education. The need for change was evident: population was increasing rapidly, the industrial economy needed an increasing number of skilled workers, and immigrants' children had to be taught English and the prevailing American social values. Local community school boards were hard pressed to meet these demands, partly because they provided education for only a small area and partly because they could not afford or were unwilling to hire educators with technical competence and experience. Only a centralized school board could marshall the resources for establishing high schools and vocational training schools, quickly provide the proper education for immigrant children and find and support a superintendent who could adapt the curriculum to modern needs. According to the current administrative precepts, only by divorcing administration from politics could modern municipal services be provided; not only must the influence of political machines be diminished, but the authority of professionals must be increased.

As these reforms occurred in the late nineteenth and early twentieth centuries the influence of educators—particularly the superintendent and other central administrators—was indeed markedly increased. While members of the central board of education now had virtually all authority over school affairs, they found the school system so large that they had to rely upon the policy recommendations of the superintendent and other central administrators. This was particularly the case for curriculum and personnel matters, about which the educators were most concerned. Occasionally, in fact, educators even forced policies on reluctant school boards by obtaining favorable state legislation.[13] In turn, the central administrators then used standards and regulations to control the building principals, who formerly had responded only to their local boards. Thus the structural changes led to administrative centralization.

Centralization also helped middle-class Americans, generally Protestants, maintain their influence over public education at a time when public services in most large cities were coming under the power of working-class political machines. By attempting to remove education from politics by abolishing the local community boards, the reformers were shielding the schools from those organizations through which working-class ethnic groups had the most influence. Moreover, by centralizing hiring and developing professional, nonpartisan standards for teachers, large urban districts became less likely to hire teachers from those families whose children could not afford to attend normal school or college. Centralization also insured that the school curriculum would serve middle-class interests. Immigrant children would be given employable skills and adapted to the prevailing American social culture through a common curriculum. Similarly,

> Where the old school had directed its energies, however patronizingly, to all young children in common, the new system was designed to benefit high school graduates, that minority completing a process whose effects presupposed completion. The parents the new schools cultivated were those of at least a comfortable middle class, hopefully mobile, who sought professional assistance in pushing their children up the ladder.[14]

Thus centralization in large urban school districts in the late nineteenth and early twentieth centuries affected social groups differently, and it established conditions against which lower-class groups were later to protest.

The Unsteady Balance

While urban education became more centralized there still remained counteracting pressures for decentralization. Despite the abolition of local community boards, parents kept pressing, sometimes successfully, to influence the schools which their children attended. Parents had access to present their grievances and suggestions through the principal, who interpreted central regulations and supervised the programs in his school. Occasionally community pressure would modify the cultural homogeneity enforced on the school system by central standards: it was not unusual, for example, for a qualified principal to be appointed on the basis of his ethnic or religious identification with the community or for history and literature books to be used which gave favorable treatment to the local nationality groups. Rather than disapprove such community pressures, principals encouraged them, for they used them to bargain for more autonomy from the central administrators. Thus the neighborhood school movement and various parent-teacher associations helped reinforce what strength remained in areal decentralization in urban areas. The balance between centralization and decentralization tipped one way and then the other, depending on the issues and personnel involved, but it never swung back to extensive community control nor toward complete central direction.

Nonetheless, since 1950 there have been renewed pressures within urban school systems for more centralization. During the McCarthy Era citizens attacked some teachers and programs as subversive, forcing educators to make tedious defenses and to exercise caution in personnel selection and course design. In the late 1950's urban educators were caught between civil rights groups and white segregationists, the former demanding integration and the latter resisting plans that would increase the number of black students in schools their children attended. That the community was concerned about subversion or desegregation was understandable, but educators found themselves poorly prepared to handle the onslaught of court suits, demonstrations, and boycotts. Being buffeted among groups of active citizens, many educators became convinced that extensive community involvement in the schools would be disastrous, and they sought refuge behind centralized administrative structures which could guarantee them autonomy.

Moreover, by 1960 urban school districts were having serious problems within the schools as well. Many students, especially lower-class blacks and Puerto Ricans, were not learning and were not getting jobs upon graduation, if indeed they remained in school that long. In the primary grades such children often scored lower on standardized tests than middle-class white children, and in advanced grades they did even less well. Upon entering high school the students were channeled into the bottom academic tracks or vocational courses. Parents complained that this was due to poor facilities and teaching in the lower grades and that the school system was perpetuating unequal treatment. Features of ghetto schools symbolized these distinctions and reinforced the parents' views: school buildings were older and lacked the facilities found in white schools; teachers were hard to recruit and often poorly-prepared when they were hired; and discipline was alternatively lax and repressive. Mounting frustration turned to bitterness when racial integration, the apparent solution to the disparity in educational achievement, was never implemented despite repeated promises of both educators and board members. With tension rapidly rising, changes obviously had to be made.

The primary response to these problems in the early 1960's was, interestingly enough, more centralization. If urban schools were failing, so modern reformers argued, the primary cause was the power of entrenched teachers and administrators who, accustomed to teaching white middle-class children, could not adapt to the changing character of the student body.[15] These educators had resisted and subverted integration programs out of fear that an increase in minority students would lower their school averages on standardized tests.[16] The reformers urged that to educate ghetto children new teachers must be hired and creative programs designed. More money, either from state or Federal sources or from private foundations, would have to be obtained to finance the changes. Most important, the superintendents of schools would have to have more authority and resources to force changes through the recalcitrant principals and teachers. If the superintendents were creative and forceful, the new reformers urged, the system would improve, while if they were conservative and cautious, problems would continue to multiply. Further centralization under the right administrative leadership was said to be the answer.

However, after several years it became apparent that reformed centralization also could not improve ghetto education. Reform-oriented superintendents were hard to find, and those who were hired often discovered they could not institute change. Lacking control over personnel selection and program planning, the new superintendents found themselves hemmed in by state regulations, uncooperative administrators, and tradition-oriented teachers who resented outsiders trying to give advice. Recommendations were diluted or ignored, and the harder the superintendents pressed for reform the less support they received on other projects. Superintendents simply lacked the political and administrative resources to bring about reform.

The problem was not solely financial. Additional money was becoming available from a variety of sources: state grants-in-aid were increased for both general operating expenses and specialized programs and Federal aid was sharply increased under Title I of the Elementary and Secondary Education Act. Private foundations, anxious to stimulate change, provided money for demonstration projects. However, these additional funds were not as significant as the reformers had estimated since much of the increase went directly into educators' salaries, thus reinforcing the very personnel who consistently blocked reform. While obviously in the long run higher salaries would draw more qualified teachers, in the short run they had little impact.

This is not to say that reformed centralization produced no changes, for curriculum experimentation rapidly increased in ghetto schools. However, since many experiments were uncoordinated and poorly planned, it was difficult to know what worked and what did not. Even the successful projects were tried on a scale too small to effect the ghetto as a whole. Children grew confused and few showed real progress, while their parents became cynical about the programs' extensive publicity and inflated promises.

Thus, despite more centralization, black and Puerto Rican children still scored poorly on standardized tests and still had difficulty obtaining jobs or entering college. Rising class and racial tensions magnified these problems and reduced parents' trust of existing administrators. In some schools communication became impossible: parents whom educators asked for advice suspected attempts at cooptation, while educators to whom parents forcefully complained dismissed the critics as irresponsible. Occasional acts of lying, bigotry, and violence by both parents and educators convinced each side of the need for uncompromising firmness. Most important, these disputes occurred in a period when opponents were becoming organized. Parents found in neighborhood associations what teachers found in union locals—protection against personal attacks and encouragement to challenge critics. By the late 1960's education politics in ghettos had become polarized.

Two Models of School Decentralization

Challenges to centralization in urban school systems are now common, and in some places they may be too strong to divert. One group of critics, principally black parents and community leaders, finds the present centralized system unresponsive to the needs of their children and yet too powerful to be reformed. Black people have found they lack the skills and power to influence the central administrators, while at the same time their efforts for local reform are undermined from above.[17] They argue that if the schools are to educate the children they must be controlled by the local community: authority over school policy must be decentralized to lay boards locally selected. Another group of critics, principally teachers and some principals in the individual schools, finds the present centralized system both cumbersome and bureaucratic. They cannot obtain needed supplies and personnel, let alone get better ones, and they are prevented by the central staff from making curriculum and teaching reforms that would improve instruction. According to this group, if the schools are to educate the children they must be controlled by the local educators: authority over school policy must be decentralized within the administration. Thus the controversy involves a choice between two different decentralized models, community control or administrative decentralization, as well as the presently centralized structure. Of course, in practice, an administrative structure need not match one model precisely; most will contain elements of all three. However, to understand the issues and strategies of decentralization disputes one must first recognize the basic demands of different groups.

Proponents of centralization still exist, of course, and in many cities they retain considerable influence. They include educators who would lose authority or their positions under either model of decentralization, such as central supervisors, curriculum specialists, or personnel or budgeting staff members. Moreover, people who now have influence over the central staff or who otherwise agree with its policies will also be likely to oppose decentralization. These will often, though not always, include the superintendent of schools and those board of education members who want to retain the access they would surely lose if decision-making were divided among numerous schools or communities. White parents' organizations interested in preserving current school policies often are firm supporters of the present structure. Finally, educators within the system who presently have good relations with central administrators or who want to be promoted to central positions will continue to favor centralization. Other educators lack these connections or goals but fear that any decentralization will diminish their power: some school principals, for example, worry that under administrative decentralization the teachers might dominate them while under community control the laymen might.

It is wrong to see these proponents of centralization as any more self-interested than proponents of either form of decentralization. While it is true they are concerned about their positions and influence, most are also convinced that educational reform can in the long run come only by centralization. They argue that the failure of urban schools lies not so much with centralized direction as with low pay and depressing working conditions. In the long run there must be more money, while in the short run there can be compromises where advocates of decentralization have valid objections. The school system should indeed devote more resources and personnel to ghetto schools, encourage more blacks and Puerto Ricans to become teachers, and develop a more responsive curriculum. If criticism mounts, then a protracted defense is in order: the bureaucracy can persist longer than the critics can, just as it did in the 1950's.

With administrative decentralization the locus of political authority remains with the single, city-wide board of education. No community boards need be established, and indeed no structural changes may be necessary. In practical terms, however, there is a significant shift of influence from the centralized administrators to the field administrators—the district supervisors, building principals, department chairmen in individual schools, or even the teachers. Field personnel under administrative decentralization attain the power to make decisions which formerly were made, or at least cleared, by central administrators. For administrators, decentralization will be significant to the extent that they can prepare and administer their own budgets and do their own hiring and promoting. For teachers, decentralization will be significant to the extent that they can design their own curricula. Of course a central administration must remain to apportion funds among the individual schools, set minimum standards, and promote coordination. However, these centralized limitations are not inconsistent with local flexibility if field personnel are actively involved in policy formation, if they have wide latitude in applying general policy to particular cases, and if they have discretionary funds to spend.

Administrative decentralization may, but need not, involve closer cooperation between schools and their communities. Under some versions local advisory boards may be appointed to convey criticism and offer suggestions, while under others principals and teachers may have more citizen contact merely because they have more power and become better access points. Increased cooperation need not occur, however, if educators feel that their newly-won autonomy must be protected from community activists.

The primary proponents of administrative decentralization are field educators who would gain autonomy and influence. Teachers have long been concerned with the expanding central staff controls over the curriculum, which not only increase their own paperwork (since they must verify that they have been following central directives) but also reduce their professional flexibility. They find it more difficult to assign what they think best or to vary their schedules and approaches. Worse yet, teachers have found they have very little influence over, let alone communication with, central staff members: directives and forms descend more readily than complaints and suggestions ascend. Greater professional autonomy for teachers has been one of the important demands of teachers' unions in urban areas. Unions, in fact, find it both a good recruiting device and a useful demand to put before the central board of education.

Principals find themselves divided by proposals for administrative decentralization. On the one hand they are given greater administrative authority and more influence, but at the same time they are charged with more responsibility. For some, the trade-off is adequate: having the confidence of their staff and anxious to try new programs, they welcome the greater freedom. Others, however, fear that their increased influence may not be sufficient to handle problems for which they will be blamed. At the present time principals can pass unpopular decisions up to central administrators, or at least say they do, but under administrative decentralization they will have to assume full responsibility themselves. Decentralization may, in short, reduce the extent to which these principals can play central pressures off against local ones.

The community control model of decentralization involves more substantial shifts of formal authority and influence. The single, city-wide board of education transfers authority to boards of education in separate communities throughout the city, which then assume some of the legal responsibility for the schools within their district.[18] The central board remains in a federal relation with local boards, retaining some authority in the various policy areas. The important question obviously is how much authority will be retained centrally and how much will be devolved to the local boards. At the very least, significant decentralization requires extensive local control over budget and personnel policy, since the quality of education depends so much upon who the teachers are and how the scarce funds are apportioned. The central board, on the other hand, would retain authority ro raise revenue and divide the funds among the community districts. Moreover, it might operate special schools, provide auxiliary services, settle boundary disputes, and, perhaps, construct new schools.[19]

Furthermore, state and Federal controls over public education, limited as they are, would continue. Thus it is inaccurate to assume that school decentralization will create *autonomous* community schools; it will merely shift policy formation to the local level. The unsteady balance between centralization and decentralization, which we have seen to be long characteristic of urban school districts, is merely to swing in the decentralized direction.

What is critical about the community control model is that authority to shape educational policy rests not with field educators but with laymen serving on district boards. Such boards can be selected in a variety of ways: direct election, indirect election through district assemblies, or appointment by the central school board or by municipal officials. Board seats in turn can be restricted to parents or other local residents, or they could include representatives of community organizations, teachers, or even students. "Community control," however, implies that at least a majority of local board seats will be held by local residents locally selected, and that the selection process will permit some degree of citizen direction and accountability.[20]

The primary advocates of community control of education are parents and leaders in black communities, who are concerned with improving the education given their children and with assuming control of institutions now run by whites but serving primarily blacks. Racial distrust is quite important in the demands for community control: while white parents under similar conditions would have similar complaints, the quickening politicization of ghetto areas provides black leaders with both additional motivation and direction for their reform drive. At the same time, these black leaders are joined by numerous black educators and some young white liberal educators who see that their own influence and effectiveness would be increased. Finally, elected officials who consider these groups their primary constituents are also likely to support community control.

Advocates of decentralization in urban school districts are thus split into two groups, those favoring administrative decentralization and those favoring community control. In general, educators favor the former and parents and community leaders favor the latter, although, as has been mentioned, there are important exceptions. Both members of the board of education and the superintendent play a pivotal role in school decentralization. If they want to maximize their direct personal influence or if they approve of the policies of the central administrators, then they would undoubtedly work to maintain centralization. On the other hand, if they feel that good education requires basic structural changes, then they would prefer a form of decentralization. Even those who prefer centralization, however, may realize the limitations of their own influence over the central staff, and they may recognize the political liability of defending centralization against criticisms of field educators and parents. Advocating a limited form of decentralization which combines both some community control and more discretion for teachers may, in fact, be a useful strategy to prevent either central administrators, teachers, or community leaders from dominating particular issues.

Basic Political Issues

Proponents of continued centralization or of either the two models of decentralization disagree in part because they conflict on basic political issues. Three such issues will be discussed here: the conflict between democratic control and professional autonomy; the conflict between substantive and procedural values in policy-formation; and the conflict between community development and societal integration.

70197

The most fundamental conflict underlying the dispute over decentralization is between democratic control and professional autonomy. Both values are important in American political culture; indeed, as was pointed out above, they have been the source of continual conflict in public education over the past century. The argument for democratic control can be simply put: administrators of government services ought to be accountable to citizens as a whole for the policies they enact and implement. This should be the case particularly for public education, which consumes such a large percentage of governmental revenue and plays such a critical role in preparing children for adult life. Advocates of community control assert that their model alone insures such accountability by placing educators under the watchful eyes of a local school board which has the authority to set personnel, budgetary, and curriculum policy. Neither centralization nor administrative decentralization, on the other hand, clearly permit such accountability. We have already seen that with the growth of large school systems members of the central board of education must struggle to direct and control administrators and teachers. Under administrative decentralization, with more policy-formation occurring in the individual schools, they would have an even harder battle. Moreover, even if board members could reasonably control the educators, it is not clear that parents could easily influence the board members, particularly if they were appointed. While parents could be placed on local advisory committees, they would still not have any actual authority to limit the educators.[21]

The argument for professional autonomy asserts that educators, like doctors or lawyers, cannot perform their tasks well under close supervision of laymen. While the latter may be legitimately concerned about education, they lack knowledge and experience of what occurs in the classroom. According to this argument, it is sufficient for citizens to set broad limits to educational policy, such as what shall be taught or how much should be spent, but beyond that they are likely to hamper the expertise of teachers. Consequently, either centralization or administrative decentralization is preferable to community control, since both minimize the extent to which parents and community leaders can interfere with educational policy.[22]

How valid are these opposing arguments? If the test for validity were the vehemence with which the arguments were asserted during the New York teachers' strikes, one would have to conclude that their validity is unquestionable. Analysis rather than ideological fervor, however, indicates that we can accept the theories of democratic control and professional autonomy only with qualifications.

To begin with, it is unlikely that even under the community control model a community will actually "control" educational policy-making. The often-mentioned analogy is with suburban school districts where, it is argued, white parents are able to run the schools. But this is precisely what does *not* happen in the suburbs: suburban public education, even under a community control model, is by and large shaped by the teachers and administrators.[23] Lay members of suburban boards lack the expertise and the time to shape most policies; occasionally they carefully investigate a particular, controversial matter, but generally they just review educators' own decisions and handle routine, trivial questions. Suburban board members have their greatest influence on revenue and school construction questions, two matters on which local community boards would not even be involved. There is little reason to anticipate that community boards in urban areas would be more influential than suburban boards: while they may be able to change those practices which now produce so much hostility and tension, on the whole they too will have to rely upon their educators.

Moreover, even if laymen could control the educators this control is unlikely to be "democratic" or "community" in any more than a formal sense. In the suburbs, as is likely to be the case in urban communities, laymen who do have some impact on school policy are few in number and only vaguely accountable to the citizens as a whole. Of course suburban board members are elected, as they would be in urban areas, but typically only after a campaign devoid of issues and by a meager percentage of the potential electorate. Most citizens simply do not become involved or have much influence. Thus under community control there is danger that only a local elite of educators and board members will determine school policy.

Similarly, we can accept the argument for professional autonomy only with qualifications. To begin with, educators themselves are divided over the issue of autonomy, with many—especially young blacks and liberal whites—believing that good education can occur only when there is extensive interaction with the community. Teachers trained to educate middle-class white children can be useful in ghetto schools only if their traditional isolation from the community is reduced. To preserve autonomy in the face of confusion and disruption is only to perpetuate the mistakes which cause the problem in the first place.

Furthermore, professional autonomy has often been used to protect practices which are most unprofessional. In New York, for example, giving the educators autonomy in hiring practices has meant that qualified black and Puerto Rican teachers cannot easily obtain key administrative positions.[24] Teachers' organizations, which are often instrumental in shaping professional goals, have long sought tenure laws and automatic salary increases, which both protect and reward poor teachers. Most important, parents who feel they have legitimate complaints about how teachers relate to their children find that "professional autonomy" is used as an excuse to avoid explanations, let alone reforms. Professional autonomy, then, is a strategy with which educators protect their own self interest while thwarting the interests of the children and the community.

Given these qualifications, some validity remains on each side of the two opposing arguments. The community control model of school decentralization will permit more community influence over school policy, even if that influence may not be very democratic or sufficient to overcome the expertise of the educators. Centralization or administrative decentralization, on the other hand, will insure more control over education policy by teachers and principals, even if that control may be used for unprofessional ends. This conflict is both pervasive and insoluble, and it will frustrate attempts to achieve agreement on administrative structure.

The controversy between professional autonomy and democratic control is related to a controversy between substantive and procedural values in policy-formation. Advocates of administrative decentralization argue that a decision-making procedure should yield decisions which are "good," and that any particular procedure is to be judged simply as instrumental toward that end. The substance of a policy is thus more important than characteristics of the procedure by which it is made. Since, the argument continues, over the long run educators make the best decisions about education, then it follows that a procedure which maximizes their influence will over time yield the best policies. Thus administrative decentralization, which grants wide discretion to field educators, is preferable to community control, which permits unknowledgeable interference.

Proponents of this view are the first to admit that ghetto education is poor, and they admit that some ghetto teachers are not doing their job properly. But the main problem, they feel, is not that there is too little contact with the community, but that ghetto schools are poorly financed and managed. If significantly more money were available, then better teachers could be hired, fewer children put in each class, and more auxiliary and remedial services provided. Administrative decentralization by itself will not provide more funds, but it will provide better management: the teachers and principals within the individual schools will have more influence in setting and implementing policy for their school, and the central administrators will be less able to interfere. While it is true that educators as a group disagree about the aims and methods of teaching, administrative decentralization will permit the ordered diversity in which improvements can be made.

Contrary to this argument, however, is the view that decision-making ought not be judged solely by the policy it produces, but that certain procedures are desirable because they have significant side-effects. In particular, extensive citizen participation is valuable: it is argued that only by regular, meaningful participation can individuals become aware of what is occurring in the community and develop the skills and understanding necessary to make a rational contribution.[25] Moreover, it is argued that participation enables an individual to develop his personal values so he can act as his own agent, not unwittingly as someone else's. This theory is currently appealing to black theorists, who feel that only through participation in black communities can black people begin to shed the values and perspectives inculcated into them by white society. Advocates of this theory naturally favor the community control model of decentralization, since it alone permits extensive citizen activity.

The validity of the former argument turns on one critical question: how possible is it to identify "good" educational decisions? Should we really assume that educators make the best choices? While everyone agrees that education involves acquiring some basic skills in reading and mathematics, there is actually little agreement beyond this about what "good" education is. Some people assert equal resources ought to be devoted to all children, while others argue that more ought to be given those who are brighter or more skilled. Some feel schools should concentrate on training in marketable skills while others urge that they should simply develop critical awareness. History, some insist, should be taught to yield knowledge of the past, while others maintain that it should be taught to instill maxims for the future. Disagreement on these and other basic questions indicates that the central methodological assumption of those who support substantive evaluation is false: one cannot judge which decision-making procedure is best by simply referring to the quality of the decisions it produces. Thus it cannot be argued that field educators will necessarily produce good decisions about urban education once influence over policy-formation is decentralized to them. Indeed, an administrative model which grants extensive autonomy to principals and teachers and minimizes the influence of other people raises the danger that a closed elite will come to determine public education policy.

Alternatively, the argument that participation is so critical depends not so much on the extent of citizen participation as on its character. The anticipated advantages of participation—awareness of one's own preferences and of what is occurring in the community, and the acquisition of political skills and understanding—are likely to occur only if the participant is regularly active, if he finds his activity efficacious, and if he is forced to consider opposing points of view. These conditions, however, rarely occur in suburban school politics, and they are unlikely to occur in urban school politics, either.[26] Individual activity is unlikely to be regular because it is so hard to participate in school politics: nonpartisanship precludes the political organizations which could provide advice and support; and election campaigns, which rarely involve issues, are dull. Most activity is left by default in the hands of board members and educators, none of whom want to encourage critical participation. Moreover, what action there is generally is not efficacious: individual citizens find it difficult to have much impact on educational policy, especially given educators' concern for professional autonomy, and they find it equally frustrating to try to rally community support. In the short run ghetto communities may have extensive participation (many do now) as citizens press to have long-standing grievances corrected; in the long run, however, they are unlikely to have any more than suburban areas.

Finally, what participation there is rarely forces one to consider opposing points of view. Aside from meetings of board members and educators there are no regular exchanges on policy problems, and the few confrontations that do occur frequently are emotional and tend to reinforce previously-held opinions. Given the likelihood that a community control plan would divide the single urban school district into numerous relatively homogeneous districts, the possibility is small that there will even be divergent social groups to provoke confrontations.

Thus the claims of advocates of each side are vastly overrated. One cannot simply assert that educators make "good" policy choices about public education, nor can one plausibly argue that citizen participation in school politics will be either extensive or beneficial to the participant.

Finally, there is a conflict between community development and societal integration. Advocates of community control often argue that citizen control of the local schools can be the first step toward the community revitalization necessary to solve complex social and economic problems of the ghetto. In the 1960's reformers attempted to use centralized governmental services to tackle some of these problems, but they had little success. In part this was due to bureaucratic resistance and poor funding, but it was also due to inadequate knowledge of local conditions. The solution of ghetto problems, the argument continues, depends upon knowledge that can be obtained only by living in the community and upon inter-agency coordination that must be handled locally. To attack poverty successfully, in other words, policy-formation and implementation must be devolved to the local community. Control over education is seen as the critical step in this transformation because of the salience of the school in the local community: it dominates the lives of the children, it draws deep concern among parents, and, with its extensive personnel and supply needs, it is a potential source for economic rejuvenation. The schools could become social centers for the children and training centers for adults, and they could provide employment for both teachers and para-professionals.

Advocates of centralization or administrative decentralization, on the other hand, argue that community development is illusory and that in the long run the crisis of the ghetto can be solved only by external resources and gradual integration of indigent minorities into the larger society. Internal community development is unlikely, so the argument goes, because ghetto communities have high population mobility and economic and social problems caused largely by outside forces. Increasing the power of the people in the local community is not going to reduce unemployment, for this depends much more upon Federal economic policies and municipal tax levels. Similarly, strengthening the local community is not going to decrease significantly the steady influx of the poor from other areas or prevent crime. Those communities which do not have these problems are not more powerful but only wealthier: it is a matter of money, not power. Advocates of centralization argue that the solution is to provide more money, both directly through increased employment opportunities and national assistance of some sort or other and indirectly through expanded governmental services. Adoption of a national tax-sharing program, for example, could provide substantial revenue for both state and local services. Advocates of decentralization, while agreeing with this argument of the centralists, also feel that the lack of expertise and coordination of centralized governmental services is hampering ghetto reform. To them the solution is not to establish community control but to decentralize policy-formation of the services to field personnel and to promote more decentralized inter-agency cooperation. Advisory committees can build in citizen knowledge without threatening the necessary administrative cohesion. Advocates of both centralization and decentralization feel that community control would balkanize the center city at the very time that problems of governmental services can be met only by planning and decision-making on a wider, metropolitan basis.

This conflict between community development and societal integration is too complex to be adequately handled in a short paragraph or two. Nonetheless, several comments can be made about both arguments. First, and most important, both theories appear to be valid only to the extent that the reforms they urge are thoroughly implemented; *i.e.,* that ghetto dwellers actually do obtain control of important governmental services or that administrators do obtain sufficient revenue and coordinating authority. Halfway measures are unlikely to be successful. Communities will not become revitalized if residents can control public education but not law enforcement or housing policy, nor will government agencies solve social and economic problems if they are not reorganized and refinanced. Recent political experience suggests that none of these other reforms are likely to occur, regardless of what the structure of the school system is. Municipal services are most unlikely to be broken down by separate communities; bureaucracies are quite resistant to reorganization; and more funds for domestic social programs will not be made available. In general, it is best not to cast the debate over administrative reorganization of city schools in terms of general social and economic reform.

However, it is likely that community control of the schools will very quickly change the character of political interaction in ghetto communities. Citizens will no longer trace all problems in the schools to a repressive white society, hostility and tensions are likely to diminish as reforms are made, and future debate over education policy will be less likely to be as ideological as it currently is. Moreover, other governmental agencies, anxious to head off community control of their own services, will probably make minor reforms and adjustments to placate some of their critics. Granting more power to black communities is a quick way to split them into separate factions that will argue with each other. In these senses community control of education could have profoundly conservative implications: the presently mounting anger of ghetto residents may be diverted so that more significant reforms will not occur.

On the other hand centralization or administrative decentralization would prevent the balkanization of public education in urban areas, and they would keep the possibility open that there might be metropolitan solutions to educational problems at some time in the future. Minor cooperative programs already exist in some metropolitan areas, and more will be started. Of course it is unlikely that such areal cooperation will aid ghetto communities unless the political power of blacks and Puerto Ricans continues to grow and racial divisions in the society as a whole become less marked. Advocates of metropolitan solutions, however, must ask themselves whether reforms can be delayed this long without provoking severe political disorder.

Strategies

Participants in a struggle over decentralization follow various strategies to protect and further their interests. Unless a referendum is held on the issue, which is unlikely, very few of those whose interests are affected will be able to determine what structural changes will occur. To influence those who will decide—the superintendent, the board of education, or the state legislature—interested parties appeal for political support and issue threats and sanctions. The manipulation of public images is the most significant strategy, since if people are convinced their interests are going to be adversely affected they will put pressure on the decision-makers. Interest groups manipulated public images for three ends in the New York City dispute: to create solidarity within their own group, to split their opponents, and to build popular support. Thus the United Federation of Teachers characterized the Ocean Hill-Brownsville conflict as a dispute over "teacher rights" and "due process of law," rather than "community control" in an attempt to draw the support of black and young white liberal teachers. To split the potentially wide support for local control, the UFT raised the spectre of black extremism before lower-middle class Catholics and of anti-semitism before Jews. To build broad public support the UFT stressed repeatedly that community control would create turmoil in the schools, citing disruption which has been occurring in the demonstration districts. Black community leaders, on the other hand, stressed "local democracy" and "community control" in an effort to rally community support for the local governing board; they tried to split the UFT by arguing that good education in the ghetto requires extensive participation of black parents. To build popular support the black leaders attempted to manipulate the widespread concern about education and the future of ghetto schools. Indeed, the intense ideological fervor of the New York dispute can be directly attributed to these strong public image campaigns.

Influencing the public commission that recommends a particular decentralization plan is another strategy for attaining political support. This can be done either directly, by placing advocates and supporters on the commission itself, or indirectly, by making clear to the commission what provisions will or will not be acceptable. Experience in New York suggests that the recommendations of a commission will serve more as benchmarks for debate than as proposals that ultimately are enacted. This is partly due to the difficulty of devising a plan that will be acceptable to the numerous interested groups, and it is partly due to the realization of the interest groups that skilled campaigning might win an even better plan. Nonetheless, since the ultimate decision-makers may rely upon the commission's recommendations, it is still useful to attempt to influence them.

Threats and sanctions may be effectively combined with appeals for political support. Customarily the threats assert that dire problems will arise should a particular proposal be adopted: teachers will strike or resign their positions; lecturers will preach white racism or anti-semitism; children will be mis-educated or become unruly; parents will start demonstrations or boycotts; etc. Given the racial and class tensions in cities, most of the threats will be persuasive if they are frequently repeated and supported by "examples." Teachers have the strongest threat that is credible since by striking they could close schools throughout the city, send the children back home, and raise endless problems about schedules, college requirements, etc. Given urban teachers unions' recent militancy, board members and school officials are likely to believe strike threats, even when striking is forbidden by law.

Actually imposing sanctions is more difficult because this could undermine campaigns to create a good public image. However, interest groups are occasionally forced to enact them to keep their threats credible and to satisfy their members' desire for retaliation. In the New York City dispute participants attempted to maneuver their opponents into making minor mistakes so retaliation would then appear justified: local governing boards would seize upon deficiencies common to all teachers as grounds for dismissing union teachers, while the UFT would point to the hostility of black leaders they had frustrated as grounds for abolishing the demonstration districts. Sanctions which destroy a favorable public image may still be successful if, like teachers' strikes, they are strong enough that opponents will sue for peace.

In general, advocates of continued centralization or administrative decentralization have significant strategic advantages. Proponents of centralization need not rally supporters to their side as long as they can split the opposition and defeat proposals for reform; indeed, as long as there is no change their interests will be protected. Administrative decentralization involves only internal administrative changes which school districts can usually enact without obtaining approval from either the state department of education or the state legislature. Alternatively, proponents of community control of schools must appeal to the state legislature to amend the state school code. In general, legislatures have always been reluctant to grant wider local control over governmental services; they will be even more reluctant to do so against the arguments of the professionals and the fears of middle-class whites. After all, the principal proponents of community control are black activists, who have never had much influence in state capitols. The New York State Legislature flatly rejected community control proposals in the spring of 1969; it even failed to protect the three existing demonstration districts. One can predict that community control of urban education will not be widely adopted throughout the country.

*

The dispute over decentralization of urban schools is in large part a dispute over who is going to run public education in cities. Central board members and central administrators are vying for control against field educators, and in turn both groups are struggling against community leaders and parents, principally blacks. Although none of these groups are unified, most have substantial support from their members or followers. It is wrong to characterize these contestants as primarily concerned with their own positions and influence, though of course that is part of their motivation; instead, what separates them are disagreements over basic educational and political issues. Three of the latter have been discussed in this paper: the conflict between democratic control and professional auton- omy; the conflict between procedural and substantive values in decision-making; the conflict between community development and societal integration. These political conflicts, though basically insoluble, will become temporarily settled as one group or another gains influence to determine school policy. Consider- ing the importance of the stakes, one can anticipate bitter fights wherever the dispute occurs.

FOOTNOTES

[1]The major exceptions to this include the indirect impact of two funding programs, aid to Federally impacted areas (1950) and the National Defense Education Act (1958), and the restrictions on religious instruction and racial segregation invoked by Federal courts.

[2]United States Bureau of the Census, *Statistical Abstract of the United States* 1968. 89th annual edition (Washington: U.S. Government Printing Office, 1968), 406. Consolida- tion has sharply reduced the number of local school districts from 127,649 in 1932 to 21,782 in 1967. The number of districts varies considerably by state, with Alaska and Hawaii having just one each but others having over 1,000.

[3]Roscoe Martin, *Government and the Suburban School* (Syracuse: Syracuse University Press, 1962), 7.

[4]For an introduction to the methodological problems of studying centralization and decentralization see James W. Fesler, "Approaches to the Understanding of Decentraliza- tion," *Journal of Politics,* vol. XXVII (1965), 536-566.

[5]For the panel's recommendations see Mayor's Advisory Panel on Decentralization of the New York City Schools, *Reconnection for Learning,* November, 1967. Accounts of the teacher strikes over the Ocean Hill-Brownsville demonstration district can be found in Maurice Berube and Marilyn Gittell, *Confrontation at Ocean Hill-Brownsville* (New York: Praeger, 1969) and Martin Mayer, *The Teachers Strike, New York 1968* (New York: Harper and Row, 1969). A general bibliography on the New York dispute and school decentraliza- tion in general is in *The Center Forum,* vol. III (May 15, 1969), 30-32.

[6]New York City is a consolidation of the city of New York, the city of Brooklyn, part of Queens County and Richmond County, as approved by the state legislature in 1897. Previously, in 1874 and 1895, sections of the Bronx were annexed to the main city. See A. Emerson Palmer, *The New York Public School* (New York: MacMillan, 1905), chaps. 31 and 34. Annexation in Pittsburgh occurred in 1906, when the city of Allegheny was added to the original Pittsburgh (though the school districts were not combined until 1911).

[7]Pennsylvania State Department of Public Instruction, *Report of the Survey of the Public Schools of Philadelphia,* vol. II (1922), 4-6. After 1867 central board members were selected by judges of the Court of Common Pleas.

[8]J. Thomas Scharf and Thompson Westcott, *History of Philadelphia,* vol. III (Philadelphia: L. H. Everts, 1884), 1936-1937.

[9]Palmer, *op. cit.,* 184, 243.

[10]Pennsylvania State Department of Public Instruction, *op. cit.,* 6.

[11]Palmer, *op. cit.,* 185-186.

[12]For an account of standard administrative precepts at this time, see Herbert Kaufman, "Emerging Conflicts in the Doctrine of Public Administration," *The American Political Science Review,* vol. L (1956), 1057-1073.

[13]See the discussion of the Davis Law on uniform salary schedules in Palmer, *op. cit.,* 280-283.

[14]Robert H. Wieber, "The Social Functions of Public Education," *American Quarterly,* XXI (Summer, 1969), 159-160.

[15]For an illustration of this culture split in the Boston schools, see Peter Schrag, *Village School Downtown* (Boston: Beacon Press, 1967), chap. 4.

[16]David Rogers, *110 Livingston Street* (New York: Random House, 1968), chaps. 8-9.

[17]For an account of central staff reprisals against community demonstration districts in New York, see Miriam Wasserman, "The I.S. 201 Story," *The Urban Review,* Vol. III, no. 6 (1969), 3-15.

[18]If the central school board transfered all authority to the local boards, complete political decentralization would occur; in other words, the single school district would be split into numerous autonomous ones.

[19]For examples of suggested division of functions see recommendations for the New York City School System, especially Mayor's Advisory Panel on Decentralization of the New York City Schools, *op. cit.,* and the New York City Board of Education's *Plan for Development of a Community School District System for the City of New York,* January 29, 1969. These recommendations were hampered by the absence of detail, an omission that is likely to cause controversy, and the vagueness of the criteria by which functions are apportioned.

[20]For a review and critique of the Bundy Panel's recommendations on local board selection see Robert F. Lyke, "Representation and Urban School Boards" in Henry Levin, ed., *Community Control of Schools* (Washington: The Brookings Institution, 1970).

[21]For an account of this problem in New York City, see Jeremy Larner, "I.S. 201: Disaster in the Schools," *Dissent* (January/February, 1967), 27-40 and Rogers, *op. cit.,* chap. 10.

[22]A variation of this urges that administrative decentralization is preferable to centralization since it grants more autonomy to those educators directly involved in teaching. Many of the reforms instituted by superintendents in the early 1960's were strongly opposed by educators in the field, who either were threatened by the administrative and personnel changes or were upset with the haste and confusion.

[23]See Roscoe Martin, *op. cit.,* especially chapter 5; and Robert F. Lyke, *Suburban School Politics* (Unpublished Ph.D. dissertation, Yale University, 1968), especially chapters 7-9.

[24]David Rogers, *op. cit.*, chap. 8. One regulation which the educators have enacted, for example, requires administrative positions to be filled from lists of applicants who have passed an infrequently-given examination, even though other better-qualified applicants may be available.

[25]Graeme Duncan and Stephen Lukes, "The New Democracy," *Political Studies,* vol. XI (1963), 156-177.

[26]Lyke, *Suburban School Politics,* 185-188.

THE POLITICS OF SCHOOL DESEGREGATION*

Robert L. Crain

The Response of the School Superintendent

One barrier to the civil rights movement is the school superintendent. During the civil rights controversies, ten different superintendents served in our eight cities. Seven can be said to have acted autonomously, without board instruction, in rejecting demands of the civil rights movement; in contrast, only three stand out as having urged their board to take a liberal position.

In studying the statements made by these superintendents, three themes recur very regularly. The most common is the insistence on a "color-blind" policy of ignoring racial distinctions. Thus superintendents have opposed referring to schools as segregated or integrated and have argued that taking racial censuses of either pupils or teachers would be illegal or at least embarrassing to both students and staff. Plans that require the schools to attempt to obtain integration have been accused of being discriminatory. One Buffalo board member's statement, that integrating Woodlawn Junior High School would discriminate against Negro students by limiting their numbers in the new school to make room for whites and that these students "should not be sacrificed on the altar of racial balance" reappears, in less colorful language, in the statements of several superintendents. All eight cities in our sample have some sort of open enrollment policy; in several cases it was adopted as a result of demands for school integration. Yet in only two cases is the plan actually keyed to a racial criterion. Everywhere else, transfers are allowed only on the basis of overcrowding and available space, and in most cases the school system does not attempt to determine whether such plans increase or reduce integration. The exceptions are Buffalo and Newark, where students transferring from predominantly Negro schools are given priority.

Although seven of the eight cities use busses to transport students out of crowded schools, and in each case the result is to increase integration, yet in none of the cities is the racial composition of either the sending or receiving school considered officially as a criterion in arranging such transfers. Compensa-

*Reprinted from Robert L. Crain, *The Politics of School Desegregation* (Chicago: Aldine Publishing Company, 1968); copyright ©1968 by National Opinion Research Center.

tory education programs for the culturally deprived are also officially color blind. Very frequently, pointed reference is made to poor whites or other non-Negro minorities in order to advertise the fact that the program is not for Negroes per se. (This is why the Pittsburgh annual report's statement on compensatory education is so unusual.) In extreme cases, school superintendents have sometimes managed to speak at length about integration or civil rights issues without ever using the word Negro.

Coupled with this attention to color blindness is the stress placed on a narrow definition of the function of the school as "educational," rather than "social." This is most clearly expressed in Spears' statement that the bringing of students together in the classroom is a necessity of teaching, but the effects of the resulting interaction between students are not within the purview of the educational system. The school administrator expresses great reluctance to "expand the function of the schools" as demanded by color-conscious plans.

The third theme which recurs in the statements of school superintendents, although not as often as the first two, is an extreme defensiveness about the schools, coupled with an intolerance of "lay" criticism. Thus some school administration reports seem to delight in pointing out errors made by their critics. Frequent references are made, not always with justification, to the inability of lay persons to make decisions on problems requiring educational expertise. Finally, the defensiveness of some school staffs is reflected in their unwillingness or inability to engage in coherent dialogue—criticisms are frequently answered with either flat disagreement or vague, off-the-point replies, or replies with vast quantities of irrelevant detail. The two most striking exceptions are Pittsburgh's Marland, who has regularly engaged in long conversations with civil rights leaders and supplied highly specific and clear information on racial issues, and Buffalo's Manch, who openly admitted that there was no particular computer mythology involved in the selection of a school boundary for the Woodlawn school.

On the basis of our interviews and the documents collected, we propose that these three themes taken together represent one sort of ideal type of superintendent behavior. Obviously, no superintendent behaves this way at all times, and some school administrators do not fit the ideal at all. If we try to capture all three of these themes in a single phrase, we could say that they represent components of a narrow and defensive definition of their occupational role. What are some possible explanations for this ideology?

We should consider the possibility that the ideology is just a device to conceal anti-Negro sentiment. This strikes us as unlikely, however. The private attitudes of the superintendents, as expressed on our questionnaires, are not particularly conservative on racial issues. Further, the men who are more liberal on race are just as likely to express the values we have discussed here as are the more conservative men; there does not seem to be much correlation between the racial attitudes and the ideological position we have defined here.

A much more reasonable hypothesis is that the superintendents feel insecure in their positions and react accordingly. This could easily be the result of their social backgrounds. The only channel into the school superintendency is through the ranks of teaching. This means majoring in education in college, usually teaching school for several years, and then rising through administrative posts. This restricts the number of persons eligible for the post dramatically. First, they must be male in almost every case. Education is a woman's field, and male students who major in education tend to be of low socioeconomic status. Any school superintendent will, then, be highly mobile socially, and he may bear strains associated with his position in an unprestigious and feminine occupation. It is hard to imagine that the big city school superintendent anticipated becoming a highly paid executive when he entered teachers college. We know of no relevant data on the occupational attitudes of men who are highly mobile, but it seems reasonable that they might have difficulty accepting the responsibilities of their position and might feel insecure about their ability to stay in office.

There are other important reasons why an administrator might develop a defensive ideology. As a teacher, he is solely responsible for the success or failure of his students, and unlike the college instructor, he must deal directly with their parents. Other occupational roles, such as doctors, lawyers, and ministers, require direct confrontation with clients, but usually their professional competence cannot be so easily questioned. The teacher, however, is not obviously doing anything that the parent is incapable of doing. Furthermore, he has few or no criteria by which to determine whether he is doing a good job. He is also subject to a second criticism—not only is he not teaching Johnnie well enough, he may be teaching him the wrong way. For in at least some cases, he is the harbinger of foreign values—classical learning or middle-class behavior patterns, for example. Fortunately for the contemporary teacher, these "foreign values" now seem widely diffused through the society. Parents want their children to go to college, and if they must learn certain subjects to get into college, the parent is agreeable. But the present generation of superintendents began teaching in the 1920's, when this problem may have been much more serious. The problem is complicated by the fact that the teacher must resist parental intrusions in the classroom while at the same time urging the parents to "take an interest in their child's education."

Thus the teacher must develop values to protect himself from being required to justify the material he teaches and the grades he gives. The professional ideology of the teacher does this—by insisting on certification, on methods courses, on rejecting the use of lay persons in teaching roles, and, in extreme cases, in the theories that preschool education by parents may retard the child.[1] Whatever the legitimacy of such a position, it enables a teacher to resist the criticism of parents and of citizens' groups. In addition, the use of educational testing may help the teacher to justify his actions; if his students don't learn as much as the parents expect, it is because of their low I.Q.'s.

When a teacher becomes a superintendent, he again finds himself in conflict with the community, this time as represented by a school board, which he sees, often correctly, as conservative and traditionalist.[2] The simple dichotomy between policy and administration is a false one; the superintendent finds himself spending part of his time trying to persuade the board to adopt his policy ideas, and more time trying to protect himself from board interference in ongoing administration.

If a profession is made up of men who share common needs for a defensive ideology, the profession will develop such an ideology. In addition, the profession as a whole may need such defenses. The public school system has had to deal with a variety of encroachments. It has had to contend with corruption in politically sponsored systems. It has fought with the public on Deweyism, on the teaching of reading, on vocational education, on the teaching of German during World War I, on communism in textbooks, and a host of other issues. Keeping politics out of schools has now become a watchword.

The educational profession and many individual superintendents have responded to these conflicts in three ways: (1) by narrowing their frame of reference so that they can silence critics by refusing responsibility for increasing juvenile delinquency, moral decline, and the lack of patriotism of its graduates; (2) by trading low priority values, about the rights of labor or of Negroes, for higher priority values such as freedom of curriculum reform; and (3) by developing the claim that expertise is required to make school decisions, so that critics can be ignored.

The pattern of a defensive profession made up of low status men who have had to resist public demands throughout their careers is present in big city school systems, but it was even clearer in the small town America of the 1920's and 1930's. The foreignness of education, the demands of parents on teachers, the absence of academic freedom, and the conservatism of elected school board members—all the factors we have listed—were exaggerated in the dense social network of the small town. For the teacher, *Stadt luft macht man frei.* And curiously enough, the recruitment pattern for big city school superintendencies tends to attract men from small town and farming backgrounds. First, the rural or small town high school student, presumably because of his more limited occupational horizons, is more likely to go into teaching. In addition, if he begins teaching in a small town (where he is one of the few male teachers), he can more quickly rise to a principalship and become a superintendent at a young age. Thus the small town teacher gains administrative experience while his big city colleague is still in the classroom. Big cities want experienced men as superintendents, but experienced men can only be found in the small cities; the men who become superintendents in small cities tend to be teachers in smaller cities, and the men who teach in such cities tend to be born there.[3]

This argument is supported by an analysis of college seniors choosing educational administration in 1961 (Davis and Bradburn, 1961). Only a tiny fraction of college freshmen (0.2 per cent) chose educational administration as a career. This number increased through the four years of college very rapidly, but even as seniors, barely enough students selected educational administration to fill the demand. Only 5 per cent of all persons going into public education specified educational administration; this would imply a ratio of one administrator to twenty teachers, which is probably too low. The population was too small to make accurate estimates possible, but we do find the following statistically significant differences: Students who chose educational administration were from poorer families, and from families where both parents have low educational attainments. Of thirty occupational careers, educational administration students were lowest in father's education; even students choosing nursing and agriculture were higher. They were also overwhelmingly rural; students from farm areas were twice as likely to choose educational administration as were students from metropolitan areas. Students oriented toward educational administration saw themselves as religious, conventional, and not intellectual. A majority intended to put off graduate training until after they had taught for at least a year.

We can also document this pattern by examining the biographies of the men who direct the schools that participate in the "Great Cities" research program (Table 10.2). The eleven superintendents listed in the 1964 edition of *Who's Who* can be divided into two groups—the "locals" and the "mobiles." The three "locals" all grew up in large cities and began their teaching in the city where they are now superintendents. Of the remaining eight, six were born in small towns, only two went to urban universities, and seven began teaching in small cities. They spent a median time of eight years at the rank of teacher or principal. Notice that three of these men deviate from this pattern conspicuously. Calvin Gross is a mobile urbanite, the only superintendent who began teaching in one big city and then wound up as superintendent in another. Samuel Brownell also differs from the other mobiles, since he went on immediately for a doctorate without pausing to teach. He is possibly the only man in this list who could have had a clear picture of his future career at the time he took his bachelor's degree. Sidney Marland's career resembles Gross's and Brownell's in that he also took less than the usual eight years to move into central administration. The presence of these three deviant cases actually tends to support our general thesis, since these three men are highly respected by the critics of the "educational establishment." We have one final bit of data to bolster our argument. Five school superintendents gave us background data that included their father's occupation and the educational attainment of their parents. Of the five, two were the sons of farmers, one of a small town merchant, and two of blue collar workers. None of the five had fathers who attended college, although three had mothers who had at least finished junior college.

Table 10.2   Careers of Prominent School Superintendents

City	Name	Place of Birth	Undergraduate College	First Teaching Position	Number of Years as Teacher or Principal	Age at Advanced Degree	First Administrative Post	Age (1963)
Locals:								
Los Angeles	Jack P. Crowther	Salt Lake City	Univ. Utah	Los Angeles	8	M.A.-46	Asst. supt., Los	54
Buffalo	Joseph Manch	(In Poland)	Univ. Buffalo	Buffalo	12	Ed.D.-45	Staff, Buffa.o	53
Philadelphia	Allen Wetter	Philadelphia	Temple Univ.	Philadelphia	22		Dist. supt., Phila.	63
Mobiles:								
Washington	Carl Hansen	Wolbach, Neb.	Univ. Nebraska	(In Nebraska)	20	Ed.D.-38	Asst. to sup--, Wash., D.C.	57
San Francisco	Harold Spears	Snayzee, Ind.	Wabash College	Evansville, Ind.	No data	Ed.D.-37	Supt., Highland Park, Ill.	61
Baltimore	George Brain	Thorpe, Wash.	Central Wash. State	(In Wash. State)	6	Ed.D.-39	Asst. supt., Belle-vue, Wash.	-
Milwaukee	Harold Vincent	Knox, Indiana	Greenville College, Illinois	Asst. principal, Wash. Springs, S.Dak.	11	LLD.-54	Asst. supt., Canton, Ohio	66
Chicago	Benjamin Willis	Baltimore	George Wash. Univ.	Henderson, Md.	12	Ed.D.-49	Supt., Denton, Maryland	62
Deviants:								
Detroit	Sam Brownell	Peru, Nebraska	Univ. Nebraska	Principal, Peru, Nebraska	2	Ph.D.-26	Supt., Grosse Pointe, Mich.	63
New York	Calvin Gross	Los Angeles	UCLA	Los Angeles	4	Ed.D.-36	Supt., Weston, Massachusetts	44
Pittsburgh	Sidney Marland	Danielson, Conn.	Univ. Connecticut	West Hartford, Connecticut	3	Ph.D.-41	Supt., Darien, Connecticut	49

Thus we see that the interaction between civil rights leaders and school superintendents has the preconditions for conflict. They literally do not speak the same language. In addition, both live in a world hostile to them and are unlikely to be very patient in dealing with each other. In six of the eight cities, school integration quickly became a conflict between the movement and the superintendent. In St. Louis and Baltimore, the superintendent wrote rebuttals to the charges of the civil rights leadership which were received angrily by the protesters. In Newark, demands that the superintendent be dismissed were made even before the first school integration incident occurred. In Lawndale and San Francisco, the superintendents flatly refused the first demands made upon them. Finally, in Bay City, the superintendent, McDonough, was criticized by the movement, although his successor has taken a more liberal position than his board and has not been criticized as much. Only two superintendents, Manch and Marland, have held the respect of the civil rights leadership (and Manch fell out of their favor after Woodlawn).

The School Board and the White Voter

But the school superintendent, in almost every one of our cases, has found that racial policy was taken from his hands by the school board. In six of our cities we can mark a point when the major decision which most influenced the outcome of the school integration issue was made not by the superintendent, but by the board. In some cities it is easy to locate such a point—in Baltimore, for example, when the school board assumed responsibility for negotiation with the civil rights leadership, or in Newark on the two occasions when the board members and the mayor met with the civil rights leadership to reach a compromise. In San Francisco the board's ad hoc committee presented a report which was, according to one NAACP leader, a "pleasant surprise" after Spears' earlier speech. In Bay City the superintendent's recommendations were disregarded. In Buffalo, while it is true that the school superintendent supported the final plan to segregate the Woodlawn school, it seems likely that he would not have done so if the board had not made its own position clear. In St. Louis, it is harder to trace out the relationship between the board and the superintendent, but the board, not the superintendent, appointed the citizens' committee which made the recommendations on which the compromise was reached, and we have other evidence to indicate that the superintendent was advised by the board to take action to meet the demands. In the remaining two cities, Lawndale and Pittsburgh, there has been no evidence of any disagreement between the board and the administration, but in both cities the administration stays in close touch with the school board and seems to be responsive to its will. Both these cities changed superintendents without changing policy on civil rights.

We cannot easily characterize the "typical" school board in the way we have the "typical" superintendent and the two types of civil rights leaders. As we have seen, board members vary considerably in their backgrounds, motivations, and attitudes toward school integration. Further, board members are in an ambiguous situation, where there are few clear guidelines to permit them to reach a decision easily. There are several reasons why there are no convenient guidelines.

The typical school board is not closely knit. It ordinarily meets to handle the legal paperwork of the schools; at irregular intervals it makes specific decisions about a particular school or on a particular policy. But it can be thought of as making school policy only in a firefighting fashion. If an issue comes up, it acts; otherwise, it does not. It may not take a position at all on some of the most fundamental issues of school policy, simply because those particular policies have not been made salient by community discussion. The result is that the school board members do not, either as individuals or as a group, have a highly articulated educational policy. Almost every time they oppose the superintendent, or the superintendent comes to them for guidance, the board has some difficulty making a decision. Every issue is different and every decision can take a good deal of time. The school integration issue is a good example of this.

The typical school board avoids issues that are not important, if for no other reason than to save time for issues that are. The result is that in virtually every city the initial complaints of the civil rights movement are ignored. Even Pittsburgh did not take action on integration until the second time the issue was brought up. Of course, the board then appears to be defending the status quo. By the time the civil rights movement begins to make noise, they can rightly claim that the school board has been ignoring the problem, and the school board begins to discuss the issue with one strike against it.

The second step the school board may take to avoid lengthy discussion of an issue is to refer it to the superintendent. As we have already pointed out, the superintendent and the civil rights leadership do not make a good partnership, and in none of our eight cities was the issue resolved at this level. In the typical case, the civil rights movement interprets the superintendent's remark as a flat rejection of their request, or even as an insult. Thus, by the time the board realizes that it must itself handle the issue, tempers are already frayed on all sides.

When the board does begin to consider the issue, it must first develop ground rules for its decision-making process and a frame of reference for its decision. This is difficult, principally because the issue is different from most that the board faces: it involves the total community, it has strong emotional overtones, and it is general, rather than specific. If the board adopts the standard tactic of holding public hearing in an effort to determine what the citizens want, it may not receive much help. Two school systems used an outside committee of citizens at this point. St. Louis appointed such a committee only a few days after the issue opened. In Lawndale the Citizens Committee was appointed at the request of the civil rights movement.

In other cases, the board or a special committee of board members may attempt to formulate policy without the help of outsiders. In such cases, if the committee members attempt to serve as a fact-finding body, they may be overwhelmed by the reports of the administration, and become mere spokesmen for the administration position. (For example, the report of the board subcommittee in Baltimore was considerably more cautious than the board's behavior only a few months later; this despite the fact that the subcommittee members were quite liberal in outlook.) If, however, the board attempts to develop a position independent of the administration, it will soon be in relatively uncharted waters. Left to its own devices, the board must develop a philosophical position on the school integration issue.

One might argue that the board's situation is not so ambiguous; that the board realizes that the white parents will not tolerate school integration; and that it therefore has the simple, if not easy, job of trying to squelch the civil rights movement. Actually, this does not seem to be the case. First of all, we know that some elements of the white community supported the civil rights movement in most of our cities. In addition, we know from several national surveys that northern whites express support for integration. For example, an NORC poll taken in 1963 found 75 per cent of northern whites saying "same schools" to the question, "Do you think white and Negro students should go to the same schools or to separate schools?" More to the point, another poll found only 7 per cent of northern whites saying they would object to sending their child to a school with a few Negro students, and only 34 percent would object if the school were half Negro (Erskine, 1962; Hyman and Sheatsley, 1964). We can also see from our eight case studies that segregationist opposition was not an overriding factor. In Baltimore and St. Louis, the opposition to school integration appeared principally after the school integration decision had been made; in both cases the opposition was short-lived. Since these are our most southern cities, we would expect the opposition in other cities to be even weaker. The opposition to school integration in Bay City and Lawndale appeared only after the board had made it clear that it would not integrate the schools in question; in these cases the segregationists played the role of supporting the school board rather than opposing them. (When one of the leaders of the Woodside homeowners' association in Lawndale ran against a school board member in the election, he was eliminated before the runoff election.) In Buffalo the petitions opposing the integration of the Woodlawn school were submitted before the board took a final decision on the matter, but they were in support of board member Parlato's proposal. In all three cases the white parents' groups appeared only after their point of view had been taken by either the school board or some members of the board. They did not initiate the opposition. In effect, the school board recruited their support in two cases.

When the anti-integrationists are in opposition to the school board, they can be squelched fairly easily. San Francisco is perhaps the most striking case. The Committee for Neighborhood Schools protested plans to increase the number of whites in Central Junior High School and also opposed bussing of Negro students, but the school system did bus Negroes into the junior high school where the Committee was strongest, and there was no public opposition. Obviously, these anti-integration movements are weak; they are not self-initiating except in the border cities and usually do not survive their first defeat. (Contrast this with the reaction of the typical civil rights movement to rejection of demands.) We might even go so far as to advance this hypothesis, which the data in all our cases seem to fit: that the school board can mobilize community support for its position, *regardless of whether that position is segregationist or integrationist!*

If the incidents described in the eight cities are representative, we can hypothesize that, generally, white parents will not protest integration as long as (1) the school their children are to attend is not predominantly Negro; (2) white students are not transferred out of their present schools; (3) white students are not forced to attend schools located in the ghetto; and (4) neighborhood racial stability is not threatened. To this we might tentatively add one qualifying statement—whites may protest if they feel that the school integration program is too obviously a surrender to Negro political power. This statement is still somewhat oversimplified; we do not mean to suggest that this is a hard and fast formula. But this "formula" might explain why in at least seven of our eight cities, Negroes are traveling into all-white neighborhoods to attend previously all-white schools without community objection.[4]

Thus we see that the board is free to take action within broad limits. It will not be under much pressure from segregationist groups while it is making its decision. At the same time, the civil rights movement is not exerting much pressure either. At least it is difficult to argue that the demonstrations and other tactics of civil rights groups are particularly frightening to the school board. In most cities court suits were filed, but they were either dropped or settled out of court in every case. In both Bay City and Buffalo the state government was brought in, and in the case of Buffalo this seems to have forced the board to act. (In both cities state action came after our interviewing, so we have only newspaper reports of the action.) But in at least five cities the board was in little danger of being overruled by higher political authority. Picketings, sit-ins, and street demonstrations are embarrassing to the school board only if the school board chooses to be embarrassed. (In St. Louis the rush-hour march was a minor public inconvenience.) The ultimate weapon in the civil rights arsenal is nothing more impressive than a one-day school boycott. In contrast, when the school board deals with a teachers union, it is often threatened with a strike of indefinite duration; the National Education Association can even take action to discourage new teachers from entering the system.

Finally, the school boards in most of these cities operate independently of other community leaders. Only in Newark did the mayor take an active role in negotiating a settlement. In Lawndale, Bay City, and San Francisco the mayor expressed some dissatisfaction with the way the schools were handling the issue, with little effect. Lawndale and Bay City have independently elected boards, so that the mayor has very little power. In San Francisco, Mayor Christopher's letter in support of integration was presented to the school board, but it is difficult to know how much effect this had on the board. In Baltimore the city council threatened to call the school board down for having been negligent enough to have to use widespread bussing to solve its overcrowding problems. However, the mayor managed to squelch this issue. In general, we do not think that any of these boards were greatly influenced by other city officials. Thus the school board is free to act within a very broad range of options.

We have suggested that the typical board has no clearly articulated philosophy of education. In fact, school boards seem to behave in a highly pragmatic fashion. They move from one issue to another as issues become urgent. But the first question raised by the civil rights movement is a philosophic one: Should school boards intentionally attempt to integrate schools, or should they continue to operate in a color-blind fashion? In all eight cities the school boards have been asked to go on record to (1) recognize the existence of segregated schools, and (2) promise to do something about it. Such a statement meets some of the more symbolic goals of the civil rights movement; it puts a governmental body on record as opposed to discrimination, not only in the schools but in effect in housing as well, and commits it to making a demonstration of its belief in racial equality.

No clear educational arguments can be made either for or against such a policy statement. Until the publication of Coleman (1966), there were very few data indicating that Negro children learn more or derive other psychological benefits from being in integrated schools. On the other hand, no educational argument suggests that the integration of schools is a bad policy. The school board thus makes its decision without any particular rationale. An obviously important question is, "Does the board trust the motives of the civil rights movement?" They may feel that the movement is "really" asking for immediate integration of all schools, or something like that. The roots of these differences in perception lie in the view the board members have of the civil rights movement, and these roots appear in the tone with which the board carries out the negotiation and in the wording of the statement that they finally issue.

Normally, the board is next faced with a concrete issue—a particular school or policy becomes the issue. There are fewer elements of ambiguity, but there is also more pressure on the board to try to anticipate the reaction of whites. At this point, the board is likely to look first for tactics to establish firm ground rules for the negotiation by defining the issue in either "legal" or "educational" terms. One school board chose to file suit to determine the legality of the existing policies. Other boards have not actually filed suit, but have stressed legal interpretations of their action. For example, the board might charge that a proposal for integrating schools is unconstitutional. The school board may also attempt to redefine the issue in the terms of the educational profession by developing a plan for compensatory education.

The action taken by the board will tend to be a compromise; frequently it is a compromise that gives the substance of integration without the form. The board may, for example, choose to integrate a particular school, explaining carefully that this was not done to increase integration, but only to relieve overcrowding. (This was the standard Pittsburgh approach.)

Whether the board meets the demands of the civil rights movement depends again to a considerable extent on the perception the board has of the movement. If it decides that the movement does not have the support of the Negro community, or that it is shortsighted and unreasonable, then the board may feel there is at least a good possibility that its proposals are unsound, and ignore or attempt to refute them. Or the board may feel that it has been insulted by the movement and take steps to defend itself.

Thus the board, operating without any clear guidelines or educational policy, hunts for a pragmatic solution, one that will keep the schools functioning and satisfy the various complainants. In doing so, it reacts more than anything else according to its general attitude about the Negro revolution. And it is this feeling which sets the "tone" of the action and determines the response of the movement.

FOOTNOTES

[1]Harper Lee satirizes this in *To Kill a Mockingbird;* her treatment of the teacher who forbids the child's father to teach her to read reflects a disrespect for the teaching profession which is common in twentieth-century writing.

[2]Vidich and Bensman (1958) paint a portrait of a local school administrator as an innovator constantly straining to get his conservative board to support some new step. One study of school board members in Illinois found that 28 per cent of the board members stated that one factor in the board's rejection of a candidate for school superintendent was the candidate's "unsound educational views." In addition, the study notes, "It was particularly noticeable during interviews with board members that they were especially conscious of the need for the candidate's having a background which would fit the community. Most boards expressed the quality desired in these terms: 'We wanted someone who would fit into the community and become a part of it—someone who would be happy here.' " (See Baker, 1952, pp. 69-71.)

[3]Baker (1952) notes that even boards of education in very small communities place high value on previous experience in considering candidates for superintendent; in fact, 53 per cent of the superintendents in systems employing ten to nineteen teachers had been superintendents prior to coming to their present job. Baker writes, "This emphasis [on having experience as a superintendent] seems somewhat unrealistic in terms of recruiting young men." And later he notes, "There is little question that boards are seeking young men

as superintendents." Thus we see that the small town teacher is probably the only one who can climb the ladder fast enough to be both young and experienced, as these boards wish.

[4]The eighth city, Lawndale, began bussing in 1966.

B. POLITICS OF EDUCATION IN SUBURBS

SCHOOL GOVERNMENT *

Roscoe C. Martin

The Board as an Instrument of Democracy

... One may tell any story one wishes to tell about the manner of functioning of the school board, for the chronicles of public education afford bountiful documentation for almost any interpretation. There are, of course, countless success stories, but there are also many horror stories. The purpose here is to examine the board as an operational agency, in an effort to arrive at some judgment both of its effectiveness and of the doctrine which supports it.

Concerning the method of choice of the school board, several subjects suggest themselves for attention. First the nominating process, as we have seen, is so free and easy as to appear to open the door to candidacy for almost any qualified person who might decide to make the race. In practice, however, the guarantees of access often turn out to be window dressing; for local imperatives frequently add requirements concerning class, status, color—and political affiliation—which are unknown to the law. A recent survey by an NEA commission of inquiry tells how in Indianapolis (a city of almost half a million) nominations for election to the Board of School Commissioners were controlled for thirty years by a self-appointed citizens' committee of fewer than two hundred.[1] The report is not explicit on this point, but the implication is clear that the committee represented powerful financial and commercial elements. In a suburban city in an upstate New York metropolitan area nominations were controlled for a like period by the single major industry which dominated the economic life of the community. In both instances the slates normally ran unopposed, and never during the thirty-year period was there serious challenge of the ruling clique in either city. A basic feature of democracy is the right of access—not to public office, of course, but to the privilege of competing for public office; and to deny such access is to reject democracy in the very beginning.

A second feature of the public school electoral process which warrants attention is the practice of holding school board elections separately. From the point of view of the schools, separate elections make possible the concentration of energies and resources on educational affairs. They permit candidates to

*From Roscoe C. Martin, "School Government," in *Government and the Suburban School,* Syracuse University Press, 1962, pp. 45-63; 95-101. Reprinted by permission.

146

announce and run their campaigns as custodians of the schools, and to propose issues and choose sides within that limited framework. They emphasize the independence of the schools, setting them apart from any and every other public activity. Separate elections serve all these purposes well, but this is not the whole of the story. They may also emphasize the cliental nature of public education, in that they bring to the polls most citizens immediately and directly interested in the schools—that is, parents with children in the public schools. Moreover, they render the whole electoral process—choice of candidates, selection of issues, management of the campaign—more subject to control by the schoolmen than it would be if the drama of school politics were played on a larger stage. One result of the system appears in lack of public interest and small voter turnout. Not uniformly, of course, but often a school board election takes on the appearance of a managed production, a *pro forma* observance with little of content to whet the public appetite. One observer reports evidence that the school administrators favor a small and mannerly election, finding in nonparticipation a sign of public satisfaction with the conduct of the schools. "This arrangement," he concludes, "while it has had the advantage of giving the choice of school board membership over to those persons most interested in and friendly toward the school, may not be an unmixed blessing."[2]

A third feature worthy of note is the school election's professedly nonpartisan character. The whole public school system, indeed, is characterized broadly as nonpartisan, and so it is in the sense that, for the most part, it proscribes political party labels. A particular school system likewise may be nonpartisan in that candidates normally do not announce as Republicans or Democrats, nor are they elected nor do they serve as such. But partisanship does not consist only in public profession of allegiance to this or that political party; on the contrary, partisan issues (sometimes party issues as well) often arise in their most virulent form in overtly nonpartisan systems. Moreover, the organizational leadership-and-responsibility vacuum resulting from nonpartisanship often is filled by factions which are as odious as the old-style political machines the schoolmen seek to avoid.[3] Skimpy budgets have been approved, low tax rates maintained, textbooks banned, library holdings purged, subjects for classroom discussion screened, and loyal administrators and teachers fired for allegedly subversive activities by "nonpartisan" school boards. Vincent Ostrom years ago demonstrated that, with respect to the Los Angeles Board of Education, nonpartisanship was a myth whose single achievement was the removal of political party names and symbols from the school electoral process.[4] The mayors queried for this study, accustomed to seeing nonpartisanship (and partisanship) for what it is, bestowed the label of nonpartisan on no more than 60 per cent of the school boards. To them, 22 per cent of the boards appeared to have Republican majorities, 18 per cent Democratic majorities.

If, as we have suggested, nonpartisanship is not always what it seems, then a case can be made for ascertaining what goes on in fact and bestowing on the process a descriptive and accurate label. Public confidence is not served by use of a prestigious title to distract attention from a shabby product. In the central New York suburb above referred to, a local politician was accused of having introduced politics into school board elections. He not only confessed his guilt, but boasted of his achievement. His rationale was persuasive. "What I did," he said, "was to throw out a company-controlled school board in favor of a board elected by the people. I substituted a real contest for the mock contest which had prevailed for thirty years. I introduced *public* politics into a system where *private* politics had been the rule." The result of this revolution is that the community now has a choice between two lists of candidates for the school board, one Republican, one Democratic. Schoolmen aver that the school system is not a strong one. Was it, then, stronger when it was run by the company? The implications of any such conclusion for local control of the schools, and in a larger sense for democracy itself, are fearful. Nonpartisanship is deserving of more searching examination than it has received to this point, for there is more to its practice than meets the eye.[5]

The exclusively educational orientation of the public school system brings in its wake two consequences for democracy which, though unanticipated, are nonetheless grave in their portent. The first arises from the public schools's cliental base: from the fact that, serving as it does a particular segment of the total population (*i.e.,* parents with children of school age), it associates itself primarily with that segment in all its undertakings. The school's reason for being is the child, and child and parent are of course inseparable. An earnest effort is made to justify public education in more inclusive terms—as a program in training for citizenship or for adjustment to society, for example—and so to broaden its popular base; but when all is said and done the most effective tie which the school has is that with the parent.

It goes without saying that this is a two-way street; for if the schools are basically dependent upon parent support, the parents on their part recognize a deep and lasting debt to the schools. Whatever the schools achieve or fail to achieve, they remain the child's custodian for a long twelve years, and the parents are sharply mindful of the obligation thereby assumed.

Public education, then, is in essence a special government program run by and for and with the valiant support of that segment of the population comprising parents with children of school age. The populace at large is keenly conscious of the limited and special character of educational service. Time and again respondents to the citizen questionnaire employed in this study replied in this vein: "I am a single woman and have no interest in the schools." "I used to take an active interest in the schools, but my children are all grown now and I haven't paid any attention to school issues in years." "I have two children in parochial schools, but none in public schools. No interest."

The implication of the proposition that the schools are the basic concern of parents with young children is, of course, well understood by such parents. It is also accepted by them. In the citizen questionnaires completed and returned, a much larger percentage of parents with children in school professed a familiarity with school affairs and participated actively in those affairs than of persons without children. Sixty-six per cent of parents with children in the public schools voted in their communities' last school board election, compared with 44 per cent of those without children. Seventy-one per cent of parents with children voted in the last school bond election, 55 per cent of those without children voted. A considerably higher percentage of parents with children attended school board meetings than of parents without. The testimony suggests that the schools are considered to belong to families with children, for the obligations of school citizenship normally are left to, as they are assumed by, those families.

All this may be thought good by some, but it raises certain problems. . . . The consequences of the single-minded commitment of the public school system are grave. They may be summarized thus:

1. Concentration on the needs and desires of the school cliental group tends to divide the population into two groups: those who are served by and who are concerned with the public schools and those who are not.

2. Creation of a special and sharply defined public school clientele results in both advantages and problems; for if the school's public is thereby isolated and its "community relations" target clearly delineated, by the same token an active element of fluidity is injected into the clientele and the target is converted into a moving one. The arithmetic of it is that, in a typical school system, there will be a turnover of one-twelfth in the parent group each year. But simple arithmetic does not tell the story accurately, for the "freshman class" of parents is much larger than the "graduating class," since incoming pupils far outnumber those departing. Thus is the ever-present task of citizen education, difficult in any case in a democratic system, additionally complicated for public education.

3. Heavy emphasis on the public school program over the course of more than a century has tended to produce an educational monolith: in the nation's image of its public school system, in goals sought, in methods employed, in professional practice.

4. A corollary appears in the election of school boards whose members, nourished in the traditions and committed to the ideals of the public school system, are uncommonly respectful of those who articulate those traditions and ideals. Nowhere else in American public life is the professional accorded greater deference than in the public school system.[6] The import of these consequences for such concerns as support for public education, progress through critical examination of ancient doctrine and receptivity to new thinking, and democracy in the public school system is worthy of more thoughtful examination than it has thus far received.

Note has been made of the prominence of professional, financial, and business representatives on the boards of education. (Eighty-two per cent of the school boards included in the sample studied contained members of those classes, but less than 11 per cent had semi-skilled, unskilled, and service workers as members.) In part this reflects the social and economic composition of suburban society, but in part it demonstrates the status required for board membership. The conclusion seems inescapable that there has not been much change in occupational representation on the school boards in the last thirty-five years. Writing in 1927, George S. Counts found:

> The important boards are dominated either by those who control the economic resources of the country or by those who are associated rather intimately with the economically powerful classes. In other words, the ordinary board is composed, for the most part, of merchants, lawyers, bankers, manufacturers, physicians, and persons in responsible executive positions.[7]

The data available for the occupational analysis of suburban boards in 1961 do not permit quite so sharp a characterization, but they point unmistakably in the direction of Counts' general conclusion.

It is clear that the typical suburban school board represents the economically and socially advantaged of the community. It represents the advantaged in educational preparation as well. What is not equally clear is whether this is the kind of board the suburban school needs: whether this is the kind of body that will ask relevant questions about the school program, that will bring imaginative action to bear on pressing social problems, that will recognize the basic issues of democracy and do battle in their behalf in the name of the public school. One might fear that such an organ rather would tend to favor the safe and tested course of business-as-usual, as a prototype board did in Indianapolis.

Politics and Participation

Throughout our discussion of the school board, the role of the citizen has provided a continuing undertone. Let us now bring the subject of citizen participation forward on the stage and observe it in its own right. It will prove advantageous in the beginning to examine the term "politics," which is among the most slippery of words. This is because it is employed with such reckless abandon by all kinds and classes and degrees of people that it has lost all semblance of scientific meaning in popular usage, hence has meaning only in reference to the context of a particular use. It is one of those universal words that means whatever the user wishes it to mean, within a very broad connotative spectrum.

In one of its commoner senses the word is employed to characterize the activities of the big-city political organization, as in the phrase "machine politics." In this instance it is used very largely for pejorative purposes, for in non-technical writing or conversation one almost never speaks well of machine politics. It is necessary forthwith to reject the concept of politics as practiced by such notorious operatives as Charles Murphy of Tammany Hall, Big Bill Thompson of Chicago, Thomas Pendergast of Kansas City, and Boss Hague of Jersey City; for "politics" and its various derivatives are misused when employed to characterize the conduct of men active on the near edge of crime. These men and others like them normally were extreme partisans who professed fealty to the Republican or the Democratic organization as circumstance required or convenience directed. Through their activities they helped to create the model of politics which schoolmen loathe, but to concede that they were politicians in any allowable sense of the word is to submit to perversion of a term basic to the democratic lexicon, one necessary and wholly proper to analysis of the democratic process. Politics as the legacy of the big-city machines of an earlier day—for they have been almost uniformly either destroyed or reformed beyond recognition—has no place in the present discussion.

In another sense politics means the manipulation of human relations to achieve institutional goals, or mayhap personal preferment or profit. Here invocation of the term may be legitimate, for it may be used to describe what goes on not only in a quite literal but in a technically accurate sense as well. Its common employment, however, to cover a wide and heterogeneous range of activities scarcely makes for responsible usage. Moreover, as in the first instance, the word is commonly used here in a depreciatory sense: seldom is one complimented to hear his activities or those of his organization characterized as politics, and seldom is compliment intended.

In yet a third sense, the sense in which the word is used in this study, politics is nothing more (nor less) than the contest which develops around the definition and control of policy. "Policy" is itself, of course, a term with variable meaning. It may be applied to private as well as to public undertakings, hence there may be said to be church policy or industrial policy or union policy, and so church or industrial or union politics. Obviously we are concerned here with policy in its public connotation, and in that broad domain we are interested only in public school policy—and public school politics. The political system is the framework of arrangements through which politics is conducted. As in the case of politics, we apply the political system concept in the present context to the public schools. To define a term is not of course to endow it with fixed significance for all time and every place, but only (or chiefly) to indicate its changing meaning with varying circumstance. For all our care in definition, *politics* continues to offer at best a moving target, its meaning affected—indeed sometimes determined—by the context in which it appears.

Under the broad definitions proposed above, it is obvious that every undertaking where important issues of policy arise has both its politics and its political system. Of public education, indeed, it may be said that the management of the public schools in a significant sense *is* politics; for politics centers on the principal foci of decision-making, and public school administration is fundamentally a process in which decisions are arrived at and implemented. Politics therefore may be said to be essentially *a way of looking at* the public school system and its management. With this view of politics most schoolmen might be expected to agree, for they are well aware of the political nature of much of public school administration, particularly of the policy decisions made there. The politics they reject is that practiced by (or in) other governments, quite specifically the "political" politics of the city. This suggests the possible usefulness of a distinction, from the point of view of the school spokesmen, between internal politics, or politics as practiced within or by the schools, and external politics, or politics as practiced in other agencies and units of government. The concept is covered by the terms "school politics" and "general politics." One schoolman suggested that the difference is one between politics and Politics. The distinction is almost as naked as that between our politics (good) and their politics (bad), though such a formulation would of course evoke sharp protest.

One senses that the politics anathematized by the schoolmen is that of the big-city machine of yesteryear, whose ghost continues to haunt municipal democracy long after death has departed the archetype. This is to perceive politics in the worst of the three senses examined above; it is, moreover, to give currency to standards of public morality long since discredited and by now almost universally rejected. The habit of thought among schoolmen which places school politics on one level and urban Politics on another and lower level is deserving of careful reappraisal.

In the course of this study samples of suburban citizens, mayors, presidents of local Leagues of Women Voters, and officials of local Chambers of Commerce were asked this question: Employing the word "politics" in a broad sense, to what extent are the public schools involved in politics? The question produced answers that were suprisingly uniform. Some three out of ten representatives of each category believed that the schools are not involved in politics at all. Somewhat more than half believed them to be involved to only a limited degree; but from 10 to 14 per cent thought they were involved to a considerable extent, and from 3 to 7 per cent believed them to be "up to their ears" in politics. Exceptions to these generalizations were provided by parents with children in school, four out of ten of whom believed that the schools were not involved in politics at all. It might be reasoned on the one hand that citizens who are most closely associated with schools find no politics there, or on the other that school patrons have learned well the age-old doctrine that there is no place for politics (and therefore no politics) in the public schools. The mayors were next kindest in general, though in the end harshest with respect to the all-out-involvement category. The League presidents withal were the most severe in their judgments regarding school involvement in politics. It may not be insignificant that because of long-standing League interest in public education and innumerable surveys of individual school systems, these people are probably as well informed on the public schools as laymen could be expected to be.

Politics—defined as "the contest which develops around the definition and control of policy"—in the public schools assumes many forms and crops up in many places: in the purchase of a new school site, in the award of contracts for the construction of a new building, in laying out bus routes, in choosing one textbook over another, in determining what groups may use the school auditorium for what purposes, in deciding what emphasis to give the athletic program. For present purposes, the discussion will be confined to those places in the complex decision-making process where the citizen participates directly. In this area, four major points of contact can be readily discerned: first, nomination and election of candidates for the school board; second, referendum votes (on a proposed bond issue, for example); third, attendance at school board meetings, or at meetings arranged by the board (such as a special budget hearing); and fourth, pressures on school authorities, both representative and administrative.

The issues which excite citizen concern may be classified broadly as perennial and episodic. One would expect that, in public school affairs as elsewhere, the citizen would place his interests as taxpayer in the forefront. Analysis of the material at hand corroborates this hypothesis, for both League presidents and Chamber of Commerce officials gave economic matters top ranking as public school issues. Both put the school tax rate in first place, school building and expansion programs second, bond issues to support such programs third, and the school budget fourth. Teachers' salaries ranked fifth among the perennial issues. There was, therefore, a remarkable congruence of judgment regarding the primary issues, all of which, be it noted, are of an economic character.

The respondents indicated no particular interest in curriculum, textbooks, subversive activities, personalities, athletics, race relations, and independence of the schools, other possible issues proposed as worthy of rating. This suggests that these areas provide a reservoir for what we have called episodic issues—issues which emerge under unusual or special conditions and shortly subside. Thus it is not textbooks which cause concern, but a particular textbook under a special set of circumstances. It is not subversive activities which excite the people but an overt act, actual or rumored: that a teacher has assigned for reading a piece of UNESCO literature, for example. It is not athletic programs as such that provoke a state of public apoplexy, but the loss of a football game to an old and hated rival. An episodic issue may arise overnight at any time and as quickly die away. Its chief characteristic, indeed, is its ephemeral nature, which in fact warrants the characterization of incident rather than issue.

The agencies through which citizen concern finds expression range from political parties to *ad hoc* committees. The former are generally banned under the tradition of nonpartisanship; the latter require no attention. Between these extremes is a broad spectrum of community groups which manifest interest in school issues. We know from observation that the League of Women Voters is among the most active of such groups, although League presidents and Chamber of Commerce officials placed the several service clubs at the head of the list. Next they placed taxpayer groups, and after that the Chamber itself. Next came school alumni, religious, and patriotic organizations. Significantly, both listed labor unions last. Both also had large miscellaneous categories, indicating that the preconceived classification was far from inclusive.

The most frequent method of expression of interest is the time-honored recourse to the board of education. The next most frequently employed tactic is appeal to the superintendent. Direct pressure on the teachers ranks third. If a grievance is not redressed through these normal channels of protest, then mass meetings, public attacks, and, in extreme cases, taxpayers' strikes may be employed. Only rarely is appeal taken to a higher authority, and that only after all possible courses of local action have failed to produce the desired result. Challenge at the polls, through opposition candidacies or slates for the school board, is a remedial measure not infrequently taken, though in normal circumstances a more amicable course is preferred.

All this superstructure of machinery and procedure may seem scarcely warranted by what follows, for its fruit in vigorous citizen interest and action is meager indeed. Ten questions bearing on popular participation in school affairs were addressed to the citizens to whom questionnaires were sent for this study. The responses were illuminating but hardly reassuring. Half of those replying did not know how long their school superintendent had served, well over half could not name the president of their school board, two-thirds did not vote in their community's last school board election. Bearing out the thesis that greatest interest is associated with economic issues, the number of voters in the last school bond election stood at 71 per cent; even so, 26 per cent did not know whether or not the bond issue was approved by the voters. Seventy-seven per cent of those responding stated that they never attend a meeting of the school board, and less than 3 per cent professed to attend often. Well over half confessed that they did not belong to the Parent-Teachers Association or other similar school patron groups. As was to be expected, parents with children in school led citizens without children on all criteria of interest.[8] Nevertheless the knowledge of and participation by school patrons, though distinctly superior to that of non-patrons, were of a low order: for example, 55 per cent did not know the frequency of school board meetings, and 68 per cent reported that they never attended such meetings.

Both interviews and observations conducted for this study corroborate this testimony. So do the findings of other studies. As a single illustration, a survey made by the Stanford University Institute for Communication Research by contract for the U.S. Office of Education found that about half of the voters "show no evidence of any participation in school affairs and no interest in such participation." No more than a third took part actively in school affairs, and the extent of knowledge about the schools was reported to be "only slight." "This is not an encouraging picture," the study concluded gloomily.[9]

The picture drawn is charged with portent for the public school and its future. We pass by that subject, important as it is, in favor of brief comment on a topic more directly pertinent to the immediate problem. If the public school system, widely regarded as the prime exemplar and the chief defender of democracy, has itself failed to provoke significant citizen interest and participation in school affairs, what, in terms of school experience, is the outlook for democratic government in large?

From one point of view, the evidence suggests that its champions have claimed too much for public education as the embodiment of democratic ideals and practice. Some school systems undoubtedly have achieved a good working model of democracy, in terms both of the internal conduct of school affairs and of effective public responsibility; but have they excelled, say, the cities of Palo Alto, California, and Rockville, Maryland, in these respects? Has the typical suburban school, indeed, either practiced or served democracy any more faithfully than the typical suburban city? Notwithstanding that claim frequently made that the schools are more democratically run and more responsible to the public than the city governments, the evidence at hand makes this at the least an open question; and there are credible witnesses who would answer it in the negative. Of the eleven "All-America" cities selected "for their citizens' exemplary conduct in the 'game' of civic progress" by the National Municipal League and *Look* magazine in 1961, four were central (metropolitan) cities and four were suburbs.[10] The myth that the public schools are uniformly more democratic, in terms of citizen participation and public accountability, than the cities is years overdue a critical reevaluation.

This line of thinking leads to further meditation on the subject of politics and the schools, for democracy and politics are inextricably related—the two, indeed, are reverse sides of the same coin. In the present context, politics may be taken to concern (a) the process of governance within the schools, (b) the process by which the schools are controlled by and held responsible to the people, or (c) the process of decision-making as it relates to other governments. The first is essentially a closed system, in the sense that it has to do with power relations inside the schools; here school boards deal with administrators and administrators with teachers, normally with little or no involvement of other governments. The second tends to be regarded by schoolmen, and indeed to operate, as a closed system also, with limited access to candidacy for the school board, separate elections, an electorate dominated by school patrons, and a practice of leaving school affairs almost entirely to the board of education. Both systems fit the definition of school politics offered above; with politics in these limited terms schoolmen find little quarrel.

It is politics in the third sense—that is, general politics as practiced in and by other governments, and particularly by the city—that accounts for the choleric attitude of the schoolmen. Any contact between urban politics and the schools is held to be destructive of sound educational practice; and since the city is widely conceived to be dominated by politics, it is natural and easy to bring it within the interdiction. Distrust of the city, its political system, and its government long since completed the journey from tentative formulation through habit of thought to state of mind, and may be said now to permeate all professional school thinking from the highest rationalizer of public school doctrine to the lowliest classroom teacher. The bitter and denunciatory attitude of the school forces toward urban politics strikes at the very foundation of democratic government, and collaterally of the public school system as well. It may be the dilemma will be resolved; if so, one would not expect it to be through the efforts of the schoolmen. To deal with a dilemma, one must first recognize its existence.[11]

The Professionals

The Office of Education's 1955-56 survey of suburban city schools reported a total of 1,387 administrators, 99,011 classroom teachers, and 8,039 miscellaneous professional employees—librarians, guidance workers, school psychologists, health personnel. These constitute the suburban schools' professional staff, which is the concern of this section. We shall exclude the miscellaneous category and shall concentrate instead on the administrators and teachers. As before, emphasis will be placed on the governmental rather than the specialized educational aspects of the professional staff and its work.

The thesis to be developed here is that the public school administrators and teachers constitute an educational bureaucracy, in that they possess the attitudes and attributes normally associated with bureaucratic behavior. This is to describe a condition, not to levy a charge, for all government is staffed by bureaucrats, which is but another name for civil servants. Public school administrators and teachers, being government employees, are therefore both civil servants and bureaucrats, whether they wish it or not. But "bureaucrat" and "bureaucracy" have been absorbed into the language as terms suggesting an introversion which places the interests of the service group above those of the group served. Some have charged that schoolmen are bureaucrats in that sense too.

It may be argued, indeed, that bureaucracy (in the invidious sense) is a natural concomitant of professionalism. Thus the most advanced professions are those most affected by sclerosis: by certitude of the rightness of any professional course or stand adopted, impatience with any contrary view, and suspicion of all criticism. Who so rash as to challenge the admirals on naval affairs, or the doctors on hospital care? It is ironic that the achievement of professional maturity is frequently accompanied by the degenerative process which has come to be called bureaucracy.

Yet so it is over wide professional expanses, and so it is with the teaching profession. For the developments which over the course of a century closed the doors to intruders, produced powerful professional associations, generated a pride in workmanship, eventuated in confidence and respect for calling—these same developments were accompanied by secondary effects which in the aggregate produced an advanced spirit of bureaucracy. Profession and bureaucracy achieved realization side by side among the public school teachers.

Evidence to support this conclusion is not far to seek. A brief flashback into public school history will disclose its nature. Early there was the central assumption that public education is a *unique* function of government. From this single basic proposition has grown the elaborate mythology with which the public schools are surrounded today: that public education, being a unique public function, must therefore be accorded separate and special treatment, that it is dangerous for the public school to be associated with any other public undertaking, that the schools must have nothing to do with general politics, that the schools are both the prime exemplar and the chief champion of democracy. The mythology can be elaborated at any length, but these major tenets will suffice to recall its central nature. It will be understood that what is here called mythology is not mythology at all to those who profess it, but sound and tested doctrine instead. The mythological origins of the doctrine are in truth all but lost in the mists of history, though its heavy freight of tradition attests its uncertain beginnings and its experimental development.

Four bureaucratic progeny of the public school mythology may be singled out for brief mention. First is the reverence for form, at whatever expense to substance. This reveals itself in deep respect for procedural rules, affection for familiar things, and suspicion of innovation. Second is the brisk defensiveness which flows spontaneously from sensitivity to criticism. This state of mind arrays the schoolmen, as the defenders of the public school faith, against the critics, even the sympathetic critics, who are regarded almost uniformly as attackers. This leads inevitably to the we-they dichotomy: we who defend the public school *vs.* those who seek to destroy it. Third is the bland assumption of professional rightness, manifest in the invocation of tradition and in *a priori* reasoning—the assertion of firmly held beliefs as facts.[12] Fourth is the homogenized character of the practitioners—their common origins, their uniform (and well nigh universal) belief system, their uncommon loyalty and dedication to the pursuit of common goals. The principal instruments in the homogenizing process are the teachers colleges and the university departments of education, and after these the professional associations.

A companion product of the long road to profession is a well-trained, seasoned bureaucracy with a universal body of doctrine and a firm commitment to its observance and expansion. If the teaching profession has not yet achieved the monolithic qualities of medicine or the law, it is nevertheless well along the way toward attainment of that professionally enviable status.

The traditional role of the superintendent, the chief of the public school's professional staff, has changed in two important respects in recent years. It might be more accurate to say that increased understanding enables us to see the superintendent's role more clearly and more realistically than it was perceived three decades ago, and that increased understanding has brought with it a new appreciation of two important aspects of that role. First, the superintendent has emerged during the last few decades as the leader rather than the servant of the school board. His is no journeyman's job, and he is no handyman merely to do the bidding of the board once policy has been established. On the contrary, he is at least as much a policy maker as he is a manager in the narrow sense; for he enjoys an expertise, a professional reputation, and a community position which combine to give him an almost irresistable voice in school affairs.

Alan Rosenthal has made a significant study of this subject. He divides school issues into two categories: esoteric, which, being professional or technical in nature, have a narrow-audience appeal, and exoteric, which, being more broadly political in nature, have a wide-audience appeal. The former we may call internal (school-centered), the latter public. Regarding internal issues, Rosenthal found the influence of the superintendent to be truly overwhelming; except in extreme circumstances, it simply does not occur to anyone to question his recommendations or his actions. Concerning public issues his influence is less in evidence but scarcely less effective; for he defines the issues, proposes acceptable alternatives (and rejects those not acceptable), provides ammunition for the school spokesmen, and in the end implements the decisions reached. Rosenthal concludes that "school matters are and probably will continue to be the special preserve of the educational experts. Their pleas of impotence notwithstanding, the educators run America's schools."[13]

Second, the school superintendent has emerged of recent years not only as an influential policy-maker but also as an active politician in the popular understanding of that term. The recent history of a suburban school system in upstate New York is instructive on this point. A taxpayers' group, which arose to challenge the school budget, procured the resignation of the superintendent, a man of unquestioned competence as an administrator but of limited popular appeal. The Board of Education replaced the departing superintendent with the school's business manager, who was strong where his predecessor had been weak. His active "community relations" program, together with his flair for atomizing incipient opposition, has raised the school to a level of public support not hitherto enjoyed. A successful superintendent is almost by definition a skillful politician. Schoolmen are strangely loath to concede this simple proposition, though the annals of public education are filled with incidents which testify to its soundness.

The emergence of a powerful leader in the person of the superintendent has brought with it a concomitant decline in the position of the school board. There is a reciprocal relation between administrator and board which tends to ensure that as one grows in stature the other will diminish. Passing by any possible adverse effect of this trend on democratic government, the bureaucracy views it with equanimity. To both administrators and teachers, but more especially to the former, it signifies the professional coming-of-age of the superintendent along with acceptance by the board of the fundamental role of expertness in managing the affairs of the schools. The superintendent is happiest when he is working with a tame board; he has one increasingly as he consolidates in his hands more and more responsibility for policy leadership within the board and public representation without.

Interestingly, these two major developments in the role (or in public perception of the role) of the school superintendent are paralleled by comparable trends in the city manager profession. There, too, the manager has emerged as a master bureaucrat on the one hand and a master politician on the other. This is to say simply that, in city management as in school administration, the policy role of the chief administrator has undergone substantial amplification in the last quarter-century.

Classroom teachers are not to be compared with superintendents for surface influence—for the weight of their voice in determining high policy, for arguing that policy before the school board, for expounding it before the public. Yet their role is not to be minimized, for they have a significant part to play in school government. For one thing, they comprise an overwhelming percentage of the school bureaucracy and so through dint of sheer numbers wield great influence. They constitute a bulwark of support in any school political campaign. They are the principal link between the superintendent and the board of education on the one hand and the school patrons on the other. Through their relations with the Parent-Teacher Association they have a regularized channel of contacts which for the superintendent and the board must be chance and intermittent. As bureaucrats, they close ranks behind the superintendent for the furtherance of educational policy and the solidification of public school doctrine.

It is in the classroom, however, that they exert their greatest influence. Here the student learns that the schools are sacrosanct, that any criticism of public education is an attack on the foundations of the republic. Here he learns, too, that government (particularly city government) is a sorry business and politics unclean. It is in the classroom, in short, that the antidemocratic freight of the schoolmen's doctrine makes its greatest impact on the young citizen. The destructive consequences of this antigovernment attitude could have been foretold with complete assurance; unhappily, they are now a matter of record. They are to be seen in citizen ignorance of public issues, in absence of interest in public affairs, in failure to take part in the democratic process, in scorn of government and contempt of politicians.

Sorry citizen performance is of course not to be laid at the door of the schools alone; instead it is a vector resulting from many forces and factors; it is a product, so to speak, of individual life experiences. But providing life experience for the child is close to the center of the schools' announced purpose. It is difficult to exonerate the school system from a major share of responsibility for prevailing civic attitudes. We reap in the adult citizen the fruits of the seeds sowed in the school child.

Of Power and Politics

Education's peaceable kingdom was not achieved by sudden flight, but resulted rather from arduous and purposeful effort exerted over a very long period of time. Not to put too fine a point on it, the leaders of education have erected for their enterprise a fortress which seems all but impregnable. It is the purpose of the present section to examine briefly how this came about.

It is a truism among students of government that an institution (whether agency or program) operates under conditions not wholly of its own choosing. Some years ago John Gaus spoke perceptively of the ecology of public administration.[14] Employing the term in the dictionary sense of "the mutual relations, collectively, between organisms and their environment," Gaus identified seven ecological conditioners of administrative action. More recently Wallace Sayre, speaking directly to the subject of public education, referred to "a 'field of forces' which determines (an organization's) strategic and practical opportunities for survival, or effectiveness, or goal-accomplishment."[15] His field of forces contains six major elements, including the "rules of the game" (the legal and conventional rules under which public education is conducted), the state government, the local government, the groups at interest, the political parties, and the educational bureaucracy. Clearly these are among the principal ecological factors which determine the organization and manner of operation of the public school system—or, with appropriate modifications to suit fresh features, of any other public undertaking.

It is the task of the public school spokesmen to identify and appraise the impact of these several elements, to classify them as to whether they are friendly, unfriendly, or neutral toward the public schools, to isolate and minimize those found to be unfavorable, to maximize those judged to be favorable, and to innovate as changed circumstances warrant and opportunity affords. The process of minimizing unfriendly forces (or weaknesses) and maximizing friendly forces (or strengths) calls for the possession and judicious use of power. The process by which power is brought into play we may call politics.

The cause of public education is abetted in the first instance by its structure. The preceding section treats of this structure at sufficient length for present purposes. We need note simply in passing that those who concern themselves with education are not required to evince interest in any other public program: there are no foreign candidates to clutter up the ballot, no strange propositions to obfuscate the issues. The schools are separate and independent, and their managers are in a position to demand of their public the utmost in attention, loyalty, and support.

What has been said of school independence in the community is almost equally true at the state level. There is found a department of education under the direction of a state superintendent or commissioner. There is found also, not uniformly but increasingly, the familiar board of education. It is the goal of the schoolmen to drive a wedge wide and deep between the education department and all other state departments and agencies, to the end that education may come to enjoy at the state level the independence which the local school district has so long known. One level up, the story is comparable: in Washington, the schoolmen favor the elevation of the Office of Education to departmental status, and there is wide support for a national board of education.[16] The strength of conviction with which the doctrine of independence is held at the federal level is indicated by the resignation of the Commissioner of Education some years ago partly in protest against the consolidation of several individual technical libraries, one of them that of the Office of Education.[17]

The steady pursuit through many years of this isolationist policy has resulted in the withdrawal of public education into a world of its own: not the figurative withdrawal which special programs frequently effect but, to the extent practicable, physical isolation as well. With its retirement from the workaday world of government, the public education system has achieved its own rules, its independent organization, its separate personnel (separately trained and certificated), its own self-prescribed standards, its own criteria (also self-defined) of success and failure, and to a very considerable extent its own separate system of financing. *Imperium in imperio* would hardly be accurate as a description of the status of the public school system, which in truth strives toward a parallel rather than a contained system of government. If the striving has not been universally successful, the goal nevertheless remains clear. And if the ostracism of all government not dedicated to public education was not an intended consequence of the goal sought, it nonetheless stands as a proximate result of the means employed.

The structure of public education ensures that the public schools will be able to command instant attention and that they will be clearly and continuously visible. The strategy which has grown up to accompany school independence is designed further to assure both that the schools will be elevated in the public esteem and that they will be brought and kept under a particular kind of control. These goals are sought first by unending emphasis on the professional character of education. The expectation that the professional educators would carry this torch is not disappointed.

Insistence by the schoolmen on a special course of training for those desiring to enter the teaching profession is the first instrument employed. Such training is both highly specialized in subject matter and rigorous in the time required for its completion, so that in the first instance none will undertake teacher training except those who wish to make a career of teaching, while in the second one so trained will not be equipped to pursue effectively any other calling. Moreover, the prospective teacher's professional training must be undertaken at an approved specialized institution, normally either a university department (or school) of education or a teachers college. At the end of the period of training the neophyte receives a certificate, either by examination or (more often) by the simple fact of graduation from an approved institution; and there is no teaching in the absence of a certificate. Thus is entrance into teaching controlled largely by the profession itself.[18]

A second instrument which emphasizes the special character of education is found in the several professional organizations of educators. There are local, county, district, state, regional, and national associations of classroom teachers and, as the area grows to the point where numbers warrant, of administrators, business manager, librarians, and so on. A nationwide professional tent is provided by the National Education Association, which draws together in one grand structure a large part of the vast empire of educational organizations. These various organizations, state as well as national, publish scores of professional journals and conduct hundreds of meetings each year. Further, they maintain school lobbies, which oftentimes are highly effective, again at all levels.

The message conveyed by the professional advocates of education, whether individual or institutional, is (in the present context) two-fold. First, education is a unique enterprise which cannot be administered in conjunction with any other function of government. Second, it is a highly technical undertaking which requires the services of a trained and experienced teacher/administrator corps. The educators hear other messages as well, but these two are fundamental to the furtherance of their profession.

Once the professional character of education was firmly established, it appeared advantageous next to maximize the role of the bureaucracy in the educational establishment. Three courses have been found effective in the pursuit of this purpose. First, the bureaucracy has sought with success to circumscribe the function of the board of education in favor of greater scope for professional action. Originally conceived as the maker of educational policy for the school district, the board has so far succumbed to the tendency toward professionalism that it has become more often a tool than a master of the professional hierarchy. Quite specifically, the school board in normal circumstances is lost without the leadership of the superintendent, who brings to board deliberations not only professional counsel but also a body of data (regarding financial needs, for example) developed by the bureaucracy. The National School Boards Association serves as the principal institutional agency for the education of board members. In view of the turnover in board membership, its services as adjunct to the school bureaucracy in the instruction of school trustees are not inconsiderable.

A second device employed in the elevation of the bureaucracy is found in the limitation of the representational and (even more important) the interpretational functions to professional schoolmen. Once again the emphasis is on the professional character of education, on the consequent technical nature of the problems it generates, and hence on the need for professional training and experience for any who may assume to address those problems. Thus one who ventures to voice an opinion without a certificate is reckoned an intruder, and is set aside as a presumptuous fellow. Only licensed prophets may speak *for* education, while those who speak *of* education command both more respect and a wider audience if they are possessed of a license.

Finally, the bureaucracy seeks to maximize internal issues, concerning which it is conceded almost a monopoly both of credible data and of sound point of view. Such issues—course of study, equipment needs, class size, teaching methods, library purchases, discipline, and so on—relate to precisely the professional areas in which the bureaucracy is presumed to be most and laymen least competent. That schoolmen prefer to concentrate on internal problems is not a matter of wonder, for that is where they are most at home. They can dominate the conversation so long as they can limit it to technical subjects.

Now and again, however, external issues, though minimized by the bureaucracy, come to the fore. Against such occasions the earnest efforts of the schoolmen are permanently directed toward destroying the credibility or at the very least limiting the role of "outside" organizations. Foremost among the organizations excoriated by the public school spokesmen are political parties, which in method and purpose are held to be foreign to the world of education. Sayre uses the descriptive term "unstructured community," observing that the schoolmen feel more secure when dealing with an amorphous public than when talking to Republicans and Democrats.[19] With such a public the school spokesmen have a better chance both of naming the subject to be discussed and of keeping the conversation on a technical level where professional considerations may be expected to prevail.

Further, an unstructured public affords a favorable environment for erection by the schoolmen of their own structure, one tailored specifically to the needs of the schools. The school's citizen structure is symbolized most notably by the Parent-Teacher Association which, part bureaucrat, part lay in composition, constitutes an effective bridge between school and public. It is not without significance that the PTA is more amenable both to narrow (technical) definition of the issues and to bureaucratic influence than would be a continuing general-purpose organization comprising a cross-section of the community.

Through the two principal devices of isolating the public schools and maximizing professional influence, the educational bureaucracy has achieved notable success in driving the public school structure toward a monolith under oligarchic control. It is to be doubted, indeed, whether the bureaucracy plays so important a role in the governance of any other public undertaking in America. Frank Munger, in his analysis of community power,[20] points out that the effectiveness of such power (indeed the very existence of power in any operational sense) depends upon the possession of one or more of its significant elements, the willingness to bring those elements into play, and the rate and efficiency of their use. Judged by the Munger model, the school forces in a particular community—centering in but in nowise confined to the bureaucracy—must be reckoned the focal point of an effective system of power. Such power is, of course, limited to decisions involving school problems, but there, under normal conditions, it is paramount. The power wielded by the schoolmen resides chiefly in their roles of initiators of issues in the first instance, expert advisers and aides to the nominal decision-maker (the board of education) in the second instance, and implementers of the policies agreed upon in the end. The function of the school board, which is almost wholly dependent upon the bureaucracy over broad technical areas, normally is limited to providing the center span of the bridge between initiation and implementation. The action it takes is important, to be sure, but usually it is *pro forma.*

Now and again, as we have observed, an issue gets out of hand and comes before the people for an airing, and sometimes for a decision. On these rare occasions "public" politics forces its way onto the stage, the board of education advances (or is pushed) to the fore as the spokesman for education, and the schoolmen retire to the wings until the hubbub has subsided. The superintendent and his aides, though skillful and experienced at the infighting which characterizes "school board politics," step out of character when they essay roles of leadership in the public forum. This is, of course, the theory of it; in point of fact, the successful superintendent is a good politician in the public acceptance of the term as well as a good administrator in the professional sense. He is a public energizer as well as a technical activator of power.

Reflection on power and politics in the public school system leads to meditation on the educators' concept of democracy. Note first that schoolmen operate within the confines of a narrowly circumscribed special-interest structure. Traditionally they do their utmost to construct a stockade around the public school domain, and to make the wall as nearly impenetrable as possible. Note second that they proceed then to delineate the issues to be debated in an equally narrow and special-interest fashion, so that there is virtually no congruence of either interest or content as between an educational issue and one arising in connection with any other public undertaking. The upshot of these policies is that education comes to rely almost exclusively on an educational clientele. The public school patron is excised from any possible general citizen context and is asked to support his school without reference to events or needs in the wide world beyond education. Such a system, with its slanted emphasis and its limited horizons, would seem to promise a specialized citizenry which would be anemic with regard to the governance of education and myopic with respect to democratic government at large.

FOOTNOTES

[1] National Commission for the Defense of Democracy Through Education, *Indianapolis, Indiana: A Study of the Sudden Forced Resignation of a Superintendent* (Washington: National Education Association, 1960).

[2] William Ellis Gould, "A Study of School Board Elections in Santa Clara County" (School of Education, Stanford University, unpublished Ph.D. dissertation, 1953). See especially Chapter X. The sentence quoted occurs on p. 210.

[3] The gruesome vendetta which has beset the public schools of one spanking new suburb would seem enough to cast at least some small doubt on the system of election. See Joseph F. Maloney, *"The Lonesome Train" in Levittown* (University of Alabama: University of Alabama Press, ICP Case Series Number 39, 1958). But see also a news story published in the *New York Times* of January 11, 1962, in which, under the headline "Schools Analysis Chides Levittown," a commission of the National Education Association identifies the problem with the absence of skilled lay leadership.

[4] Vincent A. Ostrom, *School Board Politics. An Analysis of Non-Partisanship in the Los Angeles City Board of Education* (University of California at Los Angeles, unpublished Master's thesis, 1945).

[5] A recent study pleads for an end to nonpartisanship in municipal elections, citing the importance of party organization in developing vigorous leadership, arousing popular interest, rallying the people in support of (or in opposition to) a program, bringing criticism effectively to bear, and providing a vehicle for the exercise of public accountability. See Marvin A. Harder, *Nonpartisan Election: A Political Illusion?* (New York: published by Henry Holt and Company for the Eagleton Foundation, 1958).

[6] This theme is developed in the section titled "The Professionals," below.

[7] George S. Counts, *The Social Composition of Boards of Education* (Chicago: University of Chicago Press, 1927), 74.

[8] Peter and Alice Rossi found a similar condition in Bay City, Massachusetts. Among parents with children enrolled in the local public schools, 51 per cent revealed high interest (as defined by certain specific criteria) in public school affairs. For parents with children in local parochial schools the proportion was 28 per cent, while for adults with no children or with children enrolled in other than local schools it was 21 per cent. See Peter H. and Alice S. Rossi, "Some Effects of Parochial School Education in America," *Daedalus: Journal of the American Academy of Arts and Sciences,* 90 (Spring 1961), 300-28.

[9] Richard F. Carter, *Voters and Their Schools* (Stanford University: School of Education, Institute for Communication Research, 1960), 7 and 16.

[10] LI *National Civic Review* (March 1962), 113.

[11] There is scattered evidence that a modest fissure may be developing in the near-solid school front. Thus William Ellis Gould, in a doctoral dissertation written in the field of education, argues that "(the) tendency on the part of the schools to abjure politics ... is in

error and tends to result in less skillful administration." He concludes that "this 'holier-than-thou' attitude concerning other realms of governmental activity has developed to the place where it is a matter for serious concern by those who wish the schools well." *Op. cit.,* 179. No reason has been found, however, to suppose that this view is held by more than a handful of the professional observers of the public school scene.

[12]As in these sentences from a widely used textbook on educational administration: "Even if good results can come from any type of board, if there are good people on it, it is best to have an elected board. No activity as important as public education should be removed from the control of the people, as tends to happen with an appointed board."

[13]Alan Rosenthal, "Community Leadership and Public School Politics: Two Case Studies" (Princeton University, unpublished Ph.D. dissertation, 1960). The passage quoted appears at p. 498.

[14]John M. Gaus, *Reflections on Public Administration* (University, Alabama: University of Alabama Press, 1947), Chapter 1.

[15]Wallace S. Sayre, "Additional Observations on the Study of Administration," 60 *Teachers College Record* (November 1958), 73-76. This is as incisive a comment on what a political scientist regards as the realities of educational organization as has come to my attention.

[16]Vigorously voiced by James E. Allen, New York State Commissioner of Education, in testimony before the House Subcommittee on General Education. See *The New York Times,* May 2, 1962, 33.

[17]"The Office of Education Library" in Harold Stein, ed., *Public Administration and Policy Development* (New York: Harcourt, Brace and Company, 1952).

[18]Education is not alone in the influence wielded in internal affairs by its practitioners. Medicine and law afford examples of professions which govern themselves, at least in considerable measure. Neither, however, is as *public* as education, whose status as a function of government sets it apart.

[19]*Op. cit.,* 75.

[20]Roscoe C. Martin, Frank J. Munger, and others, *Decisions in Syracuse:* Metropolitan Action Studies No. 1 (Bloomington, Ind.: Indiana University Press, 1961). See especially Chapters I and XIV.

EDUCATIONAL DECISION-MAKING IN
SUBURBAN COMMUNITIES*

David W. Minar

Our concern here is with the steps through which demands are processed and either turned aside or converted into authoritative policy statements. A simple approach to decision-making, and one that we will in general follow here, is to describe it as a series of actions leading through the interpretation and presentation of demands, delineation of alternatives, development of information about the consequences of following alternative courses of policy, and the making of choice itself. These steps follow some original impetus to action and may or may not issue in some explicit policy output directed toward the change of behavior.

The focus of the present study.—The above paragraph simply describes a set of categories through which the processes of political organization and action may be viewed. These will, in general, guide our treatment of school government in the chapters that follow. The phenomena of politics, of course, vary from system to system and from time to time. Thus the character of any portion of the political system is problematic: there are alternative modes of condition and action to be found in any of the categories outlined here. Basically, the task set out for our research is to describe school systems in terms of these categories and search for systematic patterns of variation among them.

The project reported here is, of necessity, somewhat more confined in scope than these terms might suggest. It is focussed on the decision-making process and in particular on certain aspects of that process. While it touches in one way or another on nearly all the phases of school politics, it is not an attempt to develop a comprehensive picture or to present evidence about a wide range of variations in system characteristics. Despite the generality of perspective with which it has been introduced, this work is by no means intended to be a general discussion of school government.

Specifically, the project was designed to seek answers to the question, what variations in the style and content of the decision-making process and in the division of authority are to be found among school systems whose social-struc-

*From *Educational Decision-Making in Suburban Communities* by David W. Minar, pp. 6-11; 47-56; 125-135. Reprinted by permission of the author.

tural contexts differ? The question was pursued through comparison of four suburban elementary school districts in Cook County, Illinois. The theoretical and empirical base for this research was laid by an earlier extensive study of school politics in a sample of 48 elementary districts in the Cook County area. In that study, voting data were gathered on board elections and bond and tax referenda for the five-year period 1958-62. From these data indicators were developed for each community of level of popular participation and level of dissent on referenda and elections. These were then run against aggregate socio-economic characteristics, school system characteristics, and selected and limited features of the decision-making system. A more detailed account of the procedures and findings of the earlier project may be found in Appendix A to this report.[1]

Analysis of the data described revealed substantial relationships in the sample districts among the three major variables investigated, namely, collective electoral behavior, socio-economic characteristics, and decision-making. Generally speaking, districts with high levels of voter participation were also those with high levels of dissent, i.e., high proportions of votes cast for losers in board elections and high proportions of "no" votes in referenda. These also tended to be districts low on aggregate indicators of social status, including family income, education, and occupation. Some social characteristics, including urbanism, mobility, and size of district, bore no significant relationship to political behavior. Districts with low levels of dissent (and participation) were likely to be communities of high status and also places where candidates for board positions are nominated by caucuses, these being employed in half the communities in the sample.

Interviews with superintendents turned up certain limited but revealing evidence about processes of decision-making in these districts. In low conflict, high status districts it appeared that superintendents had a great deal of latitude for independent action. Boards in such places were inclined to validate the superintendent's actions and to be concerned chiefly with broad policy issues. Boards in the high conflict, low status districts, on the other hand, were more often described by superintendents as hard to work with and likely to meddle in "administrative" matters.

A hypothetical explanation of this association between propensity to conflict on the electoral level, social characteristics, and organizational styles links them through what we have called resources of conflict management skills. These we suppose to be associated with certain kinds of occupational and educational patterns and to consist of perspectives and experiences that prize specialization, division of labor, delegation of authority, and technical expertise. Low conflict communities, more plentiful in these resources, are those better able to suppress conflict in the electoral process and develop mechanisms for low-friction control of the entire governing activity. Rival hypotheses are plausible, but in the face of the evidence do not seem equally so.

Against this background, the present study was conceived to push the line of inquiry a step further. This stage of research has consisted of intensive examination of the political process in four school districts selected so as to vary certain aggregate community characteristics. As indicated above, the focus falls on limited aspects of decision-making, though descriptive material on other phases of politics in these communities has also been gathered. Essentially, however, we are interested in the ways in which low conflict-high status places and high conflict-low status places conduct their school business, in the techniques, devices, procedures, relationships, and contents that distinguish the work of school boards and administrations in these kinds of communities. These questions may be summarized in terms of two general concepts: style of decision-making and division of labor.

By style we mean the manner in which the decision-making process is conducted. Styles may be more or less regularized, more or less formal, more or less hostile. Boards may operate on a more or less open basis, with participation by a wide or narrow range of people. They may give attention intensively or extensively, devote themselves to large policy questions or to small matters of detail. A more detailed set of sub-categories will be set out below as we present data.

Division of labor is a narrower and more concise concept, and also one in more common use.[2] Basically, the problem here is who does what in the governmental process. In school government, given the legal and traditional framework in which it operates, the problem of division of labor is essentially a question of the respective relationships of board and administration to the various aspects of decision-making. The authority of the two are differently derived, that of the board coming from the legitimizing device of democratic elections, that of the superintendent from his professional qualifications and practical operating responsibilities. They may be described as formal and technical (or expert) authority roles. While their legal relationship is clear, their relationship in operating behavior may vary over a wide range, from all-but-complete dominance by the board on the one hand to all-but-complete dominance by the superintendent on the other.

With only four cases in our sample, we are in no position to test hypotheses or generalize findings. However, to make more explicit the theoretical framework of the research discussed in the chapters to follow, we might give some advance indication of the nature of relationships we would expect to find between community structure and decision-making system. On the basis of what was said above, i.e., on the supposition that some districts bring conflict management skills to bear on school affairs and some do not, we anticipated differences in style and division of labor as follows.

Low conflict, high status districts: less formal procedures, more done on basis of implicit understandings; wider participation in decision-making; more attention to broad policy, less to detail; more latitude for decision and independent action by superintendent; less time devoted to district work by board members; more discussion by board of curriculum and community relations, less of finance, personnel, and administration.

High conflict, low status districts: more formalized procedures, more attention to written policies; restricted participation; divided votes; more attention to detail, less to broad issues; narrower range or latitude for action by superintendent; more board discussion of finance, personnel, less of curriculum, community relations.

Generally speaking, these predictions have been borne out by our research, though with a number of qualifications. These will be noted and, where possible, explained in the substantive chapters that follow.

The Interpretation and Presentation of Demands

Demands are potentially stimuli to action. They may provide the decision-making system to which they are directed with the impetus to do things. No policy-making body, however, can react to all the stimuli that might be thrust upon it. For reasons of time, if nothing else, the messages that come to the governing level of a complex organization must be screened through some filtering process. This is particularly so if the policy-making body can, by its nature, devote only limited attention to the organizational job it has to do. Thus, for a body like a school board the filtering process is an ever-present part of the equipment with which it faces its tasks.

The function of filtering may be carried out in a planned, purposeful, and rational way, or it may occur accidentally. It is not our intention to suggest that filtering is necessarily done effectively or even consciously. Further, it may be done by application of any one or a combination of a large number of criteria, either thoughtfully applied or otherwise. These criteria might include, for example, legal requirements, cultural constraints, professional judgments, and personal prejudices. Whatever the criteria, however they are developed and applied, the point is that the process of selection goes forward as the system functions; priorities are inevitably set as business is fed to the decision-making apparatus.

This is the role of that part of the governing process to which we refer as the interpretation and presentation of demands to the policy-making body. Fundamentally, the questions are, who does it, how, and by what criteria? The answers to these might vary greatly, of course, from system to system. Our examination of school districts will proceed in terms of three interrelated aspects of the process: agenda-setting, the supplying of information, and the making of recommendations.

Agenda.—Agenda are, according to the dictionary, "things to be done." We mean here to include those things that reach the official or semi-official attention of school district policy-making bodies, i.e., board and top administration acting together. Questions about the agenda of such bodies are also questions about problems that might reach their attention but do not. These are the problems "screened out," problems ignored or turned aside. The boundaries of the agenda-setting process are thus obscure. As we cannot, with the information we have, know the parameters of the demand structures of our sample districts, we cannot definitively gauge their potential agenda. We can, however, say some things about the active face of the process and the way it seems to be carried out in these systems.

In the first place, it should be noted that there are categories of agenda items that are relatively fixed, that require consideration at some given time. Some of these are minor or may easily be treated as such, e.g., the approval of minutes, meeting by meeting. Some are routine but may be blown into major proportions, depending fundamentally on the attitude of the board toward staff work. Thus the payment of bills, a task that requires board approval, is handled summarily and formally in some districts and becomes the subject of extensive discussion in others. Finally, some fixed items, particularly the preparation of the budget, are of clear and major proportions. The employment of new teachers also falls in this set. Whatever style the board may use in handling these matters of fixed agenda, there is little discretion to be exercised by anyone in putting them on the schedule for board consideration.

Only a small portion of agenda items are fixed in this sense. Beyond these the agenda are subject to discretionary choice, although some will inevitably force their way into eventual consideration. In every district in the sample the superintendent fulfills the function of preparing formal agenda for board meetings. These may be more or less detailed and more or less subject to practical revision during the course of discussion. The agenda for District C were not made available for visitors at board meetings (probably for the simple reason that few people visited the board). It appeared that these agenda, however, lacked specificity; to some extent, so did those used in District D. Districts A and B, however, tended to work off relatively detailed agenda that usually provided firmer control of the flow of business. The members of Boards A and B and to a lesser extent D received extensive documentation on proposed items of business in advance of meetings.

The selection of items for inclusion appears to reflect the superintendent's estimate of the time likely to be put into fixed routine matters, his estimate of probable deviations from the specified flow of business, and his sense of the appropriate character and range of board interests. Where routine matters were handled with dispatch, agenda were likely to include more extended presentations on policy items, especially on matters of educational program. Where routines were discussed at length, such policy items seldom appeared, and boards tended therefore to be steered away from broad questions and to receive less information on the broad aspects of program. Superintendents in the former kind of district appear to see the boards as forums for discussion and vehicles for communication, while those in the latter seem more inclined to use boards as decision-making machines. In the latter cases the question does not seem to be one of concealment of information by the superintendent but one of pre-emption of the attention of the board by business of a different level. The difference lies at least in part in sophistication in the use of machinery and in part in perspectives on the role and use of staff work.

In District A, where there is high reliance on the staff, the board stays close to the superintendent's rather detailed agenda. Items are likely to include questions of educational policy, and the discussion sometimes moves to a fairly high level of abstraction. While the style of this board appears to be very open, discussion tends to stay relevant. In a sense, the appearance of openness is deceptive. The general effect is one of very effective but never strident or repressive control of business by the superintendent.

District B perhaps presents the most interesting case in the sample. Here the style is fundamentally the same, but the counterforces are much stronger. The board tends to stay relevant, but hostility toward the superintendent and organized pressure from the community bring about some deviation from this pattern and generate some protracted discussions of relatively routine questions. Nonetheless, the superintendent does introduce questions of educational policy, if in a somewhat more formal way than his counterpart in District A, and the board pursues them vigorously. The over-all impression created by this situation is one of ambivalence that clearly reflects the ambivalent structure of community characteristics. As a later chapter will show, the result has been very long meetings and development of some rather elaborate process-management devices. District B, in other words, seems to strain toward the District A mode of operation, but only with difficulty and partial success.

In District C agenda tend to be very ineffective in screening and controlling business. Here the superintendent makes less effort to fix the subjects or course of discussion, and little effort to introduce policy questions or program discussion. The process is thus protracted, detailed, and unstructured, and the occasional efforts of the board president and superintendent to keep it otherwise are usually fruitless.

District D, on the other hand, tends to see business well-controlled but on generally low-level problems. The superintendent's agenda are more detailed and effective than those of District C, but they seldom move to abstract questions or to policy problems. The focus of the process seldom strays far from routine matters, and those are usually routine matters screened by the superintendent.

Interestingly enough, the business of Districts C and D tends to be determined almost entirely within the authority system. Districts A and B, especially the latter, are much more likely to see matters introduced from beyond the authority system itself, i.e., from the community, staff and line employees, and other units of government. As the discussion above would suggest, in District B such items are often disruptive of the control system, in District A seldom so. It may also be inferred, though it cannot be proved that the business of these latter districts is more likely to arise from "professional considerations" as distinct from administrative compulsions, i.e., it is likely to come from the latitude felt by the professionals in the system to seek program innovation.

In summary, in all the sample districts the superintendent is the chief agenda-setting functionary. They vary, however, in the kinds of business they try to introduce and the effectiveness with which they control the flow of process. Some of the consequences of these variations will be discussed in chapters to follow, where other aspects of decision-making are considered.

Information.—A second aspect of the demand-presentation process is the provision of information. Basically, this information may be of three kinds, bearing on the nature of the demands in question, the range of appropriate action alternatives, or the relative costs (or consequences) of various alternatives. The first kind has to do with the interpretation of demands, with such matters as the sources and weight of pressure to take up a given problem or follow a given course of action. In some cases this is a simple and obvious kind of information, as in those situations where the demand is routine. In other cases it involves elaborate political assessment of the context of the system. Information of the second kind defines the problem or item of business in action items. It tends to determine the framework within which the problem is seen, to structure business by setting limits to the range of consideration or perspective brought to bear. Again, this may be a routine matter or a matter of some complexity, and the difference is not necessarily one of the "magnitude" of the problem involved. Some decision-making groups are capable of making a mountain out of a molehill, others of making a molehill out of a mountain.

The third kind of information mentioned above, information about the costs of alternative courses of policy, is potentially the most complex, and probably the most variable both among systems and among items of business. It provides the equipment by which policies can be judged as to the probability of their reaching desired ends. If the definition of the problem delimits the standards by which action is to be judged, information about alternatives indicates what means may satisfy those standards. It is at this point that knowledge, experience, and professional belief enter the picture most clearly, and it is here that the history of the past and the accomplishments and failures of other systems become most pertinent. The output of a decision-making process, policy choice, depends as well on the adequacy of the information available as on the judgment in selection that goes into choice.

Observation of our study districts suggests that relatively little thought is given to information of the first two kinds. Information about demands is likely to come from both the superintendent and board, the former because of his central position in the communication system and the latter because of the political nature of their roles and the fact that they define themselves to one extent or the other as representatives of the community. Both superintendent and board are able to "create" demands by identifying or stimulating needs. When community influentials were asked to whom they would address a question or suggestion about school policy, both the superintendent and board were commonly mentioned. Only respondents in District D varied significantly; all but one of these mentioned only the superintendent. Superintendents tend to trigger the automatic processes of routine demand detection—those having to do with reports, formal legal requirements, etc. For the most part, however, the provision of information about other demands seems to be shared by administrators and board, all of them tending to rely heavily on their "feel" for their districts.

Information on the nature and range of alternatives tends to fall largely within the province of the superintendent, as a consequence of his control of agenda and probably of the time and experience he can devote to the policy-making job. It is interesting to note that in two of the districts (B and C) the board's attorney was often present at meetings and when present was often called upon to define alternatives, sometimes on problems not strictly "legal" in character. The attorney was employed, in other words, as an alternative-defining expert. In Districts A and D the board attorney did not attend meetings, and his advice, when sought, was usually filtered through the superintendent. In A and B, other staff advice (from business manager or facilities man, for example) sometimes helped directly to settle problems of this kind.

It should not be supposed, however, that superintendents are always able to impose their definitions of alternatives successfully. As our foregoing discussion of agenda implied, the boards in Districts A and D seem least likely to go beyond the definition of the problem supplied by the superintendent. Even here, however, exceptions were noted. In District A, for example, a proposal that the system cooperate in a university survey of brain-damaged children, treated by the superintendent as a question of scientific interest and responsibility, was converted by the board into a problem in community relations. Hardly a major issue in the life of the district, this was probably the most serious set-back suffered by this superintendent during the period of the study. District B's board was inclined to fight with itself over the tendency of some members (one in particular, sometimes followed by others) to convert questions into ideological issues. This tendency was usually suppressed, but at a price. The board in District C fairly often transformed relatively minor issues (the making of a long-distance telephone call or the selection of floor tile, for example) into major moral questions. In effect, this reflects the power of the boards (especially in Districts B and C) to revise the superintendent's agenda.

The provision of information about the costs of courses of action is most basic, and also hardest to pin down to empirical evidence. Only here and there do interview materials indicate that boards are dissatisfied with the amount or quality of information they get from their administrations. Only two board members in District C and one in each of the other districts mentioned inadequacy of information in a specific way. The comment from the District A respondent was to the effect that the relations of board and superintendent had been too good, so good that it was hard to get requests for information treated seriously.

It is apparent that all superintendents in the sample try conscientiously to supply adequate information for the making of choice. Three of the four mentioned this in interviews as one of the basic responsibilities of the chief administrator, the exception being C. Observation and informal discussion suggest that the boards of Districts A and B are provided with wider-ranging information on educational questions, innovations, data on the experience of other systems, etc. The superintendent of one of these is co-author of a noted textbook in the education field, and his command of the literature is exceptional. Probably Superintendent B is pressed hardest for information of both a specific and a general technical sort. In both these districts a considerable amount of sophisticated educational information is pumped into the system, perhaps more than a lay board can effectively use. Their scale makes it possible for them to employ larger administrative staffs than C and D, a fact particularly important in the information-gathering process.

Board members themselves may be and often are sources of information of this order. In this respect boards differ in style and resources. Both District A and District B have lawyer board members, for instance, while neither C nor D do. Districts A and D each have three women, B has one, C none. Lawyers, women, doctors, plumbers, etc., have specialized pertinent information they may plow into the decision-making process. Generally speaking, it appears that board members are less likely to impose their own technical information on their boards in the higher status districts than in the lower status ones.

Recommendations are information of a very specialized kind—information about the assessment of a problem made by the person from whom the recommendation comes. The significance of recommendations flows from the behavior that follows them. For this reason we will reserve our discussion of recommendations for the chapter that follows, where decision-making behavior will be the principal topic. Let it be noted, however, that recommendations play a major part in the governing process of the school districts we are studying.

Conclusions

In the foregoing chapters we have summarized in some detail the characteristics of decision-making in four sample school districts. On a great many counts these are found to vary rather widely. The basic hypothesis of the study, stated in Chapter I, was that such variations are systematically related to the characteristics of community context, and especially to certain status-related community expectations that are reflected in the style and division of work of the authority system. At a very general level these expectations are supported by the findings, but with qualifications that merit examination and interpretation.

The limitations on our ability to draw conclusions are obvious, and they were inherent in the study design at the outset. They arise in the first instance from the size of the sample, which prohibits generalization and makes the control of many variables virtually impossible. They also spring from the fact that the sample districts were selected off a continuum of aggregate behavioral characteristics and could not therefore be either perfectly matched nor perfectly differentiated. This latter is a limit that inexorably imposes itself in one way or another on efforts to compare complex real-life systems in a fairly thorough fashion. Despite these built-in problems, there remains much to say about apparent relationships among variables and the implications of these for school system government and for other aspects of community political life.

All things considered, District A presents an almost "perfect" typical picture of the low-conflict system at work. In almost every aspect it fulfills the expectations of such systems set out at the beginning of the project. Its demand structure is both vital and orderly; the thoroughly organized caucus system provides assurance that school office will not be filled in a haphazard way, and a set of organized groups attend to the less formal side of demand presentation and system-monitoring functions. The district has a fairly effective set of regularized contacts with other units of government and institutions of community life. The board itself is apparently attuned to and representative of the constituency, at least in some gross sense, and it has provided the community with superintendents that fit the political picture well. While the system does not lack the means to make demands felt, these means are highly structured; the structures themselves, the fact that they exist, and the ethos of the sub-culture act in combination as a powerful conflict-suppressant. Thus the system seems both open and controlled.

At the level of the authority structure this last description also applies. The board works openly, quickly, and informally, its atmosphere unconstrained and congenial, its major attention going to curriculum and community relations questions. The superintendent has much administrative latitude and policy initiative, and the subtle relationship of administrator and board competencies and responsibilities seems well-understood on both sides. The role of the board in this district might almost be said to be more consultative than decision-making, and in respect to the community it tends to perform as a shock and responsibility absorber. Staff assistance is ample and well-used. The educational program of the district is stable and highly innovational, perhaps partly in spite of and partly because of a high rate of teacher turnover and what appears to be an intense level of achievement aspiration in the community.

The situation of District A is in many ways one of luxury, for the system has an abundance of relevant resources available to it. District B's condition is that of a system basically similar in some respects but under a set of pressures not present in A. B is, in the first place, somewhat lower on the status ladder, i.e., its population contains a somewhat lesser proportion of certain occupational, educational, and income attributes. It is also larger in size, though we have no reason to believe that size in itself is a relevant variable. In some ways B may also be more heterogeneous, though in some ways it is not; the power of heterogeneity as an explanatory variable depends upon the particular definition given it. The pressures that tend to make District B behave differently from District A, however, seem to be two: relative scarcity of resources, and ideological dissent.

Like District A, B has a structured set of demand vehicles, but these have shown a rising level of dissensus in very recent years. The institutions of demand presentation, indeed, have served to focus and clarify dissent, creating the pseudo-party situation mentioned earlier. The scarcity of resources has made the system more vulnerable to threats (in part simply by multiplying the occasions for dissent) and the existence of ideology-based demands has focussed dissent and given it some organizational cohesion and thrust. It has probably been this combination of characteristics that has introduced instability into the decision-making system.

The response of the authority system can be described at two levels. On the one hand, conflict both from outside and within the system has grown more explicit, with more ruffled relationships and less tidiness about decision-making. On the other hand, certain tactical compensations in the decision-making system are evident, introduced consciously or unconsciously to keep the system operating as much as possible in a low-conflict mode. Thus meetings are longer, procedural formalities tend to be preserved, committees are used actively if with some misgivings, audience presentations are invited at board meetings, and some decisional work is screened from public view. These characteristics at least in some degree manifest the use of organizational skills on the part of the board and administration.

For all the tension present in this system, however, it still demonstrates many basic similarities to District A. The board tends to focus its attention on curriculum and community relations problems and to show more interest in broad policy problems than in administrative detail. Under the cover of surface conflict the administration preserves much latitude of action and exercises much fundamental policy initiative. The basic division of responsibility and the needs and strengths of technical expertise appear to be a matter of agreement among nearly all those in authority. The board has not, however, protected and reinforced the administration against community criticism. Some of its collective defenses have crumbled in the face of community pressure.

District B perhaps typifies the low-conflict system undergoing change. Its established procedures of demand aggregation and presentation focus and even magnify dissent; in this sense it is a lively and responsive system. Within the authority system it has developed some "corrective" techniques, but these hold the structure together only tentatively and at a price. How long such a situation can be sustained is problematic.

District C is in many ways an extreme representation of a high-conflict system in operation. At the electoral level its dissent is haphazard and unstructured. There appear to be no particular reasons for or cohesion to conflict in the community; the system itself has ample financial resources and our research detected no overt or covert ideological pressures. Few groups or individuals present demands to the board, which on the whole operates almost in a vacuum as far as external forces are concerned.

Yet internally the system operates in a tense, hostile, and unstructured way. Board meetings are long and chaotic and marked with evidence of mutual suspicion. The board spends most of its effort on detail, paying little attention to educational problems and policies and showing much concern with facilities. The superintendent's scope of freedom is limited, there is little evident respect for his expertise, and he is often cast in the role of shop steward rather than operating executive. The "tone" of organizational relationships and the decision-making procedures are radically different from those of District A. What the system seems to lack at all levels is structure, settled, easy understandings about relationships, and the application of organizational skills.

Of all the districts in the sample, D is easily the most deviant from prior expectations. Given its record of electoral dissent and its status level, a simple prediction from our basic hypothesis would have pictured it in much the same fashion as District C. In terms of electoral conflict and group activity it does not appear much different from C, and its per-pupil tax base is much lower, a factor that might be expected to induce conflict. Yet its decision-making system bears little resemblance to C's, and superficially it has some of the same characteristics as A's. The board is quiet and generally acquiescent to the leadership of the president and superintendent. The atmosphere in which it works is friendly and relationships are usually smooth.

On some dimensions, however, District D performs in a manner of its own, quite distinct from A and somewhat similar to C. Its interaction rate is slow, and it lacks the easy give-and-take of A. Interactions are heavily weighted toward president and superintendent, with the balance of the board quiet and rather uninquisitive. The board's attention goes proportionately less to community relations than A and B's, and proportionately more to personnel and facilities. In this respect it is more like C, though less facility-oriented. Of all the districts, D spends the most interactions on "administration," a category that includes chiefly formalistic and trivial matters.

In summary, the position of the District D superintendent is an unusual combination of elements. His freedom to administer and supply policy leadership are great, the board tending to be compliant, particularly on broader issues and educational matters. In effect the board tends neither to control him very closely nor to prod him to action. There are, however, some evidences of dissatisfaction on both sides, a sense that perhaps the board is not playing the full role it should. Both the board and superintendent convey the wish that the board played a larger part in the system's work, and the board sometimes displays a tendency to "peck away" at him on small matters. In both focus and style the system does not enjoy the settled, understood relationships of the low-conflict situation.

The question remains, of course, why District D shows these ambiguous characteristics. A number of explanations occur, all of which probably reflect some portion of the truth. In part the situation doubtless arises out of the personality qualities of the participants, particularly of the superintendent, who has handled a difficult assignment with skill and with a style of his own. More will be said below of the role of this variable. In some part, too, the total character of this system is probably the product of the change through which the community is and has been going. Like District B, District D may be a mutant of its type because of the impact of certain change processes.

Examination of the data suggests yet a third possible explanation of the behavior of District D, one that fits both the approach principally utilized throughout our analysis and some of the indications to be found in the literature. It may be that the peculiar decision-making picture in District D manifests the characteristics to be expected in the more urbanized place. It will be noted in Table 2 that community D ranks considerably higher on a composite index of urbanism than the other test districts; in fact, it lies near the top of the entire distribution of the original 48 suburban districts. On some individual variables related to urbanism, this community is also quite different from the others in the smaller sample, notably on owner-occupied dwelling units, single-family structures, dwelling units built since 1950, and women in the labor force. Only on fertility does it fail to occupy an extreme position, falling somewhat above A and somewhat below B and C. The link between urbanism and system behavior may be through the greater disattachment or disinvolvement of the more urban man. While there is no reason to expect the urban dweller to be less interested in the fate of his children, he might be expected to have fewer ties into community life and into the structure of community activity. He is less likely to be a home-owner and direct payer of property taxes. Given the nature of his dwelling unit he is less likely to "neighbor"; the fact that the women of the community are more likely to work cuts the level of their interactions in the local area.

The result may be a lessening of attention to and pressure on the local system of decision-making, especially with reference to school business. To put the matter in another way, the local demand structure may relax in the urbanized area as people's chances for social contact decline. What we are proposing is that this is the situation we find reflected in District D, where little in the way of demand behavior is detected and where the board therefore seems to operate in a vacuum. At the same time, the system retains, if in a rather quiet way, some of the distrust of expertise expected in a lower status place, and it lacks the organizational and communications skills that might give it an atmosphere of confidence and informality. These links between level of urbanism and decision-making style are thin, to be sure, but they suggest some intriguing problems for research in local government.

There are, as we noted early in this chapter, a number of other factors that may account for the variations we find among these systems, factors that we cannot, given our sample size or the data at hand, adequately evaluate. One of the most obvious of these is personality, i.e., the personal qualities and styles of the principal actors in the various systems. There can be no doubt that this must have some influence on the way the systems react. Still, on the basis of impression, we would propose that personality can for the most part be regarded as a system feature, as a part of the whole that does not usually introduce disconsonant behaviors and attitudes. Board members are selected out of a common social context (elections are at-large, it should be recalled) and superintendents recruited "to type." This is not to discount the personality variable but to suggest that it is an intervening force that may set limits to a system but probably does not usually determine its over-all character. To illustrate the point, it seems unlikely that if Districts A and C were to switch superintendents (a most improbable event), A's system would come to look like C and *vice versa.* Likewise, it is doubtful that Superintendent D, for all the skill he has demonstrated in his present district, would change the basic character of system B by his presence there. Some elements in the situation would surely alter, but its tensions and ambiguities would linger on, at least until substantial policy outputs and institutional innovations were felt by the system.

Out of this account of the characteristics of decision-making in four school districts, a variety of propositions may be drawn. The following perhaps convey the central thrust of our analysis:

1. The form of the school decision-making system is heavily conditioned by the social context in which it is set. Context-related variations in style, atmosphere, content, and division of work in the decision-making process are notable even among districts within a common framework of legal limitations and shared culture.

2. A principal factor that differentiates systems appears to be the degree to which organizational skills are applied to the political process at both the demand-aggregating and decision-making levels.

3. The application of these skills reflects (a) their availability in the community context, and (b) community expectations as to the means and ends of doing public business.

4. In general terms, the application of organizational skills is manifest through the regularization or "structuring" of the political process.

5. Low-conflict systems appear to have more "orderly," more managed, and more issue-related modes of demand aggregation and presentation.

6. Low-conflict systems grant wider decision latitude to technical-administrative personnel.

7. The boards in low-conflict systems are more oriented toward school-community relations and curriculum problems, in high-conflict systems toward physical facilities.

8. The low-conflict decision-making system under pressure tends to move toward the use of more overt conflict-management devices.

9. A higher level of urbanism in the community may result in a low level of demand behavior and hence in passivity in the governing body.

What has been said in these pages may convey a sense of inevitability about the processes of school government and the relationships and consequences they involve, but such is not our intention. There is nothing here to suggest that the introduction of different factors into a system cannot change its character in important ways. Indeed, our account of these four systems illustrates variety in itself, and it cannot touch the potential effect of circumstances not present in this particular sample.

It has not been our purpose to evaluate systems of government, nor to propose prescriptions to correct one condition or another. However, it seems appropriate to suggest ways in which changes in the basic relationships in some school governments might come about. It is commonplace to suppose that American society will continue to experience rather rapid rise in general levels of education, of income, and, by some standards, of urbanism. This rise will presumably be accompanied by redistribution of greater proportions of the working population into specialized and technical occupational careers. In other words, the community of the future may expect to have more of the "status" attributes of the Community A of today. If this is the case, and if the local community retains the power it now has in educational policy, the key figure in school decision-making will increasingly be the professional educational administrator. Such a prospect raises vital questions about the preparation of administrators and about the prospects for local democratic control.

The effects of such a social change could not, of course, be expected to be either immediate or even. Given metropolitan residential patterns, there are some places where they could not be expected to take hold except in the very long run. During this transitional period, participants in school processes, both administrators and board members, might be encouraged to develop organizational skills. These are now widely recognized in the training of educational administrators, but they are accorded little conscious attention in the recruitment and socialization of board members. Some of the potentials for planned change along this line are obvious.

It is not so clear, however, that the consequences of such a development would be universally acclaimed. If our analysis is correct, the raising of the level of participant skills would shift the distribution of work in the system toward a more generalized and permissive role for the board, leaving the administration with a greater share both of policy initiative and of operating control. Thus it seems doubtful that movement in this direction would satisfy the urge for more effective community control of educational decision-making wherever or for whatever reasons that urge may exist. This is in essence another way of raising the question of the relationship between community demands and technical-bureaucratic power. The "structured" situation of the low-conflict community, with the board playing an advisory role founded on its position in the communication channels between technician and constituency, may be the most likely pattern for the future. If this is so, the burden of responsiveness and responsibility will fall most heavily upon those who occupy administrative positions.

FOOTNOTES

[1]David W. Minar, "School Community, and Politics in Suburban Areas," in B. J. Chandler, *et al.,* eds., *Education in Urban Society* (New York: Dodd, Mead, 1962), pp. 90-104; David W. Minar, "Community Characteristics, Conflict, and Power Structures," in Cahill and Hencley, *op. cit.,* pp. 125-143; and David W. Minar, "The Community Basis of Conflict in School System Politics," (ditto; Center for Metropolitan Studies, Northwestern University, Evanston, Illinois, n.d.).

[2]Neal Gross, Ward S. Mason, and Alexander McEachern, *Explorations in Role Analysis: Studies of the School Superintendency Role* (New York: John Wiley and Sons, 1958); and Neal Gross, *Who Runs Our Schools?* (New York: John Wiley and Sons, 1958).

POLITICS WITHOUT POWER: THE DILEMMA OF A LOCAL SCHOOL SYSTEM*

Robert T. Stout and Gerald E. Sroufe

With rising tempo in recent years, educators have been entreated to "enter politics." Such exortations have proven largely irrelevant, for, regardless of the ideological preferences of schoolmen, politics has come to education. It is the thesis of this paper that educators are being required to make decisions about one of the most sensitive political questions, segregation, and that they have almost no resources for dealing with this issue. This is to say that many local systems are finding themselves in the political arena without sufficient political power.

Why is it that the local school system is often devoid of political power in dealing with the segregation question? How does it seek to compensate for lack of a political base in making controversial decisions? What may be suggested as the likely outcome of conventional strategies adopted by local systems? We have tried to examine these questions through study of a local system which sought to resolve a situation of de facto racial imbalance, Daly City, California.

School desegregation is widely feared by school administrators and school board members as a dangerously disruptive issue. Such fears are well grounded, as conflict over desegregation often serves to mobilize persons who otherwise take no interest in the schools, and to antagonize elements of the community who normally support school bonds and tax referenda. Withdrawal of traditional support groups coupled with opposition from elements about which the schools need not normally be concerned often deprives the local school system of a power base sufficient to meet a political crisis.

In suburban communities such as the one we have studied, conflict engendered over the desegregation question may become intense. Here the schools are the most visible and expensive community service, and perhaps the most actively scrutinized by supporters and dissidents alike. The issue of a policy regarding racial balance in the Jefferson Union High School District illustrates both the explosiveness of the issue and the development of a power vacuum as a result of the controversy.

*Robert T. Stout and Gerald E. Sroufe, "Politics Without Power, the Dilemma of a Local School System," from *Phi Delta Kappan*, February 1968. Reprinted by permission.

Demography: Customary Villain

Prior to 1950 Daly City had been relatively small, white, and virtually self-sufficient. The advent of a new freeway resulted in rapid growth, and concomitant engulfment of the traditional political structure. Only 30 percent of the families living in Daly City in 1960 had lived there in 1955. Early "post-freeway" immigrants were typically lower-level white-collar workers who desired a home of their own, a yard, and "a good education for their children." Their desires were partially vitiated by their middle- to lower-middle-level incomes, but they appeared willing to tax themselves for "good education." Their median family income was about $7,700 a year and they had completed about 11.8 school years. About 65 percent identified themselves as white-collar workers. Almost 60 percent were either foreign-born or had foreign-born parents whose native tongues were predominantly German and Italian.

Since 1960 the population patterns have shifted somewhat. Because of its proximity to San Francisco, Daly City has been attractive to Negro families and families with Spanish surnames. While in 1960 less than two percent of the citizens were classified as nonwhite, now almost 20 percent are so classified. Typically, the major increase has occurred in "Old Daly City," where the purchase price of houses is $4,000 to $5,000 less than in other parts of the community.

"Old Daly City" is served by Jefferson High School, the original high school for the district. The newer sections of Daly City are served by Westmoor High School, which was occupied in 1957 following an immigration of over 6,000 persons in the years 1954-56. Although only about 20 percent of the total student population is nonwhite, more than 70 percent of the nonwhite students attend Jefferson High School, while less than 20 per cent attend Westmoor High School. Seen another way, over 40 percent of the students at Jefferson are nonwhite, while less than 10 percent of the Westmoor students are so classified. Short of intervention by school officials, the percentage of nonwhite students attending Jefferson could be expected to increase substantially during the next few years; some of the elementary feeder schools had already become heavily nonwhite.

On August 23, 1965, the Board of Trustees of the Jefferson Union High School District appointed 26 citizens to an advisory committee. The board charged the committee with the study of overcrowding at both Westmoor and Jefferson High Schools, attendance boundaries for a proposed new high school, and "related ethnic and economic segregation problems." A member of the Board of Trustees appeared before the committee and asked them specifically to consider "how our district will prevent, if present trends continue, Jefferson High School from becoming a de facto segregated school."

The immediate antecedents for the board's action were a 1963 ruling by the

California State Board of Education that ethnicity be considered in drawing school attendance boundaries, and the report of the Jefferson Union High School Teachers' Association Committee on De Facto Segregation. The teachers' report requested that the board officially acknowledge the 1963 state board ruling and "create a study group on school boundaries . . . composed of teachers, administrators, and lay citizens."

Several features of the board's action are of special interest. First and most remarkable, the board was not forced to establish the committee as a last-minute effort to head off a crisis. Negroes were not sitting-in, marching, or even attending school board meetings. In fact, there was no organized minority group position, public or private. A second interesting point is that the board acted despite the unfortunate and well publicized experiences of two nearby communities. In these communities the desegregation efforts were of questionable success, and the political controversy of great magnitude.

Further, despite the fact that they were not forced to take any action, and despite the bitter experiences of nearby school systems, the Daly City board went far beyond customary limits in issuing their mandate to the Citizens Advisory Committee. They did not ask the committee to decide whether desegregation was desirable or necessary, but to draw up a plan which would desegregate and which would prevent segregation in the future.

The Citizens Advisory Committee worked for seven months, and in February and March of 1966 its recommendations were presented at three community meetings. The substance of the committee's recommendations was that an exchange of students take place between Westmoor and Jefferson. The community response was predictable and predictably onesided. The parents of Westmoor students did not want their children to attend Jefferson. The community had moved from a state of calm to a state of potential controversy.

The grounds for opposition to the exchange plans are familiar. Parents at Westmoor had a proprietary interest in *their* high school, an interest fostered by the system's policy of constructing small (1,500-2,000) high schools. One (white) citizen stated that as a taxpayer he had a right to send his children to Westmoor. A second source of opposition stemmed from the fear of a lower-middle-class group who envisioned a status loss if their children attended a school with lower-class children. One mother was quoted to the effect that her family had worked hard to be able to afford a home in the neighborhood served by Westmoor. This fear was exacerbated by the anxiety parents felt about sending children into the "tough" environment of Jefferson.

Opposition was also based upon more easily answered fears. These involved the distance from home to school, transportation, and the breaking up of friendship groups developed in elementary school.

In addition to these expressions of anger, the parents of Westmoor students accused the citizens committee of having arrived at its conclusions in secrecy and with disproportionately few representatives of the Westmoor position. Perhaps more than anything else, the charge of imbalance on the citizens committee effectively destroyed the usefulness of the committee report. The Board of Education, responding to its own long-held and public position of "democratic decision making," voted to table the report.

Extending Search for Support

The powerlessness of the board in effecting its chosen strategy was now becoming apparent. The board believed that it could not simply disregard the opposition of the Westmoor parents, nor could it claim that the citizens committee report represented a consensus of the larger community.

In an attempt to share the decision-making responsibility with a larger segment of the community, the Board of Education invited 132 citizens to constitute a second citizens committee for the study of district problems. Only 68 citizens agreed to serve, the great majority of whom were from areas served by Westmoor. Believing that this committee would be no more "representative" than the first, the Board of Education attempted to bolster its position by seeking assistance from a nearby university.

Analysis of Political Problem

The board's problem was to find sufficient support to effect a decision of great importance to the larger community. As is suggested in the following analysis, traditional sources of power were unavailable to the board, and efforts to identify and encourage new sources proved exceedingly difficult because of the complexity of the "community" and the controversial nature of the issue.

The three traditional sources of power utilized in effecting school decisions were unavailable in dealing with the desegregation question. The power ordinarily accruing to the superintendency by virtue of the superintendent's presumed expertness was vitiated because many consider desegregation a social rather than an educational issue. The superintendent is hampered further by the fact that evidence of educational benefits accompanying desegregation, though increasing, is yet limited. The support of traditional backers of the schools, PTA's and other civic minded boosters, was denied the board because these groups were themselves split on the question. That only 68 persons could be recruited to serve on a committee to study the problem, most of these with a ready axe to grind, is evidence that there was little hope of relying upon accustomed support from the public-spirited. Finally, the board could not utilize the power of its own legitimacy as official decision maker because it was unwilling to make a decision. The board was reluctant to make a unilateral decision which might embroil the community in conflict apart from evidence of strong outside support.

The board sought initially to garner additional power through the mechanism of a citizens advisory committee (hereafter CAC). Such an approach has earned educators' respect, partly because it satisfies the precepts of local control and democratic decision making, and partly because it often works. The question of how it works is seldom considered. We must do so here because we have an instance in which the invoking of a CAC seems an inappropriate strategy in the face of a fractured power structure.

If one of the main purposes of a CAC is to promote consensus through cooptation during periods of political decision making, it is well to explore some limitations of such a group. In the first instance, if its purpose is to engender consensus it can ill afford prolonged conflict. This means that its members must be carefully chosen on the basis of their shared values, or through selective attrition members will leave the committee, or compromises must be struck. In Daly City the last two phenomena occurred. However, as an issue becomes more crucial to a school, as time becomes less of a resource, and as the content of the issue becomes more emotion-laden, compromise may be both difficult to achieve and potentially disruptive. With respect to desegregation, for example, many persons on both sides of the issue are unwilling to compromise; they equate compromise with defeat.

A second limitation derives from the criteria for membership on a CAC. If membership is to be representative, how is a selection procedure to be devised? A suburban area such as Daly City is highly fractionated socially and geographically. There are perhaps a dozen "home owners' associations" devoted to keeping up the standards of their housing tracts, all located within somewhat larger municipalities. These groups identify primarily with their tracts, since for most of them the tract supplies personal and cultural support. Further, intermediary groups such as service clubs may enroll members who do not live in the school district. Unlike a self-contained community where small-business owners are residents, many of the local entrepreneurs live in other school districts.

Finally, the high rate of turnover among residents makes representation a curious concept. The basic question is, "Who is representing whom?," when over the course of a year or two a constituency changes radically.

On the other hand, if the purpose of a CAC is to allow local influentials to legitimize school decisions, selection is again a problem. The most interesting question concerns the basis of influence in a school district like Jefferson. In a small suburban community, unlike a major city, there are few rewards to be dispersed by the political leaders. The consequence may be that political control is unsteady and political leaders cannot be counted on to deliver their constituents. Thus political influentials may be influentials in name only. The local business elite, to the extent that it lives out of the community, is also a group of possible shadow influentials. Further, they cannot be legitimately included in a committee which does not directly consider business affairs. The corporate executives who commute to the city might be considered an influential group. But their influence is vitiated by their relative invisibility to the whole community and their residential instability. While they have occupational and educational status, it is difficult to attribute working influence to them. With a composition of quasi-influentials and some PTA leaders, a CAC has few mechanisms of control to assure its decisions will be accepted by the community. Other than personal ties, there are no restraints which can be used to "bring into line" dissenting residents who may also possess personal resources of occupational and educational prestige.

Finally, a CAC in such a community is highly vulnerable to charges of unrepresentativeness. Lacking substantial interlocking mechanisms among intermediary organizations, lacking political control over constituents, and with a high turnover of residents who have no occupational ties to the community, a suburban area such as this is fertile ground for a kind of mass-society response to decisions. Given the school's addiction to democratic decision making defined as participatory decision making, a school board cannot get true representation, nor can it ignore charges of autocracy. It is not surprising that the Daly City board rejected the report of its first CAC and attempted to appoint a second composed of 132 members, a number so large to be almost meaningless when compared with such committees in Chicago or Pittsburgh.

Frustration of Powerlessness

The strategem of a CAC is successful when it combines the trappings of representativeness with the legitimacy of community influentials. In Daly City it proved impossible either to identify and garner true influentials or to obtain representativeness. Having failed to muster sufficient power through the citizens committee route, the board turned to another time-tested strategem, involving the prestige of a university.

The university was given what turned out to be a double role: to develop a plan or plans, and to gain community acceptance for it, or at least to try to prevent overt resistance to it. The latter role was never explicitly defined and sufficient resources were never invested to accomplish it. In effect, the university's role became one of identifying possible dissidents and attempting to persuade them that the plans which were developed were not threatening or were for the ultimate good of the community. Two problems are immediately apparent. Identification of possible dissidents or support groups is hampered by the mass-like political and social structure. Neighborhood groups seemed to be the most likely candidates for either role, but the multitude of neighborhoods requires a large investment of resources in order to insure contact. As a compromise strategy, especially vocal neighborhood groups were contacted and presentations were made to the members. In addition, meetings were held in the high schools under sponsorship of the PTA. This latter strategy seemed not to be effective because of the self-selection of the audience.

A second problem is that desegregation is threatening to many people and rationality is a weak argument. Further, the lack of a real "crisis" in the community (the concern was to *prevent* de facto segregation) robbed an argument of some of its urgency. Finally, an appeal to a mobile population with respect to the ultimate good of the community is almost ludicrous. If a man has been and expects to be mobile, his long-term interest in the health of the community is likely to be low. In addition, if by moving to the next suburb he can avoid sending his children to an integrated school and can continue to enjoy the conveniences of a suburban region, he has no reason to be concerned about community welfare.

The ultimate response of the university representatives was to present to the Board of Education three alternative plans for preventing de facto segregation. For each plan there were also presented estimates of educational consequences. The university personnel had not been successful in generating massive community support for any of the plans, although one had met with less resistance than the others. Nor had the Board of Education been convinced that it had to act immediately. Consequently, the university report was acknowledged by the board and no action was taken.

Subsequently, the board held more public meetings in order to gauge the desires of the community and to attempt to develop support for positive action. Unable to accomplish either objective, the board referred the university report to a teachers' study group and asked them to develop a plan. Lacking solid support from the community, lacking political or personal power to insure acceptance, having been failed by the university, and needing some influence resource to legitimize its action, the board's referral was predictable. Although without much power, teachers as a group have some influence. Further, the board in utilizing the recommendations of the teachers develops several new arguments. For example, the board could argue that the success of any educational plan depends on willing implementation by the teachers and that such willingness is more nearly assured when the plan is developed by them. The board can also argue that a recommendation based on the combined educational expertise of a group of professional educators is, for the board, an extremely persuasive recommendation. Not surprisingly, however, the teacher's recommendation was an extremely conservative one which does not resolve the issue; their recommendation defers the question until some unspecified future date.

Conclusion

What we believe we have observed in Daly City is the failure of four political strategies as the board attempted to insure a priori community acceptance of its action. We believe the strategies failed because they were predicated on the board's attempted reliance on traditional sources of support: the superintendent's expertise, educational well-wishers, and knowledgeable outsiders. This reliance, we believe, was further predicated on the board's public adherence to "democratic decision making." The failure of the Jefferson High School Board and the failure of other boards in dealing with controversial political questions requires us to reconsider schoolmen's understanding of the democratic process. It would seem that participatory democracy is well established in American political ideology but that schools are the only public decision makers continuing to rely on this model as standard operating procedure.

In so doing the board makes itself too accessible to citizens. Unlike a large city, access by citizens to this suburban Board of Education appeared to be relatively easy. The advantages of such an arrangement are obvious and have been extolled by many writers in school administration. However, there are some disadvantages. If we accept the notion that a board of education cannot satisfy the demands of all the citizens, the question becomes one of differentiating among demands. The board is then faced with the dilemma of choosing among demands with little information about their source. That an individual alleges that he is a spokesman for a group is not necessarily useful information. How is the board to gain knowledge of the size of the group, the spokesman's authority to speak for them and, ultimately, his ability to control them? More generally, how is a board to separate noise from demands which rest on a substantial support base? In many growing suburban communities the lack of mediating organizations casts the board onto its own resources and intuition to gauge the strength of a pressure group. Perhaps one of the reasons that suburban educational conflicts are often so intense is that the board must wait for extremely powerful groups of angry citizens who have coalesced around a long-brewing issue to make themselves known before it can estimate their strength. In a sense, there can be no accurate warning system based on a board's access to the leadership of stable pressure groups. At one moment a board faces a demand of unknown persons with unknown resources, and at the next moment it must face a movement. The intricate system of reliable and accurate pressure group channels evident in legislatures appears nonexistent.

Democracy requires total access to the decision-making structure (i.e., to the positions from which decisions are made). This is not at all the same as total participation in actual decision making. Indeed, the policy of referring controversial questions to the electorate, for resolution outside the legitimate decision-making structure, is anti-democratic in that it is anti-governmental. Democracy requires that the electorate be in a position to hold public officials responsible; it presumes that elected decision makers will make decisions.

Educators have long been entreated to enter the game of politics; it appears that now they must be entreated to play the game the way it is meant to be played.

A SUBURBAN SCHOOL SUPERINTENDENT
PLAYS POLITICS

Lesley H. Browder, Jr.

Occasionally school men consciously attempt to influence the outcome of decisions made by the voting public. Such behavior may be considered "playing politics." This behavior is exemplified in the case that follows. Taken from a true experience, it is about a suburban superintendent playing his own brand of politics and attempting to influence the outcome of a local election. The focus of the reader's attention is invited as much to the administrator's behavior as a practitioner—how he thinks and feels, what he sees or does not see, what guides his actions, etc.—as it is toward gaining further insight into suburban politics.

Observers of administrative behavior have noted that such political activities are not considered "proper" of, by, and for school administrators.[1] At the same time, they note that politics per se has been, is, and probably will continue to be played by practicing school administrators, albeit their own brand of politics. It is ludicrous to suppose that men possessing enough vigor and aggressiveness to seek major positions of public responsibility will fail to take active interest in the outcome of public decisions affecting their life and work.

Yet "active interest" does not automatically imply consciously attempting to influence the outcome of a publicly-made decision through commonly understood political practices. Indeed, although political scientists cry out in anguish when school men insist that the schools must be kept free of politics,[2] there is a certain earthy wisdom appreciated by practitioners in maintaining this position. Two major reasons for attempting to preserve publicly this folklore and for keeping observable political action of school men at a minimum are: (1) the element of risk to the player of politics; and (2) the relative benefits derived in keeping the image of the public schools as a unique function of government. In turn, clusters of assumptions buttress these reasons and frequently appear to influence practitioner behavior.

Assumptions presuming an element of risk state:

(1) that known commitment by a public official to a cause outside the community's consensus of what is appropriate involvement for his

position is risky—win or lose (i.e., he runs the risk of making enemies, many of whom willingly dedicate themselves to his removal from office on later occasions);

(2) that, in the playing of politics, certain obligations to people may be incurred or implied which place the integrity of the professional school man under strain on later occasions when the debt is presented to him for payment in the form of favor;

(3) that if the school administrator inserts himself into a political event too far, frequently he becomes the issue, and the outcome of the vote determines whether he will remain in that community; and

(4) that if the issue is stormy, a school administrator who is too clearly identified with one side of the issue loses the option of playing the "great compromiser" and "healer-of-wounds" after the crisis has passed and people must again face each other in working relationships.

Assumptions presuming benefits from maintaining an image of the public school as a unique function of government state:

(1) that "politics" per se, because it is believed to be popularly conceived as a sordid business conducted by amoral men bent on furthering their own ends, has an image not appealing to school men and seen as detrimental to their position lest the public paint them with the same brush;

(2) that the higher social status and salary generally accorded school people by the public is better maintained and somewhat dependent upon a situation where the schools are regarded as unique rather than where the schools are seen as merely an extension of the same local government that provides dog catchers and sanitation departments;

(3) that, in a moral sense, the interests of the public schools really are better served by keeping politicians "out" and high-minded professional educators "in," serving in the best interest of the children;

(4) that in regard to maintaining a tighter hold on control over the public school system, the image of "unique function" allows greater leverage for control by the professional school administrator than an image acknowledging that the schools are "ripe for the picking" by dilettante and professional politicians; and

(5) that the "unique function" image provides the schools with a stronger competitive position for tax funds wherever voters are allowed to express a choice of priorities among government agencies in the allocation of scarce resources.[3]

That some of these assumptions may be erroneous is perhaps inconsequential in determining the elements of school administrator behavior. The folklore of the practitioner is heavily oriented toward insulating schools and school men from the taintings of "politics" in the popular sense. These powerful norms of practice mean, among school men, that unless you are willing to risk your position in an all-or-nothing gamble (a gamble that should only be made in a morally correct cause), you should not play politics. A corollary piece of advice states: If you do play politics, don't get caught.

To capture the flavor of the action as well as to sharpen understanding of administrative behavior, in part oriented by the practitioner's folklore, the material is conveyed in semi-story form as seen through the eyes of the superintendent as the situation unfolds. Because of certain embarrassments likely to arise if persons and places are too closely identified, names and other non-critical factors have been changed in this account.

How a Decision to Play Politics Was Made

In the middle of his second year as Commuterville's Superintendent of Schools, Walter Bronson faced a critical situation. Conviction that action was needed and that he himself would have to cause it materialized on the morning of January 22nd, 1969, after two sleepless nights of reviewing the situation in Commuterville, suburb of a large eastern city.

Bronson sensed that a tide was running which, if left unopposed, could seriously alter the course of education. He noted four elements in this tide: (1) there had recently been a power shift in the community; (2) the Board of Education had become the new focus for political activity; (3) at this time the Board was having its own troubles; and (4) a newly-formed taxpayers association emerged as a threat to the schools.

1. *A Shift in Power*

   Where political "power" (i.e., the ability to determine the behavior of others, even against their wishes) at the municipal level was concerned, the Township of Commuterville might be classified as having a "factional power structure."[4] That is, where "big policy" in the township was determined, two major factions in the community could be identified with relatively few people in both groups directing the course of events within their respective spheres of influence.

   A predominantly Republican town with a population of 12,000, these factions might be characterized as "progressive" and "conservative" forms of Republican politics. Generally, however, the influence of national politics was negligible. In the presidential elections of 1968, by a two-to-one ratio, Commuterville voters cast straight Republican ticket votes. From a rough survey conducted by the town's high school students on election day, it was discovered that 55% of those voting had voted last in the presidential election of 1964. Even more important, less than 40% could name *any* public official in the township. Clearly township politics did not dominate the interests or concerns of the majority of Commuterville's voting residents. It might not be unfair to say that to the majority of the residents, Commuterville provided a residence in which to sleep and entertain friends, a school system for their children, and few other intrusions into their lives. By Bronson's estimate, probably less than 2,000 adults in the township could be considered interested or even moderately informed about political happenings in the community.

While clear-cut distinctions are hard to draw, the two major opposing camps might be described as follows:

a. *The Progressives:* More cosmopolitan, generally college educated, well-travelled, tending to be employed in the city and nearly always holding executive positions, this group dominated the nine member Board of Education. Their influence was also felt in the local historical society, the Boy Scouts, and the P.T.A. Until recently, they had succeeded in driving the Conservative group to the wall, having unseated some well-entrenched members of that Conservative bastion, the powerful five-member Township Committee. Representing a more mobile population, a major problem for the Progressives was their tendency to be mercurial and loosely organized (although not as loosely organized as the township's leaderless Democrats, several of whose members could be found wistfully allied with various Progressive causes). Exhibiting broader vision and interest in community development, this group did not tend to reduce all issues to cost figures. They could be counted upon to take a longer view of future services to the community. Five men may be identified as having formerly held power in this group through their unusual influence. Three of these served on the School Board.

b. *The Conservative group,* on the other hand, more closely represented the purely local interests. Several large manufacturing plants in town employed people from the West Commuterville district of the township. Comprising about a third of the township's population, this less-mobile blue-collar district gave balance to the otherwise white-collar township, giving the township a heterogeneous socio-economic makeup. Its civic leaders, coming from the foreman ranks of the local manufacturing plants, frequently acted as the front men for the power holders of the Conservative group. This district's voting strength could be counted upon as a block of support for the organized Conservative group. The leadership of the Conservative group was held tightly by three or four men with a hometown local attorney, Edward Fingers, holding considerable power. Represented in this leadership group were the major local real estate, banking, and merchant interests. After a disasterous outmanuevering for control of the pivotal Republican Club four years before by the Progressives, the Conservative leadership preferred to use front men and work behind the scenes. Their influence was particularly felt in the police and highway departments, most of the township's municipal agencies (with the clear-cut exception being the Board of Education), the Chamber of Commerce, the Lion's and the Elk's Clubs, and the volunteer firemen. In the sense of playing politics as popularly conceived, the Conservatives controlled the municipal patronage system and showed marked interest in who got what jobs and which contracts—a feature of local politics which the Progressives generally cared little about, except where the schools were concerned. Thus, the intrusion of the Progressives into the Township Committee's activities was resented. When Conservative power was severely challenged and sharply curtailed four years before, the rallying cry of the Progressives had been to "end fingerism," an attack not easily forgotten by the powerful Conservative leader, Edward Fingers.

As frequently happens in times of relative tranquility when the major aims of the dominant group have been achieved, Progressive strength began to dissipate. Complications in business affairs outside the Township, company transfers, and the usual citizen apathy that settles after victory began to have effect with the passage of time. The torn Republican Club was re-united, but attendance at the club's meetings saw fewer and fewer Progressives. By the fall of 1968, the Conservatives were in a position to move strongly once again. The previous year, in a spirited contest for the election of officers, the Conservatives won control of the club. The apathetic Progressives, squabbling among themselves, did not challenge the control and by the next election, an entire Conservative slate, selected by an entirely Conservative controlled nominating committee, was elected without a single dissenting vote. With the decision of one of the two Progressive members of the Township Committee not to seek re-election because of personal business pressures, the path for regaining control of the Township Committee opened again over token Democratic opposition in the 1968 elections. By January of 1969, the Conservatives had majority control of the Township Committee. Interestingly, many of two years before. A rough-spoken man with a quick temper, his candidacy received little encouragement from township Democrats. Among the signers of his petition were a teacher who had been pressured to resign the year before and a group of this teacher's friends. A frequently outspoken-but-not-understood participant at civic meetings, the maverick Democrat was not considered a serious threat.

(2) Two of the petitions were clearly the Conservative group's candidates. Edward Fingers' signature was included on both petitions which carried identical names in the same order of signing. Both the candidates and the petition signers were from the West Commuterville district. Neither candidate had previously been heard from or known. These Conservative-backed candidates had to be seriously regarded.

(3) The fourth candidate, Louis Slippriano, was unknown in terms of his political affiliations, but not unknown to Bronson. The Superintendent met Slippriano at a Woman's Club Christmas dance in early December. Bronson was aware that Mrs. Slippriano was one of the P.T.A.'s tireless workers. However, for reasons unknown to Bronson at that time, Slippriano seemed to pump the Superintendent hard on many topics. Bronson, more than a little annoyed at the ceaseless barrage of questions, eventually cut off the conversation. At the time, Slippriano gave no indication of his intention to be a Board candidate. The filing of his petition, therefore, came as a surprise. The signatures on his petition also were somewhat surprising, including several names prominent in the P.T.A., names usually associated as supporters of the encumbent Board members. A further surprise came in early January when Bronson answered a midnight phone call from the press. In a printed release and press interview Slippriano had attacked the Board on several issues, including the "failure of the Board to release school test scores comparing Commuterville children to other communities." Slippriano contended that he had "asked Bronson last month to release the scores and was given a very tentative answer." Although Bronson remembered being asked some questions about test scores at the Christmas dance, he felt certain that Slippriano had not requested him—and knew it—to release such scores. Slippriano's twisting of facts, his attack on the Board and his support from important members of the P.T.A. made him a dangerous candidate in Bronson's mind.

3. *Troubles for the School Board*

Early January also witnessed a crisis on the Board. In September, against the office-holders of key municipal committees, the Republican Club and the Chamber of Commerce, were identical. At the same time, Progressive strength and organization nearly disappeared. For example, among the first acts of the newly-elected Township Committee was the abolition of the Township's Progressive-sponsored position, Business Administrator, filled by a conscientious appointee having a tendency to put contracts "out to bid" which formerly had been handled under the patronage system favoring local interests. The mild protest of the Progressives to this and other actions led Bronson to feel that a definite shift in power had occurred in Commuterville by virtue of apathy and default.

2. *A New Focus for Political Activity: The School Board Election*

Although Bronson had noted shifts in the political power of the community, he was not concerned. Then one December afternoon as the superintendent sat at his desk, a man brushed past his secretary and through the office door. Standing before him (hat on, cigar protruding from the corner of his mouth, gold watch chain stretched across an ample paunch), was Edward Fingers. Fingers informed the Superintendent that he wanted five petitions for the up-coming board member elections. Each year three of the nine school board seats came up for three-year term elections. Among the three board members seeking re-election this year were the incumbent President and the First Vice-President, Temple Martin, a key Progressive leader and outspoken enemy of Fingers—two of the Board's most valuable members in Bronson's judgment. A former attorney for the school board, Fingers must have known that the superintendent did not carry such petitions in his office (such matters were the province of the Secretary of the Board of Education). Although the conversation was polite (Bronson had met Fingers at Chamber of Commerce meetings and felt on friendly terms with him), it was not a cordial Mr. Fingers. The Superintendent felt this meeting was calculated, including Fingers's ignoring an offered ash tray and dropping cigar ashes on the floor. A message had been delivered to the messenger boy: the Conservatives intended to challenge the Progressive's hold on the Board of Education.

By deadline time forty days before the February 11th election, seven petitions, each signed with ten voting resident's signatures, had been filed in the Board Secretary's office. Three represented incumbent Board members. Whereas only one politically unaffiliated person had challenged incumbents the previous year, this year there were four challengers. The affiliations of three of the four challengers were immediately identifiable:

(1) One was a maverick Democrat who ran unsuccessfully for the Board

the protest of several members, the Board had decided to negotiate with the Teachers Association by subcommittee. The purpose of the negotiating subcommittee was, in part, to allow the Board "second-thought" options with the teacher's negotiation committee (which also had to return to its membership before an agreement could be completed). With some manuevering around among the board members by the group's dominant members, a three-member subcommittee was chosen with the Board's President and First Vice-President, Temple Martin, on it. Much ado was made about "guidelines" (particularly salary guidelines) which the negotiating subcommittee would follow and which were agreed-to by the subcommittee as part of the salve placed on the reluctantly compromising members who desired to negotiate as a full Board anyway.

As the negotiations got underway, the wisdom of a tightly-knit subcommittee seemed rapidly apparent in dealing with the one hundred-and-one page listing of teacher negotiation demands. Long, hard, biweekly nights of negotiation filled October, November, and December.

Finally, in the early morning hours, three days before New Year's Day, the last major hurdle of the agreement was passed. It involved a teacher salary increase of 24.9%—considerably in excess of the subcommittee's "outside" maximum of 10%. At the time, Bronson strongly urged the subcommittee members to call an emergency meeting of the entire Board to discuss this settlement before more than the most tentative form of agreement was passed with the teacher group. But the tired subcommittee expressed the thought that certain "hard-nosed" members of the Board would pull the entire agreement apart. The Superintendent was overruled. Agreement was reached. And the subcommittee later met with a committee-of-the-whole to explain the "tentatively" agreed upon contract in full.

To say that it was a difficult meeting would be an understatement. On the one hand, there was the subcommittee, frazzled from the months of hard, grinding work, returning with a contract of tentative agreement which all negotiating parties felt was a fair and honorable piece of work. The subcommittee was proud of the agreement. They were not ready for the strong blast of censure they received from several Board members. Expecting congratulations (and only some mild reprimands for the salary settlement), the subcommittee was stunned—"we were kicked in the teeth"—by their reception.

On the other hand, Board members not participating in the grueling work did not appreciate the efforts made. The 24.9% increase for teachers was "unconscionable." The disregard for the Board's negotiating guidelines was an "outrage." The heated discussion came close to exchanging blows. Many unfortunately chosen words were exchanged in the venting of hurts and angers.

In the end, the Board ratified the agreement, but a badly split and demoralized Board remained in the wake of the agreement. Even worse, both a personally hurt President and First Vice-President were considering withdrawing their candidacy for re-election. Their devoted service seemed rewarded with ingratitude, criticism, and insults. A despondent attitude settled on the Board.

The presentation of the 1969-70 budget on January 6th by the Superintendent to the Board did not lift this despondency. The projected 20.5% budget increase (due largely to the negotiation settlement) was no cause for elation. Whereas the previous year the Board had responded positively to the proposed budget, this year a kind of reluctance even to review the massive document manifested itself. The concentrated reviewing sessions scheduled by the Superintendent were ignored. Whereas the year before, the entire Board had been interested and involved in developing the budget newsletter to the community, only two members bothered to meet with the Superintendent this year. In sum, the Board looked and acted defeated.

4. *The Emergence of the Commuterville Taxpayers Association*

Among other signs that appeared somewhat disturbing to Bronson was the presence of increasingly large groups of people at the public meetings of the Board. Whereas the previous year, seldom more than a dozen persons attended the regular meetings, suddenly attendance doubled and tripled. Although the Board generally seemed to appreciate this flattering attention, Bronson felt uneasy. He did not perceive this growing audience to be a cheering section for the Board. The occasional note of hostility that came through the casual questions did not escape the Superintendent's attention.

Then, on a January 19th, a Sunday morning, the Superintendent began to receive telephone calls from various parts of the community. Friends called to say that persons were distributing leaflets hostile to the school. Urging "taxpayers" to "voice your protest," the flyers, bearing the notation, "paid for by the Commuterville Taxpayers Association," attacked by name the three incumbent Board members standing for election, teachers' salaries, the "ridiculous" school budget spiral, high-salaried school administrators, a "secretive" Board, and the increased need for school personnel. It asked: "Is Commuterville sick or is the Board of Education?" And although the flyers illegally bore no names of the Taxpayers Association's membership, some persons seen distributing the flyers were from the Board's newly increased audience while others were active members of the Conservative-controlled Republican club. Also reported seen among the distributors by several persons was Louis Slippriano.

To Bronson, the distribution of these inflamatory flyers was the first positive break in an otherwise relieved trend toward outright defeat. Even though several members of the Board had themselves asked similar questions as those posed in the flyers, the volatile attack from an otherwise unidentified group angered the Board. While the splits on the Board did not disappear, the emergence of an outside group publicly attacking it (and by implication, all its members) gave a disjointed Board an issue against which to close its ranks once more. The attack on teachers' and administrators' salaries also brought these otherwise apathetic groups to their feet. It appeared to Bronson that without this over-zealous Conservative attack, the will to struggle against what otherwise appeared to be inevitable had been sparked. The problem now was how to fan the spark into something bigger.

It was these concerns that led Bronson to come to these conclusions on the morning of January 22nd:

(1) that the Conservative group's hostility toward the Board of Education was apparent and that the vendetta-like approach of the Conservatives promised to convert Board of Education meetings into political wrangling sessions similar to those that marked the Township Committee meetings (while such meetings make good press, few persons realize the tremendous strains placed upon their participants. Bronson did not look forward to the kind of name-calling, accusations, innuendoes, and petty personality clashes characteristic of the Township Committee meetings);

(2) that the possible loss of the three incumbent Board members, aside from questions about their political views, would be a blow to education—the kind of education that Bronson believed-in professionally (all three incumbents were seen as Board members of high caliber by Bronson);

(3) that the possible gain of the three Conservatives (regarding Slippriano as a Conservative) on the Board would increase the already-present likelihood of a further split on the Board, making it difficult or impossible for the Superintendent to advance significantly his evolving plan for educational development in the township (an important part of Bronson's plans depended upon reasonably solid backing from the Board);

(4) that, unless something was done, the budget and the three incumbent Board members would be handily defeated in a one-sided contest pitting an organized group against a vulnerable Board of Education. (According to the local tradition, Board of Education candidates—both incumbents and challengers—run as independents without political endorsement or highly organized campaigns. Bronson feared that the incumbents, running

as independents and having no other organized support groups beyond their personal friends, would lose in this new game.)

As Bronson further reviewed the situation, he could not locate any organized group currently active in the Township to resist the Conservative onslaught. The Progressives were disunited and out-of-the-picture. The Democrats could not be considered. The P.T.A. group of supporters had been conveniently compromised by Slippriano's candidacy. Although many of its members could be counted upon to rally to the standard—if one could be raised—it appeared unlikely that the P.T.A., as an organized group, would move actively to support strongly the incumbents and the budget.

What was needed, Bronson thought, was a newly organized political force in the community, devoted to saving the schools from partisan politics (at any rate, the kind of politics that characterized the Township Committee). In a naive way, he wished that some altruistic group of concerned citizens would simply materialize, recognize the school was in danger, rally the people who cared about education (as opposed to politics per se), and vote the incumbents back into office, passing the budget at the same time.

Oriented by the profession's norms, Bronson wanted to have, where the schools were concerned, supporters who were *purely school supporters*—not Progressives, Conservatives, Republicans, Democrats, or any other political label. While he recognized that this desire might be naive, he did not consider it totally impossible. Familiar with James Coleman's theoretical work, *Community Conflict*, Bronson believed that every public institution had ready-made groups of supporters and attackers with a third otherwise neutral group.[5] In Commuterville the attackers were organized, the supporters (beyond the Board, teachers and administrators) uncertain, and the majority of the township unconcerned. With the election three weeks away and nobody stepping forward to rally the school's supporters, Bronson decided that he would have to act.

The Superintendent Acts

Arriving at his office on January 22nd, Bronson immediately arranged to speak to each of the incumbent candidates that day. His aim was to sound-out each candidate's desire to be re-elected; if "yes," to ask if each would object to running for election teamed with the other two incumbents; and if they would object to the Superintendent's quiet organization of a citizen's support group for their candidacy and the budget.

From the conversations, Bronson learned that none of the three had made extensive plans to promote their own candidacy. All three were depending upon traditional tactics to succeed: (1) an appearance at the P.T.A.'s "Candidate's Night"; (2) two or three "cottage party" meetings held by their friends; (3) one or two position statement releases to the press; and (4) the fact that they were incumbents on the Board of Education.

Bronson questioned this strategy by pointing out: (1) that only fifty persons (and half were staff people) had attended the P.T.A.'s "Candidate's Night" last year; (2) that the appearance of the two strongly backed Conservative candidates (i.e., backed by Edward Fingers and the voting strength of the West Commuterville district) and the vigorous campaign that Slippriano was making (already large batches of Slippriano campaign literature and newspaper ads were appearing) would mean more than a few meetings and press releases would be necessary; (3) that the 20.5% budget increase, based largely on salary increases given school employees, might make being an incumbent of the Board of Education unpopular with many voters; and (4) that it was unlikely that any of them or the budget stood much chance of succeeding without the rapid emergence of a citizen support group with a plan of action. All three separately agreed with this observation of the situation. They urged Bronson to move ahead. And Bronson did.

Working late into the night on January 22nd and 23rd, Bronson developed a campaign strategy consisting of an interrelated series of programs to be undertaken in phases from January 24th to February 11th. Analyzing the voting patterns for school elections in the township, Bronson noted that, over a fifteen year period, only twice had the election results surpassed a total of 1,000 votes. It was not uncommon for as little as 5% of the registered voters to cast ballots with about 15% to 20% being average for Commuterville. If the voting patterns held, then it was anticipated that a total vote of between 675 to 900 votes might materialize from the 4,500 registered voters. However, because of the involvement of Edward Fingers and the strong push shown by the Conservatives, Bronson anticipated that this election might surpass the 1,331 record vote level and probably would be close at best—if enough time remained to get the support group organized and functioning. Accordingly, Bronson's strategy was to aim at locating and delivering on election day 850 positive votes by the support group. The series of interrelated programs aimed at identifying and delivering this vote.

Among the ground rules Bronson attempted to employ in building the support group were:

(1) that the stated purpose of the organization was the election of the incumbents and the passage of the budget;

(2) that the officers of the organization be Commuterville citizens unconnected with either the school's or township's politics;

(3) that the organization composed of concerned Commuterville citizens be known as "S.O.S." ("Save Our Schools"), as a counterforce to the Taxpayers Association, and that S.O.S. would function without mention or ridicule of the other candidates or groups; and

(4) that after the 1969 elections, S.O.S. would dissolve.

In drawing these ground rules, Bronson—perhaps naively—was very concerned that S.O.S. not become a continuing political organization. He really was not concerned about attempting to redress the political balance of the township. He merely wanted to protect, as well as he knew how, what he considered to be the best interest of the township's public schools. At the same time he was worried that the campaign would become "dirty" in the sense of name-calling and other sordid political activities that gentlemen do not do. Two of his other concerns were that out-of-office local politicians would attempt to seize control of S.O.S., using it for their own purposes, and that the Superintendent's identification and connection with the organization had to remain unknown or otherwise vague. Bronson knowingly accepted these risks.

From his planning efforts, it was possible to make several important estimates. Estimates for each program of manpower, money, materials and timing were carefully drawn. A key ingredient to the entire operation was the small "Coordinating Committee," a control center maintaining the discipline and pressure necessary to have each program completed in correct order and sequence. It was Bronson's hope to be, in fact, *THE* Control Center. The publicly visible members of the Coordinating Committee were to serve as chiefs over the several programs whose activities Bronson could coordinate and synchronize with the use of his management network system charts.

By paying close attention daily to critical elements in the campaign, Bronson felt considerably higher gains could be realized than the 850 vote goal. For example, it was possible (with the use of some data processing equipment) to develop lists of "potential supporters" for telephone teams in each of the three voting districts to contact. A "potential supporter" was a combination of registered voter (no sense in courting people who could not vote) and parent of a public school elementary child (hypothesizing that the school's strongest supporters could be found among young parents of primary age children). The potential voter lists could be further refined by noting those registering as Democrats and Independents with the street address and township district (newer vs. older families and parts of town) helping to suggest what sort of Republican the voter was likely to be (Progressive or Conservative). Using these calculations, a target group of over 1200 "potential supporters" could be singled out for special attention and solicitation with an expectation of a fairly high conversion rate to active support.

Where these "potential supporters" were clustered conveniently, it was possible to contact some known supporter who could be prevailed upon to hold a "cottage party" or informal meeting in someone's home for about thirty persons to attend, meeting at least one of the Board's incumbent candidates and discussing the budget. Those who could not be reached by personal contact with the candidates at cottage parties would be solicited by telephone.

To expedite telephone work, a format was designed to cover essentials rapidly and invite those desiring further information to one of two large S.O.S. membership meetings scheduled to handle such individuals.

While the cottage party and telephone solicitation teams attacked the problem of contacting identified "potential supporters," two other groups—the flyer distribution teams and the materials development group—were to work on the general public. A study of bus routes proved helpful in determining how the flyer distribution teams might operate to best advantage. The small materials development group was to prepare flyers, telephone solicitation formats, news releases, campaign literature, and attend to placing newspaper advertisements. Both these "general public" groups aimed at soliciting membership in S.O.S. as well as support for its objectives.

With 850 positive votes pledged by election day, the use of voter challengers (allowed by law) working as a team was to aid in keeping a running tally on the delivery of pledged votes. Prompter teams, kept up-dated by the challengers, would telephone the untallied pledged voters. At the same time, transportation-babysitter teams stood-by to bring pledged voters to the polls, providing transportation and babysitting service where necessary. Wherever possible, no pledged vote was to be allowed to escape.

It was an ambitious plan. It called for close attention to detail and time sequence. Practically viewed, it was too ambitious a plan for a group of concerned citizens to undertake alone. But Bronson was not counting solely on the efforts of concerned citizens. The largest immediate reserve of manpower was the school system itself—board members, administrators, and teachers. It was to these groups that he first moved to test support.

By Thursday evening, January 23rd, he had sounded-out key people on the administrative staff. The next afternoon, accompanied by another administrator, he met with five leaders of the Teachers Association. Talking in vague terms about "the possibility that some civic group might appear," professional protocol was maintained. Nevertheless, communication was clear. The Association membership was polled to locate those individuals who would be willing to work actively—again, as individuals unconnected with the Association—for "a community organization" that supported the incumbent Board members and the budget. Sixty persons volunteered.

At the same time another problem was solved. A commitment of strong teacher attendance at the upcoming Budget Hearing on January 27th and the P.T.A.'s "Candidate Night" on the 29th was promised to off-set the possible embarrassment of being greatly outnumbered by the opposition. A strong support group, Bronson knew, would also help bolster the Board's sagging spirits.

Before the meeting between the Superintendent and the Association ended, one of the affluent teacher leaders suggested that "if some citizen group should decide to organize," he would like to make a sizeable financial donation to its efforts. It was a profitable meeting.

On Saturday morning, January 25th, the Superintendent met with the three Board candidates. The candidates had asked two other Board members to attend also. Personal obligations prevented a sixth Board member from attending. The uninvited Board members, the candidates had decided, were uncertain quantities regarding their allegiance.

The Superintendent's campaign strategy was enthusiastically received. A listing of citizens who might be initially approached to form S.O.S. was developed. Although many names were discussed, Bronson was surprised at a list of only thirty names: it was shorter than he expected; it included many local out-of-office politicians; and the few other citizens were neighbors.

One Board member mentioned that he had already talked to "some of these people." He suggested a relatively unknown citizen in town to act as chairman of S.O.S.'s organization meeting. This person could also serve as the link between the Superintendent and S.O.S. Both the Board and the Superintendent were seemingly to have no connection with S.O.S. It was agreed that the Superintendent would meet with this person the next day, review the plans, and turn over the contact list of names to him.

Preparing for the second meeting that afternoon with the entire Board to review plans for the Budget Hearing Monday night, Bronson had misgivings. He disliked having to depend upon a citizen unknown to himself and the candidates. Also, he was concerned that the candidates, now excited about the campaign, had obviously been talking to out-of-office politicians. Instinctively, Bronson was uneasy with this turn of events. From the morning's discussion, it appeared that out-of-office Progressives and Democrats were anxious to use a figure-head group of lay citizens to press forward the larger battle for domination of all township politics. This purpose went beyond Bronson's limited objectives. He felt the campaign was moving out of his control.

On Sunday morning, January 26th, Bronson met with the chairman-to-be, Bill Whisp. An energetic man, Whisp quickly reviewed Bronson's plans. He mentioned that he had contacted the Board member who recommended him and agreed to be chairman. He then told the Superintendent that he would be unable to attend the initial S.O.S. meeting because of an out-of-town business trip. Leaving that afternoon, Whisp did not know how long this trip would take, but had arranged for his next-door neighbor, an airline pilot, to substitute for him. Bronson could meet Monday with the pilot and up-date him. In the meantime, because the pilot was currently flying, Bronson was told that the pilot's wife, Alice, would "handle things" (i.e., take care of the contact list and arrangements for the meeting). "Alice, you know, lost out as tax collector in the '67 Republican primary," Whisp mentioned. Bronson's anxieties increased.

Monday afternoon, the Superintendent met with Alice and her husband. The contact work and other arrangements had been completed. Not unexpectedly, several of the lay citizens contacted were sympathetic but afraid "to get involved in anything political." Alice also contacted a few more persons not included on the list but did not volunteer their names. In addition to the overall strategy, the agenda and conduct of the organization meeting were discussed. Bronson agreed to get materials prepared for the meeting which he could not risk attending.

On Tuesday morning, Alice called to say that the airline had unexpectedly called her husband to fly that day! Who was now to serve as temporary chairman for the vital S.O.S. organization meeting that evening? Both Alice, because of her sex, and the Superintendent, because of his position, ruled themselves out. A new name occurred to Bronson, however—another airline pilot who might be approached.

Feeling like a high-pressure salesman, Bronson filled-in the new man at lunch that day on the political happenings of Commuterville. With a lack of enthusiasm for "getting involved," the new man agreed to act as temporary chairman, saying that there was a "remote possibility" that he too might be called upon to fly that evening.

At 5:30 p.m., the remote possibility became a reality. The third chairman of the vital organization meeting for S.O.S. had flown away. An air of desperation could be detected around the Superintendent's office.

Thus it was that at 7:00 p.m., the Superintendent found himself sitting in the kitchen of an out-of-office politician who said "yes" when asked—the sixth person approached for the job. While the politician ate his dinner, Bronson briefed him on the plans, gave him the materials for the meeting, answered a few questions, and dejectedly departed.

As 8:00 p.m. approached, the initial meeting of the "Save Our Schools" organization got underway. At the same time, the Superintendent and his wife arrived at the Chamber of Commerce dinner meeting with, among others, Edward Fingers. Although at the time Bronson believed he was to remain the major force behind S.O.S., subsequent events were to prove that he had played his last significant role in the campaign that evening.

The Campaign Roars Onward

While Bronson was struggling behind the scenes to get some sort of support group organized and running, the campaign assumed a velocity of its own. Among the events to transpire publicly were the following:

— On January 25th, a group of seventeen high school students distributed their own leaflet defending the school budget. At the January 27th Budget Hearing, a Conservative spokesman demanded to know who was using these students as "a tool or a pawn." "Who are these children to think they can get into the act? It's for grownups—we don't want any protests here!"

A Progressive responded by asking "how will we teach in a democracy that every man has a voice but they don't?" "I got two pieces of paper under my door," said another. "One was signed by the kids; no adult signed theirs" (referring to the Taxpayers Association).

Meanwhile the Superintendent was embarrassed to learn that the students had used the mimeograph machine in the central office, and—worse—Mrs. Slippriano, running off P.T.A. notices for "Candidate's Night," discovered a few leaflet rejects in the wastebasket.

— The Conservatives managed to win a victory by forcing upon the Board of Education their newly appointed Town Treasurer as Custodian of School Funds. By law, the Board had an option to appoint either the Town Treasurer or the Town Tax Collector, whichever would accept. Upon approaching the Tax Collector, a docile lady dependent upon her position for a livelihood, the Board prevailed upon her to accept this additional position and its small stipend. Within twenty-four hours after accepting the position, however, she resigned it without official explanation. The new Custodian of School Funds, now privy to the school's financial information in addition to serving as the town's treasurer, was also Vice-President of the Republican Club and—it was later learned—a key member of the Taxpayers Association.

— As a result of the organized Conservative push, an excited Temple Martin charged at the Budget Hearing that "a hack political machine is muscling in on our schools. Our community has outgrown the neanderthal politics of a machine out to destroy this school system. It has destroyed the morale of the police department, scrimped on the fire department and is now out to take over the schools." The stacked audience applauded vigorously. The temperature of the campaign rose as the level of conduct dropped.

— The P.T.A.'s "Candidate Night" was held on schedule despite freezing rains and icy roads. Only two of the incumbent candidates appeared. The Board President had notified the P.T.A. weeks before that he would be out-of-town. The other candidates simply did not appear to debate the issues and answer questions. Temple Martin, discovering latent talents as a demagogue, did not let the matter pass: "I've been here long enough to know that Fingers's candidates never appear anywhere for questions. They don't know why they're running and they couldn't answer your questions if they were here. We must not let it happen that the grubby manner of local politics is extended into the school system. The repair of streets is not the same thing as the education of our children." Again the stacked audience responded enthusiastically. The Conservatives had given up attempting to beat the Board on its own grounds. The standard answer to the press for reactions to Martin's charges from Fingers and his candidates was: "No comment."

The Conservatives had not given up the campaign however. Instead they began an unobtrusive series of door-to-door and telephone solicitations. They were selective in their concentration on portions of the community population. They relentlessly hammered on the 20.5% budget increase. Particular attention was given those homes sending children to the local parochial schools. Even among many supporters of the incumbents, the large budget increase was unpalatable. Despite a good press, Bronson felt the schools were losing ground.

Meanwhile, S.O.S. finally materialized. Even while Bronson was first meeting with Bill Whisp, the Sunday papers were carrying stories about "unconfirmed reports of a fusion group" forming to back the incumbents and the budget, "ultimately to fight (Conservative) Republicans on and off the Township Committee." A local Progressive politician was quoted: "It looks like they're starting out to save our schools, but then it may have further ramifications." Bronson winced as he read the story.

The S.O.S. organization meeting went well. Thirty-five residents attended. The press was also present. The organization, founded as Bronson intended, chose a Coordinating Committee of politically-untainted citizens. The absent Bill Whisp remained as chairman. District captains were elected. Within a short time after this meeting, a membership and manpower reserve could be counted in excess of a hundred persons (excluding school personnel). Funding by contributions presented no problems. The initial thrust of Bronson's plan was working well.

However, where Bronson himself was concerned things were not working well. A person who attended the S.O.S. meeting asked him where he was that evening: "Everyone was saying this whole idea was yours." That was not the kind of news Bronson wanted to hear, fearing public identification with the organization. At the same time, the Superintendent found it impossible to act as the control center for the operation. The Coordinating Committee, taking immediate control of the organization, suggested that it was too risky for Bronson to meet with them. Several Board members agreed, fearing to have the new organization too closely linked politically with the schools. A consensus emerged that with the launching of S.O.S., the Superintendent had taken enough risks. With mixed feelings—relief, disappointment, and hurt—Bronson had become a spectator by the end of January.

The Campaign Concludes: Election Day

During the final week of the campaign, both sides remained publicly quiet but otherwise busy. The Conservatives were criticized for "moving underground," but this tactic and "no comment" answers were effective in terms of raising no new issues or outcries.

The projected plans of S.O.S. changed also during this period. Because the necessary daily attention from a network control center was lacking, many of the programs had to be modified or curtailed. Absentee leadership raised problems, as did loosely organized teams and missing "follow-up" procedures. Neither the "potential supporter" listings nor the telephone solicitation formats were employed. Records of identified supporters and membership lists were only partially maintained. The full manpower of the organization was never tapped or realized. A few members did the work of many. Despite these shortcomings, however, S.O.S. was functioning.

In the closing days of the campaign, the only peculiar event Bronson noted was the behavior of Louis Slippriano. Running a hard campaign pace, Slippriano personally canvassed large sections of town. His campaign literature appeared everywhere. Then, on the Friday before the election, he surprisingly approached Bill Whisp and asked for S.O.S.'s endorsement of his candidacy. Although Fingers's candidates and the Taxpayers Association endorsed him, Slippriano's own literature endorsed only himself. A close reading of his literature revealed not much more than the fact that Slippriano stood for "sound education." As he later boasted to Bronson, "getting elected is simple—all you do is start walking and shaking hands, find out what's buggin' the voter and tell him you'll fix it. One side of the street is as good as the other. All you have to worry about is getting elected." When Whisp asked him about his earlier work delivering Taxpayer Association flyers, Slippriano flatly denied it. A dumbfounded Whisp invited Slippriano to an S.O.S. meeting to "explain himself further," but Slippriano said he thought it "wiser" not to do so.

Two days later, Slippriano appeared at a Sunday Republican Club campaign party. Here, lest there be any doubt, Edward Fingers, with his arm draped over Slippriano's shoulder, formally announced his endorsement of Slippriano's candidacy. For Mr. Slippriano, "all you have to worry about is getting elected."

A large snow storm reduced much of Sunday night's and Monday's last minute campaign efforts, but not all. As anticipated on the eve of election day, the Taxpayers Association again came forth publicly with another leaflet. Timed so that its charges could not be answered or challenged, the leaflet endorsed all three of Fingers' candidates. This time, unlike the first public leaflet, it was signed by a four-member "Executive Committee." Coincidently, all four held membership in the Republican Club (including the Club's Secretary and Vice-President). Three also held appointments from the Township Committee while the fourth was Treasurer of the Chamber of Commerce. The attorney for the Taxpayers Association served also as President of the Republican Club and Secretary of the Chamber of Commerce (for which Edward Fingers acted as Counsel, fulfilling this duty as well on the Township Committee). The only other noticeable difference in this flyer from the one three weeks previous was the use of more accurate financial data, resulting from the efforts of the Board's unwelcome new Custodian of School Funds.

February 11th finally arrived. A snow-covered town voted. Despite all his efforts to anticipate the outcome, Bronson found himself unable to predict the results as he returned that evening to the central office to await the official results.

The scene was memorable. Masses of people filled the building. Reading faces as he entered, the late-arriving Superintendent felt immediate alarm. The Conservatives looked smug and jubilant; the S.O.S. people grim. Neither group spoke to the other. Temple Martin was ashen-faced and stammered when he spoke. The first trickle of results gave strong indications of a clean sweep for Edward Fingers and the Conservatives.

When all the votes were tabulated, a record school election vote was recorded in Commuterville: 1652 ballots. The budget was defeated by a three-to-two ratio: 952 votes "against," 643 votes "for." The crucial Board member elections were as follows:

Candidate	Endorsed by	Votes Cast	Outcome
1. Louis Slippriano	(Fingers, Conserv. & Taxpayers)	863	Elected
2. Board President	(S.O.S.)	777	Elected
3. Temple Martin, Board Vice-Pres.	(S.O.S.)	762	Elected
4. Conservative No. 1	(Fingers, Conserv. & Taxpayers)	721	Defeated
5. Board Member	(S.O.S.)	707	Defeated
6. Conservative No. 2	(Fingers, Conserv. & Taxpayers)	672	Defeated
7. Maverick Democrat	(Independent)	276	Defeated

Bronson's reaction to these results was: "Well . . . I did my best." Both groups departed for dreary "victory celebrations."

Aftermath and Conclusion

With the election over, several new situations faced Commuterville:

(1) *The Election Results:* As a minor note, the Conservative Candidate who placed fourth (being defeated by Temple Martin by 41 votes) demanded a recount. The Conservatives felt cheated by the results. From later conversations with their various leaders, Bronson learned that they had expected a clean sweep for all their candidates as well as for the budget. No vote change resulted from the State-conducted recount.

(2) *The Budget:* By law, the Board had to do something about the defeated budget. It had to be re-submitted to the voters. The Board re-submitted it

uncut. An exhausted S.O.S. made a token support gesture while an enraged Conservative group pressed forward new attacks on the unpopular 20.5% budget increase. To no one's surprise, the budget was defeated again on February 25th, by a vote of 882 "against" and 498 "for." By law this second defeat placed the matter in the hands of the Township Committee. They cut the budget 5.8%. A stubborn Board, refusing to accept this cut and exhausting their last legal option, appealed the Township Committee's action to the State Commissioner. As time passed with these manuevers, Bronson, without consulting the Board, called Edward Fingers on the phone. They talked for an hour. No mention was made of settlement figures by Bronson, who avoided Fingers's questions on this matter and spoke only of attempting to "settle things down" in Commuterville. Two weeks later in mid-April, a quick settlement was reached in a brief meeting at the Commissioner's office. A 3.6% cut in the budget was sustained—a safe and negligible amount, Bronson felt.

(3) *The Fate of S.O.S.:* To Bronson's surprise, the Save Our Schools organization stuck to its founding principles, dissolving after the election. Many of its leaders, however, began efforts immediately to establish a new organization—"Interested Citizens for a Better Commuterville." Progressive politicians seemed particularly interested in the more broadly based objectives of this new organization and expected to challenge Conservative candidates for the Township Committee. Among other things, S.O.S. did produce some new faces on the Commuterville political scene. And it had stalemated a determined, organized drive by an established political group in its brief two-week operation.

(4) *The New Board:* The election automatically led by law to the Board's reorganization meeting where officers are appointed for the year until the next annual election. The previous two years the Board had simply voted to retain its same officers in uncontested appointments. Bronson fully expected the same action this year. Temple Martin frequently did the unexpected, however. He told his colleagues that, because of the recent acrimonious election, it was necessary for the Board to change its public image. Therefore, he, under no circumstances, would accept the Board's Presidency. It is doubtful to Bronson that anyone present had seriously thought of Martin as Board President. However, with much awkward fumbling around, another Board member was elected President. The suddenness of this change, occurring in less than ten minutes, obviously stunned and hurt the noncontroversial former President and several of his friends. Interestingly, Temple Martin was returned to his old position as Vice-President. While it is doubtful that the change significantly altered the Board's public image, it did alter its manner of operation. With the

addition of Slippriano and the change of the Presidency, the Board appeared to become more unsettled. The discussions were heated. The struggle for power and influence in the new configuration intensified. Hard days lay ahead Bronson thought.

As Walter Bronson looked back upon the election and his efforts to influence it, what could he conclude? A troubled Bronson concluded that he had done his best, but remained uncertain about whether he should have done anything at all. Was he right to undertake such an effort? Did he even have the right to do such things? He did not know. On the one hand, he felt guilty for violating a professional norm. On the other, he was proud of acting out of conviction. He believed he saw a need in his community and moved literally to "save our schools." That several of his calculations (the needed 850 votes, for example) were incorrect and some of his fears groundless (e.g., the professional politicians never did assume real control of S.O.S.) were perhaps, in retrospect, minor errors and faulty perceptions. But was it a major error to save a Temple Martin? He was not always certain. At least he had helped to stir an apathetic township to some degree. Maybe that was good. Probably the Conservatives would be back next year. At any rate, other problems needing Bronson's attention had arisen. Next year would have to wait.

FOOTNOTES

[1] See, for example: Roald Campbell, John Corbally, and John Ramseyer, *Introduction to Educational Administration,* 3rd edition, (Boston: Allyn and Bacon, Inc., 1966), pp. 276-81.

[2] See: Thomas Eliot, "Toward an Understanding of Public School Politics," *American Political Science Review,* (December, 1959), pp. 1032-51.

Roscoe C. Martin, *Government and the Suburban School,* (Syracuse, N.Y.: Syracuse University Press, 1962), pp. 59-60.

[3] It is interesting to note a Louis Harris Poll on government spending. Sixty percent of those polled marked "aid to education" as the last place to cut federal spending. See: "The Dollar Squeeze," *Life,* (August 15, 1969), p. 23.

[4] Donald J. McCarty, "How Community Power Structures Influence Administrative Tenure," *The American School Board Journal,* (May, 1964), pp. 11-13.

[5] James Coleman, *Community Conflict,* (Glencoe, Illinois: The Free Press, 1957).

PART II
POLITICS OF EDUCATION AT THE STATE LEVEL

INTRODUCTION TO PART II

State Politics and Education

The amount of actual and potential state control of local education is vast. The Federal Constitution asserts that education is a state function, and consequently local prerogatives must be surrendered or delegated by the states. Unfortunately, most empirical studies of state politics and education have focused exclusively on the issue of state financial aid. There has been little attention to policy making in such important areas as curriculum, certification, district consolidation, and other non-money items. Many state legislatures are very active in controlling these areas. Also, there has been only the barest political analysis of the conditions under which local schools respond to state direction.[1] Proposals for strengthening state departments of education are based on principles of administration rather than an understanding of how states actually influence local affairs.

The method of the studies to date was *not* to posit testable propositions at the outset of several in-depth case studies. Rather, findings were presented as a posterior hypothesis for further research of a larger and more representative sample of states. As Masters, et al., concluded after a study of three midwest states:

> It was hoped that if and when our hypotheses are integrated with findings from other studies, they will take us a little further down that rough-hewn path that leads to a general theory of politics, or that state in scientific development where research is conducted with a conceptual scheme or model that, for research purposes, is widely accepted within the community of scholars.[2]

With these research caveats in mind this introductory section will summarize the conclusions of our existing studies that cover New York, the New England States, and Michigan, Missouri and Illinois. The variance in political styles and structures is very great among the states studied.

215

The Politics of State Financial Aid

A recurring theme is the lack of decisive political influence over financial aid decisions of state government by any *single* education organization or group. The teachers or school administrators do not usually have the political muscle to bring about large increases in state aid. Neither do state education commissioners or sympathetic state legislators. Consequently, the strategy of schoolmen in many states has been to devise some means to achieve consensus among the various interest groups outside of the maneuvering of the normal state legislative process.

State politics have been characterized by attempts at alliance formation of different education interest groups and in some cases the establishment of a united state-wide organization. The aim of these coalitions is to aggregate enough political influence from different sources to insure a total amount sufficient to enact proposals. The coalitions or statewide organizations have tended to be temporary and for specific purposes. But time, money, skills, and ideas have been marshalled. The case studies in this part demonstrate that if coalitions are not formed the policy outcomes are likely to be negative from the educators point of view.

Who comprises these coalitions? The core membership is usually the state teachers' association, the state school boards' association, school administrator groups, and the state PTA. In some states, such as Colorado and Pennsylvania, these are the only members. In other states the coalitions have a broader base of potential influence. These broader coalitions include business groups, the American Association of University Women, American Legion, Jaycees, etc. Sympathetic legislators and governors can also be considered coalition members.

As the New England study by Bailey indicates, working in the background for the coalition are frequently the "educational academics." These academics chart the goals, prepare detailed analytical information, and draft the legislation. Paul Mort of Columbia Teachers College is an excellent example from the New York case study. There are also episodic actors who join the coalition for some special issue but are not normally concerned with education. Together, all these groups have at their command political influence which rests on such impressive and varied foundations as authority, respect, friendship, rational persuasion, salesmanship, and coercion. It is little wonder that large coalitions based on a specific goal have been successful in a variety of states with different political traditions and styles.

The opposition to the coalitions is identified by Bailey's New England study as tax sensitive business groups, legislative or interest group spokesmen for rural localism, and all types of conservative political leaders and citizens who are committed to holding taxes down. Masters found that virtually no one opposes public education openly and there is no *formal* anti-school lobby. But state aid increases are costly since education is over one-third of the state budget. Significant budget increases necessitate a tax bite with impact on all voters.

Consequently, opposition is carried out through informal mechanisms rather than from standing or ad hoc organizations.

Laurence Iannaccone's selection provides an analysis of how influence is concerted among the coalition members so they are all working for the same goals. He discusses four types of statewide patterns for goal formulation and lobbying that link an education coalition to its allies in state legislatures.[3] He groups the states by the degree of alliance cohesion (or fragmentation) and the process or style by which the coalitions communicate with state political leaders. On the one pole are coalitions like New York and Illinois that have formed statewide monolithic organizations. At the other extreme are states like Michigan and California where allies cannot agree on goals and are classified as "state-wide fragmented." In the past, various educational and civic organizations in states like Illinois and New York have formed new organizations that present a united front and are the chief link to state government officials.[4] These coalition organizations, such as the New York State Educational Conference Board, formulate the legislative program and marshall information and other types of influence on the legislature. This includes lobbying by grass roots members of the various component organizations.

The impressive potential influence of the coalitions brings us to the question of what issues the broad coalitions can deal with effectively. If the alliances depend on a unity of goals—and these studies indicate they do—then increased state financial aid is one of the most likely targets. As long as the goal is a larger financial pie for everyone, conflicts among allies are less likely. But if the legislature is asked to recut the pie, or earmark increases for selective priorities, conflict is inevitable. Increasingly the demands for change in education involve categorical demands that benefit some members of the coalition at the expense of others. For instance, special programs for disadvantaged students in urban schools will splinter the education forces that include large suburban and rural elements. Teachers' organizations are concentrating on salary and fringe benefits, and consequently do not share the goals of administrators. Nor are teachers willing to have administrators or any coalition be the teachers' spokesman.

The issues of aid to religious-affiliated schools and black community control divide the traditional allies. These involve a fundamental recutting of the financial aid cake and threaten to redistribute control away from entrenched administrative interests. Perhaps the enthusiasm of groups like the League of Women Voters and the Jaycees for more education aid is diminishing as the frustration with past increases for urban education increases. The educational attainment results for many compensatory education programs have not been encouraging. Moreover, state legislative reapportionment tends to upset the rural strengths of many coalitions and teacher-administrator organizations formed several years ago.

In short, the future outlook for effective broad based coalitions is not bright.

The most promising issues in urban areas are not good candidates for agreement among allies. Moreover, "the no politics doctrine of schoolmen," discussed in the section on local policy, is not only inconsistent with reality but also self-defeating as an effective political strategy. Educators cannot be isolated from the general political system for their internal operations and expect the political system to automatically provide them with the necessary financial resources. If the schools must be kept free of politics, and governments must be held at arm's length, then it is not likely that the governor or state legislative leaders will wade into state level education conflicts. Nor will the mayor or city representative tend to be a leader in fighting for school aid increases from the state legislature.

If future goals are too conflict-laden to permit education-based alliances then the leadership must come from influential governors and legislators as outlined in the Michigan selection. In effect, once the education coalition is shattered influence will move to elected officials. The thrust of the selections is that educators must develop new strategies for use of their political influence and not rely on grand coalitions or what Iannaccone termed "statewide monolithic organizations." This new strategy must recognize that political skills are essential to the health of education and that political campaigning must have a high priority. Also, influential politicians at the state level must be cultivated and given favors in return for their support.

The last selection by Alan K. Campbell documents the results of the past structure of state political influence in terms of the low priority for financial aid to central cities. Indeed, as the educational attainment problems of central cities have increased state aid has decreased. On a per student basis state governments provide more aid to suburban than city school districts and this imbalance is growing!

Campbell concludes with some ominous political trends. Reapportionment will increase suburban representation. It is the suburbs that have the present state education aid advantage. The ability of cities to improve their aid position will depend on the amount and kind of political influence they can exert on governors and legislators. Yet Campbell's case studies in Chicago, Boston, and San Francisco indicate central city school boards have played a relatively small role in supporting state aid for compensatory education. Teachers are the most involved group but their concern is their own salary and fringe benefits. The Usdan study of educational power in New York State concluded that city school officials' influence was minimal at the state legislative level.[5] Masters, et al., found the same for Detroit (p. 199) as did Gittell for the five large cities that her group studied.

Campbell asserts that a broad coalition of local business leaders, school administrators, teacher organizations, and local government officials might have enough collective influence to redirect more aid to the cities. But no such coalition now exists and the inevitable conflicts that a redistribution of state aid would cause makes a grand coalition unlikely.

State Departments of Education

Empirical studies have not focused on state departments and state boards of education. Observers agree state departments are undergoing change in the direction of more power and influence.[6] The project approval powers granted to state departments by the federal ESEA are allowing them to make program decisions and exert influence over curriculum and personnel policies that were precluded under state aid formulas. Gittell's study found state aid had little impact on local innovation because it is allocated on a formula and not a program by program basis.[67]

According to Campbell the historic rural orientation of state departments is in large part caused by the rural base of state organizations of school board members, school administrators, and teachers.[8] But urban unrest and financial pressure is causing a greater concern from top state department officials. In sum, the amount and scope of political influence of state departments is an unresearched area, but the trends seem to be toward greater control of local agencies and an increased big city orientation.[9] As with the whole field of state politics of education one senses rapid change in the structure and process of political influence exerted by state departments of education.

FOOTNOTES

[1]See David L. Colton, "State Power and Local Decision Making in Education" (paper presented to the American Educational Research Association Annual Meeting, Los Angeles, February 8, 1969).

[2]Nicholas A. Masters, Robert H. Salisbury, and Thomas H. Eliot, *State Politics and the Public Schools* (New York: Alfred A. Knopf, 1964) pp. 10-11.

[3]See Innaccone, *op. cit.,* pp. 47-63.

[4]*Ibid.,* pp. 66-68.

[5]Michael V. Usdan, *The Political Power of Education in New York State* (New York: The Institute of Administrative Research, Teachers College, Columbia University, 1963).

[6]See Alan K. Campbell, "Who Governs Our Schools," *Saturday Review* (December 21, 1968), p. 63.

[7]Gittell, *op. cit.,* p. 124.

[8]Campbell, "Who Governs Our Schools," p. 63.

[9]For an analysis of the recruitment and composition of the State Board of Education, see Gerald E. Sroufe, "Recruitment Processes and Composition of State Boards of Education," AERA annual meeting, February 8, 1969. He does not discuss the influence of the Board on substantive policy. His overall conclusion is that state board elections or nominating procedures produce a singularly homogenous population of high income professionals. At the time of selection state board members do not seem to be persons with highly specific educational goals. The members appointed by the governor usually had not thought about serving. State board elections take place in an environment of public indifference and lack of information on the candidates. The state board is not a stepping stone to higher office.

SCHOOLMEN AND POLITICS: A STUDY OF STATE AID TO EDUCATION IN THE NORTHEAST *

Stephen K. Bailey, Robert T. Frost, Paul E. Marsh
and Robert C. Wood

Since World War II, building upon a long tradition of free public schooling and amid a welter of recurring tensions, the northeastern states have fashioned substantial school aid programs of varying degrees of liberality and sophistication. The formal route these programs traveled from inception to authorization is a familiar one. Bills were introduced in state legislatures, at the instigation of a governor, a legislator, or a private party. They were assigned to appropriate legislative committees. Hearings were held; reports made; formal readings scheduled for floor action in both houses; debate occurred; votes were taken; appropriations made; gubernatorial approval secured. Then the administrative machinery of state departments of education took over.

But who initiated the action? Who contacted, cajoled, pleaded and persuaded persons in positions of authority and influence? Who aroused the grass roots and then followed the school measures through the labyrinth of requisite actions? It is the function of this chapter to identify the political actors who have played decisive roles in energizing the machinery of government in the northeast states to provide increased state support for education.

Identifying the schoolmen and their friends is not always a straightforward business. Earlier it was indicated that no simple political typology built on official officeholders, private interest grups, or the articulated opinions of large portions of the voting public serves adequately to describe the drive for more state aid. Instead, actors with no formal titles, leaders without groups, groups without leaders, and sporadic waves of public sentiment are all relevant components of the pro-school movement. Their different combinations in different states offer a colorful assortment of figures entering and disappearing from the political arena.

Yet, for all the eight states, some persistent sources of strength for school aid have been observable and some recurrent types of schoolmen and their allies have been visible. Building upon the fundamental concerns of parents and the

*From *Schoolmen and Politics: A Study of State Aid to Education in the Northeast* by Stephen K. Bailey, Robert T. Frost, Paul E. Marsh and Robert C. Wood, Syracuse University Press, 1962, pp. 22-56.

citizenry at large for adequate education, pro-school interests can be divided broadly into four groups. First are the educational academics who fashion in the first instance plans for school aid and form the intellectual core of the movement. Second come the officials in state government, sometimes leaders in state departments of education, sometimes officials with other responsibilities, who adopt the school cause. The third group consists of the professional educators—teachers, superintendents, principals—and their lay supporters, school board members, PTAs', and school betterment groups and the coalitions which those interests strike. Finally, there are the "surprise" actors, individuals and associations engaged in pursuits not normally aligned with public schools but which for numerous and subtle reasons make common cause with the schoolmen.

It is these actors who in the end have been responsible for the enactment of the programs the last chapter described. But each group displays quite different characteristics, holds different motives and plays different parts, and an exploration of the composition in some detail is needed before an accurate understanding of their behavior can be divined in the recent past and today.

Scribblers and Their Friends

"In the beginning was the word." It is impossible to account for the rapid growth in state aid to education in recent decades without reference to a tiny group of dedicated academics who have attached their enthusiasm to their brains and have energized movements for state aid in the Northeast.

J. M. Keynes concludes his *General Theory of Employment, Interest, and Money* with a tribute to the power of economists and political philosophers. "Practical men," he writes, "who believe themselves to be quite exempt from any intellectual influences, are usually the slaves of some defunct economist. Madmen in authority, who hear voices in the air, are distilling their frenzy from some academic scribbler of a few years back."[1]

The story of state school aid in the Northeast is a living tribute to Keynes' insight, for if we are to search out the origins of general state aid legislation of the past generation, the trail with fascinating regularity leads back to a group of academic scribblers at Teachers College, Columbia University, in the years immediately after World War I. The most significant scribbling appeared in two books: George D. Strayer and R. M. Haig, *The Financing of Education in the State of New York,*[2] and Paul R. Mort, *State Support for Public Schools.*[3] These two books outlined the need for additional support for education and proposed formulae by which such aid could be equitably administered. The authors, by their writings, by consultancies to public officials and education commissions, by the drafting of legislative proposals, and by placing their protégés in strategic places in professional associations and state agencies, enormously influenced the course of educational policy throughout the Northeast—and beyond—in the forty-year period now ended.

Perhaps of all people Paul R. Mort was the schoolmen's schoolman. Without denigrating in any way the contribution of other powerful academics, it is fair to say that no single human being in the twentieth century had a more profound effect upon state educational finance than Paul R. Mort. A pipe-smoking angler, salty and often blunt in expression, Paul Mort for forty years was inflamed by a passion to upgrade public education through the particular avenue of public finance. Technically on the staff at Teachers College, Columbia, Professor Mort spent his life as an itinerant catalyst. It was he who translated research findings into the Cole-Rice Act and the Friedsam Act of the mid-twenties in New York State. With his love of statistical puzzles, it was he who directed scores of research projects at the behest of educational professional associations, citizens' study groups, and official state agencies and commissions. In the Northeast alone, his ability to create politically viable formulae, backed with elaborate statistical analyses, influenced the development of educational finance policies in all of the eight states. In the two states of New York and Rhode Island he towered above any other single individual as the master-mind of existing state aid legislation.

It would be a mistake to limit Paul Mort's contributions to his academic scribblings—seminal as these were. Certainly it was his creative imagination in the construction of state aid formulae which was his most evident contribution to the development of public policy. The foundation, equalization, and incentive aspects of existing state aid legislation are in no small measure the result of his productive mind. But Mort's contribution went far beyond this. Although he would have discounted the claim, he was one of the great political movers of his own proposals. His acute instinctive political sense and his personal charisma led him to fashion a series of educational juntas which in state after state were the prime movers and energizers of political action. Almost from the beginning of his career he sought out and identified himself with key individuals in professional associations and in state departments of education who constituted a necessary link between ideas and political action. Where forceful individuals were lacking in key positions, Mort saw to it that wherever possible his own protégés from Teachers College were insinuated into key roles. There is hardly a state department of education in the Northeast which does not contain at least one of Paul Mort's associates. Beyond that, as an educational consultant, Mort influenced the thinking of officials and research associates in the professional associations and education departments of all the northeastern states.

Yet, if it is important to recognize the crucial role which Mort played as an individual, it is equally important to know that he was not alone in performing the creative function of school politics. Other scribblers and consultants have played vital, if not as spectacular, parts in shaping state aid plans and masterminding the strategy for their adoption. Now they appear in sufficient supply on the campuses of the schools of education in great private universities of the Northeast, and in teachers colleges, that the Mort role is close to being institutionalized, indeed has been since the 1940's.

The principal companion figure to Mort was Alfred I. Simpson of Harvard, originally a Mort protégé, but subsequently a leader in his own right. Indeed, one long-time school observer, estimating the work of the academics, remarked "you divide New England states at any rate, into Harvard and Columbia territory. Massachusetts and New Hampshire have been where A. I. Simpson left his mark. Rhode Island and Maine are the scenes of Paul's great victories."[4] And, in New York, Mort was joined by George Strayer and Robert Haig. In New England, Cyril Sargent of Harvard collaborated with Simpson and assumed in large measure Simpson's role upon the latter's death. In Maine, William Bailey of the School of Education at the University of Maine has been influential. And, as the schools of education expand their teaching and research programs in administration and finance, this breed of scholar-activists will continue to be produced.

One other type of consultant needs to be briefly identified: the public-relations expert, called in by school people to assist in the promotion of campaigns for better school laws. Serving schoolmen as he does other clients with political problems, the public relations expert is perhaps best regarded as a mercenary and he is by no means universally employed. But in Massachusetts, Eugene Belisle, head of the Department of Public Relations at Boston University, worked side by side with Sargent in promoting that state's great push for a minimum education program in the late 1940's. And the J. C. Jacobs Co. performed similar services in the Maine push for new school laws in the mid-1950's. This participation, if nothing else, demonstrates that schoolmen are keeping up with the political trends of the times.

State Educational and Political Officialdom

If the scribblers and consultants have the crucial role in designing new state aid programs and suggesting strategies for their legislative enactment, they cannot go it alone. They need contact and support from individuals and groups possessing greater political influence than academics and salesmen can muster. Typically, their first couplings are made with officials within the formal structure of those parts of state governments and of state political systems most intimately concerned with educational policy. In short, as proponents for state aid push forward, they soon touch base with state educational agencies.

Again, in canvassing the behavior of these organizations, the similarities are impressive. But here, more than with the first group, differences in structure and program, with important implications for our understanding of educational policy-making at the state level in the northeastern part of the United States, need to be highlighted.

As to gross similarities, a glance at the basic structure of government in the eight states in the Northeast reveals substantial uniformities—in some cases, virtual identities. These patterns spring from a common constitutional heritage dating back to revolutionary times and from a common administrative heritage of more recent origin.

Each state of course has a governor. Each state has a bicameral legislature. Each state relates governor and legislature ambiguously to formal instruments of educational supervision: boards, commissioners, and departments of education. In each of the states there exists a board of education, although not always called by that title.

State School Boards

State school boards vary in size from thirteen in New York to seven in New Hampshire, Vermont, and Rhode Island. In all states except New York members are appointed by the governor, either with or without some form of legislative consent. In New York State alone, members of the Board of Regents are elected by the legislature.

Although the eight states vary widely in terms of office for board members (from five years in Vermont to thirteen years in New York), these terms uniformly extend beyond the terms of any one governor or legislator, and, perhaps more important, members are elected in every state for overlapping terms.

There is considerable variation in the formal responsibilities of state boards of education in the Northeast. In terms of the range and monolithic character of its operations, the Board of Regents of the State of New York is unique. The New York Board enjoys independent executive, legislative, and judicial power of such scope as to bring into question its consonance with American constitutional principles of separation of powers and checks and balances.

At the other extreme is the complicated maze of educational administration in the state of Massachusetts in which the Board of Education must compose itself into three overlapping structures in order to do legal business covering collegiate and vocational as well as elementary and secondary education. In addition, the State Board must live with autonomous units such as a School Buildings Assistance Commission, a Youth Services Board, a Board of Educational Assistance, and trustees of the Lowell Institute of Technology which have their own separate jurisdictions. Beyond this, two other technical institutes in Massachusetts have their own boards.

Other state boards of education fall somewhere between the administrative patterns of New York and Massachusetts.

But whatever the scope of legal power and concern, each state board, by constitutional and statutory provision, has a general mandate to encourage and supervise public education within the confines of the state, and to make recommendations to the governor and the legislature for the improvement of education. However formal and nominal the powers of state boards of education may be in reality, their place in the chain of legal authority makes them significant factors in the initiation and execution of state educational policy.

The state board's political role must be precisely understood, however. They are less independent forces in their own right than sympathetic responders to the executive and administrative officials they oversee. Rhode Island is an extreme case in point. A recent governor and a board member have both complained that the board "rubber-stamps" departmental action, and is a passive agent in school policy-making. The rule is that strong commissioners of education, exercising forceful professional leadership, have a ready sounding-board and supporting officialdom in their state boards.

These observations suggest that as the policy-making—or, at least, policy-sanctioning—state agency for schools, boards are best understood as a statutory link between government and schools. Any official position taken by the commissioner must carry the explicit or implicit stamp of his board's approval. After all, in law the commissioner is the board's executive secretary, acting on its behalf and at its discretion. While practice may construe the relationship differently, statutory formalities are not to be winked at.

But the basic fact is that the visibility of state boards of education as bodies politic is generally low. For the most part they act as sounding-boards for educational ideas and programs rather than as active participants in the political process of consent-building. Exceptions exist. In New Hampshire, the Board chairman has recently been so bold as to ask the legislature for 30 per cent more money for state aid, a fruitless, if not quixotic, gesture. In Connecticut, many State Board members have testified before legislative committees and have spoken tirelessly before civic and educational groups. But, in Vermont, contrarily, public opposition by the State Board to a new aid formula helped to kill whatever slight hopes it had of passage. Most typically, board members can be expected to record on cue their support of the commissioner's program when it comes up for discussion before legislative committees. Members of state boards in the Northeast do not sit in the councils of the mighty in school politics.

Commissioners and Departments

The key educational official in each state is called commissioner. Except in New Jersey, the commissioner is appointed by the board. In New Jersey he is the direct appointee of the governor. A tradition of professionalism frequently attaches to this office in contrast to the lay backgrounds of state board members. In New Hampshire, for example, strong professional administrators—frequently from out of state—have characterized departmental leadership throughout most of this century. In the area as a whole, Allen, Morrison, Butterfield, Engleman, Fuller, Hill, Buley, McCaffrey, Ritch are names known as educators first, with or without the additional status of native sons which some of them enjoyed.

The commissioner in turn supervises the state department of education, which carries out the various functions which law and administrative rulings mandate. Although departments of education in the Northeast vary substantially in size, they all perform certain core functions. A comparison of organization charts of the various departments reveals a recurring list of divisional and bureau titles: Instruction, Vocational Education, Administrative Services, Teacher Certification, Special Education, Higher Education, Finance, and Planning and Research. The peculiar nomenclature in each state reveals the historical development of legislation and of administrative reorganizations. These, in turn, have often reflected the views and recommendations of professional educators from university schools of education, and of professional associations.

Perhaps of particular importance to this study is the fact that in each state department of education there are at least a few individuals, with varying titles and under varying administrative units, who have as their special responsibility research, planning, and administration in the general field of state financial aid to local school districts. It should be noted, also, that there can be found in each state department one or more key individuals (sometimes the commissioner, sometimes the deputy commissioner, sometimes the departmental attorney, sometimes others) who have as one of their special responsibilities the cultivation of strategic and tactical relationships with the governor (and his budgetary staff) and with key legislative leaders concerned with matters of educational finance policy. It is this political role of the department, often working through the state board, as in New Hampshire and Rhode Island, sometimes moving through other channels as in New York, Connecticut, and New Jersey, which is the focus of attention here.

This "political" orientation of the educational agencies is, of course, not surprising. In spite of the relative independence of board, commissioner, and department of education in each state, there are scores of ways in which the major constitutional instrumentalities of the state impinge upon the activities of the state education agencies. This is most particularly true in the field of educational finance. The amount that a state spends on education is ultimately determined not by the recommendations of the education agencies, but by political decisions taken at the level of the governor and the state legislature. So, although activities of the key officials in the state education agency may be highly relevant to the success of educational finance policies, the final, determinative action is legislative and gubernatorial.

The Political Officialdom

This need for school agencies to engage in a broader arena than their legally independent status would suggest indicates a second linkage made among pro-school interests and introduces another set of actors: political officialdom or, more precisely, governors and legislators. Here the political flavor of the schoolmen becomes even more apparent. Whatever their role as chiefs of state, governors are partisan political figures. However harmonious legislative bodies may be, their capacity to do business and to insure even a modicum of political responsibility is heavily dependent upon the partisan political structure of the state and of the partisan leadership structure in the two houses of the state legislature. This is true even in the states of northern New England in which one-party domination is a long-standing item of state political life.

The cardinal political fact in the region is that partisan political machinery has been fused with a constitutional system of representation which has given inordinate power to rural, small-town, suburban and overwhelmingly Republican forces in parts of every state legislature save two. This fact produces special tensions in the states of Connecticut, New York, and New Jersey whose populations are either evenly balanced between the two major parties, or in which a largely big city, Democratic popular majority feels itself thwarted by the over-representation of suburban, small town, and rural Republican interests in at least one branch of the assembly.

These tensions are heightened by the frequent existence of Democratic governors in these states. These governors, elected of course at large, must somehow develop public policies in cooperation with politically divided or hostile legislatures. As noted later on, the politics of educational finance in the Northeast has frequently centered in the executive-legislative struggles of split partisan majorities. This drama is usually personalized in the minority leaders in the upper houses; the speaker and floor leaders in lower houses; and strategically placed committee chairmen in both houses on the one hand, and the governor and his party stalwarts on the other. Often, the struggle is quite as apparent when the governor and the legislative leaders are of the same party; a tribute to the differences in constituencies and historical habits between the two major branches, as well as to intra-party factionalism which so often builds around competing, strong personalities.

Out of this maelstrom of conflicting partisan and institutional interests, schoolmen nonetheless must co-opt some influential spokesman for their goals. This they do in the Northeast in several ways: working on party leaders to have their aims recognized in party platforms, joining hands occasionally with other interest groups, doing staff work for legislative and executive branches alike. But most typically, the procedure has been to persuade governors and key legislators to espouse their cause.

It would distort reality to suggest that leading politicians are always among the staunchest friends the schoolmen have. But over and over again our studies have shown the energizing influence of governors and the power and importance of key legislators. Furthermore, political parties in states where such organizations count have taken important stands on educational policy. Even in those cases where partisan reaction has been derivative, one must assign credit to political friends of schoolmen who have given priority to education's cause.

As far as gubernatorial support is concerned, a long list of the names of recent chief executives can be enscribed on the schoolmen's honor roll: in Connecticut, Chester Bowles; in Rhode Island, Dennis Roberts; Muskie for Maine; Bradford in Massachusetts; Smith, Harriman, and Rockefeller in New York. Each in his own way has provided assistance and leadership on critical occasions.

Cementing executive and legislative—and sometimes party—relations has been the role of legislative leadership. Again, a survey of the eight states results in a long list of names. Walter Mahoney and Joseph Carlino, majority leader and speaker in New York, are usually counted as schoolmen's friends for reasons at least in part explicable by their school-oriented suburban constituencies. E. O. Smith for Connecticut, Ralph Mahar in Massachusetts, Rhode Island's Florence Murray—the role can be extended for all states and in depth to include at least three or four dedicated friends of education.

Sympathetic governors and legislators underwrite the schoolmen's efforts in various ways, but almost always their roles are significant. As succeeding chapters will further illustrate, Maine's success story is dominated by Republican State President Robert Haskell and Democratic Governor Edmund Muskie. The Massachusetts school victory of a decade earlier got a decisive initial boost from Republican Governor Robert Bradford. What lies outside the scope of the Rhode Island story is that the movement which created that state's Department of Education was set in motion by Democrat Governor Dennis Roberts in 1951. For nine years the state's chief executives had toyed with Paul Mort's recommendations for a separate educational agency. Then Roberts took the decisive first step of establishing a state board of education with an attendant staff.

As relevant as any of these key acts to an appreciation of the central position of political leadership in supporting schools is Connecticut's experience since World War II. The residents of that state for many years have been pretty evenly divided between the two major parties. Competition has led to thorough party organization and an uncommonly high degree of party discipline. As Lockard clearly demonstrates, intra-party disputes are ironed out in caucus whose decision is binding, and these disputes are mostly on matters of state policy.[5] Education ranks very near the top as a subject for such debate. What Connecticut has done about education in recent years, therefore, is largely the result of vigorous, orderly political decision within and between the two parties. Party actions, responding to key schoolmen, have written Connecticut's school aid history since the war.

Special Commissions

Governors, legislators, party leaders, do not always move, of course, in ways the schoolmen desire and some of their acts of apparent friendship turn out to be ambiguous. A case in point is the use of special commissions as a favorite device for politicians to get themselves off the hook. On inspection, responsible decisions can be found to be politically unpalatable or perhaps enticing political movements may turn out to have irresponsible implications. In instances like these, the study commission has real virtue even if its friendship to schools may be not immediately apparent. The virtue lies both in delaying a commitment and in involving more people—the members of the commission—in reaching a solution. The ambiguity lies in the nature of commission recommendations which, almost by definition, must bridge some political impasse. Study groups may be set up as conscious "depressants"; others have been conservatively weighted so that strong recommendations for increases in state aid will get somewhere but at the same time will free the governor or the legislature from sole responsibility. School politics by study committee has flourished in just those northeastern states where forces at loggerheads with each other had to find common ground on which to proceed. New Jersey's strongly partisan politics, for instance, beset by keen urban-rural, low tax-high expectation, state-local splits, has for years leaned heavily on research commissions as vehicles for educational decision-making. But in whatever state, if their findings are not always all the schoolmen might hope for, at least they do open ways around political roadblocks.

Although most of the northeastern states since World War II have established special committees or commissions on school finance which would illuminate the above generalizations, a typical example has been the so-called Diefendorf Committee, which wound up its affairs early in 1962 in New York State.

Called a Joint Legislative Committee on School Financing, the committee has been popularly identified with its chairman, Charles H. Diefendorf, a Buffalo banker. The committee was established in 1960 in the full knowledge of Governor Rockefeller and his Republican legislative leaders that demands for increased state aid would continue to be insistent and that a special committee might well cushion the political impact of major increases in state aid.

The Diefendorf Committee issued a staff report on December 28, 1961. The committee itself modified the report in the direction of big city demands and issued a final statement on February 14, 1962.

Legislation based upon the Diefendorf recommendations was passed unanimously in the Assembly on March 30, 1962, but with substantial modifications. From the point of view of this essay, the most important modifications involved a substantial increase in state aid over the Diefendorf Committee's best judgment. Perhaps no better indication exists of the power of the schoolmen in New York State than their ability to convince the Governor and their legislative leaders of the inadequacy of the Diefendorf proposals. But it may also be stated that the existence of the Diefendorf proposals helped to establish an ideological benchmark which gave to the political leadership of the state a bargaining weapon with which to counter even greater demands by the schoolmen.

In states where schoolmen have been weak, one of course can find examples in which the reports of special committees or commissions have been filed away as too radical. But the classic use of the special commission seems to be to construct a conservative countervailing force to the schoolmen which will at the same time provide a rationale for prudent progress in aid to education.

An examination of the personnel appointed to special committees in the various states suggests the conservative bias of such committees. The dynamics of the special committee seems to start from this conservative bias but move toward a more liberal conclusion which is still short of the demands of the schoolmen but which at least presents an entering wedge for further legislative action.

Educational Associations and Their Satellites

The sum and substance of school politics is not restricted to inner groups of academics and professional politicians. A broader arena is inevitably involved, and a third set of actors perform the role of uniting the political actionists in government to the laborers in the educational vineyard and the public at large. The hard core of this group is the professional educational associations, and, to a much lesser extent, teachers unions, often reflective of the split personality of an occupation still unsure of its status. In these states, the more professionally oriented associations claim by far the majority of teachers as members, around 90 per cent. They have professional staffs, at least an executive director and a research "figure-gathering" person, and they are active at their respective state houses. Minimum salary laws, teacher retirement plans, teacher dismissal laws occupy their attention year in and year out. So do the publication of journals, the holding of conventions and workshops, and the organization of committees. The unions are limited to the large cities and are likely to be oriented more directly to such bread-and-butter issues as single salary schedules for elementary and secondary school teachers, higher pay without regard to differences in educational attainment, and better working conditions. Except in New York, the unions rarely figure at the state level except in a line of witnesses before a legislative committee. More typically they snap at the heels of associations, encouraging them to more hardboiled stands on benefits and privileges to keep the membership rolls intact. In New York, however, the United Federation of Teachers works intermittently with organizations like the United Parents Association and the Public Education Association in developing legislative policies, and it has a full-time legislative representative in Albany. On school aid legislation, although not a member of the Conference Board, the UFT backs Conference Board proposals while pressing for a larger diversion of grants to urban areas—especially to New York City where UFT has its strength.

Between the teacher groups and the state educational officials are the "hierarchical" associations of superintendents and sometimes principals. These may best be classified as administrative-oriented, for their concern is for education as a going enterprise. They keep the local school staffs together, meet payrolls, schedule school bus arrivals and departures, speak to parents, oversee school plants, keep school doors open, make budgets and present them to school boards. Unlike the teachers, they are sure they *are* professionals, on career ladders which, when duty, advancement, or better pay call, can take them out of their districts, out of the state or even the region to new positions. Theirs is the broader horizon and the greater sophistication. Their problems are not so much with routine concerns of teaching but with the management of schools and school systems. Their recognition of the importance of state action is clear and unwavering.

Following those for whom education is a livelihood come the more diverse assemblies of laymen who for one reason or another are drawn into school affairs. The distinction is perhaps a Weberian one: they live for the schools in their public lives and not off of them. True, in the case of school committeemen, the local popularly elected officials charged with the legal responsibility of determining local school policies and perhaps ultimately accountable for their quality, the line may be blurred. Especially in a large city, a position on the local school board is often a stepping stone to a grander political career. But local school board members do not belong to the professional in-group, and not infrequently they part company with the professionals on matters of salaries, the dismissal of superintendents, teacher qualifications, merit plans for promotions, and curriculum.

Less ambiguous are the roles of the Parent-Teacher Associations in these states, and the councils of citizens, variously named, organized for "school betterment." Here the distinction is the lack of any official responsibility for the conduct of school affairs and the absence of paid staffs or a permanent budget. As between the two groups, the difference is in orientation: the first are parents, discharging the age-old concern of how Johnny is actually faring, whether he can read, and whether the school product satisfies the customers. The second group, the citizens councils, are engaged in what they consider a "higher" calling. For them the schools are an agent in the national life, a prime source of strength in our world-wide battle with the Soviets, the underpinnings of our economic system, in short, a national resource. But both groups share the frustrations of amateurs. They are uncertain as to whether or not in the eyes of the Internal Revenue System they can lobby without losing a tax-exempt status. They are not clearly informed as to the details of how the school enterprise functions. They cannot commit major portions of their time and political capital to the cause and they are sporadic in their attention.

Supplementing these groups whose pronounced aim is better schooling are other civic associations which encompass education in their general agenda. School bills sometimes become the pets of organizations not exclusively concerned with education. While state Leagues of Women Voters from time to time back school legislation, they are not the only ones to do so. State branches of the American Association of University Women, Federations of Women's Clubs,

Library Associations, Leagues for Mental Health have all been found involved with educational campaigns on occasion. Each with its own style—often social—and at its own best level—usually local—these groups and others like them can rouse considerable political influence for matters they care about. And professional politicians know it.

The Coalitions

Given such a diverse array of actors in the twilight zone between officialdom and public, it is not surprising that we find schoolmen in most of our states striving for some form of collaborative endeavor. The coalition may express itself as a permanent organization; it may be a strategic device of a state department of education, as appears to be the case in Rhode Island and possibly New Hampshire, or it may be an *ad hoc* one-time affair as in Massachusetts. But the need is obvious and the trend toward cooperative action unmistakable. The New York Educational Conference Board, the New Hampshire Joint Committee on Needs of Education, the New Jersey "Princeton Group," the Massachusetts Association for Adequate State Financing for Public Schools in the late 1940's, the Connecticut Legislative Coordinating Committee, the Maine Advisory Board, the Rhode Island Liaison Committee are all representative of the urge to coalesce.

New York State Educational Conference Board

Far and away the most impressive of these coalitions is the New York Educational Conference Board. Superficially the Conference Board is an alliance of the major educational interest groups in the state: New York State Teachers Association, New York State School Boards Association, New York State Congress of Parents and Teachers, Public Education Association of New York City, New York State Citizens Committee for the Public Schools, New York State Association of District Superintendents of Schools, New York State Council of School Superintendents, New York State Association of Secondary School Principals, and New York State Association of Elementary School Principals. In reality, however, the Conference Board is a sounding board for and a refiner of the deliberations of an inner core of seven schoolmen. Paul Mort was one of these; and few observers would argue with the statement that he was *primus inter pares* until his death in May 1962. As of this writing, the other six are Arthur W. Schmidt and Lorne H. Woollatt, of the State Department of Education; Howard Goold and Arvid J. Burke, of the New York State Teachers Association; and Everett R. Dyer and Clyde B. Moore, of the New York State School Boards Association.

The New York State Educational Conference Board was created in 1937 by the then secretaries, respectively, of the New York State Teachers Association and the New York State School Boards Association: Arvie Eldred and W. A. Clifford.

The Board was almost precisely modeled on the New York State Conference Board of Farm Organizations, which had been created in 1918 in an attempt of a half dozen farm organizations to reach unanimous agreement on broad questions of agricultural policy which involved state legislative action. The Farm Conference Board had pooled its impressive lobbying power with extraordinary success. Witnessing this strength and this unity, Eldred and Clifford saw in the Farm Conference Board a possible model for public education. These two men were particularly concerned in the 1930's with the destructiveness of the frequent misunderstandings between school boards and school teachers: school boards frequently looking at teachers' demands as exorbitant; teachers looking at school boards as penny-pinching management. The obvious area of possible cooperation between school boards and school teachers was additional state aid. Additional state aid could help satisfy teachers' demands without imposing impossible fiscal burdens upon local school boards. The solution seemed to be for the State Teachers Association and the State School Boards Association to form a united group of all state-wide organizations concerned with the betterment of education, to strive for policy unity on the single subject of state aid, and to present a united front to the Board of Regents, the legislature, and the governor.

Over the years since its founding, the Educational Conference Board has looked to the secretariats of the two major associations and to the research staffs symbolized today by Woollatt and Schmidt in the State Department of Education, and until recently by Paul Mort, in Teachers College, as the strategic and tactical core of the Conference Board's interests. Through all of this, Mort acted as the leading catalyst and synthesizer of the inner group and, through the inner group, of the Conference Board itself.

The "Princeton Group" in New Jersey

The second best example of the coalition is perhaps in New Jersey. When the present Commissioner of Education was appointed in 1952, he felt the necessity for a regular, informal communications device among the schoolmen in the state. The result was the "Princeton Group," so named merely because the Princeton Inn in the college town eleven miles north of Trenton was a pleasant and conveniently central place for all to meet.

There are five member groups in New Jersey which attend meetings called four or five times a year. They are the State Department, New Jersey Education Association, New Jersey Congress of Parents and Teachers, State Federation of District Boards of Education, and the School Superintendents Association. Each group is entitled to send four officials to any conclave of the group. Meetings are called "in turn" by the respective members, but actually it is the Department or the New Jersey Education Association which decides when it is appropriate to get together. Only the highranking officials go to the Inn. For example, the typical delegation from the State Department includes the Commissioner, the

Deputy Commissioner, and two Assistant Commissioners. The character of the meetings is wholly informal since these people have worked together in overlapping capacities for a long time. For example, all the Departmental officials in attendance had been members of the New Jersey Education Association working committees when they were teachers, and still work with New Jersey Education Association committees as state officials.

The group is more of a clearing house than a decision-making body. Here the schoolmen determine where they will agree and where they will disagree. Here also are discussed tactics, general strategy, planning, and execution of various campaigns for school improvements, and here intelligence on the political climate and on possibilities for forward motion is pooled.

The role of the State Department in the Princeton Group has always been a little self-conscious. The officials have found it a very helpful device, but in the last year or so they have been pulling away from leadership in it to avoid becoming identified as a prime mover. The organization has sub-units in several of the more important counties—little "Princeton Groups" generally brought together under the impetus of NJEA rather than of the Department.

This self-effacement by the New Jersey Commissioner indicates his recognition of several important developments in his political sphere. The first is that the "Princeton Group" has become a going concern and no longer needs to lean on the initiative and prestige of the Department. Educational officialdom will unquestionably continue to pull its own weight in the coalition, but as participants, not leaders. Furthermore, the now-established dominance in New Jersey politics of the governor, the only state officer elected at large, and his appointed "Cabinet," of which the Commissioner is a member, prohibits the latter from seeming to lead a special interest. Common sense and prudence agree that the Commissioner must play the governor's game. What some observers interpret as shrinkage of visibility can be more accurately described as political sensitivity. New Jersey seems to have achieved a flexible and comprehensive alliance of key schoolmen.

New Hampshire's "Joint Committee"

An example of a far more tenuous basis of coalescence is found in New Hampshire. Sparked by the New Hampshire Education Association, all of the state's schoolmen have come together to form the Joint Committee on the Needs of Education. Stimulated by a certain disorder in the introduction of school legislation in recent sessions of the General Court, the Committee's present aim is to insure a united front at the Capitol. With representatives from the Department of Education, the New Hampshire Supervisory Association, the Council for Better Schools, the Education Association, the State Congress of Parents and Teachers, and chaired by the Executive Secretary of the Association of School Boards, the Committee meets every five or six weeks to define school needs and to seek ways of meeting them.

It is early yet to predict whether the Joint Committee will grow into a decision-maker like the Conference Board or a clearing-house like the "Princeton Group." What is clear is that the Joint Committee has within it the potential to go either way. True, the promising new alliance has yet to agree on its tactics but its initial success in getting a fair dismissal bill for teachers has whetted its appetite for political action. Its member groups will attempt to speak with one voice and will coordinate their activities insofar as they are able. All their work has been aimed at the legislature, whose members they variously buttonhole, banquet, and address. Like the other coalitions, New Hampshire's Joint Committee is comprehensive but it still ranks with Massachusetts as representative of the states where permanency is not assured.

The other states in the area have, or have had, similar coalitions, although their life, visibility, and effectiveness have varied substantially.

Other Political and Economic Forces

Schoolmen have not only willing allies—at times they have strange allies—but also help from interest groups which on first inspection one would not expect to be in education's camp. Generally, this support occurs when the aims of schoolmen coincide with the objectives of those concerned with the structure of state finance, and especially state-local tax relations. Associations of municipal officials seeking tax relief and sophisticated taxpayers' federations often have deemed it in their best interests to shift school financial loads to the state.

Massachusetts provides the best illustration of this outside support. In its drive for a new school aid program in the late 1940's, one principal rallying point was the Massachusetts Federation of Taxpayers Associations. Established in the late 1930's, its stated objectives compare to those of taxpayers organizations everywhere: "to seek out and fight waste and extravagance in government . . . develop and demand sound and economical governmental policies and practices, to strive constantly for better legislation and improved legislative procedures, to improve the business climate in Massachusetts, to inform and educate the citizens of Massachusetts about what goes on in their government."[6] But in this generation, at least, the taxpayers have been a major source of help to the schools. In particular, the services of their municipal consultant Lyman Ziegler, and the library and research resources of the organization have been critically important in the drive for state aid. Ziegler emerges as a sort of father of school legislation. The Massachusetts Federation sees expanded school aid as a key lever in improving state-local fiscal relations, generally reducing the burden of local property taxes, and redressing fiscal imbalances between small towns and cities and larger towns.

The sort of assistance the tax group provided in Massachusetts has been provided perhaps more sporadically and indirectly in Connecticut by the Connecticut Public Expenditures Council, and by companion taxpayers' associations in Rhode Island and New Hampshire. In the latter state, John Langmuir was a crucial figure in organizing and advising the special study commissions in that state which battled for greater state aid in the late 1940's. The central point is that the guardians of the public purse are not always aligned against schoolmen. In the complicated world of public finance, school aid legislation may help to readjust state and local tax burdens and provide relief for particular taxpayers and particularly hardpressed ones. A tax group working in a public atmosphere of conservative political ideology may, on occasion, be something for educators to regard with fear and trembling. But this is not always the case. A tax group swimming upstream in a welfare state may become an important and powerful ally. And business groups other than the well-established tax federations can also prove sympathetic.

This proposition needs elaboration, for the constellation of business interests is often blindly tagged as anti-tax at all levels of government. On occasion it is. But it is certainly concerned not only with the total tax levy, but its distribution. What these interests oppose is state or local taxation which discriminates excessively against business. Throughout the Northeast local taxes are levied almost wholly against real property (over 95 per cent in most states) and revenues from them go largely to maintain local schools. Where and when local property taxes become consequential items in a company's budget, then its management becomes tax-minded. For instance, major pulp and paper industries own vast forests in northern Maine, but, since this land is classed as unimproved even though the woods enjoy expert silviculture, taxes on corporate property in this section are piddling; the Maine Pulp and Paper Association does not fret over them. On the other hand—and much more commonly throughout the Northeast— industrial associations agitate against high local property taxes on their plants and office buildings. Often these plants and office buildings are new and shiny suburban ornaments. Their home municipalities have relatively high tax rates anyway—mostly thanks to schools—and local volunteer assessors frequently regard business construction as a blessed source of local tax relief. The upshot is that in many instances corporations find themselves hit with high assessments to go with the stiff tax rates, a combination producing inordinately large tax bills. One major Massachusetts corporation, for instance, pays every year half of the local taxes collected by the middle-sized suburban city in which its home office is located. This firm, and the business associations it belongs to, would not object if it owned half the city's real property, but this is far from the case. Such discrimination appears to be endemic in all the industrialized areas of the region. And business groups are against it.

What the organizations are pushing for instead are broad-based taxes levied impartially on all sectors within the state. By definition such taxes are state taxes—most commonly on sales. Sales taxes, in particular, come to be preferred by business groups as they seek to shift burdens to the non-business sector of the community. A heavy property tax on a manufacturing concern will raise costs and make the firm's life more difficult; a sales tax does not appear to the business firm to have such adverse effects. This is not to say that all business associations are against the property tax or local governments. What they dislike is taxation that they feel discriminates against their membership—and tax discrimination, they feel, is often characteristic of local taxes whose only base is real property.

Given broad-based state taxes impartially levied, state and local Chambers of Commerce and Associations of Manufacturers have not proved unduly restive about the rising costs of school government. In Maine, for instance, a prime mover in the long and difficult campaign for greatly increased and sound financing of state school subsidies was vice-president (now president) of the Bangor Hydro-Electric Company and a director both of the Maine Chamber of Commerce and of the Electric Council of New England. A close and keen student of New Jersey state politics recently observed that he foresaw only token opposition from the state's business groups to more money for state school aid so long as the funds came from a sales tax. Connecticut's tax-minded groups feel they have already gone pretty far in shifting taxation to the state, and they claim local schools have not suffered from the shift. Responsibility and competence, not cost, are frequently the considerations of the tax-minded.

On balance, one is hard put to it to suggest that all business organizations are school-tax-minded. Many local Chambers of Commerce take relationships with their local schools quite seriously and work hard at improving them. Most national industrial associations have given a good deal of time and thought to devising and promoting programs for industrial aid to education. And, indeed, the New England Council, an organization created to promote the economy of the six northernmost states and largely dominated by business, has had for several years a man working full-time promoting all manner of business assistance to schools. A great deal of this activity, of course, lies quite outside the realm of tax policy. Lectures by industrial experts, guided tours of plants and factories, demonstrations of sophisticated equipment, scholarships, summer jobs for teachers and students come at once to mind.

On balance, it is hard to defend the proposition that tax-minded groups are implacable enemies. At specific times and places, business groups oppose taxes which appear to them discriminatory or irresponsible. When and where broad-based state taxes for school support are concerned, many business associations have been more than passive. At times they have been forces for improvement.

Conclusion

In broad strokes, then, these are the groups which are most generally aligned in the efforts for increased state school aid. Building upon the overt and latent interests in better education in the society as a whole, scribblers, governors, legislators, party leaders, teachers and their lay disciples, in sympathetic coalition with particular business interests constitute, when united, a powerful alliance. But they do not have their way unopposed. School politics generates countervailing interests, pressures, and opposition. Before it is possible to evaluate the true political skill of the schoolmen it is necessary to know who and what stands against them. The phrase "who and what" is deliberate, for the identification of counterpressures is tantalizingly difficult to pin down. These are termed "depressants" and their characteristics are outlined in the chapter which follows.

DEPRESSANTS: IMAGINED AND REAL

In view of the steady increase in general state aid to education in the Northeast since the end of World War II, it may be argued that depressants have been singularly unsuccessful. On the other hand, most schoolmen would argue that state legislatures would have gone much further than they have in state aid had it not been for both overt and invisible opposition.

The political process involves dynamic tensions. There are people for something. There are people against something. In the case of state aid, most of the schoolmen are highly visible even when they are unsuccessful. The problem of identifying and analyzing the schoolmen's opposition is, on the other hand, a complex and difficult exercise.

No responsible citizen ever says he is against schools—especially public schools. On the other hand, responsible citizens can and do argue that at a given time and at a given place something else is more pressing. And as we shall see, many citizens—responsible or not—argue that education should be kept local and that increased state financial involvement in local education is a threat to cherished principles of local autonomy. But the true depressants in the area of school aid seem to transcend identifiable individuals and groups. Political and economic conservatism in large sections of the Northeast is a pervasive climate of opinion which conditions the actions and reactions of men in authority. The problem in this chapter is not only to identify the specific men and institutions opposed to the demands of schoolmen for increased school aid, but to treat of some of the intangible attitudes which permeate all decision-making at the state level.

Before making this attempt, however, a highly complex and widely misunderstood alleged depressant must be discussed.

The Roman Catholic Church

What first comes to many minds as a possible depressant on state school support is the only large scale, across-the-board competition public schools have: the Roman Catholic educational system. School for school and level by level, the Church is parallel with the state. There are parochial grade schools and high schools at the local level; diocesan high schools at the regional level; Catholic colleges and universities at the level of higher education. Nor is the similarity with public education institutional only. In most parishes attendance at the Church's schools is as compulsory as the hierarchy and existing facilities can make it. And so are levies and tuitions against parishioners requested by the Church to pay for these schools and their operation.

Teaching is the expressed vocation of many Catholic regular orders. In education, the separation of church and state becomes a matter of moment when the schools of one become a complete and reasonable alternative to those of the other. The fact is that today in many a northeastern city the parochial schools' enrollment and pupil population year after year equals that of the public schools. Given the increase in the region's total population and its increasing shift into metropolitan areas, the Church's ability to keep pace both with its own parishioners and with its public counterpart presents no mean accomplishment. This is particularly true when it is remembered that, increasingly, Church schools have been forced to enter the lay market for teachers in order to find the quantity and quality of staff needed to meet the continuous postwar expansion of parochial education.

It would be easy to jump to the conclusion—as many people have—that self-interest would dictate a massive and uniform opposition of loyal Catholics to increased spending for public schools. Not only do Catholics subject themselves to what they sometimes refer to as "double taxation" for education, but any substantial advantage given to public schools in the form of higher salaries for teachers increases the competitive disadvantage of parochial school interests in attracting qualified staff to teach in Catholic schools.

Logical inference in this case is, however, not supported by empirical evidence. Certainly there have been times and places in which assumed or real attitudes of the Catholic populations and of leaders of the Church have had a depressant effect on local public school finance. But there is no evidence whatsoever that this has been the result of a conscious policy on the part of the Catholic hierarchy. Local priests and local politicians have often responded negatively to demands for increases in local public education budgets out of sensitivity to the double education burden placed upon Catholic voters. On the other hand, there have been scores of examples of Catholic laymen, Catholic members of local schools boards, and Catholic politicians taking the leadership in promoting the cause of public education in heavily Catholic districts.

It should not be forgotten that a vast number of Catholic children are still educated in the public school system. It should not be forgotten either that Catholics are also Americans and most of them have a sense of community responsibility which far transcends the limited interests of the Church.

But even if it could be proved that Catholicism by and large is a depressant upon local spending for public education, no evidence could be found in this study to support the proposition that the Church has used its influence to hold down the level of state aid to public education. There is plenty of evidence to document the Church's interest in increased state services for parochial school children—in such fields as transportation, health, and welfare. There is also evidence to indicate that Catholic interests can be affected by the nature of state aid formulae. The most explicit example of this was in Massachusetts in the late forties, when the Bishop of Fall River stated that a projected state aid bill would be the most inequitable bill the state has ever passed. But the "inequity" in the bill, in the Bishop's mind, was the fact that state aid was to be apportioned on the basis of a census of *public* school children. The Massachusetts General Court, responding to the Bishop's statement, dropped the word "public" from the phrase "public school children." The effect of this deletion was simply to increase state aid to localities with a heavy parochial school attendance. This meant in turn that all taxpayers in the area—including of course Catholic taxpayers—would pay a lower percentage of the total public school cost, with a lower local tax. Local priests would obviously find it easier to raise parochial school money than if the local tax were higher.

But an interest in the nature of a state aid formula is a far cry from opposition to state aid. For those who argue that increased state aid to public education decreases the competitive advantage of parochial schools, Catholic spokesmen can and do argue back that state aid eases the burden on local property taxes, that it provides additional income to Catholic communicants who represent the majority of public schools teachers in at least half the states of the Northeast, and that it improves the quality of education for the hundreds of thousands of Catholic pupils who still attend public schools. Furthermore, the number of instances in which Catholics have performed leadership roles in increasing state aid to public schools is impressive.

Rhode Island adopted the most open-ended state aid formula in the Northeast with a Roman Catholic priest as chairman of its state Board of Education and a Roman Catholic Commissioner of Education. Maine's Protestant legislature passed the most liberal state school subsidy in its history with the strong and active backing of a Catholic governor. Connecticut, certainly not one of the backward states in terms of state aid in the area, also has a Catholic Commissioner of Education. The pioneering attempts to create state aid formulae in the entire Northeast were undertaken in the State of New York in the 1920's. The Governor was Alfred E. Smith. Throughout the Northeast, school aid bills have been passed by legislatures most of which are overwhelmingly Catholic in at least one of their two houses.

In short, there is no evidence whatsoever to suggest that the Roman Catholic church has been a depressant upon state aid to public education. Neither is there any evidence to suggest that the Church hierarchy has taken leadership in the struggle for additional state aid, although there is substantial evidence that individual Catholic laymen have provided strong, if intermittent, leadership for the achievement of break-throughs at the state level in granting additional financial assistance to local school districts. Whatever may be true of the Church as a depressant upon local and federal public school spending—and even here the story is mixed—the Church cannot be reasonably accused of being a depressant at the level of state aid.

Tax-Minded Business Depressants

In the previous chapter certain tax-minded business groups were identified as uncommon bedfellows of the schoolmen. But this is far from a universal phenomenon. And here we turn to the first of our real depressants, for the fact is that the inclination of many tax-minded business groups is to oppose at every level of government taxes which strike them as discriminatory, or assessments which they feel are disproportionate to postulated social gains. Even when increased taxation is deemed necessary or inevitable, many business groups fight additional taxes until they are satisfied that the incidence of taxation is relatively favorable to business interests.

In New Jersey, for example, conservative business groups have begun to soften their opposition to a broad-base state tax—but only on condition that the tax is a sales tax. This single-mindedness is at loggerheads with a growing conviction among many political leaders—especially in the Democratic Party—that an income tax would be more equitable and efficient. As long as these two influential groups stand in opposition over the kind of broad-base tax to have, campaigns to get any new major state tax will be protracted. This in turn has inevitably a depressant effect upon additional state aid to education.

The same kind of condition has existed in Connecticut. In both states, the chance for increased state aid has been a victim of a more general struggle over the form of new state taxes. The implications for substantial increases in state aid to education have been quite as serious as though the schoolmen had been tackled head-on.

In some states tax-minded business interests have gone far beyond arguing over the nature of new state taxes. They have flatly opposed new state taxes of any kind. For years on end, in the state of New Hampshire, the railroad lobby led the fight against any sort of broad state taxes. In recent years the place of the railroad lobby has been taken by the Paper and Pulp Association. The most cohesive force in the entire state, tax-minded business groups, has managed to get its own way for years. This force has been so consistent and insistent in its effect upon legislative behavior that it surely must be considered one of the prime reasons why New Hampshire ranks near the bottom of the list of all states in the union in its proportion of state aid to education.

Localism

The most pervasive and persistent of depressants on state school subsidies is rural localism, whose proponents are typically overrepresented in state legislatures throughout most of the Northeast. These stalwarts are emphatically not against good schools. Their main concern, however, is to oppose, and, if possible, to thwart, the pernicious growth of the power of the state government. On their side they have, in this section of the country, three hundred years of tradition as well as the support and intensity of their own parochial mode of living. Occupied for the most part as farmers or as primary extractors of natural wealth, they are tied to fixed locations and bound by their own local preoccupations. Their legislative frame of reference begins—and all too often ends—with consideration of their own community's advantage. They grapple with law-making by applying the only standards they feel sure of—hometown benefit. Since their rooted existence, if not their manner of enterprise, is akin to that of the eighteenth century, they can speak to modern legislatures with the hallowed tones of their fore-fathers, venerable and well-tested.

These good and sincere Jeffersonians never really examine how much autonomy their schools have. At best, their address is negative; their aim is opposition to increasing state power in education. They are devoted to the antique Yankee rule of thumb that every tub should stand on its own bottom, but they do not define their terse and tidy terms. Their devotion to elementary schooling is complete and unrestrained—if their children can come home for lunch and if bus transportation is neither expensive nor long. They cherish high school education—if their youngsters are not needed at home or in the fields. They want good teachers—if their salaries, by local standards, are not plutocratic. (A Maine legislator recently felt compelled for this reason to oppose a minimum starting salary for teachers of $3200.) They flatly oppose large modern school buildings as extravagant and lush. Rural legislators find schooling on these terms expensive, different from their own education, and incomprehensibly remote. Indeed, they care too much. Schooling is the major effort of their local governments, a level of operation they love too intimately and manage too handily to delegate.

There is nothing venal in this posture. It enjoys all the respect of long and widespread usage. It is almost never espoused by legislators considering personal gain. It has philosophical roots at least as old and as positive as the Kentucky and Virginia Resolutions. It handles the routine vote-getting at election time. It is consistent. It continues to affirm the American faith in grassroots democracy. What it lacks is sympathetic and thorough examination—and translation to modern circumstances. Without this redefinition, modern rural localism with the best of good intentions works against increasing state school aid.

It does so in at least two ways with a range of effectiveness dependent on the political discipline of the particular northeastern state. The first of these drawbacks is simple non-contribution of political support—a function of lack of understanding and lack of interest. The champions of localism do not compre-

hend the educational advantages of relatively large and diverse student populations—say of no less than 500. Nor can they really accept the meaning of
large-scale urban poverty. Educational fair play has an unreal and hollow ring in
their ears. With these gaps in their understanding, modern townsmen have little
to contribute to the formation and support of responsible state school policy.
And many of them are intelligent and energetic men with a large capacity to
contribute to policy development in their states.

But their sterility as statesmen, in the exact sense of the word, is only part
of the mischief they cause state school aid. Oftentimes they actively oppose it.

Localism is not confined to the rural hinterland of the Northeast. Some
business and professional men in New Jersey, largely centered in wealthy North
Jersey suburbs, have been against taxation for school aid increases not so much
from any general anti-tax attitude as from a very real localism. They do not want
to support schools in South Jersey or anywhere away from home, and know that
this is what increases in state aid would mean under present formulae. They may
or may not rebel against high or higher property taxes at home; they at least
know where the money is spent. This local chauvinism is roundly supported by
the North Jersey spokesman, *The Newark News.*

To an almost unique degree, New Hampshire combines an aggressive spirit for
economic development with small-town settings for the daily life of its residents.
In political terms, these forces have expressed themselves in a high degree of
consciousness of the need to attract and maintain industry and a conservative
outlook on governmental activity indigenous to semi-rural circumstances. An
undercurrent of localism runs strong in the New Hampshire General Court. The
notion that the state has any real educational responsibilities and the fear that it
may be bent on wiping out the now existing 230 school districts are particular
concerns. To many small town legislators, the essence of a good education is a
little high school with its basketball team carrying the name of the town to
victory. This peculiarly up-to-date affirmation of localism finds legislative expression in justly celebrated state frugality. The General Court has systematically
frustrated the workings of aid formulae that would put more state money into
local school budgets. Add to this the failure and disinclination of the General
Court to take seriously school reorganization or to deal with any major items on
the schoolmen's agenda, and the inability of New Hampshire to mount a
comprehensive educational program becomes understandable. Since the Second
World War, the state's portion of annual total school operating expenses has
ranged between 2 per cent and 7 per cent.

In Massachusetts, émigrés from Boston to the suburbs find the tradition of
localism full of convenient ideological ammunition for little or no action at the
state level. As they come to cluster in towns inhabited by like-minded and
similarly situated neighbors, the disposition grows to "do-it-yourself" in government as well as in home repair. So Massachusetts local property taxes have

climbed to the highest in the nation, and school programs elsewhere assumed by the state are retained by the town or city in Massachusetts. To many of the most enlightened civic leaders this posture makes sense. As the process of diffusion goes on, each community can set its own style for schools, and for those that choose excellence in education, state aid is not likely to help unless it achieves the Rhode Island potential. With ample local resources, the well-off are not disposed to help the less-well-endowed communities. "Look at it this way," a former superintendent of the Newton system pointed out, "a state formula which really equalized would allow a lot of communities to upgrade their systems. The first thing they'd be after is better teachers and that would spell competition for us. As it is now, we're close to a monopoly." A few well-to-do suburbs in Massachusetts are content; towns with more to gain financially by state action may have a heavy Catholic population only indirectly concerned with the public system. In either instance, there are no strong motives for state action.

Conservative Politicians

Conservative, tax-minded legislators are both an effect and a cause of a conservative ethos in the political life of a state. Bolstered in their attitudes by editorial support from a generally conservative press, often elected with the active support of powerful business interests from one-party districts, many legislative leaders in the Northeast in turn become articulate spokesmen for frugality and localism in government. Their words are news, and a reinforcing cycle is established.

Appropriations committees, as watch-dogs of the state treasury, are often foci for such conservatism. Such committees usually take a proprietary interest in the funds they allocate. In session after session in state after state, house and senate appropriations committees rank at the top in seniority and prestige—and consequently in power. Their caution is not selective. Their axe is not aimed at school subsidies alone. But appropriations committees have a role to play, and this is often antagonistic to the spending recommendations of outside groups or of other legislative standing committees, including education committees. The priorities of education committees and appropriations committees legitimately differ in accordance with their separate responsibilities. The difference often shows up in amounts recommended by the former which are cut by the latter. A case in point occurred in Massachusetts in 1949 when a school aid bill reported out of the education committee of the legislature called for a $28 million increase. The Appropriations Committee cut the amount to $14 million. The original $28 million was chopped in half by the simple expedient of dividing the proposed distribution formula by two. Tax-conscious leaders in the legislature had performed a routine operation. The pattern is sufficiently familiar not to need further elaboration.

Competing Demands

Education is not the only item on the agenda of a state's budget. At any one point in time, the demands for additional appropriations for highways, welfare, conservation, prisons, police, courts, or any of the other responsibilities of state governments, may be insistent. The very competition for state money is frequently, at a given time and place, a major depressant upon additional state aid to education. Even when a governor and a legislature are reasonably friendly to the cause of education, the essence of governance is the allocation of resources to a variety of functions of which education is only one. The more sophisticated and insistent the demands for increased state spending for non-educational purposes, the more difficult the problem for the schoolmen and their allies.

Executive Conservatism

In more northeastern states than one this prudence has basked in explicit and decisive executive support. Vermont, New Hampshire, Connecticut, and New Jersey have all recently had governors who for one reason or another have opposed or seriously slowed down increased state spending for education. And here again the prohibition has not been selective; any other item of growing state expense would have been as dispassionately discouraged. In each of these states, the chief executive has felt compelled to hold some fiscal line or another—state expenses, state taxes, the value of the dollar. In Vermont, in 1961, Governor Keyser flatly opposed any increase in state spending for school assistance, regardless of the hopelessness of correcting inequalities without it. The governor's budget message was in detail, department by department, line by line. It was "wholly adequate and necessary to provide government services for a progressive Vermont." To go further would require "tax levies that would stagnate economic growth." State school aid grants were budgeted for $5,480,000 in 1962 and $5,540,000 in 1963, increases of $750,000 over which Governor Keyser was careful to point out he had no control. But there was no guesswork about the governor's implication: any departmental legislation would have to stay within the confines of the executive budget, or else.

In postwar New Jersey, both Governor Driscoll and Governor Meyner supported increased school aid, but at a level which did nothing to increase the percentage of the school burden carried by the state. The former imposed a budget ceiling; the latter avoided the basic revenue issues whose resolution alone would have made increased state aid to education possible.

In New York, in 1948, Governor Dewey set a flat amount of money he was willing to consider as a reasonable increase for general state aid. This was determinative, although far below the demands of the schoolmen.

In Connecticut, state school aid eased upwards six years in a row under

Governor Ribicoff; but Connecticut schoolmen inside and outside of the Department of Education are convinced that the amount of increase was far less than Connecticut's wealth would have allowed. They place the blame upon Governor Ribicoff's fiscal conservatism.

In New Hampshire, Governor Powell in his 1961 budget message went so far as to single out educators for seeking unjustified increases as he lopped $9.76 million off their state aid appropriation request.

This is essentially a kind of tax-mindedness located where it counts most. Any governor has great political power on his side. He is a hard man to fight, especially when he wants to hold the line on state finance. There is nothing pejorative in this conclusion; it is a cold fact of political life. Responsible, experienced, powerful, and tax-minded governors, and their budget officers and political advisers have on occasion acted as real depressants on state school aid in the Northeast.

But legislative and gubernatorial conservatism has been a natural function of the prudential conservatism of elective partisan politics generally. Politicians are subject to a total evaluation at the polls. Responsible party leaders cannot risk their own or their organization's standing with voters by proposing radically increased state expenditures at any one time in the absence of a strong public mandate. Strong public mandates are hard to come by, particularly for something as relatively invisible as local school subsidies. In most northeastern states, state assistance has increased steadily over the years, but the change each time has been relatively moderate, rarely sharp. This incremental speed may not be as fast as hard-pressed schoolmen might like, but it usually wins the applause of a relatively conservative press and reflects the eternal conflict within citizen-taxpayers: their desire for service; their reluctance to pick up the check. State politics in the Northeast works gradually to achieve its educational goals. In the eyes of many schoolmen, the spirit of gradualism is a depressant.

The Splintered Schoolmen

Frequently schoolmen themselves have made their own programs easy to oppose. Far and away the most common handicap to increasing school subsidies in the eight states has been the inability of schoolmen to work and speak as one for a responsible general school aid bill. Effective organization is exceptional. Most of the time in most of the states disorder and naivete are the schoolmen's outstanding political characteristics.

To begin with, public education is almost endlessly organized. In every state there exist at least four kinds of official educational agencies—the state board, the state department, local boards, and local departments. And local boards commonly have their own independent state association. These official agencies rarely act in unison. The real proliferation, however, is on the private and professional side. Every state has its education association, sometimes at war with a teachers' union in a major metropolitan area. There are state-wide associations of school principals and of school superintendents, of guidance counsellors, of teachers of vocational education, of coaches and teachers of physical education, and of classroom teachers. The public joins in the Parent-Teachers Associations and has its own councils for better schools. Associations of University Women, Leagues of Women Voters, Federations of Women's Clubs, Women's Legislative Councils all have strong concern for schooling. Associations for Mental Health and for Retarded Children represent special educational interests in many northeastern states. Furthermore, many members of these groups really care about the organizations' impact, and their officers work hard at representing the real or divined wishes of the membership. Each of these public and private groups has its own pet concern and its special momentum. The number of special educational interests stirs up a vast—and often infuriating—buzzing in a lawmaker's ears. The wily lawmaker finds it easy to ignore educators disunited—or to play one educational group off against another.

The root difficulty is that too few states have a permanent forum where ardent schoolmen can organize their interests and coordinate their activities into orderly, clear, political campaigns. More than once school groups have lined up publicly on opposite sides of the same bill. Vermont's recent experience reveals this disorganization at its starkest, but disunities of the same sort can be found in state after state. What Vermont's General Assembly was asked to cope with at its 1961 session is worth recording: both from within and without the State Board of Education, public attention had been focused on the patent inequalities of the state aid formula. No state organization had a stake in the existing one; indeed, most clear sentiment favored its revision. But here unanimity ended. Two dominant members of the State Board favored a formula that would reward local excellence—small classes, highly qualified staff, rich and diversified curriculum, and similar so-called lighthouse subsidies. The Commissioner favored an equalized minimum foundation program which would scale assistance to the wealth of the state's districts in such a way as to prevent educational poverty resulting from financial poverty. The other members of the Board wavered between these poles, ultimately siding publicly with its leaders. In the meantime, an independent advisory committee to the Board studied the problem and came out publicly on the side of the Commissioner. The Vermont Education Association, the state's most powerful professional group, refused to take sides but urged formula revision of some sort. The Vermont School Directors Association, a state-wide organization of school board members, was more in favor of the existing formula than of either of its alternatives. The dozen remaining professional groups in the state were too small and distant to make themselves heard in Montpelier. The result was a public confusion of advices, each given by associations small enough in themselves to be ignored by the legislature. They were so ignored, and an inadequate formula remains in force. The issue is not which formula might be right or wrong for Vermont. The issue is that the state's schoolmen were unable to agree on a common program and to work in harness to get it.

But it is no easy thing to get schoolmen—especially professionals—to agree on state aid allocations. Indeed, educators in the Northeast can be found in a variety of distant camps. There are backers of general state aid: state subsidies for local operating expenses, to be allocated as the local jurisdiction wishes. There are also backers of general, unrestricted school construction assistance. These two are across-the-board financial programs with few strings attached. Far and away the bulk of state school aid is of this sort, but schoolmen differ on which is needed most at a particular time.

But these general "aiders" are frequently at war with the defenders or sponsors of more limited categorical aid. Under categorical aid, funds go for special education of some variety of even for special schools—for the deaf, the blind, the crippled; for Americanization, for veterans or their orphans; for home economics or for agriculture. By and large, the amounts currently devoted by states to these restricted programs are only a very minor portion of state aid, but categories could logically be multiplied to include almost every facet of schooling. While the over-all cost of general aid as opposed to the totality of special aids might theoretically be the same, the political and institutional implications differ radically. General aid implies that schoolmen can and should stand or fall together in legislative campaigns. Categorical aid implies professional independence for every special educational interest and the devil take the hindermost. There has been no explicit comparison of the political strength of these two approaches. Universally, however, the northeastern states have moved away in the last fifteen years from bundles of categorical subsidies to general programs except for schools for handicapped children. The question is insistent, however: would not general state aid have moved faster and farther if the depressant of categorical aids—with all of the divisiveness therein implied—had not had to be negotiated?

Another major division among schoolmen splits the professionals and the trade unionists. This separation is somewhat restricted, however, in that only big city school systems have been unionized. Where strong teachers' unions have been formed, hard-headed militance is the order of the day. The emphasis is on salary scales, hours of work, holidays, and collective bargaining. Only teachers' unions have called strikes. Bread and butter issues may be rationalized on the ground that children are to benefit more from well-paid and contented teachers than from ill-paid and discontented ones; but the style of unionism is offensive to the so-called professionals in education. Teachers' unions charge professional associations with prissiness and company unionism. Professional educators accuse educational trade unions of crass self-seeking, and of demeaning the white-collar character of the teaching profession. In New York State, where the issue is hottest, the incapacity of teachers' unions and educational professional associations to work in common cause has had an inconclusive effect upon state aid. It is fair to say, however, that until December, 1961, when the United Federation of Teachers was voted the sole bargaining agent for teachers in the New York City school system, the internecine warfare in New York City among union-minded and non-union-minded educators (and even within these respective groups) seriously limited the capacity of New York City schoolmen to influence state aid policy. The first state legislative session following the resolution of the bitter struggles within New York City saw the most pronounced advance in state aid for urban areas in the state's history; and even if the prime cause for this was a shift in Educational Conference Board policy, a consolidated teachers' union in New York City provided a unity of metropolitan support lacking in previous years.

In sum, all too often political activity by schoolmen in the Northeast has been amateur politics, with all the zeal and disorder the phrase conveys. On balance, this lack of political sophistication and discipline among schoolmen assumes major proportions in depressing state assistance. Many law makers would respond favorably to financial appeals that schoolmen can make when they agree on common goals. Most legislators, small-towners or not, find it difficult to withstand coordinated pressure from their grass roots. Special pleading by splinter educational groups stirs up an uneasy suspicion of excess among responsible statesmen, whether legislators or governors. Governors may honestly disagree with responsible schoolmen on school finance, but the schoolmen's case, if orderly and well-organized, cannot be brushed aside. In many northeastern states, schoolmen have handicapped their own political success by their failure to understand, develop, and use political machinery available within their own ranks.

Conclusion

The major depressants upon general school aid, then, can be found in certain tax-minded business groups, in traditions of localism, in the conservatism of politicians responding to ambivalent public expectation, and in the disorder and naivete of educators themselves. How these depressants affect and condition the designs of the schoolmen in the policy-making process is the subject of the next chapter.

FOOTNOTES

[1]J. M. Keynes, *General Theory of Employment, Interest and Money* (London: Macmillan and Co., Ltd., 1936), 383.

[2]George D. Strayer and R. M. Haig, *The Financing of Education in the State of New York* (New York: The Macmillan Company, 1923).

[3]Paul R. Mort, *State Support for Public Schools* (New York: Teachers College, Columbia University, 1926).

[4]In an interview with Dr. Paul Mandry, Executive Secretary, New Hampshire Association of School Boards, August 22, 1961.

[5]Duane Lockard, *New England Politics* (Princeton: Princeton University Press, 1959).

[6]Massachusetts Federation of Taxpayers Association, "Conscientious Corporate Citizens Safeguard your Business Climate," (Statement of Objectives and Activities of the Association, mimeographed, undated).

MICHIGAN: THE LACK OF CONSENSUS*

Nicholas A. Masters, Robert H. Salisbury and Thomas H. Eliot

Explaining how major public school issues are decided—or not decided—in Michigan is much more difficult than it is for either Illinois or Missouri. In the latter two states, formulas have been developed to achieve consensus. The MSTA in Missouri, representing virtually all of the claimants, adjusts its demands each year to what the other participants in the decisions will accept, and consequently most of its recommendations are adopted. Similarly, in Illinois the School Problems Commission, combining the stated goals of the professional educators with a recognition of political realities is able to formulate proposals acceptable to all elements within the legislature, as well as the governor. Although it is true that a whole series of elaborate negotiations, clearances, and strategies are necessary to achieve consensus on education recommendations in these two states, each of them presents a much simpler picture than Michigan, where there is no group that has come to represent the "best thinking possible to solve the state's education problems."

In Michigan there is no continuous or regular pattern of decision-making, or at least none that is easily visible. The final outcome of recommendations cannot be safely predicted as it can much of the time in Illinois and Missouri. That is, there is no established process in Michigan to eliminate or modify the factors that cause conflict over education issues. Does this mean, then, that Michigan has a "better" or "worse" record than Illinois or Missouri? Does it mean that there is never a consensus in Michigan, or that there will invariably be conflict and unpredictability in the Michigan scheme of things? The absence of a clear, visible pattern of decision-making in Michigan does not necessarily imply that the results achieved are less impressive than those in other states or that it is impossible to bring about wide acceptance of a policy proposal or series of proposals. But each year a new pattern emerges with the outcome in doubt until final decisions are reached.

The factors that make Michigan contrast so sharply with the two other states are easily identified but not easily explained. First, the education groups that make demands on the legislature are no longer unified. Second, the failure to adopt a state-wide school district reorganization plan immediately after World

---

*From *State Politics and Public Schools* by Thomas H. Eliot, Nicholas A. Masters and Robert H. Salisbury, Alfred A. Knopf, 1964, pp. 179-227. Reprinted by permission of the authors.

War II has resulted in a situation where the wealthy and poorer districts display a considerable self-consciousness over their conflicting interests, and these divisions are reflected and articulated within the legislature when school district reorganization or state aid is the issue. Third, there is a longstanding cleavage between two ideologically oriented parties. Since one party controls the governor's office and the other controls the state legislature (particularly the Senate), and since they disagree widely over the extent and method of financing state services, their division has caused education "to divide along political lines." Finally, it should be mentioned that there is a division between the proponents of public schools and the protectors of the parochial and private schools. This division seems to be based more on economic than religious grounds, but in any event it is largely latent at present.

In this chapter we will first identify the various groups that make claims on the state concerning education and analyze the potential resources of influence of each. Secondly, we will discuss the political context in which the education interests must operate and their relationships with the governor and the state legislature. Thirdly, we will examine two issues, one involving state aid and the other involving reorganization of school districts, to determine how the aforementioned factors—lack of unity among education interests, wealthy vs. poor districts, and partisanship—have been more disruptive in this state than they have been in either Illinois or Missouri. The major question this chapter attempts to answer is why a clear decision-making pattern was not operative in Michigan.

Education Interest Groups

"I was elected to the Senate Education Committee to keep those bastards in education in line." This remark, made by a ranking member of the Senate Education Committee of the 1961 Michigan Legislature, indicates more than just his personal feelings toward public school interests; it captures the essence of the reaction of many legislators to the demands made by public school interests in Michigan.

During the past decade the groups advocating major changes in public school policy in this state have faced a legislature that was sometimes hostile, sometimes indifferent, and only occasionally sympathetic to their demands. In the face of rather formidable obstacles, the public school interests have sought, through various means, to create an alliance capable of obtaining the legislation they want. The nature of the alliance that has evolved and the potential and actual influence of each group is the focus of the study of state politics and the public schools in Michigan.

Michigan has no dominant spokesman for the public schools. It has no governmental agency analogous to the School Problems Commission in Illinois and no group which has influence comparable to that experienced by the Missouri State Teachers Association. Nor does Michigan have a state board to back policy proposals or decisions with prestigious lay support. Rather, in Michigan, demands for changes in public school policy are voiced by an array of groups that are seldom in complete agreement but which sometimes join together to push for favorable action on a particular issue. Frequently, their approach and their views as to what issues should be given highest priority differ sharply.

There have been efforts to unite the education interests behind one common authoritative spokesman. The superintendent of public instruction, seeking a broad base for the development and support of his education program, attempts to unify the various groups through an Educational Council, composed of representatives from each public school interest. The council, which meets weekly throughout the year to consider major education issues, has, for reasons which will be discussed later, enjoyed only limited success. To a large extent the various participant groups still follow their own individual programs, regardless of the decisions reached within the council.

There are two types of groups that make active demands for public school legislation in Michigan. (We did not make this distinction in Illinois and Missouri because it appeared less relevant to a meaningful discussion of school politics in those states.) In the first category are the groups whose members have *a direct tangible stake* in the legislative decisions on education questions and which *make specific demands* upon the various decision-makers. In this category the major groups are the Michigan Education Association (MEA), the Michigan Association of School Administrators (MASA), the Michigan Association of County School Administrators (MACSA), the Michigan Federation of Teachers (MFT), and the Michigan Association of School Boards (MASB).

We call the second type of group a supportive group. A supportive group has *a major interest* in education policy, but either its members are normally not directly employed by public schools or the organization does not consider itself a spokesman for the professionals. Groups of this type make fewer specific demands upon the decision-makers and do not usually initiate policy proposals, although they may exert considerable influence on the decisions reached. The significant group that falls in this category is the Michigan Congress of Parents and Teachers Associations (PTA).

The Michigan Education Association

Of the major professional education groups with a direct interest in public school legislation, one of the most influential is the Michigan Education Association. At one time, we were told, this group virtually monopolized the policy articulation process, and operated in a manner not dissimilar to the MSTA in Missouri. But the rise of separate and competitive interests within the education establishment has significantly curbed its influence. Yet with its 58,000 members comprising 85 to 90 percent of all public school professionals in Michigan, the MEA comes closest to representing all phases of the public schools.

It operates under the assumption that the political process holds the key to the ends it seeks. Its major resource is its possession of information about school issues and its ability to supply this information to decision-makers. Only rarely does the MEA rely upon the mobilization of its membership to affect political decisions. It conducts substantial research and transmits its findings to the legislature through distribution of its weekly, biweekly, and monthly publications. Its representatives testify before legislative committees and meet privately with legislators and representatives of the governor's office. The association's legislative representative, Dick Adams, is always available to supply information to inquiring legislators. The MEA also provides legislators with such services as research reports, briefing papers on education questions, and technical assistance in drafting bills.

An example of the type of service MEA supplies to the legislature is the information the association provided in 1961 on the proposed increase in state financial assistance to local school districts. The MEA had requested an eight percent improvement factor in the amount of state aid over the previous year. To support this request, MEA provided the legislators with figures indicating the condition of classrooms, income of teachers, increase in student population, financial condition of local districts—all information derived from their research which showed the need for the eight percent increase in state aid.

Legislators' comments in interviews showed that they frequently rely upon the MEA for information and that invariably they have found its data accurate and useful. Several legislators further indicated that they conceive of MEA as an informational service rather than as an education interest group. One said, "We don't think of Dick Adams [the MEA legislative representative] as a lobbyist; rather we think of him as a person who gives us good, reliable information on education questions." It would be misleading, however, to suggest that all legislative leaders view the MEA simply as a service-oriented group. In fact, a few felt that this group was the most prominent and visible lobby in the state. But this is not the general view. It minimizes the importance of information to the politician, who is in "continuous need of current information because he is at the mercy of the changes as they occur." The effect of information—or the lack of it—extends to a legislator's status with both his colleagues and his constituents. Information is significant to a legislator in two respects: it helps him, first, to arrive at what he considers the proper decision, and, second, to gauge the political consequences of alternative decisions.[1]

Although the majority of legislators interviewed were favorably disposed toward the MEA, two members were of a decidedly different opinion. The chairman of the Senate Education Committee, who regards himself as a conservative Republican, stated:

I don't look to any interest group in the state for information. I look instead to educators I know in various areas of the state. The MEA is the most powerful lobby in the state; most of the fellows [his legislature colleagues] rely on them but I don't. I don't because the MEA is partisan; I know it is not openly partisan *but* it is for spending more when we haven't got it and that is a partisan issue.

The chairman added that although he felt that most of the representatives of the MEA were Republican or "sympathetic to the Republican cause," most of the educators were not. "Republican Senators know that most of the educators in education groups are Democrats and of course this affects their decisions." Our impressionistic evidence does not, however, support the Senator's conclusions. In fact, we are inclined to suspect that most public school people are Republicans. What is significant for our purposes is that this was his perception of reality.

A Democratic legislator from Wayne County who is a ranking member of the House Education Committee felt that the MEA was "too aggressive" and that it was too biased to trust. He contended that it made very little difference whether educators were Republicans or Democrats, "that in fact they did not favor either party." He maintained that the major problem in Michigan was to find a "meaningful criterion to measure school needs."

The MEA is self-conscious about its image. Its representatives say that the organization prefers to be regarded as an information service rather than as a political lobby. Political bargaining must be done outside the purview of the rank and file membership. The leadership considers expertise its most important single source of strength and likes to think of the association as furnishing significant information to the political leaders of the state at all times. The association leadership feels, for example, that the work of a full-time research person borrowed from the faculty of Michigan State University influenced education legislation during the 1960 legislative session. But organization representatives are aware that their services are regarded with suspicion. In their view, the Senate is more "hostile" or "unfavorably disposed" than the House, and they attribute this hostility largely to what the chairman of the Senate Education Committee suggested, namely, their "partisan image."

The MEA does not, of course, rely exclusively upon specific services to legislators in order to influence policy decisions. It makes a concerted effort to create a favorable climate of opinion in support of the public schools among both legislators and the general public. For example, all legislators, regardless of party, area, and voting records, receive a personal letter from the president of the MEA congratulating them for work they did on behalf of public education. Moreover, regional representatives of the association make personal contact with the legislators in their home constituencies. At the state capitol in Lansing, the MEA does a moderate amount of entertaining. It usually holds a joint dinner for the House and Senate Education Committee members each year, where it gives a thorough explanation of the important education issues confronting the state.

In the face of a legislative crisis, the MEA has attempted to activate its membership, to make them aware of the issues, and to stimulate them to contact their representatives. In some instances, the MEA has informed incumbent legislators that they would probably lose the support of many MEA members by unfavorable votes on key issues. On the whole, however, the MEA does not make any effort to gain legislative backing for its programs by threatening legislators with reprisals at the polls. In the interviews, legislators said that this is an important resource that the MEA has at its disposal, but all stated that MEA exerted little or no perceptible influence in this manner. In assessing the organization's influence potential, an MEA representative said:

> We are successful as long as we remain nonpartisan. This has been difficult to do lately with the governor and legislature in a fight over how much money to spend. We want to spend more on schools and that makes us seem partisan. Our problem, then, is to prove that schools need the money, and information, not theories of government, is the only nonpolitical approach to this problem that will keep us from being drawn into a partisan battle.

The Michigan Association of School Administrators

If information is the major resource of the MEA, an influential membership is the most important resource of the Michigan Association of School Administrators (MASA). This group of 700 school administrators, representing 96 percent of the superintendents, assistant superintendents, and county superintendents in the state, is frequently cited by members of the House and Senate Education Committees as "potentially the most influential" education group in Michigan, although the organization has never fully realized its potential. All members of the House and Senate Education Committees contend that the strength of the MASA lies not in what services it provides for them, but rather in the *nature of its membership*. School superintendents, they point out, are respected members of their communities and are regarded as local authorities on education. Since they enjoy leadership positions in virtually every community in the state, local district superintendents generally find access to state legislators easier than do classroom teachers.

The MASA is a federated unit of the Michigan Education Association; the MEA is the parent organization, with MASA as a specialized subordinate organization within the MEA. As the MASA has grown in membership, however, it has tended to pull away from the MEA. The result is that the MEA is more teacher-oriented, while the MASA is concerned mainly with the needs and views of administrators. A basic reason for this development is that the MEA has been forced to compete more vigorously in this state with the teachers union movement. Such competition requires more active concern with teachers' welfare.

This, in turn, tends to alienate school superintendents and school boards who are facing budgetary pressures. This separation, to the degree it is perceived by the legislators, has tended to place the MASA in a stronger bargaining position for the schools as a whole, whereas the MEA has become increasingly identified as the teacher-welfare bargaining agent. MASA officials tend to view the MEA in this manner. MEA, on the other hand, prefers to view the organizational relationship as it is formally established and considers the MASA as a subordinate, specialized agency.

Because the MASA leadership realizes that legislators see its strength in terms of its capacity or potential capacity to bring grass-roots pressure to bear upon them, MASA feels that the most potent weapon in its arsenal is its ability to persuade the local superintendents to support a piece of legislation by contacting their local senators and representatives at home. From the organization's vantage point, this type of action yields more impressive results than any services or entertainment it can provide for legislators while in Lansing. As a result, the MASA leadership encourages each local superintendent periodically to discuss the problems of education with his legislators at home and to offer suggestions for solutions.

The MASA maintains contact with its local members through its ten regional chairmen. Action plans initiated by the State Legislative Committee of the association are transmitted to the local membership through the regional chairman. The committee uses this mechanism when it wants local superintendents to act.

The effort of MASA officials following the 1961 legislative session illustrates the importance MASA places on the influence of its local membership. That summer, "leadership teams" were dispersed throughout the state for the purpose of organizing local superintendents into "minuteman" units, to be on call when the MASA leaders in Lansing send down an action plan on a piece of legislation. The minutemen are to keep in continuous contact with their individual legislators, and when the association's Lansing office sends out an impulse, the minutemen are supposed to transmit it immediately to their legislators. MASA officials hope that ultimately these minutemen will meet periodically with their legislators as a forum and will keep the pressure up throughout the year. According to the executive secretary, however, MASA's greatest problem at the moment—and perhaps the greatest problem of all the public school groups—is "getting our own boys interested."

While the MASA leadership assiduously tries to cultivate more political activism on the part of its membership, it expends great effort to ensure that contacts with legislators appear locally initiated. For example, when the MASA joined the other major education groups in a crash effort to get an increase in state financial aid during the 1961 session of the legislature, the executive secretary, in a flyer to the local superintendents, urged them "to get a carload of people to come to Lansing [to] take your representative out for dinner and make the plea to give something for public education." The local superintendents were instructed as follows: *"Don't tell the legislators you are coming at my suggestion or Max Cochran's* [the Department of Public Instruction's legislative representative]. *Indicate you are concerned about financial aid for your own school."*

Not all efforts of the MASA, of course, are directed through its local membership. Association officers have active personal contacts in Lansing. These contacts are maintained, to a large extent, for the purpose of keeping up to date on legislative activity. In addition, however, the leadership discusses the MASA position with the legislators, urging their support, as well as maintaining rapport with the other public school interest groups. Although MASA does not maintain elaborate research facilities, it does provide the legislators with substantive information, when requested, on pending legislation.

Even though the personal influence and contacts of its membership are the strongest assets of the MASA, this group is hesitant, save in its recent minuteman effort, to make full-scale use of these resources through more active political participation. The association states that it does not want its members characterized as politicians, but rather as educational statesmen. Several legislators cite the association's reluctance to use its full political potential as its major weakness. But MASA officials point out that full and continuous displays of strength might, in the long run, prove self-defeating. MASA officials contend that they cannot run to the membership every time they face a difficult or closely contested issue. The question they must constantly face, they say, is "Will the members respond?" And even if they do respond, "wouldn't the extensive use of power serve only to activate and consolidate opposing forces?"

The principal difference between this group and its counterparts in Illinois and Missouri is its insistence upon an independent status within the professional education establishment.

The Michigan Association of County School Administrators

The Michigan Association of County School Administrators (MACSA) shares substantial common ground with MASA: both are affiliated with the MEA, and their memberships overlap. The county superintendent group, however, is on more tenuous ground than MASA or, probably, any other public school group in Michigan. The county school district in Michigan, as in other states, is now fighting for survival. With the expansion in the size and resources of local school districts, the county school district—whose function has traditionally been to assist marginal school districts—has experienced a diminution of responsibility in recent decades. The county school district today performs little more than a few housekeeping functions, such as taking the annual school census and collecting delinquent school taxes owed to school districts within the county. Its major substantive function—to furnish supervisory and consultative services to the local school district when requested—has dwindled in significance as the local districts have grown and developed their own supervisory and consultative staffs.

In recent years, the legislature has given county districts some new responsibilities. For example, they are now authorized to conduct cooperative programs among school districts within the county, area studies to analyze the educational conditions and needs within the county, and special education programs to bring training to children who are deaf, blind, crippled, defective in speech, mentally handicapped, or housebound. But these new functions have failed to enhance the status or insure the longevity of the county school district.

The strength of the Association of County School Administrators reflects the present condition of the county school district. The association, founded in 1924, realizes that it, too, is at the crossroads; it knows it must rebuild or perish.

MACSA has never exerted much influence at the state level; its activities have always been more county-directed. In recent years, however, because of the requirement of state action for reorganization of county districts, it has become a more active force at the state level. This contrasts sharply with what we found in Illinois and Missouri where comparable organizations had little or no concern with most state-wide policies. It has the endorsement of the other key education groups, but not their strong support. The association's access to the legislature is limited because each county district has a limited amount of patronage at its disposal. As one legislator put it, "This group has no bargaining power since county superintendents have no jobs that legislators could use to get support." In addition, even MACSA leaders contend that many of its own members have never been sure whether their primary allegiance should go to the County Administrators Association or to other professional education groups. In recent years, county school administrators have become increasingly involved in the MASA and the MEA. And recently the association longevity received another blow when the administrators from large counties split with the small county people to form their own group. Although the MACSA still has over eighty percent of the county school administrators as members, these defections have hurt.

Realizing the portents of doom, the MACSA leadership has vigorously sought the passage of an intermediate school district bill to inject new life into the county school district. This bill, which we will examine presently, provides, among other things, for the consolidation of county school districts.

There have been difficulties in getting unanimous support for the bill from within the organization, however. County superintendents who fear losing their jobs in such a consolidation have voiced their opposition to legislative leaders. This internal dissension, coupled with the weak bargaining position of the group as a whole, has rendered the MACSA's efforts on behalf of this bill ineffectual.

The leaders of the MACSA have staked its entire survival on the proposal for reorganizing the county school districts. Without it, they claim, the association will continue to decline in strength. The real dilemma facing the MACSA leaders is that the major source of the group's weakness—a low level of cohesion—is aggravated by the bill on which the organization is staking its survival.

The Michigan Federation of Teachers

The fourth major education organization in the category of groups whose members have a direct interest in the outcome of decisions that affect public schools in Michigan is the Michigan Federation of Teachers (MFT). The "teachers' union" has approximately six thousand members and is affiliated with the American Federation of Teachers. The federation, its leaders assert, is proud to be identified with the labor movement and casts for itself the role of bargaining agent for the classroom teachers in their relations with the school administration. In terms of policy, it considers superintendents to be employers and thus on the other side. "The superintendents represent the administration, we represent the teachers." Federation leaders believe that many superintendents have failed to meet their responsibilities to the teacher. Although its leaders say the organization has many goals identical with those of the MEA, they firmly believe that only an organization composed of classroom teachers exclusively can properly represent the teachers.

MFT's close identification with labor has contradictory effects. On the one hand, it helps secure support for the MFT program from legislators sympathetic to organized labor, primarily Detroit and Wayne County Democratic legislators. This is its major source of strength. On the other hand, in a state where the division between the Democrats and Republicans is ideological and is predicated on a corresponding split between urban labor interests and rural agricultural interests, the MFT relationship with urban-labor Democrats alienates outstate Republicans. Interviews with several key Republican legislators indicated that they found this group and its demands offensive. As one ranking House Republican put it, "I am highly offended by the federation's practice of calling teachers 'scabs.' "

MFT demands are occasionally inconsistent with and contrary to the position of other public school interests, in particular the interests of the superintendents and school board members. As an organization it poses a direct threat to the MEA since it competes for the membership of the classroom teachers. In fact, the National Education Association, MEA's parent group, views the teachers union movement as a major threat and has encouraged all of its state affiliates to take an active stand against its operations. The reader will recall that the same antagonism was present in Illinois and Missouri. As a consequence, the MFT does tend to alienate these interests, the result being the obvious one: sincere attempts at a closer alliance with these groups are often futile. Even with these basic differences, however, surprisingly good rapport exists between the MFT and other education groups. Again, partisanship is part of the explanation.[2] The Democratic commitment to labor—including the MFT—gives the federation some bargaining power with the other public school groups in terms of the perceived number of negative votes the MFT could potentially marshal in order to derail pet projects of the other groups. Moreover, the other education groups realize they are dealing with an organization which has considerable support and sympathy among Democrats, many of whom are dependent on or in sympathy with organized labor generally. Working relationships have thus become more imperative, particularly when the Democrats control the governorship.

Michigan Association of School Boards

The Michigan Association of School Boards (MASB) is the most rapidly growing organization among Michigan public school interests. Although it is the newest group on the Michigan scene, it should not be construed as only a minor influence. Indeed, it is quite possible that this group might, in the near future, become the most influential of all the education groups in the state. At the present time, it has access to the legislators and other public school groups view it as their strongest competitor of the legislature's attention.

A particularly notable feature about the School Board Association is its recent growth in membership. From a roster of 300 school boards in 1957, the association had mushroomed to 809 member boards by 1961, representing districts that included 94 percent of the public school children of Michigan and 90 percent of the public school systems offering classes from kindergarten through twelfth grade. In 1961, approximately 5,000 members were included in the School Boards Association.

It is difficult to identify the precise reasons for this rise in membership, but representatives of the organization and informed onlookers have some explanations. As it became clear that the state government would assume an increased share of educational policy decisions, the local school boards organized into a state-wide group to function more effectively at the state level—organizing, in effect, for the tasks at hand. They considered themselves to be the governing units for the local schools, and if part of the governing authority was to shift to Lansing, they saw their task as one of reorganizing in order to gain access at the new points of decision. The School Board Association's first major step into the state arena was to sponsor the 1957 legislation which provided for a guaranteed continuing appropriation for state financial assistance to local school districts. Political observers in Lansing indicate that the School Board Association first emerged as a strong force at that time.

Encouraged both by effective reorganizing and by success in its first legislative venture, the organization began to operate vigorously. It could then compete with other interests for the scarce fiscal resources at the state level for public schools. Some educators list as a contributing cause for the association's rapid growth and increased activity the aggressive developmental policy of the National School Board Association.

The Michigan Association of School Boards makes policy proposals only rarely. It has no research facilities to support such activity. Rather it acts as a watchdog over public school legislation that is introduced and offers its support or opposition as appropriate.

The organization sees itself as the only major education interest group that is not on the public payroll and so has no immediate and direct interest in the outcome of public schools legislation. It sees itself as disinterested and public-spirited, with only the best interests of the schools in mind. The leadership of the Association is quite emphatic on this point.

An underlying antagonism between the School Board group and the professional educators stems from the former's self-image. Viewing themselves as the only duly elected authorities for the local schools, they feel that they can best represent *both* the schools and the taxpayers; they feel that they and not the professional educators (whom they regard as their employees) should represent the schools at the state capitol. This concept of employer-employee relationship is illustrated in a statement of one of the Association leaders. In explaining why the experiment of organizing the School Board Association as a branch of MEA failed in 1947-48, he said: "It was just like General Motors operating as a branch of the United Auto Workers." And a School Board Association official observing the Education Council, a body including all key education groups, said, "I find it most disturbing that School Board officials are sitting down with all divisions of their employees."

Meanwhile the professional educators express *their* antagonism against elected governing boards. One leader in the Association of School Administrators states quite bluntly: "We are not going to let these *lay people* come down here and run things."

The differences of opinion between the School Board Association and the professional education groups flare into the open from time to time. In the showdown fight on public school appropriations in the 1961 legislature, all of the professional education groups moved to a compromise three percent improvement factor in state financial assistance to local schools, while the School Board Association stubbornly held out for its request for five percent.

Virtually all of the professional education groups whose representatives were interviewed indicated that they saw the School Board Association as something of an "antagonistic force" in the education family. At the same time, the School Board Association leaders warned their members of a "prospective MEA-MASA coalition," and urged their people to "head off this coalition." The significant variable in this regard in Michigan is the absence of any *effective alliance* in which differences can be absorbed or reconciled. Unlike its counterparts in Illinois and Missouri, no long-term and stable relationships have crystallized in Michigan.

The strength of the School Board Association springs largely from the elected status of its members. This makes an impression on both Democratic and Republican members of the Senate and House Education Committees. They reason that, in the first place, the school board officers are elected because they have strength at home; they must, in general, be esteemed members of their communities. They can translate this into influence at the state level because they do get votes at home. As elected school officials, their voice on public school matters is generally respected in local communities. Because of this, a legislator is reluctant to arouse their opposition.

If the political activism of its members is one important factor in the group's strength, another is the position of its membership in the social structure. School board members are usually property owners in their communities and often have a sizable financial stake there. As a result, they often reflect a conservative view, leaning toward preservation of the *status quo*. They usually come from and represent a selected layer of influential and relatively satisfied people in the community. In this sense, they are joined by many legislators of the same kind who share the same perspectives and enjoy the same status. In general, the school board people speak the language of the legislators. On the other hand, several legislators went so far as to say that the professional educators are usually loquacious and somewhat suspect. The fact that school board people are not on the public payroll is also a large factor in their favor. Legislators tend to view their requests as representing less self-interest and more common concern for the community as a whole.

Since its strength is largely a result of the home town prestige and position of its members, the School Board Association directs most of its activity to the individual community. The Association places great emphasis on having the local school board officials maintain constant contact with their legislators at home. When action is desired, the association leaders contact local school board people to put the pressure on. The association has not yet perfected this device but it has been improving it. It recently held a series of meetings throughout the state to activate its local memberships and will possibly demonstrate more success in mobilizing local strength in the near future.

The Detroit Public School System

Michigan's major metropolitan school district, Detroit, also constitutes a separate interest that intervenes at various points in the state's political actions. Like Chicago, St. Louis, and Kansas City, it has as its major resource of influence a bloc of urban legislators which, when unified, is able to bargain and negotiate with outstate legislators for the special legislation Detroit's schools need and desire. The Detroit public school system, again like the metropolitan systems in our other two states, has not played a highly active or visible role in deciding education matters of state-wide application, being content to leave such deliberations to other interests. However, we must report that at the time of this research and apparently because of the failure of the state's other major education interest to achieve results, Detroit in conjunction with some adjacent school districts in Wayne County has begun to "step up" its activities at the state level. "We have begun to recognize," a high official of the Detroit school system stated, "that we can no longer operate effectively by leaving state-wide decisions exclusively to outstaters. The concerns of schools in this area where most of the state's people live are vital and they demand state attention. We will simply have to take more firm action than in the past." A decision on strategy is one thing, implementation of course is another matter. The same official did not hesitate to point out that the seemingly inherent urban-rural cleavage had been effectively overcome under the old formula of area delegation bargains. "The urban-rural conflict could rear its head if Detroit pushes too hard," he said. Conceding the thinness of our data, we can report that this new strategy of active involvement, if it is carried out, will make Michigan stand in sharp contrast to school decision-making patterns in Missouri and Illinois.

Michigan Congress of Parents and Teachers

Moving now to the second category—supportive groups which have a major and continuous concern about education but whose members are not so directly affected by the outcome of education decisions—we find one major group in Michigan politics, the Michigan Congress of Parents and Teachers, commonly referred to as the PTA. Although its membership includes professionals it is nevertheless an essentially lay group and so regards itself. Although the PTA's 390,000 members make it the largest education organization in the state, the minimal level of political activism and political commitment of the membership, coupled with the purely local outlook of many of the members, reduces the group's political significance. Few, if any, politicians see the PTA as a major voting bloc. (They certainly do not conceive it anywhere near comparable in power to the United Auto Workers, which has only approximately 254,000 members in Michigan.)

In a certain manner, however, the tactics of PTA leadership render the size of its membership a source of some strength. It is a prestige group of high status, organized to promote closer cooperation between the teachers, the public schools, and the parents. In that sense, it concerns itself with a broad range of education issues, giving the nominal support of 390,000 prestigious citizens to specific programs which have been formulated by other education groups. The PTA is not in any sense a rubber stamp group, but operates with the expectation that it will be used for the benefit of the public schools—or, more precisely, in support of those proposals that win its favor. The leaders visualize the group as largely a supportive group. Consequently, PTA membership is not stimulated to militant action, but the Association relies instead on face to face contact between the PTA leadership and the legislators in Lansing.

The PTA does not have a large degree of cohesion, and since "the degree of unity sets limits on permissible partisanship," it is not surprising that the PTA is perhaps the most hesitant of all the education groups in Michigan to be identified with any partisan political activity. As one PTA leader put it: "There is absolutely no partisanship in the PTA; we do not even want politicians to speak at our meetings." In sum, the Michigan PTA is a useful friend, but not a very bothersome enemy.

Another category of groups which touch upon education—including both supportive and nonsupportive groups whose major concern is with issues other than education—will not be described in this section. Suffice it to say that these groups—organized labor, chambers of commerce, taxpayers associations, etc.—can create a broad favorable climate for education programs and they can also create a substantial residue of opposition to many proposals. Their support or opposition is sporadic, rising and declining as the issue at hand affects or does not affect their interests. Such support or opposition, especially when generated to protect perceived interests, can obviously be one of the deciding factors in some instances, as will be seen later on in this chapter. However, detailed analysis of these groups, no matter how attractive the prospects it offers, is not essential to an understanding of the public school interest group structure in Michigan. Their existence and sporadic participation can be accepted as facts of political life in the public school policies of the state.

The Superintendent of Public Instruction

No investigation of the education interest in Michigan is complete without discussing the legislative and political role of the superintendent of public instruction and the State Department of Public Instruction. With a popularly elected superintendent of public instruction, who sees his role and that of the Department as integral parts of the education policy-making process, the machinery of the Department is constantly thrust into the decision-making arena.

The Department becomes engaged in policy-making in three ways: through the superintendent personally; through the Department's legislative representative; and through the Department's own internal administrative machinery which systematically prepares policy positions.

The most overt—and the most controversial—involvement is that of the superintendent, who, since 1957, has been an elected Democrat, Lynn Bartlett. He has closely adhered to the education planks of the Democratic platform, and is perceived as presenting to the legislature partisan proposals for the solution of education problems. The Michigan legislature, on the other hand, has consistently had a Republican majority in each house. In this political environment (where there not only is a divided government, but where the parties are more ideologically oriented than in most American states), the pursuit of Democratic programs along strictly party lines spells continuous defeat. Therefore the superintendent has faced the dilemma of having to maintain a partisan stance toward public school issues in order to retain the strong support of his party and thus remain in office, while at the same time he must support a bipartisan program in the legislature in the hope of legislative victory.

The nature of the office of superintendent of public instruction compounds the difficulty. To gain acceptance and respect within the public school system, he must be regarded as an educational statesman, not a politician. This informal requirement has given the superintendent very little political leverage for the promotion of his own programs even when they bear the Democratic label. Unlike the governor, for instance, who is in a stronger political position, it is difficult for the superintendent to transfer his ballot box popularity into voter support for his programs in the legislature.

To offset this position of relative political impotence, the superintendent has attempted to fuse the education groups into a unified voice, the Educational Council, in order to present a "consensus program" to the legislature. This group is composed of representatives of the MEA, MFT, MASA, and the MASB. The council has had only a limited success. Agreements reached in the Council are not binding and on numerous occasions they have been ignored by member groups. Moreover, the MEA desires to create its own council and has tended to resent the leadership efforts of the superintendent. As a result, the superintendent has found his bipartisan education support unreliable and his program often defeated in the legislature along party lines.

The superintendent has been unable to erase his partisan image in the eyes of numerous legislators. Virtually all of the education committee members interviewed said they identified the superintendent and his programs as partisan. As a Republican member of the House Education Committee put it, "He [the Superintendent] couldn't get away from his partisanship if he wanted to; the nature of the office wouldn't allow it." He added that "the partisanship is inherent, and he [the superintendent] doesn't try to hide it." Another House Republican mentioned the superintendent's partisanship with disfavor: "The superintendent is little more than a party politician rather than an 'educator.' He has cheapened his position by engaging in lobbying activities." Democrats in the legislature look upon the superintendent's legislative efforts with more favor than do the Republicans, of course. Said one House Democrat: "The superintendent rates high among the Democrats in the legislature, and he also has some support from the Republicans. The two together could add up to a winning ticket. He wouldn't even have this strength if the office wasn't an elected partisan post."

Despite Republican antipathy to the superintendent's lobbying activity, all legislators, including Republicans, indicated that they sought out the superintendent's office for information on education issues and, perhaps with some qualifications, generally trusted the information they received.

The legislative acceptance of Department of Public Instruction information and counsel may be more attributable to the efforts of the Department's legislative representative than to the superintendent's. While the superintendent must carry the party banner, his legislative representative, Max Cochran, who is highly respected by many legislators, quietly goes about the legislature in nonpartisan garb (although it is well-known that he is a Republican), informing and advising the legislators.

The legislative representative is, in fact, a key to the Department of Public Instruction's influence. His job is to keep on top of all legislative proposals. As a result, he keeps the Department personnel, the various education groups, and, at times, the legislators themselves informed on the various public school proposals before the legislature. He prepares an analysis of each education bill.

In his role as lobbyist and legislative trouble-shooter for the Department, he maintains close contacts with the legislators. In general, the legislators interviewed indicated respect for his advice and counsel. A ranking Republican senator indicated his confidence in this way: "I have more confidence in Cochran, the Department's legislative representative, than in any other member of the Department of Public Instruction." A Republican leader in the House indicated that "Max Cochran wields substantial influence in the legislature." A freshman Republican senator indicated that he got no information from the Department of Public Instruction "except through Max Cochran." He added, "I am inclined to lean heavily on Cochran in the future because I have confidence in his information." Also, all Democrats interviewed said they found Cochran to be very reliable and helpful.

The legislative representative also functions as a catalyst in the operation of the Department's internal legislative policy-making machinery. This activity is centered in the Department's Legislative Committee. This committee, composed of a representative from each of the six divisions of the Department of Public Instruction, meets weekly during the legislative session to consider public school proposals before the legislature. The committee is a clearing house for proposals already submitted rather than a policy initiating body. Proposals presented to the Legislative Committee are referred back to each division before a committee decision is made. This allows the professional administrators to pass judgment on the proposals from their administrative point of view. Decisions reached by the committee serve as a way of keeping the superintendent informed as to how Department personnel feel and of keeping them, in turn, up to date on pending legislation. The Legislative Committee's final decisions are transmitted not to the legislature, but to the superintendent.

Department of Public Instruction personnel have some additional activities that bear on public school policy-making. These include testimony by Department personnel before legislative committees, preparation of research papers, and the drafting of legislation.

Perhaps the key to understanding the role of education interests in this state is a recognition of the following two points. (1) To a much greater degree than in our other two states, the various groups act independently. In the remainder of this chapter, we will attempt to show that at this point in time Michigan has no stable education power structure in the sense that Illinois and Missouri have. Our data suggest that until fairly recently, 1959 to be exact, a power structure consisting mainly of the MEA and its contacts in the state as a whole and certain key officials in the legislature, did indeed exist, a structure capable of keeping education issues from becoming controversial. At the time of our study, however, only the remnants of that structure remained and new groups, powerful in their own right, had begun to exercise influence and move in different directions. (2) The emergence of conflicting elements beyond merely the teachers union *within* the education lobby, coupled with broader political conflicts in the state's total political system, some of which are between the two major parties, creates a problem for the majority of the education interest groups. That problem is that this type of political atmosphere does not fully lend itself to the basic strategies of neutrality, objectivity, nonpartisanship, and low conflict appearance that most of these groups have adopted. By examining the role of these interests in the larger political context and in two specific situations, we hope to illustrate these points.

The Michigan Political System and the Education Lobby

For over a decade, the public school interests just described have operated in a political context significantly different from those in Illinois and Missouri. Although the overall objective of the professional educators in Michigan has been to minimize conflict over their demands, they have been comparatively unsuccessful. While in Illinois and Missouri, state participation in school matters has been greatly expanded, particularly in the area of finance, almost the opposite is true in Michigan. For example, state aid in support of the public schools has declined from over 50 percent of total operating costs in 1950 to less than 43 percent in 1961. Not only have the public school interests been unable to reverse this trend, they also have been unable to persuade the legislature to take any major steps in other policy areas. They could not obtain the necessary support in the legislature to adopt a foundation program; instead they have had to be satisfied with a continuing appropriation act which embodies only some of the features of the more desirable foundation program. There have been no giant strides in teacher welfare (except perhaps in teacher retirement), or local and county school district reorganization, and the state legislature has steadfastly refused, despite repeated requests, to approve of state participation in several federal programs authorized under the National Defense Education Act.

As we have noted previously, public school issues are not normally hotly contested in either Missouri or Illinois, and the public school interests have been largely successful in their efforts to achieve fairly wide consensus. Why is Michigan different? There are no simple answers, but the interviews do provide a perspective.

In the first place, in terms of expenditures for services, Michigan is not a conservative state if judged by Illinois or Missouri, or for that matter, national standards. The state government in Michigan plays a much more prominent role in the total economy of that state than do the state governments in either Illinois or Missouri. Public schools have been much more generously supported in Michigan than in either Illinois or Missouri. During the 1950's, however, general concern with public schools appears to have leveled off, at least partly because of an early impressive record of financial support. Table 1, while establishing the high dollar investment in public education in Michigan, also indicates that the state's role in educational finance has become less impressive when compared with that of Illinois and Missouri. The figures are given below. The question is why.

Table 1

PUBLIC SCHOOL REVENUE RECEIPTS
(In Thousands).*

	Illinois		Michigan		Missouri	
	All Sources	State Sources	All Sources	State Sources	All Sources	State Sources
1951-52	490,797	62,938	319,404	177,206	135,866	48,197
1955-56	437,945	105,251	528,281	256,257	200,045	72,917
1957-58	622,644	127,419	636,768	278,780	242,646	79,879

*U. S. Office of Education, *Biennial Survey of Education in the United States, Statistics of State School Systems:* Organization, Staff, Pupils, and Finances, 1951-52, Table 18; 1955-56, Table 24; 1957-58, Table 25.

"With service levels and expenditures relatively high," one Republican legislator commented, "demands for more money run into stiffer resistance." "It is no secret to the Republicans," a Democratic member of the Education

Committee said, "that Michigan is spending a lot more money for schools than are many of the neighboring states." Representatives of the various organized interests all agreed that because the state did spend considerable funds for education at all levels as well as for other services, their "demands were much more difficult to support and justify."

Several interviewees referred to various statistics to buttress their argument. For example, in per capita total state expenditures for all purposes in 1960, Michigan ranked eighteenth, spending $171.46 as compared with Missouri's $120.31 (forty-sixth) and Illinois' $120.12 (forty-seventh). In terms of per capita *state* expenditures for *all* public education, Michigan ranked eleventh, spending $66.38 as compared with Missouri's forty-second position ($32.93) and Illinois' forty-fourth position ($30.04) in 1960. Although Illinois spends more per pupil in average daily attendance than Michigan—$502.00 as compared to $440.13 in Michigan—significantly less money comes from *state* sources. (Missouri spends less than either state, the figure being $386.17 per pupil in ADA.) That is, the degree of state participation in financing public elementary and secondary schools is higher in Michigan than in either of the two other states. In 1961-62, Michigan contributed 42.2 per cent of all revenue for public schools as compared with 35.7 per cent in Missouri and 22.8 per cent in Illinois. In dollar amounts per pupil in average daily attendance, Michigan contributed $224 in 1961-62, Missouri contributed $159, and Illinois $129. In brief, then, Illinois and Missouri rely more extensively on local resources; whereas in Michigan, state resources have been tapped more often and to greater extent, despite the decline in recent years. (See Appendix I.)

Moreover, Michigan's commitments and obligations in the field of higher education are vastly more extensive than in either of the other two states. Michigan's total expenditures on education in 1960 were approximately $520,000,000. This compares with only $302,873,000 in Illinois and $142,247,000 in Missouri. Obviously, drains on the state treasury of this magnitude make the task of any education proponent, regardless of the level on which the support is sought, an exceedingly difficult one. We were told time and again by legislators that the state was "over-committed," "the funds are simply not available." Furthermore, as far as long-range planning is concerned, the educational establishment in Michigan is in disarray, which has led to some competition between the proponents of the public schools and the representatives of the institutions of higher learning (which often compete among themselves) over the state's scarce fiscal resources. Perhaps the most significant finding was not that competition exists, but that when expenditures reach these levels, most legislators are not inclined to make any distinction between money needed for public schools and money needed for higher education. Rather, we were told by one informant they think simply in terms of "how much money will the *educators* want this year."

A second major variable affecting school politics in Michigan is the pervasive conflict between the two major parties and the interests that support them. The exact nature and historical development of this conflict need not concern us here, except to demonstrate the manner in which public school policy and the public school interests have been affected. John P. White states:

> What seems to have happened in Michigan since 1928 is that a great national electoral realignment rejuvenated the previously moribund Democratic party. For a time in the late thirties and early forties, the well-fortified political position of the long dominant Republicans, coupled with the political inexperience and ineptitude of many Michigan Democrats, seemed strong enough to survive the assaults of the New Deal era. But since 1948, the Democrats have been able to produce a leadership group and a party organization strong enough to gain and hold control of the state government. . . .[3]

The emergence of the Democratic party as a dominant force in state politics has been accompanied by a realignment of the major parties. The forces that have gained control of each have succeeded in making the parties more responsible in the classic sense of the term: that is, each party is programmatic or committed to certain specific policies. Thus, in Michigan, the parties present alternatives, clear-cut alternatives, and their disparate views are reflected in the day to day operations of government.

Fiscal Conflicts

The party cleavages in Michigan relate, first of all, to political ideology and then to implementation. Much of the conflict in Michigan centers on questions of fiscal policy; more specifically, parties divide over how much money should be spent for public services generally and what type of taxes are equitable and raise enough money to finance existing or expanding programs. At various stages, these conflicts have reached crisis proportion and have become the subject of considerable national public discussion and debate. The primary protagonists—the "automobile manufacturers and rural interests versus organized labor—each identified with a political party, have not entered the political arena for the traditional prizes, but are more interested in controlling the total social and economic policy of the state government."[4]

One side is led by the Democratic party, strongly endorsed and supported by the United Automobile Workers Union, having as its principal spokesmen two of the state's past governors, G. Mennen Williams (1949-1961) and John B. Swainson (1961-62). The solid Democratic vote for state offices during the past decade, even during the Eisenhower years, is generally credited to the drawing power of one man. "If any coat-tails were important, they were those of G. Mennen Williams."[5]

On the other side stands the Republican party, in control of both houses of the state legislature during the entire period of the two Democratic governors' incumbency and prominently identified on a state-wide basis with the conservative economic interests, including General Motors, Chrysler, and the Ford Motor Company as well as agricultural and small business interests.

During the course of these years, the public school interests have operated in a political context where the economic posture of the two parties varied more perhaps than in any other state. Republicans accused the Democrats of being "fiscally irresponsible," "dominated by labor," "anti-free enterprise," and "socialistic." Democrats attacked Republicans with equal vigor and dispatch at the slightest provocation. Democrats viewed the Republicans as being "dominated by business interests," "friends of the rich and enemies of the poor," "anti-progress and pro-stagnation," "right wing and authoritarian," and "rural and backward in outlook."

Throughout the state, debates between party adversaries flared up whether it was election time or not. The debates covered a wide range of issues; the principal ones were, however, the representativeness or apportionment of the state legislature, the nature of the state's fiscal policies and concern that present policies had caused industrial enterprises to move outside the state, and "welfarism." Did this mean that the state was hopelessly deadlocked and that nothing could be done? On some issues, yes. At other times and on other questions, no.

The one major issue that persistently plagued both sides and that was never resolved during the Williams years nor during Swainson's 1961-62 term in office was the question of a state income tax as a means to finance expanding state services. There was wide agreement that additional revenues were needed and that a revision of the tax structure was in order, but the type of the tax and who was to be affected by it was the subject of the deep cleavage. To the Democrats closely aligned with labor, a sales tax or any other form of taxation which they considered "regressive" or adversely affecting lower income groups was out of the question. Similarly, the Republicans' base of support—big business, high income groups, conservative rural farmers—was during these same years vigorously opposed both on economic and constitutional grounds to any corporate or personal income tax. The present constitution provides for a "uniform rule of taxation" which some Republicans argue prohibits the enactment of a graduated income tax.

Agreement on the need for additional revenue if state services were to be maintained at present levels or raised, and disagreement on the source of the additional revenue complicated the public school interests' position in Michigan. Unlike the MSTA in Missouri, or for that matter the education groups in Illinois, the organized interests, while requesting additional state aid, could not endorse tax measures proposed by the governor without incurring direct opposition from

Republican legislators. On the other hand, to oppose the governor's tax measures might mean the loss of the Democratic support they had in the House as well as that of the governor. It would also place school interests in the untenable position of opposing the only long-range proposals that had been presented at a time when everyone agreed that increased revenues were imperative. ("We Republicans did not offer any long-range alternatives because it was the governor's responsibility to propose a sensible tax program," said a Republican spokesman. "All the Democrats did was to promise more and more and present tax proposals everyone was against, including the Democratic legislators privately.")

Neutrality on the tax question was the only alternative open to the education groups, but this too was an almost impossible position, since they had already admitted that new taxes would be necessary to increase appropriations. "The only alternative we had," a representative of MEA said, "was to present our case and try to gain bipartisan support by appealing to all sides to examine school needs critically." "In this atmosphere, the organized public school interests' chances for success," said one educator, "hinge on the extent of the conflict at the moment our proposals are submitted and on our ability to separate public school issues from other policy questions."

In sum, the fact that so many people have taken sides or believe that the conflict is irreconcilable creates the psychology that reinforces the conflict. Unfortunately for the public school interests, they have found no device in the Michigan political system for coherent education decision-making comparable to the School Problems Commission in Illinois, and no group similar to the MSTA in Missouri was able to fill the gap. Therefore, timing is of greater significance in Michigan, and if measures are introduced at a time when conflicts over fiscal policies are at their peak, *any* influence attempts may appear chaotic, unwise, and predetermined to fail.

One effect of all this has been that each organization, particularly the MEA and the State Association of School Boards, depends heavily on its state-wide campaigns to gain wide public support for school needs. This strategy contrasts sharply with the one followed by Illinois groups, which are represented on the School Problems Commission. It also contrasts, though perhaps less so, with the strategy of the MSTA in Missouri, where state-wide campaigns to generate citizen interest are used only for major and fundamental changes in the direction of public school policy, such as the foundation program in 1955.

Another effect has been that the interest groups in Michigan do not have the same symbolic advantage as do the groups in Missouri and Illinois. Although there is no anti-school lobby operating in the state capital and no one opposes the schools *per se,* resistance to school demands is more open. "We are doing enough for the educators," a Republican member of the Senate Education Committee said, "and until tax questions are settled there is no more money to give them."

Finally, in the political context, representatives of education groups point out that one of their main difficulties has been to gain political mileage from their acknowledged expertise. "We are regarded as experts on school needs all right, and have no trouble on that score, but nobody consults us on revenue-raising matters; and if we got involved in that fight, we would be ruined." The pervasiveness of conflict has further complicated attempts to maintain unity among the various organized education interests. An MEA representative summarized the situation thus:

> The state superintendent and the Michigan Federation of Teachers are with the Democrats. The Association of School Boards is for more state aid, but its membership and leaders are generally thought to be conservative and against an income tax. And to complicate matters further many groups, including the PTA, have their own view as to how much we can get or what the Senate will accept. We don't disagree on needs, we disagree on how much we *should* ask the legislature for. Certainly all of this disorganization among the education groups limits our chances for success.[6]

Conflict Between "Have and Have Not" School Districts

Although the split between the governor and the state legislature over fiscal policy tends to overshadow and receive more publicity than other controversies, a division within the state legislature itself—not based on party lines—has demonstrably affected public school policy perhaps to an even greater extent. This division is between the legislative representatives of areas which contain wealthy school districts and the legislative representatives of areas which contain poor districts. The cleavage is aggravated in Michigan because the state has never adopted a state-wide school district reorganization plan, the reasons for which will be discussed subsequently. State representatives from areas such as Grosse Point, Pontiac, and Bloomfield Hills are inclined to oppose changes in the state aid formula that would provide more state money to poorer districts on the basis of need. Conversely, representatives of the areas containing poor districts, with the general support of most education groups, favor a state aid formula weighted more heavily on the side of such equalization. These representatives feel that they have the full support of their local school officials in maintaining their position. Obviously, such a situation tends to weaken the bargaining power of state-wide organizations claiming to represent all of the claimants.

The chairman of the House Education Committee says: "This division is the most serious problem we face. The partisan fight gets all of the attention and right now it is of more far-reaching consequence, but that has in the past and will again die down and dwindle in significance."

A Democratic member of the same committee commented:

The biggest split is between the high and low valuation districts; this split is justifiable since the higher the valuation the less aid. The rift is greater in the Republican ranks than in the Democratic ranks. Our distressed aid formula takes care of the metropolitan districts, but many of the rural districts represented by Republicans don't benefit from this. If we had reorganization and eliminated a lot of these low valuation districts the picture would change, but there is so much opposition from the little red school houses and the Farm Bureau that this is not feasible on a state-wide basis; not to mention the tax problem it would raise because of the constitution.

All of those interviewed agreed that the differences between the wealthy and poor districts over the state aid formula would be reconciled only if and when: 1) the majority of poorer districts were eliminated through state-wide action or a series of local annexations and consolidations which would result, according to an MEA representative, in all new districts having "a more sound and sensible financial base"; and 2) there were a basic change in the constitutional provisions dealing with county and city tax limits, which regulate or affect school district tax rates.

Why has a state-wide school district reorganization plan never been adopted in Michigan? Representatives of the various organized interests agree as to the reasons. As one explained it:

After World War II, the state had plenty of money and in comparison with other states we were doing more. Over fifty percent of school revenue came from the state. Add to this the fact that at that time the local school district situation was not as bad as it was, say, in Illinois or Ohio. By comparison, we had fewer districts than most. Thus, there just wasn't the emergency that there was in other states.

A representative of MEA added: "The local districts were in good shape after the war and wanted local control preserved. There seemed to be plenty of money, so we didn't push very hard to change things then; but the simple fact is we did not remain in favorable comparative situations for very long and now reorganization has become a hot political football."

Although both legislators and representatives of organized interests agree that a state-wide plan might have been approved immediately following World War II, they also agree that each succeeding year made it more difficult to get one passed. In the first place, following the war a number of groups, particularly the Michigan Farm Bureau and the Friends of Michigan Schools (Little Red School House group), opposed vigorously any proposals to change local school districts by action initiated at the state level. "These groups were very vocal and swamped us with mail," a legislator asserted. "In fact, the biggest and loudest hearing ever held in the State Capitol was when the opponents of reorganization came down to tell us about it."

Despite this opposition, representatives of all of the major school interests felt they would have been successful had it not been for constitutional provisions differentiating the limits of city and county taxes. The efforts of the Michigan Municipal League, an organization representing municipal officials, were perhaps of most significance in defeating any reorganization scheme. The basis of this opposition was that inclusion of outside city-limits school districts would subject city schools to the 15 mill county tax limits, thus lowering the quality of existing city schools, which can tax on a higher level. The state Supreme Court held that inclusion of school districts located in the county would require the entire district to tax within the 15 mill limitation. Representatives of the education groups admitted that reorganization was practically impossible with such an interpretation. Their next tactic was to advocate a change in the state constitution, and the constitutional convention was considering a proposal to this effect.

Although the organized education interests in Michigan have been too weak and divided to overcome many of the forces in the Michigan political system, they are strong enough to block any proposal they consider detrimental to the public schools. In the absence of a clear test, it is, of course, impossible to say exactly what would happen, but no one disputes this view. Legislators agree that they would never initiate or attempt to push through a program without the active support of at least some of the major groups.

The Policy-Making Structure

For certain analytic purposes, one may look at Michigan's House and Senate as entities. However, the picture is not complete until the executive branch and its troubled relationship with the legislature, past and present, are considered. That large portion of state politics in Michigan which involves ideology, policy priorities, and personality has centered to a striking extent around the state's current (1961-62) and preceding Democratic governors. Because of the repercussions for education affairs, we shall focus briefly on the institutional roles of the governor and the legislature in the policy-making process.

The Governor

The constitution in force in 1962 plus certain statutory provisions require the election of seven other top administrative officials who, with the governor, make up the State Administrative Board. These offices are those of lieutenant governor, secretary of state, state treasurer, auditor general, attorney general, superintendent of public instruction, and highway commissioner. Advocates of the strong governor system find the current situation theoretically, if not always in fact, intolerable. If all state officers are members of the same party, as they have been in recent years, a strong governor may direct them as a team; however, when party membership is not identical, the governor finds his administrative powers limited to an even greater degree than already exists in the nature of the arrangement. (Governor Williams attempted to by-pass this problem in the early fifties by use of an unofficial "Little Cabinet.") Also, each of these officials has, like the governor, a state-wide constituency, which supplies the potential for party factionalism.

The governor in Michigan is elected for a two-year term; he may succeed himself indefinitely. One of the items on the constitutional convention agenda, which will be discussed below, was to increase the governor's term to four years. As the situation stood, a governor spent half of his two-year term at less than full efficiency, since he must occupy months with familiarizing himself with the administrative process and campaigning for reelection. It was one of Governor Swainson's strengths that he offered to the voter extensive prior experience both in the state Senate and in the lieutenant governorship.

Another constitutional area in which the gubernatorial powers are curbed in Michigan is that of appointment and removal of public officials. The Michigan constitution does not specify a method of creating new executive offices and filling them, although the governor may appoint persons to fill vacancies; therefore, an important aspect of the great modern-day proliferation of the state administrative services still rests in the hands of the legislature. By statute some department and agency heads were made appointive by the governor; but the Senate had held on to extensive consentual powers in this matter.

The formal delegation of gubernatorial powers in Michigan would appear to put the governor in a weak position. However, the political culture of the state provides some balance. The governor, as leader of a fiercely partisan, ideologically oriented political party, has many resources at hand. Perhaps his clearest advantage is the wide-spread attention and consideration that his proposals, fiscal and otherwise, receive throughout the state. The governor is always in a position to dramatize an issue or appeal to the public interest. G. Mennen Williams, during his six terms as Michigan governor, relied heavily on this approach rather than on any of his constitutional powers. As a result, Williams vetoed a much smaller number of bills during his tenure in office than is the average in most states.

One commentator on the small number of vetoes explains: "This phenomenon would appear to emphasize less the existence of coordinated action between the political branches than unusual awareness on the part of the majority party in opposition to the Governor of the latter's tolerance limits."[7]

One of the clearest distinctions between Williams' political style and that of his successor, John B. Swainson, was Swainson's extensive use of the veto. It did not become a factor in the educational picture, however, because the legislature has not passed any major educational legislation since the Continuous Appropriations Act in 1959.

But even though the elements of power a governor has cannot be ignored, he is not in a strong bargaining position with the state legislature. Unlike the Missouri and Illinois governors, the governor in Michigan does not dominate the revenue picture. Legislative leaders are not committed to push or to give high priority to any of his recommendations. Moreover, there is no presumption—as there is in Illinois and Missouri—that the governor's allocation of resources will be accepted. Perhaps the situation would be different in Michigan if recent governors had been more low-pressure and had not attempted to exercise broad programmatic leadership. As the situation stands, however, the institutional limitations—no patronage, the two-year term—make it possible for the legislature to thwart the governor almost at will, even while he remains politically popular and gets reelected.

Education leaders claim that Michigan needs executive leadership with more teeth in it. As the representative of one education interest put it:

> The recent governors of Michigan have been on our side and they have both been strong personalities, though Williams was the stronger. But they don't have much power over the legislature. Our governors have to spend too much time running for reelection.

According to another educational leader:

> The weakness of the governors in this state is well-known to anyone who has ever observed the legislature in this state. Recent governors have, on the whole, supported most of our proposals, but, without trying to minimize the importance of this support, I can tell you it was less than half the battle. A governor with a strong personality and strong public image still can't do much in this state even when he attempts vigorous leadership.

As we will see in the following case studies, Swainson's term in office, in relation to the legislature, can be characterized as a political impasse.

The Legislature

In contrast to the situation in Missouri and, to a lesser extent, Illinois, the Michigan political context can be called a high-pressure system, high enough to be periodically explosive. We have already discussed the orientations of political parties and interest groups in Michigan. Now we turn in more detail to the Michigan legislature as it existed in 1961.

As is frequently the case in America, under-representation of urban areas is built into Michigan's legislative apportionment scheme, and typically—at least of Northern states—rural areas tend to be Republican. As a result, the Michigan Senate is heavily Republican. Democrats have controlled it only once in the last forty years. The House is more evenly divided but overall figures for 1951-62 indicate a Republican majority of 362 to 277. Table 3 illustrates the nature of Michigan's apportionment system. Senatorial district boundaries are fixed in the constitution, and are therefore exceedingly difficult to change.

Table 2

COMPOSITION OF MICHIGAN LEGISLATURE,
1951 to 1962

	House		*Senate*	
	Repub-lican	Demo-crat	Repub-lican	Demo-crat
1961-62	56	54	22	12
1959-60	54	55	22	12
1957-58	61	49	23	11
1955-56	59	51	23	11
1953-54	66	34	24	8
1951-52	66	34	25	7
	362	277	139	61

Table 3

MICHIGAN APPORTIONMENT SYSTEM

County	*Popu-lation* (1950)	*Popu-lation* (1960)	*Represen-tatives*	*Percent of total*	*Senators*	*Percent of total*
Wayne	38.2	34.2	38	34.5	7	20.6
Oakland	6.2	8.8	6	5.5	1	2.9
Macomb	2.9	5.2	3	2.7	1	2.9
Kent	4.5	4.6	5	4.5	2	5.9
Genessee	4.3	4.7	4	3.6	1	2.9
Others	43.9	42.4	54	49.1	22	64.7

While Democrats accuse Republicans of insuring their position in the legislature with outstate Republican majorities, Republicans point to Wayne County and charge that "if all 38 legislators were chosen from equitably drawn, single member districts, their 30 percent of the total vote in Wayne County would give them between 5 and 10 of the representatives." To at least one observer, "It seems apparent that 'gerrymandering'... is not the exclusive province of one party."[8]

Fourteen years of Democratic governors and a Republican-controlled state legislature have served to aggravate, if not freeze, political disputes into such rigidities that it is now difficult for this large, diverse, and prosperous state to enact changes in public policy, especially in the much publicized area of taxation. While Democratic governors are cordial to school interests, education bills have trouble passing the legislature.

As in Missouri, the school men in Michigan, seeking favorable consideration for public school bills, have found the House of Representatives to be more receptive than the Senate in the eyes of the education lobby. The House has three or four members who qualify as experts in the field of education, one of whom is a member of the House's powerful Ways and Means Committee. Over the years of bitter partisan fights, the education interests have been able to maintain bipartisan support in the House Education Committee for most of their proposals and generally, as one representative of the MEA said, "we get a fair shake from the entire House."

During the past twelve years, the Republicans have been in the majority on the House Education Committee. On the whole, education groups in the state feel that this committee gives their needs a reasonable hearing, as well as support. One variable bearing on this may be the considerable number of committee members who come to this post with previous experience in educational affairs, either in some professional capacity or as an elected local school official. Five of the current nine members of the Education Committee have such experience, one as a local board president for twenty-three years. Another variable may be the continuity of service on this committee. Normally this is a nine-member body (Ways and Means is the largest committee with 13). From 1953-54 through 1961-62, only 20 legislators, 14 Republicans and 6 Democrats, have served.

In contrast to the House, the legislative representative of the state superintendent's office maintained that the Senate was the "toughest to crack." During the late 1950's and early '60's, the Michigan Senate Education Committee was chaired by Republicans who were self-designated conservatives. The most recent chairman, Lynn Francis, says that the "state spends too much money on schools," and believes that "most educators are Democrats." Education lobbyists do not regard anyone in the Senate as an education expert or public schools' champion in the way some members of the House are. Each particular interest has its own "friends in the Senate," but the main job, according to those who make the demands, is "to persuade the Republican Senate leaders to support their position." "This is no easy task," an MEA official commented, "and in recent years the fight with the governor has caused the Republicans to stand firmly together against further appropriations."

Republican leaders insist that they are not opposing the schools, but that unless the school groups can demonstrate a real need and gain responsible support on a state-wide basis, the lawmakers will not go along with education bills that involve expenditures of state funds or disturb local school district autonomy. To sum it up, the Senate Education Committee has been the burying ground for much school legislation sent over from the House.

Although there is nothing comparable to the "local unity norm" found in Missouri, area delegations do bargain with other area groups within the legislature, and education matters are frequently the subject of the negotiations. For example, the Detroit-Wayne County Democratic delegation in the House and Senate bargained for the "aid to distressed schools" law which helps out particular schools within a metropolitan district. Of even greater importance, the broad concerns of the Detroit school system have been protected and enhanced largely through bargains arrived at between the urban and rural delegations. And, like the pattern in Missouri and Illinois, in return for the bargain Detroit school men have not played an active role in other state public school matters. As previously indicated, however, this pattern is undergoing a change. What is "given up" in these bargains depends on the issue, but "it is certain," one legislator said, "that the city bills would not pass without some concessions being made at the time or promised for a later date." In brief, schools are the objects of informal legislative negotiations in much the same way as other issues are.

Constitutional Convention: Michigan's "Solution"

After years of agitation on the part of Michigan citizens who are aware of impending disaster if the state continues to operate under the provisions of an archaic and restrictive constitution, Michigan has just finished watching the efforts of a 144 delegation Constitutional Convention. A considerable number of issues relating directly or indirectly to the state's educational systems were debated. On the surface, expectations of striking changes in the school picture appear reasonable.

As we have noted, Michigan elects its state superintendent of public instruction on a partisan ticket. Considering the fact that the Democrats have controlled most state offices since 1956, positions on whether the superintendent should be elected or appointed may reflect either individual concern for sound educational administration or partisan desire for control of important posts—or both. Arguments over the desirability of an appointive rather than elective state board of education and superintendent of public instruction follow two lines of reasoning: one concerned with the "model" or idealized approach to the question, and the other thoroughly enmeshed in partisan power strategies.

Those in favor of changing the current status of the superintendent and board put forth arguments which have been summarized by the Citizens Research Council of Michigan in the following manner:[9]

1. Separation of these offices from the requirements imposed by running for popular election would broaden and enrich the field of candidates for the offices.

2. The requirements and functions of the offices are such as to provide little effective basis for qualified voter judgment.

3. The office of the superintendent of public instruction in particular is administrative rather than policy-forming in nature and thus should be appointive.

The other side takes the Jacksonian view that these positions are "too vital to place beyond the control of the people as exercised by direct election."[10]

The example of debate in the convention over the school superintendent's office cannot be separated from debates over the power and authority of the governor. In fact, it can be used to mask the debates over the crucial question of whether to provide for a strong or weak chief executive. And in its turn, the struggle between administrative and legislative branches relates to bitterly conflicting fiscal and economic policies. For example, constitutional provisions pertaining to earmarked funds, sales tax diversion, Michigan's 15 mill property tax limitation, and a state income tax, were all in issue at the convention. So were the short (two year) terms of the governor, the dispersal of authority in a plural executive, the myriad responsibilities of an elected superintendent of public instruction who also serves on numerous state boards and committees, and a state governmental organization which "exhibits all the weird confusion of a twenty-mule team harnessed iin the dark by a one-armed idiot."[11] And of course, all of these issues were part of the conflict between the two major parties and the interests behind them.

A number of changes in the Michigan constitutional set-up may have important implications for the public schools. Perhaps of greatest significance is that the state superintendent will no longer be elected but rather appointed for an indefinite term by an eight member *partisan-elected* state board. Also, the apportionment formulae in the House and Senate have been changed to give greater weight to population.

Despite these changes, pessimists in the state are convinced that the status quo will persist, except for the means of selecting the state school superintendent; and they believe the school lobbies will continue to operate in their traditional fragmented fashion while problems of finance and reorganization remain unresolved. That is, if constitutional revision does not lead to improvements, Michigan school interests will probably be forced to continue along the difficult but not unfamiliar road of temporary alliances, search for friendly legislators, and attempts at piecemeal amendment of existing school policies.

FOOTNOTES

[1]Forced to make choices of consequence and to minimize serious disturbances in his established relationships, the legislator is constantly in need of relevant information. Access is likely to be available to groups somewhat in proportion to their ability to meet this need. David B. Truman, *The Governmental Process* (New York: Alfred A. Knopf; 1951), chapters XI and XII.

[2]In the case of the MFT, partisanship seems accepted as a group tactic, and thus denotes a high degree of cohesion and serves to lessen the threat of cleavages along party lines within the group.

[3]*Michigan Votes: Election Statistics, 1928-1956* (Ann Arbor: Institute of Public Administration, University of Michigan; 1958), p. 118.

[4]Stephen B. and Vera H. Sarasohn, *Political Party Patterns in Michigan* (Detroit: Wayne State University Press; 1957), p. 69.

[5]John P. White, *op. cit.,* p. 111.

[6]The breakdown of unity among the members of the school lobby will be discussed subsequently in connection with issues before the 1961 session of the state legislature.

[7]Peter J. Turano, "Governor Williams' Use of the Executive Veto, 1949-1956," *University of Detroit Law Journal* (October, 1956), p. 13.

[8]Joseph LaPalombara, *Guide to Michigan Politics* (East Lansing: Bureau of Social and Political Research, College of Business and Public Service, Michigan State University; 1960), p. 35.

[9]Citizens Research Council of Michigan, *Michigan Constitutional Issues,* Report 201 (Detroit, June 1960), p. 35.

[10]*Ibid.*

[11]"Miracle in Michigan," *National Municipal Review,* XLVII, No. 7 (July 1958), p. 318.

STATE POLITICS OF EDUCATION*

Laurence Iannaccone

Evidence indicates that the education association network of power and influence used "scribblers" to produce studies, reports, and recommendations between 1890 and 1915 to solve educational problems common to the nation. A single, governmental organization did not exist to solve such problems, and the extra-governmental operation of the extra-legal associations of the educational professionals had to be employed. The similarity displayed by fifty legally-discrete and disparate state systems of education is one result of this *modus vivendi*. Each system looks much more like any one of the others than like anything else known to man. Summarily, it seems quite possible that the four types of linkage structure, found in the eleven states studied, may be all that do exist. Until more states are studied and described, the four types will be used.

The typology used turns upon the nature of the organizational structure, which characteristically links the network of educationist groups to the legislature. One may visualize a state legislature and the lobby—i.e., any set of organizations attempting to influence the legislative process—as a single, complex social system; so conceived, the legislature and the lobby are sub-systems of a larger system clustered around the process of legislation. The specific organizational units (offices, committees, and groups), which work as *key links* between the specific lobbies (and their far-flung tracery of social groups), play a central role in translating influence into the legislative process. Such a social unit, where interaction takes place linking sub-structures that comprise a larger social structure, may be called a point of tangency:

> The linkages at these points of tangency occur in the form of dyads or face-to-face groups comprised of persons who hold common membership in two or more groups (within the social system involved in legislation, thus linking these groups to the legislature) by means of a network of interaction.[1]

To classify states in the typology, the key unit of social structure will be the usual point or points of tangency which link the association network of educationists and their allies to the state legislature. The interaction customarily

---

*From the book *State Politics and Education* by Laurence Iannaccone. © 1967 by The Center for Applied Research in Education. Published by CARE, Inc., 70 Fifth Avenue, New York, New York.

taking place among those who occupy positions in this key-linkage point is used to identify the type of social structure attempting to influence educational legislation. Basically four patterns may be found in reports on the following states: Connecticut, Illinois, Maine, Massachusetts, Michigan, Missouri, New Hampshire, New Jersey, New York, Rhode Island, and Vermont.

I. The first type of linkage structure exists in Vermont, New Hampshire, and Massachusetts, although Massachusetts seems to fit the second type, too. Localism characterizes this structure and the customary interaction at the usual points of tangency linking educationists and the legislature. That is, the participants to the interaction, both legislators and schoolmen (but in particular the schoolmen), represent their school district first of all. Localism implies the existence of geographic bases and districts as essential sub-units in the associational system of schoolmen influencing legislation. Therefore, a chief distinction between sub-units, the separation or boundary lines between sub-units of a structure, would be geographic. This type is locally based. Localism, denoting geographic distinctions and bases, also connotes an attitude of provincialism, jealousy, and fierce defense of one's own home district against outsiders, especially against central government. Geographic separation among neighborhoods—the grassroots of the system of educational influence described in this type—is further reflected in the fierce independence of its units. Such a social system unites effectively to gain its ends with great difficulty when faced with extreme conditions. Even then it is likely to guard its independence jealously and to fall apart immediately after each victory. *Locally-based disparate* denotes this type of structural interaction linking the legislature and the association network.

II. The second type of organizational structure linking the legislature and profession is characterized by a state-wide pattern of interaction. Examples are: New York State, an outstanding case of this type; New Jersey, following the influence of New York State "scribblers"; and probably Rhode Island. Schoolmen customarily speak to the legislature on behalf of education. The chief distinction of the associational boundaries are interest lines rather than geography. The major components of the associational system linked to the legislature usually include the state school boards association, the NEA state affiliate, one or more state associations of school administrators, and some volunteer citizen groups such as the state PTA. Therefore, a chief distinction between the sub-units, the lines of demarcation among the component sub-systems, linked by points of tangency to the legislature, display a state-wide interest character. While representing different interest groups who could display a great deal of conflict and hostility, this type is also characterized by a high degree of consensus—a consensus mutually dependent with an organizational unit that represents the various state-wide interest groups of schoolmen and their allies. The result is a *pyramid* of associations interested in education and educational legislation—a pyramid whose apex appears where the associational system of schoolmen and their friends are customarily linked to the legislature. The *chief point of tangency* between legislature and educational interest groups is the key point of tangency between the association and interest groups involved with schools. The social structure emerging from these generalizations is the feared, condemned, and over-estimated power pyramid such as the one found by Floyd Hunter.[2] It is a *state-wide monolithic* structure.

III. The third type of linkage is found in Michigan. Unique among the eleven states, Michigan contributes an empirically logical category. If a pattern of state-wide educational interest groups and associations, united into a monolithic structure, does exist (as in Type 2), then logically a pattern of state-wide educational interest groups and associations not so united may also exist. In Michigan the logical possibility finds its phenomenological reflection. Here state-wide associations of school board members, teachers of the AFT and NEA state affiliate, school administrators, and parent groups come to the legislature disunited, often in conflict rather than consensus, injecting separate, competitive proposals into the legislative process. *State-wide fragmented* describes this organizational structure and its characteristic interaction pattern with the legislature.

IV. Illinois provides the only instance of the fourth type of linkage structure. The organizational pattern linked to the legislature is state-wide, but the link is a formal governmental unit: the Illinois School Problems Commission. The SPC is a creation of the legislature. It functions like the better-known legislative councils.[3] Because Illinois adopted the legislative council idea in 1937, it is logical that the same idea was extended to educational matters. The purpose of the Illinois law creating its earlier legislative council is stated in its preamble:

> Such legislative planning and formulation as actually obtains would, by being recognized and made properly antecedent to regular sessions, conserve legislative time, save unnecessary expense, improve ensuing debate, and restore legislature activity to the high place in government and public which it merits.[4]

Twenty years later Illinois legislated the existence of the School Problems Commission. Masters *et al.* said that the legislature brought the commission into existence because it was "anxious to find solutions for the many problems in education it faced and to avoid the constant harassment that would result from failure."[5] Membership of the Illinois School Problems Commission illustrates its essential character, as the Washington University team stated:

> The salient feature of the composition and organization of the SPC is that it includes most of the major interests that have a direct and tangible stake in the outcome of the public school decisions. It is structured to provide these interests with a formal and official voice in its deliberations.[6]

Of the seventeen members, each serving two-year terms on the commission as the law provided, ten are legislators, five are appointed by the governor, and two (the state director of finance and the state superintendent of public instruction) are ex-officio. Here a set of politically determined offices are dominated numerically by governmental representatives. The interest groups in education include the NEA-affiliated Illinois Education Association, the Illinois Agricultural Association, the State Association of School Boards, the Chicago Board of Education, and sometimes the Chamber of Commerce. However great the power of educational association leaders may be toward influencing and dominating the commission, the basic structural characteristics of the linkage are state-wide in nature. One would have difficulty arguing that chambers of commerce and agricultural associations are captured and coopted by educationists. Furthermore, the numerical strength lies in the hands of legislators; therefore, even if the SPC has been heavily influenced and near capture by the Illinois educationist group, as Masters *et al.* seem to indicate, the structural link must be treated as a type of its own government rather than extra-governmental in character. Thus, the structure is the focal point of component units of state-wide educational interest groups, governmentally brought together, with representatives who are governmental officials in their commission roles originating from independent organizations. They are a coalition. This form is called *state-wide syndical.*

Correlates of Structural Types

With some knowledge concerning the types of linkage structure, it is possible to hypothesize certain correlates of structure for further research. For example, if certain specificable differences exist among states hypothesized as related to their type of politics of education (defined by the patterns found at their respective points of tangency between the legislature and the educational interest groups), then, once a state is identified by its type, correlates of type can be examined to see if the hypothesized relationships exist. Because action in life must often be taken without full knowledge of the situation, knowing the relationship between structural type and other aspects of one's state increases a group's chances to influence policy making in the politics of education. At least, it may suggest where *not* to put one's energy.

Any discussion of classification systems should provide categories which are mutually exclusive and which exhaust the universe under consideration. The latter goal is easier to achieve if the universe for the task consists in the published reports cited earlier. Otherwise, this task falls short of its exhaustive goal. The author will not offer categories that are mutually exclusive because that ideal is only attainable at the sacrifice of categories which seem worth noting. For example, a category of political life style picks out a characteristic flavor of political behavior from each type of state. Allocation of types of state politics on the classic *Gemeinschaft-Gesellschaft* continuum overlaps political life style. One is much more global, having value for students and researchers, while the other is more specific to behavior, selecting a few aspects for attention. It seems wiser here to risk breaking down walls between some categories than to lose them altogether.

Hypotheses may be offered concerning the role which the points of tangency of the four tyes are likely to play in educational legislation. The probable power of the education lobby in each type of state may be assessed in relation to each role and each structural type. Hypotheses may also be offered concerning the legislature in each type. Aspects of the legislative process, exclusive of the pressure group operations outside its walls, will be used to illustrate the possibilities. (1) Where does the process accommodation of interests, necessary for the passage of educational legislation, take place? (2) What are the sentiments and attitudes of legislators toward education people in each type, and how do they view school people? (3) In what types of states are education people most successful with legislatures, and where do they characteristically initiate or oppose legislation?

Before answering these questions, the author warns students who may demand a mathematical derivation from premise to conclusion for the flow from theory to hypotheses that the course taken here is not the mathematic-deductive one of Herbert Fiegel.[7] Instead, the author's knowledge from reading about the phenomenological universe has invaded the neat reasoning. This analysis is *post factum* because: (1) the data were conceived, collected, and communicated to the field by an atheoretical method; (2) long discussions with graduate students touched briefly the basic ideas involved; and (3) the author prefers interacting with people in complex social systems as a basis for theory construction. The "logic" here may often be a rationalization of the data; such hypotheses do have value.

Where is the chief locus of accommodation likely to be in each of the four types? The answer is implicit in the nature of the social structure, if a specific structural type can account for the interaction patterns of the groups involved in educational legislation. Consider Type I (*locally-based disparate*): the likelihood of accommodation is low among the geographically-separated units of school districts where local pride dominates the behavior. The focus of accommodation on educational legislation in such locally-based disparate states will be *inside* the legislature, probably on the floor of each house. With Type II (*state-wide monolithics*), the accommodation of interests takes place outside the legislature but inside the monolith. The monolith's tasks will get legislation through the houses without upsetting the prior accommodation. Type III (*state-wide fragmented*) faces problems similar to Type I, for it must fight inside the legislature unless various educational interests work together (then the term "fragmented" would hardly apply). Finally, Type IV (*state-wide syndical*) will find an accommodation inside its operations. The existence of governmental members virtually insures such accommodations. This function is given to the point of tangency between the legislature and educational interests.

What are the sentiments and attitudes of legislators toward education people in each type? How do they view school people? Based on the thesis that difficulties lead to frustration, frustration to anger, and anger, in turn is directed against the perceived causes of frustration; and based on another thesis that one is often led to feel great respect for a person (especially in vote counting) if one experiences that person's power; it is possible to generalize about sentiments and concepts. In this manner, legislator sentiment toward education and education's spokesmen, and legislators' views of school people can be considered in each of the four types of states.

In the case of Type I states, *locally-based disparate* linkage structures appear automatically to involve the status of key spokesmen, which is clearly higher than the rank and file teacher status. The dominant local-view-of-the-world reinforces the notion that teachers are paternalistically controllable and that key superintendents will be respected and heeded on educational matters by legislators, particularly those nearest the chief schoolmen.

In the case of Type II states, *state-wide monolithic* linkage structures appear to legislators to represent the totality of the profession in their state. The monolithic structure resulting in a united front suggests that teachers are *a single public* rather than several publics within teaching. The warm sentiment evoked by "Mr. Chips" and the school marm in American folklore is extended to all members of the pyramid, weakening the opposition—even the fumbling weakness of the superintendent in *The Child Buyers*[8] lays the legislator open to seductive cooptation. Legislators will respond to this type of linkage as most people, including college undergraduates, do. Educationists seen as a total group will be viewed positively as very high in social service and activity, but low in power.[9]

In the case of Type III states, *state-wide fragmented* linkage structures display components approaching the legislative hearings arguing among themselves all the way. The distinctions among education's insiders—teachers and administrators, board members, and competing teacher groups—are highly visible to legislators who are often forced to take sides, thereby gaining kudos from some constituents and censure from others. Hostility toward some education groups is likely to result. In addition, a picture emerges of good and bad persons in education. Usually the "school administrator establishment hierarchy" is seen as the "bad guys" and the "poor classroom teacher" as the "good guys." The frustration which legislators must develop at their inability to find real agreement among educationists should hurt educational causes seriously; legislative stalemates could result if Type III states were not openly engaged in extensive public debate actually resulting in higher political gain for legislators acting on educational matters. This more active public interest in Type III states certainly tends to generate greater awareness of the political power of schoolmen even with fragmented association networks, and it means a greater respect by legislators for that power.

In the case of Type IV states, *state-wide syndical* linkage structures are likely to find educationists more positively valued by legislators. The continuous interaction between members of the legislature and the educational interest groups, represented on the governmental unit involved, tends to reinforce the peer relation implied with membership inside this agency. The minimal conflict on the floor (and even in committee) over many educational matters resulting from the "legislative-council" approach could simplify the legislator's task. Any governmental linkage agency, such as the Illinois School Problems Commission, would probably gain prestige. Legislators would consider it truly expert and its direction worth following. Thus, the agency would be attributed with even greater power than it actually has because of the following factors: (1) Legislators need a "fall guy." When an agency appears untouchable and above partisan strife, legislators can blame that agency for their own failure to comply with constituents' demands. "It's no use if *they* (the agency) won't approve it" becomes a convenient excuse to pigeonhole constituents' requests which seem foolish, harmful, or uninteresting to the legislator. Thus, positive sentiments toward education and its representatives will characterize Type IV as well as Type II states. (2) The attributed power, especially to the key linkage component, tends to be greater in Type IV states. The fact may not fit the attribution because the apex of Type II structural units results from a united pyramid and cooptation, while Type IV's unity is more likely to reflect bargaining among its component elements. The presence of legislators in this, however, tends to make it difficult for coalition members to move around it.

In what types of states are education people most successful with legislatures, and where do they characteristically initiate or oppose legislation? Lobbies are effective when they prevent legislation which is contrary to the interests they represent or when they secure legislation which furthers their interests. It is usually easier to prevent legislation than to pass it. Thus, a lobby with influence in the executive office might secure a veto of legislation it disapproves of, although it might lack the capacity to get a bill out of committee or through either house. Again, a lobby may concentrate its resources on a given committee in order to have it pigeonhole a measure, thus avoiding a vote on the floor. For much proposed legislation, sufficient influence to swing one legislative committee of either house is enough to prevent passage. Moving a bill through its rites of passage is frequently another matter requiring different strategies and much more influence. The relative power of lobbies becomes apparent in the distinction between the power to prevent or the power to secure passage of laws. In effect, the first question is: "Can the organized educational professionals prevent hostile legislation?" At first glance, the number of bills opposed and espoused successfully, compared to those opposed and supported unsuccessfully, appears to be an over-simplified merging of equal numbers for each legislative item without discriminating for their significance. One cannot ignore the possibility that a law opposed unsuccessfully, e.g., a proposal revolutionizing the ground rules for entrance into the profession, may have more to tell about the lack of legislative influence of an education lobby than any number of successful bills supported through the same session. It is more difficult to estimate what a lobby has avoided because it felt insufficiently influential to gain more. Here is a subtle and significant factor so difficult to compare that it seems nearly impossible. On the other hand, two factors facilitate judgments concerning the relative influence of education lobbies in one state as compared with another. If the typology does deal with truly significant differences in the type of educational politics of a state, then the variation between two types is likely to be large enough to judge. Furthermore, there are fifty states, not eleven. When data is gathered on more cases of each type, the central tendency for each type, if there is one, will become clearer. Now we are dealing with data comparing only eleven states.

Even within the limits of the eleven cases reported, certain things become clear. The *locally-based disparate* Type I states have not fared well in passing legislation although they seem successful in preventing legislation.[10] This is logically consistent with the nature of the type. Taking into account the capacity of the profession to obtain state aid, legislation strengthens this judgment.[11] Thus, Type I states may be classified as having the power to prevent but not to pass legislation.

State-wide monolithic Type II states also display the capacity to prevent legislation.[12] In addition, they have proud records of initiating education law successfully. In New York, the epitome of the type, the education lobby has been considered the strongest in the state. The question, "Is the 'box score' as good as it appears because of the power of the lobby or because of the nature of the politics of education?" is a doubt raised by the Masters report on Missouri. By graphic example, a wary football coach knows that he can impress the alumni by picking opponents who look good becuase of past prestige or performance but who are not too strong this year; if he is measured by the win-loss column, he will turn in a great record. The educational lobby of Type II states resembles such intelligent coaches at times. No one seeks the toughest battles in the legislative process whatever his sporting instincts are. The game is played for the stakes involved. Furthermore, Type II states have a monolithic educational-interest structure. This is the familiar structure of Butler and Carroll G. Pearse, described by its preferred internal politics: closed system consensus (*see* Chapter 2). As a way of life and a technique of organizational struggle, the group avoids open conflict. Thus, the sub-cultural drives, the stakes involved, the appearance of power to be lost or won all seem to compress the lobby and limit its goals. Its box score of legislative bills won and lost may be misleading. Nevertheless, the educational organizations in this type certainly have more influence over legislation than in the first. They can prevent legislation, pass a great many bills, and traditionally lead the way in acquiring monies for education.

State-wide fragmented Type III politics of education appear to have less powerful education lobbies than Type I cases; some data would argue this, but the overall data are conflicting. Here the paucity of present research is obvious. Against the weakness of fragmentation must be laid the intensity of open conflict that draws such organizations as the AFL-CIO in Michigan[13] into the educational battles; otherwise these organizations would never have been involved. The process mobilizes social power from far-flung networks not usually participating in the legislative process resulting in education law in Type II states. In any case, the structural nature of the key links between educational organizations and the legislature virtually dictates that some educational groups will be successful in their support of certain legislation, each winning and losing some battles but openly fighting in all battles. The financial data on Michigan, compared with Type II states, is much better than one might expect.[14] The lobby here must be classified as mixed toward preventing and passing legislation. If measured by its successes in representing members or clients, as the clients seem to express themselves, it is less influential than Type II lobbies. If measured by the successful yield to educational welfare, although not necessarily expressed by the schools and teachers, the lobby *is more effective*. Visible politics may be better for all concerned and more effective in expressing the true will of the people than invisible politics with more influence.[15]

The education lobby's power in *state-wide syndical* Type IV structures is surely greater than in Type I states. The need for bargaining agreements militates power in opposite directions when it comes to passing laws. The general power to prevent hostile legislation flows logically from the nature of the long-term close association and warm sentiments which are likely to result in this point of tangency. The probable cost in limiting goals after bargaining is less sure, but there must be costs in this process. More important would be the question: "Who has a chair at the table?" The Illinois case does not explore the potential limits and boundaries of the structure now composed of relatively unaggressive associational members. In any case, one essential result of coalition and bargaining is a limitation of yield comparable to accepting half a loaf in lieu of none. Thus, Type IV structures may be classified as able to prevent hostile legislation, able to pass legislation it agrees upon, but likely to undershoot its immediate potential gains for a long-term relationship. Here it is akin to Type II states. If Type IV structures do reflect the publics inside the educational interest group complex, because of its coalitional bargaining rather than monolithic consensus, it is, however likely to undershoot as far as Type II structures do.

The typology and its correlation of legislative efforts, including the lobby's hypothesized power to prevent and to pass legislation, the sentiments of legislators, and the typical loci of accommodations are summarized in Figure 2.

LEGISLATIVE RELATIONSHIPS

Structure of Key Link	I DISPARATE (Locally-based)	II MONOLITHIC (State-wide)	III FRAGMENTED (State-wide)	IV SYNDICAL (State-wide)
Correlates				
LOBBY POWER:				
Prevention	Yes	Yes	Mixed Yes and No	Yes
Initiation	No	Yes	Mixed Yes and No	Yes
LEGISLATOR SENTIMENT	Warm & Paternal to Teachers	Warm, undifferentiated	Differentiated: Critical to Administrators; Warm to Teachers	Warm, not Critical
LOCUS OF ACCOMMODATION	Legislature	Apex of Monolith	Legislature	The Group of Syndics

Figure 2. Typology of linkage structures correlated to legislative effects and appraisal.

Since the key linkage structures with their patterns of intersection mediate between legislature and interest group, the implications of particular structures and patterns are likely to be greater for the association networks tied to the legislative process than for the legislature. Although it may "call the tune" at times in certain states, *the lobby exists because of the legislature,* not the other way around! The correlates of structural type which may be hypothesized from the association network of educational interest groups are tied to the key link with the legislature and legislation. Relevant information for legislative decision making is obviously very valuable. The role played by expertise to provide prestige, peer recognition, and high informal status among legislators is cherished for its information and understanding. No one is generally expert on all legislative matters. Thus, to executive branch bureaucrats and to lobbyists information becomes an almost incalculable premium toward legislative influence, putting legislators in one another's debt. A well-run lobby can make an "expert" legislator.

At this moment in the political history of education's changing power structure, it is relevant and timely to examine several points: (1) the variations in the existence and control of information correlated with structural type; (2) the customary political life style of the educational organizations and their members, especially those models of behavior, the organizational elites; (3) the nature of the educationist elites heading each type and located at the chief linkage to the legislature; and (4) that ubiquitous German continuum of *Gemeinschaft-Gesellschaft* which Howard Becker[16] translated and transmuted as the sacred-secular continuum.

The relationship frequently seen between American ruralism and localism, as well as the arrested development of education into the twentieth century, suggests that Type I *disparate* state educational interest structures will display a dominance of *gemeinschaftlich* in contrast to *gesellschaftlich* educational beliefs, knowledge, outlook, and sense of community. Type II *monolithic* structures will be somewhat closer to the *Gesellschaft* end of the continuum than the *disparate* but still essentially *Gemeinschaft* in beliefs, etc. With the Type III *fragmented* structures, instead, secularization is found; the educational outlook, beliefs, knowledge and sense of association are clearly *Gesellschaft*. Type IV *syndical* structures are again more likely to produce *gemeinschaftlich* outlooks and beliefs. However, the nature of the associations participating will heavily influence the result, and *some of the patterns of consensus* (most likely the politics of the priestcraft) *will reproduce the aura of the sacred community,* primarily because an accommodation had to be reached under the eyes of the legislators! The *syndical* structure will not go as far toward the secular as will the *fragmented* type.

Thus, hypothesizing the characteristic verbal expression and the organizational preference exhibited by participants of educational interest groups, we can rank the four types of political structures along a *Gemeinschaft-Gesellschaft* continuum with no attempt at equal interval scaling. Type I and Type II will be very high and high, respectively, toward the *Gemeinschaft*. Type IV will blend midway between the terminals, and Type III will be nearest the *Gesellschaft* terminal (see Figure 3).

Further substantiation of the positions of the *disparate, monolithic,* and *fragmented* types allocated on this continuum is the work of Seymour Evans at New York University.[17] Evans studied the organization of schools in relation to bureaucratic theory and found that the predisposition of teachers, along a *Gemeinschaft-Gesellschaft* continuum, was related to their tendency to seek organization along a bureaucratic and pre-bureaucratic continuum. This, he noted, is related to the tendency toward union militancy or loose association. Consistent with this, Moeller noted that the rural or urban background of teachers in identical school districts predicted their adherence to the teacher's union or an NEA affiliate.[18]

The nature of the educationist elite, found at the top of the professional associations in the states of each type, follow partially and logically from their location on the sacred-secular continuum. The skills that are needed to operate each structural type, the published reports on the state politics of education, and the author's experience in the field all help to indicate the type of elite one can expect to find in these states. The *disparate* structure suggests that the highest

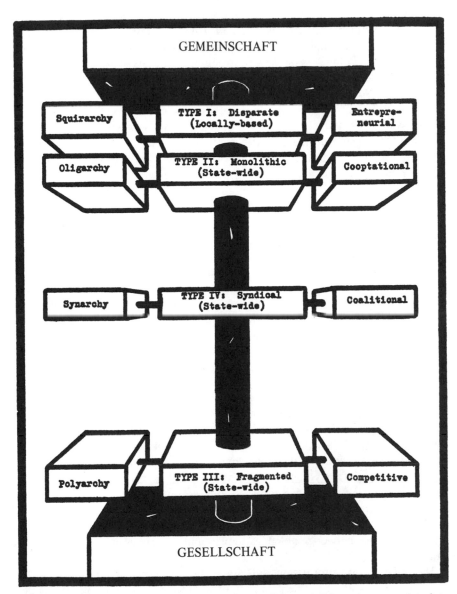

Figure 3. Types of key links in the State Politics of Education correlated to Political Life Styles and Elites ranked along the Gemeinschaft-Gesellschaft continuum. (This Area is represented in Sec. A, Fig. 1)

ranking individual superintendent, who is likely to be well paid, will be able to "phone the folks back home" to gain support for his position. This type of educationist elite is the educational *squirarchy*. Type II states remind one of Springdale in Vidich and Bensman's *Small Town in Mass Society*.[19] New York State, the classic example of Type II (and perhaps progenitor as well), still displays an educational *monolithic* structure with its apex linked to the legislature. Its leaders have been masters of cooptation and the consensus-building manipulation. Not tied to a single geographic component of the state, they tend to lead and partly govern the differing aspects of the complex educational interest system of the state. The term, educational *oligarchy*, describes their leadership. Michigan's *fragmented* structure of interests and interaction pattern with the legislature indicates a division of control, a pulling apart of leaders, a separation along interest lines, but with strong state-wide associations competing for the legislative ear. Hence, the term, educational *polyarchy* identifies this type of elite. The Type IV pattern, *syndical* in nature, is led by association representatives who are governmental officials. Its leaders are an educational *synarchy* (see Figure 3).

The political life styles are further related to each of the respective elites by their educational beliefs, forms of knowledge, outlook, and sense of community that are characteristic of each type of political structure. Therefore, by the very methods these leaders use in dealing with others in educational politics, the behavioral characteristic of the educational "squire" is *entrepreneurial*. In contrast, the political life style of those who lead and those who follow in the educational *monolithic* types rests heavily on persuasion, on the search for agreement, and finally on cooptation. Cooptational behavior characterizes the political life style of the educational *oligarchs*, the educationist elite in the type occurring most frequently. The *polyarchy* of Type III states engages in political behavior and displays a life style most familiar to those for whom two-party struggles are a normal way of life. Secularized and tougher, in fact, than the *oligarchy* of Type II states, the political life style of this group is *competitive* throughout the realm of their associational networks. *Coalitional* behavior characterizes the life style natural to the *synarchy*, with the recognition of identifiable spheres of influence accorded each group.

The *Gemeinschaft-Gesellschaft* continuum may be used to arrange the organizational types of structure found in the key point of tangency linking the legislature to the networks of educationists and correlates of these types (see Figure 3).

The control of information and its quantity at points of access to the legislative process are extremely important sources of influence in the modern legislature. By having data on this dimension alone, a researcher who had no other might pinpoint more accurately the sources of influence over the sources of legislation than he would with any other data. Again, untidy as the sacred-secular continuum is, it too is related, conceptually and phenomenologically, to the nature and control of information.

The *disparate* type of structure with the leadership of the educational squires is short of information. Because of the individualistic, entrepreneurial, localist short-sightedness of its leaders, who laud practical "horse sense" about education when they can actually evaluate a horse's points for county fairs far better than a school program, this structure relies upon folklore and myth in education for its information. The little information it has is scattered and cannot be brought to bear effectively upon the legislative process with respect to education. Quite different are matters regarding quantity, nature, and control of information in the *monolithic* state. The *monolithic* nature of the interest structure itself indicates the *oligarchy's* capacity to deliver what information it has quickly, pinpointed to a target, and specific in detail to influence the legislative process. The *monolith* has a virtual monopoly of information and, as a result, the legislature is conditioned to depend on the *monolith* for its data. The amount and sophistication of these data are high, limited only by the conceptual frameworks of the "scribblers" who historically developed the categories of information and used the theories underlying their use. (Here is the customary vulnerability of closed systems—rigid and repetitive behavior even when no longer appropriate.) To all intents and purposes, the data at hand indicate no significant difference between Type II and Type IV structures regarding the quantity, nature, and control of data that each has. Type III states are another matter. Here more information exists than is characteristically present in Type II states. Moreover, it exists in various forms, not all of which fit the conceptual frameworks of the educationist "scribblers." Other "scribblers" may help determine the flow of information into the legislative process where it functions competitively to pull the legislator this way and that way.

Summary

The politics of education at the state level consists of four basic types of structure, depending upon the nature of the characteristic patterns of interaction taking place at points of tangency which link the legislature and the network of educational interest groups in the particular state. The organizational structure of these key points of tangency was first used to provide indicators of the types that have been described in the published reports by Stephen Bailey *et al.*, Nicholas Masters *et al.*, and Michael Usdan on New England, New Jersey, New York, Illinois, Michigan, and Missouri, cited earlier. Then it was possible to identify elements related to the legislative process in educational matters and, in turn, relate these to each organizational structural type of link between the legislature and the educational interests. These correlates include the characteristic locus of accommodation about educational law, the expressed sentiments of legislators combined with their view of education's legislative spokesmen and the profession as a whole. Indeed, the extent to which the profession is seen "as a whole" was one variable in this discussion. Finally, the probability of the education lobby actually influencing the legislature became another variable related to the four types of states in the politics of education.

In a similar manner, correlates of each of the four types of organizational links were identified by "turning one's back" to the legislature—toward the associational network of interest groups tied through each linkage pattern to the legislature. The quantity, nature, and control of information characteristically available to each linkage type was noted. The educational sub-culture most consistent with the data from the eleven states and logically consistent with linkage type was used to locate the four types on the sacred-secular continuum. Similarly, the characteristic political behavior of each type—the political life style—was noted and charted. The educationist ruling elite typically found in each organizational type was noted. The whole study produces a taxonomy on the state politics of education. (See Figure 1.)

Again, remember that the empirical bases for the illustrated taxonomy consist in the reports on eleven states only, which is a limiting factor. These reports also indicate that more cases of Type II states exist than any other. This makes sense in several ways. The *monolithic* form fits the politics preferred by pedagogues. It is the closest to informal closed-system politics; unlike the *syndical* form, it does not include elected officials. Also, its form was heavily influenced by the schoolmen "scribblers," such as Paul Mort and his protégés. One would expect to find this as the prevailing pattern.

FOOTNOTES

[1] Frank W. Lutz and Laurence Iannaccone, "Power Relationships and School Boards," *Journal of Education,* Karaidudi, Southern India, IX (October, 1965), 1-9. This concept is adapted from the Solon T. Kimball and Marion Pearsell, *The Talladega Story* (University: University of Alabama Press, 1954), p. 259; *see also* Frank W. Lutz, "Social Systems and School Districts," (Unpublished doctoral dissertation, Washington University, St. Louis, Missouri, 1962, p. 6; Laurence Iannaccone, "An Approach to the Informal Organization of the School," in Daniel E. Griffiths, ed., *Behavioral Science and Educational Administration,* Sixty-Third Yearbook, National Society for the Study of Education (Chicago: University of Chicago Press, 1964), pp. 234-238.

[2] Floyd Hunter, *Community Power Structure* (Chapel Hill: University of North Carolina Press, 1953).

[3] Frederic H. Guild, "Our State Legislators," *The Annals of the American Academy of Political and Social Science,* CVC (1938), 144-150.

[4] Quoted in Guild, p. 145.

[5] Masters *et al.,* p. 112.

[6] *Ibid.,* p. 124.

[7] Herbert Feigel, "Principles and Problems of Theory Construction," in *Current Trends in Psychological Theory* (Pittsburgh, University of Pittsburgh Press, 1951), p. 182.

[8] John Hersey, *The Child Buyer* (New York: Alfred A. Knopf, Inc., 1960).

[9] Donald D. O'Dowd and David C. Beardsley, "Student Image of the School Teacher," *Phi Delta Kappan,* XXXXII, (March, 1961), pp. 250-254.

[10]Bailey *et al.*, pp. 92-102.

[11]*Ibid.*

[12]Masters *et al.*, pp. 12-98.

[13]Masters *et al.*

[14]*Ibid.*

[15]Stephen K. Bailey *et al., Schoolmen and Politics* (Syracuse, N.Y.: Syracuse University Press, 1962), p. X.

[16]Howard Becker, *Systematic Sociology* (New York: John Wiley & Sons, 1932), pp. 223-226.

[17]Seymour Evans, "Toward a Theory of Teacher Collective Organizational Behavior" (Unpublished doctoral dissertation, New York University, 1966).

[18]Gerald H. Moeller, "The Relationship between Bureaucracy in School System Organization and Teachers," (Unpublished doctoral dissertation, Washington University, 1962).

[19]Vidich and Bensman.

THE SOCIO-ECONOMIC, POLITICAL AND FISCAL ENVIRONMENT OF EDUCATIONAL POLICY-MAKING IN LARGE CITIES*

Alan K. Campbell

Population within American metropolitan areas is decentralizing. Suburbs continue to grow in population, while central cities decline or, at best, hold their own. The significance of these shifts for the education function would be substantial even if the population redistribution between central city and suburb were random relative to the socio-economic characteristics of the people involved. But this is not the case. The shifting is not only a matter of numbers of people, it also involves a sorting-out process. In general it is the poor, less educated, non-white Americans who are staying in the central city and the higher income whites who are moving out. Although the description must be qualified somewhat in terms of the size of the metropolitan area and region of the country in which it is located, the larger the metropolitan area the more accurate the description is.

It follows from these population differences that the provision of educational services is a more difficult and complicated process in cities than suburbs. Yet expenditures for education are higher in suburbs than cities. The per student expenditures for suburban areas in 1962 were substantially higher than those for central cities. For a sample of 35 large metropolitan areas, suburban expenditures per pupil were $559.42 compared to $414.46 for students in central cities. The gap appears to be increasing. In 1957 expenditures per pupil were approximately the same for city and suburb.

Although socio-economic background of students appears to be the most important determinant of educational achievement, the differences in amount of resources devoted to education apparently holds down this achievement. Correlation analysis indicates that teacher characteristics do influence student performance and higher-priced teacher talent is positively correlated with achievement.

With a declining tax base relative to the suburbs, cities find it difficult to raise additional resources for education. This problem is accentuated by the working of most state aid systems which discriminate against cities. In 1962 suburbs received $40.62 more aid per student than cities. Another difficulty is that aid appears to be partially replacive of local effort in cities, while such is not the case in suburbs.

*From "The Socio-Economic, Political and Fiscal Environment of Educational Policy-Making in Large Cities," presented at the September 1966 meeting of the American Political Science Association.

Since the evidence indicates that massive additional resources will be needed to provide adequate education in cities, and since it seems unlikely that such resources will be raised locally, external aid is vital. Federal aid is a step in the direction of providing special aid for cities but the amounts involved are small.

Reapportionment may help to increase state aid but the evidence is not clear. The political strength of the advocates of additional aid do not seem strong, particularly at the state level. School boards, for example, do not exert much influence beyond the boundaries of their own districts and tend, on the whole, to be more tax- than expenditure-conscious.

In summary, the present allocation of fiscal resources works against education in cities. The lesser resources applied to education in the cities apparently hold down educational performance, particularly in the low income neighborhoods. Additional resources, if massive enough, would probably improve educational achievement. The political possibility of finding such resources for central city education are, at best, uncertain.

Introduction

A group of faculty and graduate students at the Maxwell Graduate School of Syracuse University, with the financial support of the Carnegie Corporation, have been engaged for the past two and a half years in a study of policies and policy-making of large city education systems.[1] This paper is the first public report of some of the findings of this study. Only a few of the individual parts of the over-all study have been completed, and all will not be finished until a year from now. Further, the range of the study is so broad that one paper could not possibly encompass all aspects of it.

Since the study is not completed and because its range is so great this report will concentrate on only a few of the findings, and even these will have to be stated with caution. In order, however, that those findings which are being reported will fit into a meaningful framework the report will focus on the decision-making environment of large city educational systems. The emphasis will be on the socio-economic, fiscal and governmental environment of educational decision-making but some hypotheses, yet to be thoroughly tested, will be presented about the political environment.

It is well to stress at the beginning that the environment and the decisions which emerge from it are not really separable. Today's environment is, in part, a product of yesterday's decisions and today's decisions will help to determine the character of tomorrow's environment. For analytical purposes, however, it is useful to examine the environment as if it were an independent variable since it does provide some explanation for the policies which emerge from it. Relative to policy, the environment plays two roles. On the one hand it indicates the kind of policies necessary if certain agreed upon goals are to be accomplished, and on the other hand it suggests some of the limits on policy innovation.

A good example of this double-edged character of environment is the integration situation facing many large city education systems. Characterized by racial ghettoes the environment may dictate a policy of school integration; yet in many cities, with the Negro proportion of public school population well over half, the only means of accomplishing integration would be to redraw district lines in such a way as to combine city and suburban school populations. The political environment may make such a redrafting of school district lines impossible. Thus, the social environment dictates changes in education policy while the political environment prevents it.

In order to explain the determinative role of the environment for central city education policy-making, the interrelationship between certain environmental factors and fiscal performance and educational achievement will be presented. In order to demonstrate the character of the central city problem the differences and similarities of city and suburban characteristics will be given. The differences in educational performance between city and suburb is, in part, a result of differences in environment and, in part, a result of differences in response to similar environmental factors.

Education's Fiscal Performance

In general, it can be argued that the over-all environment during the past decade has been quite favorable to public education. The resources devoted to this function have increased substantially during this period. In this respect education has acted very much like the total state and local sector of the economy, and this sector is the fastest growing of all sectors of the total economy. Not only has state and local government increased its proportion of total government expenditures, i.e. it has grown much more rapidly than has direct federal expenditures, but has, in fact, increased its role in the total economy.

Total government purchases of goods and services constituted 19.16 percent of Gross National Product in 1964, a figure which shows a small decline from 1954 when it was 21.84 percent. In other words, the total public sector as measured by purchases of goods and services has not increased its proportion of the total economy during the past decade. Its over-all stability, however, hides important internal shifts. For this same ten-year period, federal government purchases as a proportion of Gross National Product declined from 13.96 percent to 10.01 percent, while the state and local sector grew from 7.89 percent to 9.14 percent. In relative terms, therefore, the proportion of Gross National Product represented by state and local expenditures for goods and services increased 16 percent while similar federal expenditures declined 28 percent during the past decade.

This over-all growth in the state and local sector has been made up of different performances by individual functions. Total state and local general expenditures have increased by 126 percent during the past decade while education expenditures have increased by 151 percent. Thus, the function to which the public is willing to devote substantially more than the average increase in resources is education. If education, however, is broken down into its component parts it is higher education which accounts for most of this above-average growth. In fact, local school expenditures grew 128 percent, almost the same as the total state-local expenditures, while expenditures for public *higher* education increased 290 percent.

On the basis of this data it seems fair to argue that, on the whole, public elementary and secondary education has responded to the needs of American society in approximately the same way as have other public functions performed at the state and local level. Whether or not such a response is an adequate one is not answerable by the data, but the data is important in indicating the kind of public policy response which public elementary and secondary education has produced.

These average rates of growth, however, hide important variations in school expenditures among different type areas. There are various ways in which the country can be divided to show these variations but one of the most meaningful is to divide it by its metropolitan characteristics. Metropolitan areas,[2] (the large cities and their suburbs) contain approximately two-thirds of the country's population and each area, of which there are 216, tends to constitute a separate labor market, and school districts within each area probably compare their performance to other districts in the same area.

At least partial substantiation of this "demonstrative effect" of metropolitanism is provided by the fact that the single most important determinant of per student expenditures in any central city is the expenditure per student in that city's suburbs.[3] A simple correlation of .605 was found between central city and suburban expenditures per student and when the variable of suburban per student expenditures was used in a regression analysis with other variables it was the per student expenditure variable which dominated.[4]

This relationship between suburban and city school expenditures should *not* be interpreted to mean that school expenditures in city and suburb are about the same. They are not. Rather it indicates that variations among central cities' school expenditures are best "explained" by suburban school expenditures. There may still be substantial differences between city and suburban expenditures.

In fact, these differences between city and suburban school performance is at the heart of this whole analysis but before examining it further a brief note is necessary about the differences between metropolitan and non-metropolitan educational fiscal behavior. Of particular importance is the difference in the role which intergovernmental aid plays as between metropolitan and non-metropolitan school expenditures on the one hand and between city and suburb school expenditures on the other.

On the basis of per capita expenditures for education in 1962, the latest date for which figures are available, metropolitan and non-metropolitan areas were expending approximately the same amount—$98.24 in metropolitan areas and $93.64 in non-metropolitan areas. If this data is translated into per student expenditures the difference is somewhat greater, primarily because of the higher ratio of local school enrollment to total population in non-metropolitan than in metropolitan areas. Both the age composition of the population and the fewer students attending parochial and private schools in non-metropolitan areas accounts for this greater difference in per student expenditures. In the case of per student expenditures metropolitan areas across the country spent $480.22 per student compared to $419.42 in non-metropolitan areas.

Of interest is this similarity in metropolitan and non-metropolitan school expenditures despite the greater wealth and therefore taxable property within metropolitan than in non-metropolitan areas. This phenomenon is a result of the pattern of state aid which tends to offset the differences between metropolitan/non-metropolitan taxable resources. Aid operates quite differently as between cities and suburbs. Aid to these type areas moves in exactly the opposite direction—greater aid to the suburbs than to the cities.

Central to the concern of this over-all study is this pattern of suburban/central city differences. It is central because of the problem of finding sufficient resources to bring adequate education to the culturally disadvantaged population which tends to be concentrated in the central cities of the country. The per student expenditures for suburban areas in 1962 were substantially higher than for those in central cities. For a sample of 35 large metropolitan areas, outside central city total expenditures per pupil in 1962 were $559.42 compared to $414.46 for students in the central city. The comparable figure for current expenditures were $439 for suburbs and $376 for cities. These figures are in sharp contrast with those for 1957. In that year current per student expenditures were $303 in the suburbs and $310 for cities. The difference for each metropolitan area in the sample are given in Table 1.

"Thus, in 1957 central cities were spending about the same per pupil as their suburbs, but by 1962 the suburbs forged considerably ahead. This relative growth in suburban school expenditures per student is even more remarkable when one considers that suburban school system enrollments grew between 1957 and 1962 at almost twice the rate of their central city counterparts. Indeed if account is taken of differentials in the proportions of the total population going to public elementary and secondary schools by measuring expenditure growth differentials in per capita terms, the growth in the suburbs relative to the central cities is even greater."[5]

Table I

Current Educational Expenditures per Student, Total Educational Expenditures per Capita and Total Non-aided Educational Expenditures per Capita (Tax Proxy) for Central City and Outside Central City Areas: 1962

	Current Education Expenditures Per Student 1962		Total Education Expenditures Per Capita 1962		Total Non-Aided Education Expenditures Per Capita 1962	
	CC	OCC	CC	OCC	CC	OCC
New York	$536.88	$684.34	$ 77.29	$194.05	$47.10	$127.88
Chicago	408.51	473.69	66.09	112.60	50.78	92.15
Los Angeles	437.14	555.54	101.01	174.83	64.82	72.53
Philadelphia	397.75	492.96	54.69	105.59	37.24	81.42
Detroit	461.67	434.10	93.78	128.08	70.16	88.59
Baltimore	366.07	421.61	80.50	112.82	60.67	81.21
Houston	290.09	450.35	63.75	143.85	32.42	91.87
Cleveland	370.59	459.50	65.01	113.74	58.25	100.98
St. Louis	386.58	423.73	55.31	100.70	37.11	75.87
Milwaukee	377.90	469.38	65.20	124.75	51.77	112.84
San Francisco	466.77	546.29	69.19	172.17	45.47	73.83
Boston	385.46	465.36	50.32	100.87	43.78	93.09
Dallas	301.96	325.40	74.42	100.37	47.29	61.63
New Orleans	271.87	233.05	41.74	66.63	12.68	27.62
Pittsburgh	368.00	450.98	51.19	96.05	39.76	61.52
San Diego	414.63	538.95	105.13	156.29	67.70	92.42
Seattle	409.89	415.72	89.39	138.86	46.93	58.83
Buffalo	447.03	561.20	59.27	137.32	33.82	77.52
Cincinnati	373.11	577.74	62.80	118.29	55.07	95.24
Memphis	227.58	245.71	48.74	96.59	26.54	64.25
Denver	418.30	380.74	81.19	151.07	67.13	116.37
Atlanta	272.52	287.80	57.42	90.49	36.17	51.47
Minneapolis	414.31	441.45	61.42	157.05	41.91	63.32
Indianapolis	352.87	467.92	69.83	144.17	51.30	116.28
Kansas City	409.19	350.67	75.09	156.54	54.40	126.33
Columbus	327.40	332.06	61.25	98.08	51.97	69.77
Newark	496.21	522.23	93.80	112.08	78.32	100.04
Louisville	301.44	477.73	42.81	134.33	25.28	106.31
Portland, O.	421.59	480.14	79.37	149.10	58.32	95.58
Long Beach	426.33	555.54	85.99	174.83	51.08	84.77
Birmingham	194.43	223.89	49.93	61.49	18.23	23.64
Oklahoma	269.23	291.67	67.16	83.76	43.97	70.37
Rochester	580.05	573.07	79.35	158.58	54.79	91.53
Toledo	377.71	511.85	80.08	160.51	71.54	113.00
St. Paul	415.51	441.45	58.10	157.05	40.37	55.02
Norfolk	265.43	288.65	47.42	87.51	29.53	59.23
Omaha	282.58	394.90	49.48	136.83	43.88	126.37
Mean	376.33	439.11	67.96	127.24	47.23	83.80

Source: U. S. Bureau of Census, *Census of Governments*, 1962.

This relative decline in expenditures for the education of central city students compared to suburban students has occurred simultaneously with a "sorting-out" of metropolitan population. Not only has large central city population either declined, or at best held its own, but the composition of that population has changed as well. In general, it is the poor, less educated, non-white Americans who are staying in the central city and the higher income, better educated whites who are moving out, although this description must be qualified somewhat in terms of the size of the metropolitan area and region of the country in which it is located. The larger the metropolitan area, however, the more accurate is the description.[6]

This sorting out process has resulted in a median family income for central city residents in 1959 which was 88.5 percent of outside central city income; $5,940 for central cities, compared to $6,707 for the suburbs. Although median family income for both central city and outside central city residents has grown since 1959, the gap is widening, with central city median family income in 1964 at $6,697 while for outside central city areas it was $7,772, a proportionate relationship of 86.2 percent.[7]

These nation-wide averages hide important differences between metropolitan areas which can be explained, in part, by differences in population size. Over-all, the larger metropolitan areas have higher family incomes than the smaller ones. In metropolitan areas having populations of over three million—the largest size category—the percent of families earning over $10,000 a year is almost double the percent earning less than $3,000 a year—23 compared to 12.6. Further, it is only in this category that the central cities have a higher proportion of their population over $10,000 than under $3,000, 19.5 percent compared to 15.4 percent.

As size declines, over-all metropolitan wealth declines, too. The proportion of families earning under $3,000 increases from 12.6 percent for areas in the largest size category to 20.7 percent for those in the smallest category, while the percent of families earning over $10,000 declines from 18.8 percent to 13.8 percent.

These figures demonstrate that the large metropolitan areas have less poverty proportionately than the small ones. This finding, however, is not as significant for the performance of the education function as is the contrast between central cities and their suburbs. It is these large, relatively affluent areas which possess the greatest income disparity between central cities and their suburbs. In the size category of over three million, for every 100 families in central cities earning under $3,000 there are 127 earning over $10,000. In the suburbs the comparable number of families with an income over $10,000 is 312 for every 100 families earning under $3,000. In other words, there are 185 more families with income over $10,000 in the suburbs for every 100 families under $3,000 than is true for the central cities. The magnitude of this difference in income distribution between central city and outside central city declines as the size of the area decreases and, in fact, reverses itself for the two size-categories below 250,000 population.

The differences in income characteristics between central cities and their suburbs is reflected in the educational attainment of the respective populations. Again, the contrast between central city and suburbs is substantial: 40.9 percent of central city pupils have completed four years of high school or more, while outside the central cities the comparable percentage is 50.9.

The explanation for the income and education differences between central city and suburb rests, in part, on differences in the distribution of non-white population within metropolitan areas. Although the non-white component of the American population has now distributed itself between metropolitan and non-metropolitan areas in approximately the same proportion as the white population, the distribution within metropolitan areas (i.e., between central cities and suburbs) follows a quite different pattern. It is well known that the proportion of non-whites in central cities has been increasing, while the proportion in the suburban areas has been declining. The proportion of non-whites in central cities has increased since 1900 from 6.8 percent of the central city population to 17.8 percent, while in the areas outside central cities the non-white proportion has declined from 9.4 to 5.2 percent of the total. In other words, the non-white population proportion is moving in exactly the opposite direction within metropolitan areas as the proportion of white population.

This larger proportion of Negro population in central cities helps to account for the differences in educational achievement and income between central cities and suburbs. Due to a history of discrimination in all aspects of life, the Negro has a lower income and less education than does his white neighbor. In central cities, for example, the 1964 median family income for Negroes was $4,463, while for whites it was $7,212. In 1964 the percentage of all Negroes 25 years old and over having completed 4 years of high school was 17.1; the comparable percentage for whites was 31.3.

The impact of the growing proportion of non-white population in central cities is intensified for the schools by the even higher proportion of public school enrollment which is non-white. This difference in population and enrollment proportions is a result of age distribution, family composition, and the greater tendency of white parents to send their children to private and parochial schools. In 1960, for example, 23 percent of Chicago's population was non-white, while 40 percent of its public school population was in this category. Similar percentages for other cities are: Philadelphia 26 and 47, Detroit 29 and 43, Cleveland 29 and 46, Washington 54 and 78. Since 1960 these disparities have increased and more and more cities find that well over half of their school population is non-white.

These characteristics of the school population create educational problems for central city school systems. Yet it appears that as the problems increase the resources available for solving the problem decline. They decline, at least, relative to the resources available for educating suburban children.

The differences in resources for education between central cities and suburbs is substantial. The differences in income level have already been given. There are also differences in taxable property. Data for property value is more difficult to get than for income, but scattered data demonstrate the stronger tax base in suburban areas. For example, in a recent five-year period the percent changes in taxable assessed valuation for seven cities were as follows: Baltimore, -10.5 percent; Boston, -1.2 percent; Buffalo, -1.0 percent; Detroit, -2.0 percent; St. Louis, +1.1 percent; Philadelphia, +2.8 percent and Cleveland, -3.4 percent.[8]

With lower income and a declining (or, at best holding its own) tax base, cities find it increasingly difficult to finance not only education expenditures but all public expenditures. These non-education expenditures also create greater problems for cities than for suburbs. For the 37 sample metropolitan areas the suburbs spent in 1962 $126.94 for non-education functions of government while the cities spent $161.70 per capita, a difference of $34.76. This difference makes it possible for suburban areas to devote a larger portion of their public funds to education than cities do: 55 percent as opposed to 32.4 percent.

Most surprising of all is that despite these differences the states provide more aid to suburban than to city school districts. "On a per student basis, the cities average $124.92 in aid from their state while the suburbs get $165.54, or a difference of $40.62 for every student. The relative difference is larger on a per capita basis than it is on a per pupil basis. The mean per capita aid for education is $20.73 while the comparable figure for outside central city areas is $37.66, a difference of $16.93 per capita."[9] As already pointed out, this pattern is quite different than the one found between metropolitan and non-metropolitan areas. In that case aid offset rather than accentuated resource differences as it does between city and suburb.

This difference of the socio-economic and fiscal environment demonstrates that there are differences in the environment of cities and suburbs.[10] One of the issues which emerges from this description is the interrelationship between the socio-economic and fiscal characteristics. In other words, do the socio-economic differences explain the fiscal differences? This issue is being examined by several participants in this over-all study and some tentative findings can be given.

Determinants of Central City and Suburban School Fiscal Behavior

In measuring the fiscal response of education there are a variety of ways of stating that response. One of the most common is expenditures per pupil, and to some extent this is a measure of education quality. Another measure is expenditures per capita, which indicates the over-all federal-state-local burden of school costs, while another measure is per capita locally-raised expenditures (a proxy for locally-raised taxes for education) which indicates the local burden of school costs.

The differences between city and suburb for each of these fiscal outputs are given in Table 2.

Table 2

Average Fiscal Outputs for Suburban and City School Systems
in 35 Standard Metropolitan Statistical Areas (1962)

	Suburbs	Central Cities	Differences
Current educational expenditures per student	$439.11	$376.33	+ $62.78
Total educational expenditures per capita	127.24	67.96	+ 59.28
Locally-raised expenditures per capita	83.80	47.23	+ 36.57

Source: Computed from U. S. Bureau of the Census, *Census of Population*, 1960 and U. S. Bureau of the Census, *Census of Governments*, 1962.

Through multiple regression analysis many socio-economic variables were tested relative to each of these fiscal variables. Rather than present the total analysis, the discussion will be restricted to those variables which appear important with some mention of variables which normally are believed to be important but which did not prove to be so in this analysis.[11]

As already explained, the most important determinant of central city school expenditures is suburban school expenditures. This finding is true for all three measures of school expenditures. When the level of suburban school expenditures is introduced into the regression equation it tends to overpower all the other variables. In other words, for any given metropolitan area there is a strong relationship between city expenditures and suburban expenditures. The higher suburban expenditures, the higher city expenditures are.

This finding is not a surprising one but it is, nonetheless, important. It demonstrates that city and suburban schools in the same metropolitan area are operating in the same labor market and that there is a demonstration or imitation effect which causes these two parts of metropolitan areas to emulate each other, with the influence probably running from suburb to city rather than the other way. It seems clear that the pressure for educational resources exerted by suburbia has raised the cost of education in central cities. Although central city school expenditures follow suburban school expenditures, the gap between them is, in fact, widening. Despite this increasing difference the dependent relationship contains important implications for the cost of education in central cities. As suburban school expenditures climb upward, more and more pressure will be put on the already heavily burdened fiscal bases of central cities.

Another general finding of particular importance for central cities is the lack of fiscal significance for city schools of the independence or dependence of their governmental systems. The finding is reported despite its negative character because of the tendency, in much popular literature about education, to attach great importance to governmental independence.

The significance of this variable was tested by developing a continuum from high independence to complete dependence. High independence included an independently elected board with taxing power while complete dependence included an appointed board with dependence on general city government for fiscal resources. Measured in this way it was found that the degree of independence had no influence on educational fiscal outputs; not on per student expenditures, per capita expenditures, or per capita locally-raised taxes. It may well be that the independence-dependence issue is important relative to other educational policy matters but as far as fiscal policy is concerned it is not, with only one possible qualification to this generalization being necessary.

That qualification relates to the proportion of total city expenditures (education and non-education expenditures) devoted to education. Apparently independence does result in a somewhat larger proportion, although not a higher level, of public expenditures for education. In other words, independence does not raise the absolute amounts spent for education but does give to education a larger proportion of the total city public expenditures. It is possible that some would count this a factor in favor of independence. But is it? It means lower expenditures for such non-education functions as police, fire, welfare, housing, all of which are related to the general well-being of the community and may also, as will be shown later, have direct relevance to the performance of the education function.

Turning now to the variables which were used to analyze the fiscal variations for both city and suburban education, the most important is personal income. This variable is significant for all measures of educational expenditures in both cities and suburbs, although perhaps it is more important in explaining suburban than city expenditures. This importance of income for educational fiscal outputs is but one of the findings in the over-all study of large city education which demonstrates the fundamental significance of personal income for educational performance. Not only does it influence the amount of money spent for education, it is also the single best indicator of student performance as will be shown later. Income, which probably serves as a proxy for many other family characteristics, is apparently a measure not only of resources available for education but of the willingness of people to use their resources for education and of motivation for educational accomplishment by students.

Another variable, the enrollment ratio, i.e., the proportion of population in public schools, does influence the various expenditure measures differently. It is positively associated with both per capita measures, per capita expenditures and per capita locally-raised school taxes, but is negatively associated with per student expenditures. In other words, as the enrollment ratio increases, per capita education expenditures, both total and locally-raised, increase but per student expenditures decline. A high enrollment ratio, therefore, calls forth more fiscal effort on behalf of education but the increased effort is not sufficient to make per student expenditures as great as they are when the enrollment ratio is lower. Stated another way, when a high proportion of students attend parochial and private schools the expenditures per student are higher in public schools than when the proportion attending non-public schools is low.

Intergovernmental aid plays a more complicated role than the other variables and in some ways a more crucial one since it is directly controllable by public policy decisions. As would be expected, aid is positively associated with per capita educational expenditures and per student expenditures in both cities and suburbs; but if locally-raised expenditures are examined, the difference in behavior between city and suburb is revealing.

The issue is whether aid acts to reduce local school tax effort or is additive to that effort. In the case of suburbs it seems that aid is almost entirely additive. One study of 1957 data found that in suburbs for every one percent increase in aid there was a reduction of only .03 percent in education taxes. This same study found that for central cities there was a reduction of .15 percent for every one percent increase in aid. A more recent study, using 1962 instead of 1957 data, found the reduction in central city school taxes to be .42 percent for every one percent increase in state aid while the comparable decrease in the suburbs was only .18 percent.

Stated another way, increases in state aid result in higher total educational expenditures in both city and suburb, but the increase is much greater in suburbs (almost the full amount of the aid) than it is in cities. As education aid for cities increases, particularly federal aid, this behavior pattern becomes particularly important. To the extent that aid results in reductions in local effort, the policy purposes of the aid are undermined, at least in part.

It has often been hypothesized that non-education public expenditures have a dampening influence on education expenditures. Much of the argument for independent school districts is based on the belief that an independent tax base for education aids school districts in overcoming this supposed influence of the non-education fiscal burden. Although a weak relationship was found between non-education expenditures and all measures of education expenditures for both cities and suburbs, in no case was the finding sufficiently strong to be significant. Non-education expenditures do not appear to hold down, in any significant way, education expenditures in either city or suburb.

Finally, the influence of owner-occupied housing was examined. It has often been suggested that home ownership tends to hold down tax levels, particularly at the local level where property taxes predominate. For non-education expenditures and taxes this hypothesis is true. It is not true for either education expenditures or locally-raised education taxes in either cities or suburbs. Apparently there is a greater willingness on the part of the public to support education than non-education services when the tax bill is paid directly through taxes on local property.

In combination, these variables explain a good deal of the variation in both city and suburban school expenditures. The range is from 83 percent explanation for variation in central city current expenditures per student, when expenditure levels in the suburbs are included in the equation, to a low of 33 percent for cities in the case of locally-raised education taxes when only income, enrollment ratio and state aid are included in the equation.[12]

Although this range of explanatory power is quite wide, indicating that some types of fiscal outputs are more easily explained than others, it is clear that many of the important variables have been isolated. Whatever policy goals are sought in the education field, it is clear that some of these variables will have to be influenced if agreed-upon policy goals are to be accomplished.

Finding the Resources

The participants in the Large City Education Systems Study are not experts in learning theory or teaching techniques and, therefore, make no recommendations in these areas. As political scientists and economists, however, judgments can be made by them about the need for additional resources. The evidence, although perhaps not conclusive, strongly indicates the need for the infusion of rather massive resources into disadvantaged schools.

What are the political possibilities of such resources being allocated to the areas of obvious need? The comments on this question will have to be tentative. The political portions of the Large City Study are not finished but a few findings are beginning to emerge. They are not, however, sufficiently firm to merit more than brief comment.

Perhaps the most important single generalization relative to the political potential for change is a negative one. The present fiscal responses to socio-economic characteristics and the system of local school government tend to reinforce each other. The decision-making unit at the local level, the school board, responds not to the general problems of its metropolitan area or of its state but rather to the district which it serves. Since these districts tend to homogeneity in socio-economic characteristics, particularly in the suburbs, the inevitable result is a pattern of resource allocation which reflects the nature of the districts involved.

A redrawing of school district lines, causing the districts to reflect more accurately the total population distribution of the metropolitan area, would change this environment, and might cause a more equal distribution of educational resources between city and suburb. The growing demand by national educational leaders for metropolitan-wide school districts is based on the belief that this would be the result.

The political possibility of this partial solution being adopted is not great. There are no substantial political forces at the appropriate level of government demanding it. But even if there were, its potential for accomplishing the right kind of change in resource allocation is not great. It is true that a redrawing of boundaries to include city and suburb in the same district might raise expenditure levels in the city. It might simultaneously lower expenditures in the suburbs. It seems clear that the present competitive situation, which is particularly important among suburban school districts, but which, as has been shown, does have some impact on central city school expenditures, causes per capita and per student expenditures to be higher than would be the case if common, metropolitan-wide school districts were established. In other words, metropolitan-wide districts might lead to greater equality in suburban and city expenditures but might simultaneously lower average total expenditures. City expenditures would be higher, suburban expenditures lower.

To correct the present distribution of resources, however, requires more than simply equalizing expenditures between city and suburb. The need is for an unequal distribution of resources in order to accomplish genuine equality of educational opportunity. Such a goal raises a serious ideological problem for the educational community. The California report explains this dilemma when it says, "With respect to the adequate provisioning of slum schools, one factor is the view of local school authorities that each school, regardless of the nature [of] the pupil clientele served, must be equally treated. It is said that the public demands that staffing ratios, expenditures for instructional materials and supplies, etc., be approximately the same for all schools of a given grade level. Further, this view is reinforced by the code. Section 1054 of the Education Code, Statutes of 1963, states: 'The governing board of any school district shall maintain all of the elementary day schools established by it, and all of the day high schools established by it with equal rights and privileges as far as possible.' "[13]

There has been a gradual moving away from this equality concept with the acceptance of compensatory education as an appropriate policy goal. Thus far, however, the resources involved have been small.

Even assuming the policy acceptance of the goal of increasing and reallocating resources in accord with educational needs will not guarantee the effectuation of such a policy. Such new and reallocated resources will have to be raised either at the local level or aid, state and federal, will have to be substantially increased.

The kind of increased local tax effort which would be required to meet the needs described here seems highly unlikely. The fiscal bind in which most cities find themselves is well known. Further, the behavior of the city school boards in the cities studied indicates that they are more tax- than expenditure-conscious. There seems to be a tendency to calculate how much tax increase the community will tolerate rather than to concentrate on the expenditure levels necessary to do the educational job.

A school principal in New York City describes the situation well when he says: "I have regard for the Board of Education, but it has never fully recognized that it ought to be functioning as the representative of the children—all children, but most particularly poor children, who have the fewest representatives in power. The Board should continually be making strong statements about the urgent need for money and services. So far, the Board has represented education in a taxpayer's style. It ought to keep haranguing the city to the point at which a real exploration takes place of how to get the essential funds. Sure, there'd be some complaints from parts of the citizenry, but it would be useful to get those complaints out into the open. And the middle class as a whole would not really oppose this kind of push. The middle class is always passive—alienated from its own beliefs. It doesn't even know it *has* beliefs until things are stirred up. We ought to make education *the* basic industry in this city."[14]

Whether school boards fight as hard as they should for increased expenditures is perhaps a moot point. The difficulties, however, of raising substantial additional funds locally are sufficiently great that it seems unlikely the funds will be raised at this level.

This conclusion means that if the resources are to be found they will have to come from outside; from either state or federal aid. Further, that aid, if it is to serve the problem of education for the disadvantaged, will have to be pointed specifically to this problem.

Two findings about aid made in this study are relevant to its potential for dealing with the problem. The first is the present aid pattern. It discriminates against cities. If aid is to serve the purpose outlined here, this characteristic will have to change. The other relevant finding about aid is its impact on local school expenditures. It does raise these expenditures but not as much in cities as the full amount of the aid. If the aid is intended to be fully additive to local effort, therefore, policies will have to be adopted to accomplish this end.

The more important issue, however, is whether aid can be made to reflect the kinds of problems which it must solve. Thus far aid at the state level has not moved in that direction. There is, however, some evidence that state legislatures are beginning to think in terms of compensatory education. New York, Illinois and California have all begun to move in this direction. The amounts of money involved thus far are small and compensatory education does not appear to have much political strength at the state level.

It is believed by some that reapportionment will aid in correcting the present distribution of aid as between suburbs and cities. Ever since the Supreme Court decision insisting on the one-man one-vote principle, there has been much speculation as to what the increase in metropolitan representation in state legislatures will do to state policies and through such policies to state-local and local fiscal outputs. The uniformly higher aid pattern outside of metropolitan areas, when measured on a state-by-state basis, is consistent with the pre-reapportionment representation pattern.

More complex is the situation as it relates to suburban areas. Although these areas are underrepresented in state legislatures, even more so than central cities, they have done relatively well in terms of the amount of state aid they have received. This result is undoubtedly related to the historical situation when these areas were, in fact, rural and to the set of functions which state legislatures have over the years decided to aid. These aided functions make up a larger part of the packages of services in suburban areas than in central cities. The suburban areas thus receive more aid relative to their fiscal burden than do central cities.

Since reapportionment will increase suburban representation, it follows that the present aid advantage which these areas possess might be retained or even enhanced. On the other hand it is possible that a reapportioned state legislature will be sufficiently metropolitan-oriented to show concern—not only for suburban problems but for those of the city as well. The result could be an increase in education aid as well as other types of aid to central cities. The evidence on this point is not yet in.

In part, the ability of cities to improve their aid position will depend on the amount and kind of political influence they can bring to bear in state legislatures. As a part of this total study of large city education, a series of case studies on the role of central city school boards relative to increasing the amount of aid for their jurisdictions have been undertaken. These studies are not yet finished but it is clear that the Boards of Education in Chicago, Boston and San Francisco played a relatively small role in supporting state aid for compensatory education. In the case of Illinois, the Superintendent of Schools from Chicago did play an active role but his Board was little involved.

Once the resource issue moves away from the question of local tax rates school boards seem to play a relatively small role. School administrators, apparently, are somewhat more involved and perhaps most involved of all are organizations of teachers. The role of teachers, however, is not usually concerned with the issue of the increasing of aid to disadvantaged schools. They are more concerned with such matters as salary scales, pension systems and working conditions.[15]

There is some evidence that some city leaders, particularly those involved in the economic health of their city, have become increasingly concerned about the quality of education provided in their cities. The relationship of education to economic development is believed by many of them to be an important one. There are, therefore, a number of cities, of which Atlanta is one, where efforts are being made by these leaders to get from state legislatures greater school aid.

If this movement should spread it is possible that a coalition of local business leaders, school board members, school administrators and teacher organizations could bring substantial pressure to bear on behalf of increased education aid to cities. No such coalition now exists.

Finally, there is the issue of federal aid. The present federal aid program is designed specifically to deal with the problem of the education of the disadvantaged. Politically this aid has grown out of national rather than state and local political forces. It is a product of the demand for increased aid from national professional associations, plus other national interest groups. The major breakthrough occurred in 1965 when the church-state issue was sufficiently compromised to permit both the National Education Association and Catholic groups to support the program.[16]

The issue about federal aid, therefore, is not one of principle but one of adequacy of funds. The demand for funds from other government activities, particularly the Viet Nam war, has undoubtedly held down the increase in resources allocated by the national government to education. Again there is no evidence of any strong activity on the part of local school boards to increase federal aid.

Although external aid appears to be the only means by which the resources necessary for dealing with the kinds of education problems which face this country can be provided, it is by no means certain that sufficient aid will be found to meet this need. The evidence is not yet clear. Perhaps the pattern of political behavior of state legislatures and the national government will show itself more clearly in the next two or three years. In the meantime the principal spokesman for education at the local level, school boards, seem to be playing a relatively minor role. There is no evidence in the studies we have undertaken to indicate that this role is going to undergo any drastic change.

In summary, the present allocation of fiscal resources works against education in cities. The lesser resources applied to education in the cities apparently hold down educational performance, particularly in the low income neighborhoods. Additional resources, if massive enough, would probably improve educational achievement. The political possibility of finding such resources for central city education are, at best, uncertain.

FOOTNOTES

[1] A brochure describing this study may be obtained by writing to the Metropolitan Studies Program, 607 University Avenue, Syracuse, New York 13210.

[2] The Census Bureau definition of metropolitan area and of its component parts is followed throughout this study. That definition is as follows: "Except in New England, a standard metropolitan statistical area (an SMSA) is a county or group of contiguous counties which contain at least one city of 50,000 inhabitants or more or 'twin cities' with a combined population of at least 50,000. In addition to the county, or counties, containing such a city or cities, contiguous counties are included in an SMSA if, according to certain

criteria, they are essentially metropolitan in character and are socially and economically integrated with the central city." In New England, towns are used instead of counties.

[3]David Courtney Ranney, "School Government and the Determinants of the Fiscal Support for Large City Education Systems," Ph.D. dissertation, Syracuse University, 1966.

[4]*Ibid.*, pp. 175-176.

[5]Seymour Sacks and David C. Ranney, "Suburban Education: A Fiscal Analysis," to be published in *Urban Affairs*, Fall 1966.

[6]For a complete discussion of these differences relative to size and region see Advisory Commission on Intergovernmental Relations, *Metropolitan Social and Economic Disparities: Implications for Intergovernmental Relations in Central Cities and Suburbs* Washington, D.C.: U.S. Government Printing Office, 1965).

[7]U. S. Bureau of the Census, *Consumer Income*, Series P-60, No. 48, April 25, 1966.

[8]For further discussion of this see Alan K. Campbell and Philip Meranto, "The Metropolitan Education Dilemma: Matching Resources to Needs," to be published in *Urban Affairs*, Fall 1966.

[9]Sacks and Ranney, *op. cit.*, p. 7.

[10]It should be noted that the lumping of all suburbs together hides important differences among suburbs. There are suburbs which possess many of the same socio-economic characteristics as cities have and as a result many of the same kinds of problems.

[11]The material for this section of the report is drawn principally from Ranney (Dissertation), Sacks and Ranney, *Op. cit.*, and Campbell and Sacks, "Metropolitan America: Fiscal Patterns and Governmental Systems," to be published by The Free Press of Glencoe.

[12]The Beta coefficients for a variety of variables relative to the various measures of educational expenditures used here are given in Appendix I.

[13]Senate Fact-Finding Committee, *op. cit.*, p. 60.

[14]Ilentoff, *op. cit.*, pp. 82 85.

[15]An analysis of the role of teacher organizations is being done as a part of this over-all study: Alan Rosenthal, *Pedagogues and Power: Teacher Organization in Five Large Cities*, to be published Spring 1967.

[16]For an analysis of the constellation of political forces which produced the Elementary and Secondary Education Act of 1965 see Philip Meranto, *The Politics of Federal Aid to Education in 1965: A Study in Political Innovation*, to be published Spring 1967.

PART III

POLITICS OF EDUCATION AT THE FEDERAL LEVEL

INTRODUCTION TO PART III

Overview of Readings

The selections in this part concentrate on all aspects of the federal policy making process for education. The initial selection by James Sundquist presents a detailed historical analysis of the legislative politics of federal aid legislation. He focuses on the substance of the various proposals and the political forces that blocked or advocated the bills in Congress.

Sundquist's congressional analysis is supplemented by two selections that focus on executive policy, direction and innovations during the administration of the landmark Elementary and Secondary Education Act legislation. Bailey's case study explores the impact of a vast increase in administrative responsibility on the organization, personnel qualifications, and orientation of the Office of Education. Bailey's study also illuminates the importance of federal agencies and ad hoc Presidential task forces (composed of non-government consultants) in designing substantive legislative proposals.

A central concern of both Sundquist's and Bailey's studies is the types and amounts of political influence (often mobilized by changes in the substance of the legislation) needed to overcome obstacles to federal aid. Bailey stresses that the man who concerted and aggregated political influence for ESEA was the Commissioner of Education, Frances Keppel. Keppel was an influence broker who included or excluded various components and substantive aspects of the legislation in order to aggregate enough allies to insure passage. The major education interests held together in support of ESEA as they have in legislative victories at the state level described in the previous part. A key factor, however, was the 1964 election to the House of 80 liberal Democrats pledged to the enactment of federal aid to education.

After an education bill is passed and the administrative agency is reorganized there is a vast amount of policy made by administrators through federal regulations and guidelines. Bailey and Mosher highlight the Office of Education's attempt to impose regulations and guidelines restricting the number of children who could participate in the Title I programs. By restricting the participants, OE hoped to insure a high per pupil expenditure. But OE did not have enough

321

political influence to sustain its policy and had to make large concessions to the chief state school officers. Indeed the right to promulgate federal administrative regulations and guidelines does not necessarily give federal agencies sufficient flexibility to shape the legislation according to their interpretation of Congressional intent. There are the same kinds of negotiation and bargaining in the administrative process as Sundquist describes in the legislative process.

The passage of ESEA demonstrates the predominant political influence that an innovation minded executive branch can have *under favorable political circumstances.* Indeed, ESEA was changed very little by Congress. Sundquist's selection, however, demonstrates that many earlier attempts at passage of federal aid were reworked substantively in Congress and subsequently died there. In short, the passage of ESEA is not a good indicator of the real or potential influence Congress wields over education policy. Prior to 1965 the three obstacles of race, religion and fear of federal control had made Congress a graveyard for federal aid bills. Sundquist analyzes how these political obstacles were overcome.

The Influence of the Federal Courts

The role of the judiciary cannot be overlooked in describing the political system for public education. Alan K. Campbell noted that "in the field of education, no single public decision has had more impact than the Brown *vs* Topeka decision requiring the desegregation of the schools."[1] This decision was made during an era when the federal executive and legislative branches were immobilized by political conflict over desegregation. Indeed the courts have exercised leadership in educational policy in areas where a political consensus has not evolved. Almost every week a federal district court rules on a Southern school district's plan for desegregation.

Sundquist's selection highlights the influence of Supreme Court decisions on the compromise on aid to private schools in ESEA. The court enunciated concept of aid to the child as distinct from aid to the private institution proved to be acceptable politically as well as legally. It is to the courts, moreover, that groups must turn who want to challenge the Office of Education's administration of ESEA aid to private school pupils.

It is possible that we are on the verge of another court decision with as significant an impact on education as the Brown decision. School boards in Chicago and Detroit have brought cases arguing that the present state aid formulas for education in their states should be declared unconstitutional. These suits, with implications for state aid allocation formulas in a majority of our states, are based on the equal protection clause of the Fourteenth Amendment.[2] They imply that the state has a vastly greater constitutional obligation to its school children than it presently accepts. Equality of educational opportunity obligates the state to provide each child with an equal chance for an equal educational outcome, regardless of disparities in cost or effort that the state is obliged to make in order to overcome such differences. In view of the Coleman report this could require more state aid for disadvantaged as compared to advantaged children.

Future Issues in Federal Aid to Education

The debate between Representatives Quie and Brademas explores perhaps the leading issue in federal aid in the seventies—general versus categorical aid. Sundquist's section presents the political background of the general aid debate, while the two Congressmen argue the substantive merits of each position. Both men stress that from a political standpoint one cannot advocate general aid without confronting the religious issue of aid to private schools. General aid implies federal support for teachers salaries, construction, and general operating expenses with few federal restrictions. Such general support, unlike ESEA, runs afoul of the Constitutional prescription for separation of church and state, and potent political forces who object to bolstering church-related institutions. In view of the financial pressures on Catholic education and the closing of several elementary schools, it seems unlikely that a general aid proposal could pass without considerable conflict over assistance to private schools.

The selections in this volume pertain to an era of large scale innovation for federal education policy. The political breakthroughs in the early sixties led to a massive outpouring of federal money and programs. Each subsequent year the ESEA of 1965 was amended and even more new programs were added to an already large base. Yet the federal government in 1969 provided only 7% of the total support for elementary and secondary education.

Almost all existing federal aid is categorical and consequently involves "program politics"—as contrasted to federal aid distributed through formulas (which is the predominant pattern for state aid). For example, federal programs are directed specifically at disadvantaged children, laboratory equipment or library books. The impact of this categorical aid is noted in a study of innovation in five large cities:

> It is clear that the emerging role of the Federal government through the Office of Education is an external force promoting the greatest change in the large city districts that have been witnessed in the course of their history... Compensatory education was virtually non-existent prior to federal aid. The proliferation of experimental programs can be traced directly to the influence of federal aid policies. Preschool education is now widely accepted under "Headstart" auspices.[3]

As Congressman Brademas emphasizes, opponents of federal general aid claim it will only result in "more of the same" educational programs.

A continuing federal impetus for change in local educational programs depends in large part on significant increases in appropriations. Elementary/ secondary education is a vast national enterprise with total expenditures in excess of $27 billion. Consequently, $20 million demonstration programs cannot have significant national impact. Federal programs must continue to grow rapidly in size, if they are to approach the impact that ESEA and its amendments had (over $1.5 billion of new money the first year). Local school systems have made program adjustments in order to receive their present level of federal funds. A substantial expansion of these new federally stimulated local programs (such as compensatory education) depends primarily on the ability of federal education programs to grow and diversify. Given the military expenditure demands, however, the outlook for the immediate future is for reduced federal influence on local education compared to the middle sixties.[4] In fact, federal appropriations for elementary/secondary programs have decreased since 1966. As of 1969 authorizations for most programs were double the actual money available.

It appears that there is a small role for the federal government to play in two increasingly important educational issues—teacher strikes and community control of schools. Sundquist's analysis highlights the potent political force of the American value of local control of education. Indeed, this entrenched local control viewpoint would appear to preclude federal directives that schools be decentralized or that teachers' strikes be ended. The federal role will probably be confined to "seed money" for stimulating "community control," and perhaps a mediation and conciliation service for teacher disputes.

The increasing militancy of teacher organizations will also have an impact on the shape of future federal aid bills. Sundquist's selection demonstrates the wide political appeal that school construction aid *per se* had in the 1950's and early 1960's. Clearly, any type of bill that emphasizes school construction is now less acceptable to a militant teaching profession that wants emphasis on instructional salaries.

The growing imbalance in per pupil revenue potential and expenditures between the lower funded central cities and the higher per pupil expenditure suburbs will cause major political conflict over the equitable distribution of future federal aid bills. Proposals are now pending in Congress to provide a great deal of federal support for cities and less relative support for suburbs. This is the essence of equalization but it will tend to splinter the united front mounted by educational organizations for the passage of ESEA. Existing state aid formulas favor suburbs. Consequently, under a plan of general federal revenue sharing with the states, a political conflict will develop over internal state distribution for education. The Nixon administration has supported the concept of revenue sharing, but safeguards and restrictions will be needed if federal aid for education is not to compound the damage done to central cities by current state aid formulas.

Any major decision on future federal aid policies must consider whether to put a priority on the increased funds for the existing base of categorical programs for disadvantaged children or to substitute general types of support. This decision on priorities may well be the most important education issue facing the new administration. Moreover, it appears that substantial increases in integration in the North and West will require a federal monetary incentive as a "carrot" to overcome local political obstacles. A federal decision to attack racial imbalance with seed money will reinforce the current priority for disadvantaged children.

ESEA included Titles III and IV directed at educational research and demonstrations. These programs have been cut back in the last two fiscal years after two initial years of large growth. As Bailey's case study indicated, Titles III and IV were viewed by the designers of ESEA as the change agent of the federal aid package. However, shortly after project approval for Title III was transferred by Congress from the federal level to the states, Title III's growth ended. Federal policy makers will have to face the issue of whether Title III should be revived or a new vehicle designed to stimulate educational change from the federal level.

As of FY 1969, of the $12 billion spent by the Federal government in education, less than 1% is spent on educational research and related efforts. In many instances, however, ESEA caused new local programs to be started and changed the local curriculum content.[5] The local education policy making process has not been structured politically to promote significant and continuous educational change. Consequently, a federal program emphasis that does not have a specific innovation focus would exert a different type of influence on local schools than ESEA.

FOOTNOTES

[1]Campbell, *Who Governs Education,* p. 64.

[2]See David Kirp, "The Poor, the Schools, and Equal Protection," *Harvard Education Review,* 38 (Fall 1968), pp. 635-668.

[3]Gittell *et al., op. cit.,* p. 127.

[4]This will also mean a reduced federal influence on future state education policy and state departments of education as discussed in the previous section.

[5]Gittell *et al., op. cit.,* p. 127.

FOR THE YOUNG, SCHOOLS*

James L. Sundquist

Year of Consensus: The National Defense Education Act   *(1958)*

"I ask you, sir, what are we going to do about it?"

With this blunt question, Merriman Smith of the United Press opened President Eisenhower's news conference of October 9, 1957, five days after the Soviet Union launched its first sputnik into orbit.[1] The President's response that day did not mention education. But later, in two television addresses to the nation, he referred to the shortage of highly trained manpower in scientific and engineering fields as "one of our greatest, and most glaring deficiencies,"[2] and "according to my scientific advisers ... the most critical problem of all." The Soviet Union, he said, already had more persons in these fields than the United States and was currently "producing graduates ... at a much faster rate." The problem was one for the whole country but, he promised, "the Federal government ... must and will do its part."[3] Under the menace of the orbiting sputniks, the raucous partisanship of the school construction debate dissolved, and within a year the Congress had enacted the most important piece of national education legislation in a century.

Congressional consideration of the National Defense Education Act (NDEA) began with two bills introduced almost simultaneously at the end of January 1958—one a Republican bill written within the Department of Health, Education, and Welfare, the other a Democratic bill written on Capitol Hill under the supervision of two close friends from Alabama, Senator Hill and Representative Elliott. Both bills provided scholarships for college students, with preference to those in specified defense-related fields, and assistance to educational institutions to improve instruction in those fields.

On the administration side, "the origins of the NDEA are traceable back at least as far as the 1955 White House Conference on Education," according to Elliot Richardson, who as assistant secretary of HEW was responsible for developing the administration version of NDEA.[4] He might have gone back further. A year before the White House conference, President Eisenhower himself

*From James L. Sundquist, *Politics and Policy: The Eisenhower, Kennedy and Johnson Years.* Copyright 1968 by The Brookings Institute, 1775 Massachusetts Avenue, N. W., Washington, D. C. Reprinted by permission.

had advanced the idea of scholarships. Asked at a news conference about reports that the Soviet Union was outstripping the United States in training scientists, the President responded: "Here is one place where the government should be very alert, and if we find anything like that . . . I believe the federal government could establish scholarships. . . . I am just saying what could be done, and, possibly, will have to be done. I don't know."[5]

When the decision was made to limit the White House conference to elementary and secondary education, those interested in higher education proposed a separate study. The President responded by creating a President's Committee on Education Beyond the High School, headed by Devereux C. Josephs, a life insurance executive and former president of the Carnegie Corporation, and the question of federal scholarships became a part of its agenda. That committee estimated that 100,000 able high school graduates each year were not going on to college for primarily financial reasons, but recommended that the federal government stay out of the scholarship field (except for an experimental "work-study" program for 25,000 to 50,000 students) until other sources had a "fair trial" to see whether they could multiply existing scholarship funds several-fold.[6]

In June 1957, as soon as the Josephs report was available, Secretary Folsom appointed a task force within HEW headed by Commissioner of Education Lawrence G. Derthick to review its recommendations and draw up a legislative program. Rejecting the caution of the Josephs committee, the task force proposed federal scholarships. It also emphasized the early identification of talent through strengthening of testing, guidance, and counseling services in secondary schools. The Derthick program was in draft form at the time of sputnik. At that point, a major new program was developed for grants to the states for improvement of high school science and mathematics instruction.

On the congressional side, support for a program of federal scholarships had been steadily rising. Early in 1956 Democratic Representative Melvin Price of Illinois, chairman of a Joint Committee on Atomic Energy subcommittee, published a Library of Congress study with a warning "that the United States is in desperate danger of falling behind the Soviet world in a . . . life-and-death field of competition" and called for a "crash program" for the training of scientists and engineers.[7] Citing data from that report, Senator Earle C. Clements of Kentucky, the Democratic whip, introduced a bill for 5,000 federal scholarships in science and engineering. The following year, more than a dozen scholarship measures were introduced in both houses, and Representative Elliott, the sponsor of one of them, scheduled a series of Washington and field hearings during the late summer and fall. It was in the midst of these hearings that the news of sputnik came.

On that date, Lister Hill was in Berlin. When he returned, on top of the papers awaiting his attention was a memorandum from the chief clerk of his committee, Stewart L. McClure, suggesting that sputnik be made the vehicle for carrying an aid-to-education program through the Congress. Hill agreed. He told a staff group headed by John S. Forsythe, committee counsel, to assemble a bill that, besides linking education to defense, would "steer between the Scylla of race and the Charybdis of religion." This they did, piecing together suggestions from individual scientists and educators and their organizational representatives in Washington and taking what they liked from the drafts of the administration bill that Richardson supplied them—making bigger and better, of course, the more appealing sections of the administration proposal. In accepting the title "national defense education act," Hill observed that his colleagues would not dare vote against both national defense and education when joined in the same bill.

The administration bill, called the "educational development act of 1958," was introduced on January 28 by Senator H. Alexander Smith of New Jersey and Representative Carroll Kearns of Pennsylvania. Two days later, the national defense education bill was introduced by Hill and Elliott. The Democratic bill was broader and considerably more generous in the student aid provisions, the Republican bill more generous in its aid to schools. The Hill-Elliott bill called for 40,000 new four-year scholarships a year, at a flat $1,000 stipend; the administration bill provided less than one-fifth as much money for the program, but since the stipend would be variable depending upon need, perhaps one-third as many scholarships. The Hill-Elliott measure also authorized $40 million a year for student loans and $25 million a year for work-study programs. For graduate fellowships the administration bill provided a slightly larger program.

Considering that the two bills were defended as national defense measures, it is noteworthy that neither restricted its assistance to students in defense-related fields. The Hill-Elliott bill required only "special consideration" for students with preparation in science, mathematics, or modern foreign languages; the administration bill had "preference" for those prepared in mathematics or science. Once chosen, however, the students could study what they pleased. The administration bill put no limitations whatever on its fellowship program.

Both bills authorized funds, to be matched by the states, for improvement of guidance and counseling in the secondary schools and for the training of counselors, with no striking dissimilarities in scope and purpose. In aid to the states for the improvement of instruction in defense-related fields, the administration bill provided $150 million a year and permitted aid for teacher salaries, while the Democratic measure provided only $40 million and restricted its use to purchase of equipment and minor remodeling of facilities.

During this period, other bills were floundering on partisan differences much narrower than these. But Hill and Elliott, on the one hand, and Folsom and Richardson, on the other, had no intention of letting that happen to the education bills. They had established informally a collaborative relationship during the period when the rival but parallel proposals were being drafted, and once both bills were in, the formal negotiations could begin.

The two bills by no means met with universal acclaim. The National Education Association, in December, had proposed a general aid bill both for school construction and for raising teacher salaries, providing $1 billion in the first year and $4.5 billion by the fourth year, and was rallying professional support behind it. Congressional supporters of federal aid were cool to the long-term and technical nature of the educational development bill; they wanted a more spectacular "crash" response to the challenge of sputnik. But these critics had no choice; they knew that they would get, in 1958, a combination of the Hill-Elliott and administration bills or nothing at all.

Scylla and Charybdis were successfully skirted. The NAACP[8] again proposed a "Powell amendment" but it was not pressed in either committee. Protestants and Other Americans United for Separation of Church and State expressed "apprehension" that scholarships for use in sectarian institutions of higher education might set a precedent for similar scholarships in elementary and secondary schools. They were also "apprehensive" at the eligibility of private colleges for teaching equipment and materials.[9] But the points were not pressed. When Senator Purtell offered an amendment suggested by the National Catholic Welfare Conference authorizing loans to private schools for teaching equipment in science, mathematics, and modern foreign languages, it was accepted by the committee without opposition and survived unnoticed through the floor debate.

By midsummer the two committees, working in an atmosphere of rare harmony both internally and with the administration, produced their separate compromises and approved them by lopsided bipartisan majorities. Only three members of the House committee—Republicans Ralph W. Gwinn of New York, Clare E. Hoffman of Michigan, and Donald W. Nicholson of Massachusetts—signed a minority report. Of the Senate committee, only Barry Goldwater, Arizona Republican, and Strom Thurmond, then a Democrat, of South Carolina, said it went too far. Goldwater's minority report follows in all its eloquent simplicity:

> This bill and the foregoing remarks of the majority remind me of an old Arabian proverb: "If the camel once gets his nose in the tent, his body will soon follow." If adopted, the legislation will mark the inception of aid, supervision, and ultimately control of education in this country by federal authorities.[10]

The debate, in both houses, centered upon the student aid provisions. Republican members of the committee, with Stuyvesant Wainwright of New York as their spokesman, had taken the precaution of checking the amended bill with President Eisenhower and found he had two objections—the number of scholarships had been increased by the committee compromise, and half the stipend, or $500, was to be granted regardless of need. The members of the bipartisan committee bloc agreed to yield to the President's terms, and the changes were made in the House bill when the debate opened. With that change, Wainwright assured the House that "the President supports" the bill.[11] Nevertheless, Walter H. Judd, Minnesota Republican, proposed to strike the entire scholarship section, retaining only the student loans from the Elliott bill. "Any boy or girl bright enough to merit a scholarship is good enough to be able to pay a low-interest loan back without difficulty or hardship in an 11-year period after his graduation," he argued. "Any boy or girl who is not sufficiently competent to be able to pay back such a loan . . . is not good enough to deserve a free scholarship."[12] The amendment carried on a division vote, 109-78. On signing the bill, President Eisenhower complained that Congress "did not see fit" to approve his scholarship proposal, but later, in his memoirs, he wrote that the Judd amendment "was, I thought, a good one."[13] The Senate accepted, 46-42, an amendment by John Sherman Cooper, Kentucky Republican, limiting scholarships to $250 a year, with any aid above that amount in the form of loans. In the Senate-House conference, the Senate gave up the truncated scholarship program entirely.

What began as a scholarship bill, now devoid of scholarships, breezed through both houses. The vote was 62-26 in the Senate and, on a recommittal motion, 233-140 in the House. Comparing the House vote on the National Defense Education Act with the vote by the same Congress to kill the school construction bill in 1957, the major difference lay in the return of thirty southern and border state Democrats to the support of aid to education.[14] Folsom and his staff, as well as Hill and Elliott, had entreated the liberal forces not to kill this bill with an antisegregation amendment, and Powell had responded by agreeing to limit his antidiscrimination amendment to the student aid provisions of the bill, to which nobody objected; he did not propose to disqualify segregated schools from the school aid provisions. The Republican vote showed a net shift of five members to the favorable side, but a majority of Republicans were still in opposition, 95-86. In the Senate, a clear majority of both parties supported it.

"An historic landmark," Majority Leader Lyndon Johnson termed the bill just before the Senate vote; "one of the most important measures of this or any other session."[15] Subsequent appraisals agree—not so much because of the specific provisions of the NDEA but because of the psychological breakthroughs it embodied. It asserted, more forcefully than at any time in nearly a century, a national interest in the quality of education that the states, communities, and private institutions provide. "The Congress hereby finds and declares," said the preamble to the act, "that the security of the Nation requires the fullest development of the mental resources and technical skills of its young men and women. . . . The national interest requires . . . that the federal government give assistance to education for programs which are important to our national defense." Henceforth, as Elliot Richardson put it, "discussion . . . no longer centers on the question of whether or not there will be federal aid. Rather, the debate has shifted to the two factions who agree that there should be federal aid but who divide sharply over the form in which it is to be provided"—that is, short-term aid for specific needs, as in NDEA, or a permanent sharing of the total costs, as proposed by the National Education Association.[16]

The NDEA experience also demonstrated how a consensus for national education legislation could be formed. Once these thresholds were crossed—or, from Senator Goldwater's point of view, once the camel's nose was under the tent—other and bolder measures could, and did, follow. But before they followed, several more years of frustration were to intervene.

More Years of Frustration   *(1959-62)*

Arthur S. Flemming, who became secretary of HEW in August 1958, took office at what, for an advocate of aid to education, was a most unpropitious time. The National Defense Education Act did nothing to solve the school construction "crisis" that the Republican administration and the congressional Democrats both acknowledged. The backlog of school building needs remained. But politics, which had been adjourned long enough after sputnik to permit passage of the NDEA, resumed with doubled force when the question of general aid for construction or teacher salaries was again considered.

"History will smile sardonically," said Robert Maynard Hutchins, "at the spectacle of this great country's getting interested, slightly and temporarily, in education only because of the technical achievements of Russia, and then being able to act as a nation only by assimilating education to the cold war and calling an education bill a defense bill."[17] But that was the way it was. The political deadlock made the country, whether "interested" or not, powerless to act.

The Flemming Bill—and the NEA-Democratic Alliance. In the 1958 campaign President Eisenhower centered his attack on what he called the "spending wing" of the Democratic party, using such epithets as "left wing government," "extremists," and "political radicals."[18] At the same time he issued a stringent directive to all departments to hold down their spending proposals for the coming year. So when Elliot Richardson set out in midcampaign to put together a 1959 education bill for Flemming, the ground rules were clear—whatever was done must be accomplished, for the most part at least, outside the budget. Moreover, Richardson was by this time convinced that the school construction crisis had now moved up to the college and university level, and a public school grant program on the scale of the 1957 administration bill—even assuming the President would support it—would leave nothing for higher education. The compromises he had negotiated with the House committee in previous years were now out of the question, and he launched a search for alternatives. Out of this reexamination came a complicated proposal to offer federal grant assistance to needy districts—those that could not, with a "reasonable tax effort," finance their own schools—but to spread the budgetary impact over twenty to thirty years by letting the districts borrow and then making an annual federal contribution, matched by the state, to debt repayment. Thereafter, the districts, insofar as possible with the same tax effort, would repay the federal and state "advances." Even this proposal violated the President's "no new spending programs" edict, but with an assist from Vice President Richard M. Nixon—who reportedly argued in Cabinet meeting that the Republican party could not afford to go into the presidential campaign with no education program at all—Flemming won the President's grudging assent. The proposal was submitted to Congress by Flemming, unheralded by any word of support in any presidential message. This was the first time since 1954 that the President had not personally recommended an education bill—a "visible waning of support," in Representative Udall's words,[19] that was noted by Republican as well as Democratic members.

Virtually isolated within the administration, Flemming was even more isolated on Capitol Hill. Still smarting from the President's campaign attacks on spending, and buttressed by their landslide victory and by repeated polls showing strong public support for federal aid to education, the congressional Democrats had no intention of accepting a program that saved President Eisenhower's balanced budget by spreading the spending out over two or three decades of his successors' budgets. They simply refused to take the proposal seriously. On the floors of both houses and in hearings reminiscent of those on the Hobby bill of 1955—but more heavily laden with partisan acrimony—they ridiculed the measure as an unworkable subterfuge.[20] As in 1955, educational organizations likewise could see no merit in it. Among the dwindled ranks of Republicans, some sought a bill along the lines of the 1956-57 compromises while a large bloc wanted no legislation at all. That left only a handful of Republicans—who, under the circumstances, were without influence—to fight for Flemming's measure.

The majority of congressional Democrats had, by this time, joined in open alliance with the NEA—which could claim to speak for over 700,000 voting teachers. Two Montana Democrats, Senator Murray and Representative Lee Metcalf, had introduced the NEA's bill for a multibillion-dollar program of aid for school construction and teacher salaries, and that bill was rapidly achieving the status of a party program measure among northern and western Democrats. Metcalf, in a blunt speech to the NEA's annual convention in 1958, had told the teachers they would have to enter the arena of political action if they were to get federal legislation. They had been bested by the U.S. Chamber of Commerce and its affiliates, he told them, because the businessmen had actively supported congressmen who opposed federal aid while too many educators took the "peculiar attitude . . . that political action is somehow not a proper activity of good citizens."[21] The NEA tacitly accepted the challenge. More vigorously and systematically than before, it identified to its members the congressional "friends" and "enemies" of the Murray-Metcalf bill. Their bill, because it gave the states the option of using part or all of their federal funds to raise teacher salaries, had far more appeal to NEA's membership than did the earlier Kelley construction-only bills. Congressmen began receiving mail from teachers and resolutions from their local organizations,[22] and one by one the supporters of school aid became committed to that specific measure.

In June 1959 the House Education and Labor Committee reported the Metcalf bill, scaled down to about $1 billion a year, as a strictly Democratic measure opposed by all the committee Republicans.[23] Senate committee Democrats were, however, split. Four, along with Republican Cooper, had joined Murray in sponsoring the NEA measure. But others argued that only a construction bill could be passed; the National Catholic Welfare Conference had made clear that aid for teacher salaries, which it regarded as "inherently nonterminable," would raise the issue of aid to private schools which the temporary emergency construction measures had successfully skirted.[24] Chairman Hill felt that aid for teacher salaries, likewise, was much more likely to raise the aid-to-segregated-schools issue. Until he was sure his view would prevail, he exercised his chairman's prerogative not to call a meeting. Bendiner notes that Majority Leader Johnson's "considerable powers" were also used to limit the bill to construction.[25] Finally, as the session approached its end in September, the committee did meet and approved, by the vote of all the Democrats and three Republicans,[26] a $1 billion construction bill sponsored by Senator Patrick McNamara, Michigan Democrat.

The House Democrats who reported the Metcalf bill knew it had no chance of clearing the Rules Committee. Solid Republican opposition in the Education and Labor Committee assured equally solid Republican opposition in the Rules Committee, and without at least one Republican vote the bill could not win approval, since two of the eight Democrats on the eight-to-four committee— Chairman Smith and William M. Colmer of Mississippi—were sure to vote, as they always had, against any general school aid bill. So the bill languished in Rules for the remainder of the year[27] and, when Congress adjourned, the indefatigable Cleveland M. Bailey (Democrat of West Virginia), the subcommittee chairman, set out to draft a compromise that would command enough bipartisan support to both pass the House and win President Eisenhower's approval.

In March, Bailey brought forth his compromise—a three-year emergency, construction-only measure like those of 1956 and 1957, but with each state permitted a choice between receiving its funds as flat grants or as federal commitments for debt service on the pattern of the administration bill. He claimed no administration support, however, and only Frelinghuysen among the Republicans voted for the bill in committee.

While the House committee was reversing its field to exclude teacher salaries from its bill, the Senate had moved in the opposite direction. The NEA promised that if a bill "embodying the principles of the Murray-Metcalf bill" were not enacted, it would "endeavor to make this matter a major issue in the political campaigns of 1960 so that the American people may again express their mandate for the enactment of such legislation in 1961."[28]

Senate Democrats relished the prospect of their party's entering the 1960 campaign as the staunch and proven friend of three-quarters of a million teachers. Senator Joseph Clark of Pennsylvania agreed to sponsor an amendment to revamp the McNamara bill on the lines of the Murray-Metcalf measure by permitting the bill's funds to be used for teacher salaries as well as for construction. Without difficulty, he lined up twenty-one Democratic co-sponsors.[29] When the roll was called on the amendment, the result was a 44-44 tie, and Vice President Nixon ultimately cast the deciding vote in opposition. Some said that Majority Leader Johnson prevailed on a Democratic opponent of the bill to switch his position to the favorable side to assure a tie vote, so that Nixon would be forced to personally kill the amendment.[30] In any case, the vote solidified the Democratic-NEA alliance. Only five of the thirty-two Republicans voted for the Clark amendment, while the northern and western Democrats were unanimous except for J. Allen Frear, Jr., of Delaware, Carl Hayden of Arizona, and Frank J. Lausche of Ohio. And the Nixon vote served further to dramatize the sharp partisan division.

In the debate on the amendment the Democrats accepted also the new rationale for federal aid to education. The Clark amendment was not premised on the assumption, explicit in all school aid debates since 1955, that the federal government could solve the school "crisis" by pumping money into school construction for a few years and then retreat to its previous position of unconcern. "Let us not kid ourselves, let us be candid, let us face the facts," said Clark. "This educational crisis is not going to be with us merely for next year or for only 5 years from now. It is going to be with us for the rest of the lives of those of us in the Senate. . . . Mr. President, the educational gap will not be closed until we undertake a massive Federal aid to education program."[31] State and local debt, he pointed out, had more than quadrupled in the thirteen years since 1946, rising from $13.6 billion to $55.6 billion, while the federal debt had risen only 4 percent. Similarly, state and local tax revenues had increased 232 percent in twelve years while federal budget receipts had climbed but 74 percent and, in relation to the gross national product, had actually declined. Without federal aid, Clark contended, the states and localities could not raise the $1.5 to $2 billion additional required every year for the next ten years.[32]

After Nixon's vote killed the Clark amendment, Senator A. S. Mike Monroney, Oklahoma Democrat, came forward with a modification that would reduce the funds by 20 percent and authorize the program for four years only.[33] These concessions picked up support from seven Democrats, including Lister Hill, and three Republicans. In this form the bill was passed.

At the other end of the Capitol, it required a threat by school aid supporters to resort to "calendar Wednesday" procedures[34] before Howard Smith would agree to call a meeting of his Rules Committee to consider the Bailey construction-only bill. When it met, the balance had shifted just enough to clear the bill; one Republican, B. Carroll Reece of eastern Tennessee, who had heard from educators in his district, voted with the six pro-aid Democrats to provide a 7-5 majority for sending the bill to the House floor.[35] Compared to previous engagements there, the debate was mild. A Metcalf amendment to substitute the Senate-passed bill, with the funds cut in half, was ruled out of order as not germane. The Powell amendment was adopted. As in 1956, Republicans who had supported the Powell amendment—seventy-eight in all—then voted to kill the bill. But this time they lost. The bill passed, 206-189.

The victory was accounted for entirely by the changed composition of the House since the 1958 election. A comparison of the 1960 vote with that of 1956 (when the Powell amendment was also in the bill) shows an actual loss of support among the congressmen who voted on both occasions. The Democratic votes were stable, with a net shift of one to the favorable side, but the Republicans recorded a net switch of eleven from yes to no. The percentage of support within the dwindled Republican minority thus fell from thirty-nine to thirty-two. But these losses were more than offset by the almost unanimous support of Democrats who replaced Republicans in 1959. Of these, forty-three voted for the bill and three against.[36]

For the first time in the twentieth century, then, both houses of Congress had passed a general aid-to-education bill. The outlines of a compromise in a Senate-House conference seemed clear: the Senate would drop its teacher salary provision and the House would give up the Powell amendment. But the conference never convened; the House Rules Committee refused permission—thus overriding the expressed will of both houses. Reece of Tennessee and James W. Trimble, Arkansas Democrat, switched to the opposition in a 7-5 vote against the bill on June 22. In the ten remaining weeks of the session, positions only hardened.

Several factors influenced the Rules Committee decision. At a meeting of Republican congressional leaders with the President on June 9, it was agreed that the Republicans would not accede to a conference unless they were assured in advance that the conference committee would report a bill the President could sign; otherwise they would suffer the embarrassment of an Eisenhower veto of an education bill at the outset of the 1960 campaign.[37] The failure to obtain any such assurance accounts, presumably, for Reece's vote. Trimble may have been influenced by the Powell amendment. A third factor was the lukewarm support of the bill by the NEA. With the conference committee foreordained to give up the aid for teacher salaries won on the Senate floor, the organized teachers, as they had said in their November statement, preferred to take their chances in the coming election. A new president, with a fresh mandate, might get them the bill they wanted; if they settled for a "half a loaf" construction bill, many years might elapse before they would have another chance as favorable for aid for salaries. Liberal Democrats likewise "preferred a campaign issue to a watered down bill," according to Munger and Fenno.[38] Some of the Democrats also welcomed the Rules Committee action as a powerful argument to be used in attempting a reform of that committee in 1961.[39]

The Kennedy Program—and the Church-State Issue. As the campaign progressed, Senator Kennedy exploited the education issue with increasing zest. In speech after speech he read the record of Republican votes against school construction bills, climaxing each assault by denouncing the vice president's "tie-breaking vote killing a Democratic bill giving the states money to increase teachers' salaries."[40] In the first Kennedy-Nixon debate, Nixon had been asked about that vote. "We want higher teachers' salaries; we need higher teachers' salaries," Nixon responded; "but we also want our education to be free of federal control. When the federal government gets the power to pay teachers, inevitably, in my opinion, it will acquire the power to set standards and to tell the teachers what to teach." Not so, said Kennedy in rebuttal; the amendment had proposed aid "without any chance of federal control" because the money was paid in a lump sum to the states.[41] The NEA stopped just short of endorsing Kennedy, giving wide distribution to literature that made clear that Kennedy supported the NEA position on federal aid while Nixon did not.[42] As the campaign was closing, Kennedy devoted an entire speech to education, boldly promising that "in 1961, a Democratic Congress—under the leadership of a Democratic President—will enact a bill to raise teachers' salaries . . ." as well as pass "an adequate bill for school construction."[43]

But it was not to be. The debacle of 1961 was a worthy successor to those of 1956, 1957, and 1960. The legislative process depends not only upon readiness to compromise but upon room for maneuver in consensus-building, and by 1961 important forces became "locked in" to fixed and diametrically opposed positions on an issue that had been quiescent during the 1950's—aid to parochial schools.

Because he was the country's first Catholic president, John Kennedy was locked in from the beginning. In his climactic confrontation with the Greater Houston Ministerial Association, he had said: "I believe in an American where the separation of church and state is absolute—where no Catholic prelate would tell the President (should he be a Catholic) how to act . . .—where no church or church school is granted any public funds or political preference."[44] After the campaign, in which Kennedy's Catholicism had been the single most important issue, Kennedy remarked that whether the "unwritten law" against a Catholic president was to be permanently repealed—rather than temporarily set aside— would be determined by his administration. If he appeared to yield to the church hierarchy in the conduct of his office, the religious issue would be used against any future Catholic candidate.[45] Accordingly, when he sent his education bill to

Congress on February 20—essentially the construction-salary bill passed by the Senate in 1960 scaled down to $2.3 billion over a three-year period—he was categorical: "In accordance with the clear prohibition of the Constitution, no elementary or secondary school funds are allocated for constructing church schools or paying church school teachers' salaries."[46]

But the Catholic hierarchy had likewise become locked in. During the Eisenhower period the religious issue had remained abeyant as long as legislative activity centered on short-term aid for school construction; but now, with a very real possibility that a president strongly committed to school aid could succeed in inaugurating a permanent and growing flow of federal funds to education, the stakes were high and the church moved rapidly to rally its political power. Three days before the inauguration, Francis Cardinal Spellman of New York denounced the recommendations of President-elect Kennedy's task force on education, which proposed aid only to the public schools, as "unfair," "blatantly discriminating," and "unthinkable," as making Catholic children "second-class citizens," and as embodying "thought control" by compelling a child "to attend a state school as a condition for sharing in education funds."[47] Catholic diocesan newspapers took up the cry. On March 1 the National Catholic Welfare Conference declared its opposition to any federal aid program "which excludes children in private schools." The bishops did not seek grants but, said Archbishop Karl J. Alter as their spokesman, "we hold it to be strictly within the framework of the Constitution that long-term, low-interest loans to private institutions could be part of the federal aid program. It is proposed, therefore, that an effort be made to have an amendment to this effect attached to the bill."[48]

Reacting to the vigor of the Catholic demands, non-Catholic organizations quickly became locked in also. On February 22 the general board of the National Council of Churches, whose constituents claimed 38 million members, adopted a statement saying: "We do not . . . consider it just or lawful that public funds should be assigned to support the elementary or secondary schools of any church. The assignment of such funds could easily lead additional religious or other groups to undertake full scale parochial or private education with reliance on public tax support." The statement expressed flat opposition only to "grants" for nonpublic schools, but Gerald E. Knoff, in presenting the board's statement at House subcommittee hearings, said he was "very sure that a great majority" would be opposed to loans also, "deeming such loans to be an outright departure from long-cherished principles of separation of church and state." "Unhappy accumulated experience," he said, showed that concessions such as those made in the college housing program, the National Defense Education Act, and various state enactments inevitably led to other concessions. For that reason, "what may be constitutional may not be wise."[49]

The two parties in the Congress, it should be added, also had taken fixed and irreconcilable positions on aid for teacher salaries. Once aid for salaries became a major partisan issue in the campaign, dramatized by the first Nixon-Kennedy debate, Democratic and Republican campaigners—which included all House members—became committed to the views of their respective presidential candidates. Even the bipartisanship of 1956 and 1957 in the House was impossible now. The Democratic bill had to aid salaries as well as construction, and that assured the administration a solid bloc of opposition votes no matter how it might resolve the religious controversy.

The President appeared surprised and irritated by the forcefulness of the attack on his program by his own church. "I do not recall that [during the Eisenhower administration] there was a great effort made . . . to provide across the board loans to an aid to education bill," he complained to a news conference, "and I am concerned that it should be made an issue now in such a way that we end up the year with, again, no aid to secondary schools."[50] If the Congress wanted to consider the question, he made clear, it should be in a separate bill.

While Catholic and non-Catholic organizations devoted their energies to generating a flood of emotion-laden mail to members of Congress, the administration sought a way out of the dilemma. HEW Secretary Abraham Ribicoff and Special White House Counsel Theodore Sorensen opened conversations, through an intermediary, with the bishops, and out of these talks a strategy emerged: the public school bill would proceed as planned, but the Congress—not the President —would initiate a private school loan program as an amendment to a measure extending the life of the National Defense Education Act.[51] That act had already breached the aid-to-private-schools barrier in providing loans for equipment for science, mathematics, and foreign language teaching, and the new program would merely extend the aid to the construction of facilities for the same purposes. An HEW brief had indicated that aid in this form would be constitutional. Accordingly, on April 25, President Kennedy formally recommended the extension of NDEA, with the pointed suggestion that "it is also appropriate that the Congress consider other proposals" as amendments. But by no means were all Catholics ready to compromise on any terms that provided their aid in a bill separate from the one that carried aid for the public schools. Ribicoff swung over to their position. On the day debate opened in the Senate, May 16, he and Lawrence F. O'Brien of the White House legislative staff, supported by Majority Leader Mike Mansfield of Montana, argued for combining the two bills. But Wayne L. Morse of Oregon, manager of the President's public school bill, felt that such a tactic presented the greater danger, and the two-bill strategy prevailed. Senator Morse then skillfully steered the public school bill to passage, 49-34. The division was almost identical with that of the year before.

In the House the intransigent positions of the opposing religious groups were reflected far more sharply in the positions of individual members than was the case in the Senate. Hugh Douglas Price has suggested the basic reason: Almost every senator, save those in the South and one or two western states, must represent both Catholics and Protestants, but many House members have constituencies made up almost wholly of one or the other religious group. Thus, on the parochial school issue, "compromise was accomplished *within* most senators themselves, but would have to be negotiated *between* members in the House."[52] The Boston district represented by Majority Leader John McCormack was almost wholly Catholic, the rural district represented by Speaker Rayburn almost wholly Protestant. As it developed, more significant was the fact that three of the eight-man administration majority on the Rules Committee[53] were Catholics representing heavily Catholic districts (James J. Delaney of Queens Borough, New York City; Thomas P. O'Neill, Jr., of the Boston-Cambridge district once represented by John F. Kennedy; and Ray J. Madden of Gary, Indiana) while three others were Protestants from southern districts with few Catholics and strong sentiment against aid to parochial schools (James Trimble of Arkansas, Homer Thornberry of Texas, and Carl Elliott of Alabama). Even a House member who becomes majority leader still represents his district—it was McCormack who assumed generalship of the legislators seeking aid for parochial schools.

The House Education and Labor Committee approved the public school bill in May, with the Republicans now unanimous in opposition. The apportionment formula was revised, but the committee avoided every other hazard. Powell himself led the fight in committee against the "Powell amendment," sponsored this time by Republican Frelinghuysen.[54] The spotlight now centered on the fifteen members of the Rules Committee. Delaney and O'Neill first voted with the seven opponents of federal aid to delay action until the NDEA bill with its private school loan provision was ready for action. But on July 18, when the latter bill was also before the Rules Committee, Delaney cast the deciding vote with the opposition coalition to kill them both. Describing the loan program as "just a little bit of a sop" for the Catholics, he demanded a truly "nondiscriminatory" grant bill. Moreover, he had no confidence that, if he approved the public school bill, the private school-NDEA bill would survive as a separate measure.[55] Many members were happy to be relieved of the responsibility of recording their votes on the two bills, which by then had generated hundreds of thousands of messages to representatives from their constituents. *Time* quoted a southern member as saying, "when Delaney cast his vote, you could hear the sigh of relief all over the Capitol," and congressmen were shaking Delaney's hand for hours afterward.[56]

In an attempt to salvage something, the administration retreated to a 1961 version of the old Kelley bill—a one-year program of aid for school construction, but not for teacher salaries—and its sponsors on August 30 attempted "calendar Wednesday" procedures. But this was a bill almost nobody liked. "Woefully inadequate," the NEA called it. The Republicans, former supporters as well as consistent opponents, saw no reason to back it. The solidifcation of their opposition, as compared with previous votes on school bills, made the difference. Only 6 of 166 Republicans voted to take up the bill (compared to 44 of 136 voting for the school construction bill in 1960). The Democrats managed to attract 17 southerners who had voted against the 1960 bill—while losing 6 nonsoutherners (only 2 of them Catholics)—but it was not enough. The Republican-southern Democratic coalition prevailed, 242-170, on a vote not to take up the bill on the House floor.

The following year President Kennedy went through the formality of again recommending his school legislation. But nobody had any stomach for another round of religious warfare. Neither committee gave the matter any serious consideration.

In the postmortems the blame was well distributed. Each side of the religious argument, of course, charged the other with intransigence. But could the parochial school issue have been avoided somehow, or resolved before it reached the fever point? Nobody has explained how. "They expected a miracle and I couldn't produce a miracle," was Ribicoff's summation. "It was impossible to bring together a majority for a bill when most members didn't want one."[57] Bendiner concluded, "There is no reason to suppose that without the trickery of the Rules Committee an agreement would not have been reached in 1961."[58] But this seems too easy a conclusion. The Rules Committee, by the time the religious feud had boiled up, was not an unrepresentative sample of the full House. Seven of its fifteen members were opposed to both the bills before the committee—reflecting closely the division of the House. Of the other eight, three were reportedly insisting upon *no* aid to parochial schools, and Delaney and O'Neill were demanding *some* aid as the price of support for the public school measure. If Delaney had not killed the bill in committee, would not many Delaneys among the eight-eight Catholics in the House (not to mention non-Catholic Democrats with Catholic constituencies) have joined with the Republican-southern Democratic coalition to provide the margin of difference on the House floor? There is no mathematical way to compromise between *none* and *some,* and the impossible would have been even harder to accomplish on the House floor than in committee.

The New York Times editorially blamed "legislative irresponsibility and inept executive leadership."[59] Price, unlike Bendiner, absolves the Rules Committee with the comment, "a bill could always be brought to the floor by other means," and observes that "the one point on which all could agree was the lack of presidential leadership." The President "apparently decided to knuckle under," he says, but also adds that Kennedy could have prevailed on this issue "only at the cost of disaster for much of the rest of his program, sharpened religious cleavage in America, and seriously endangering his own reelection prospects." Even a strong president, Price concludes, "must choose his showdown battles with care."[60]

But even this balanced judgment as to presidential power evades the substantive question: For precisely what kind of measure could the President have battled successfully? Price does not tell us, saying only that it would have embodied the President's "national" view of the matter. Yet the President tried two different positions, each presumably a "national" view. He began by offering the Catholics *nothing;* some Catholics responded by demanding *equal* treatment, others by asking for at least *something.* He then offered them *something*—and only intensified the Protestant insistence that the Catholics be given *nothing,* while leaving the Delaneys among the Catholics still demanding *equal* treatment. The switch of positions did not help, and laid his administration open to charges of duplicity and ineptness, but it is not clear how remaining adamant in the original position would have succeeded either. Every president has found that there are limits to the effectiveness of the tactics of pressure and coercion that Price suggests Kennedy could have used successfully; they were at least tested, without avail, on Delaney. "He had no interest in bargains or trades," writes Sorensen.[61] Perhaps a Protestant president-elect, if he could have fully anticipated the fury of the religious controversy, would have been able to find and include in his original program the *something* that would satisfy the preponderance of Catholics while not arousing the preponderance of Protestants. This had been accomplished, after all, in the National Defense Education Act—and was to be accomplished again in the education legislation of 1965. But the *something* could only have been found through conversations with the interested parties, including the Catholic bishops, and how could Kennedy—given the circumstances of the campaign—begin his tenure as the first Catholic president by opening negotiations with the hierarchy over ways to breach the wall of separation between church and state? Moreover, a bill that could have averted the religious quarrel would, in all probability, have had to be a measure other than the NEA general aid bill to which the Democratic party, as a matter of political inevitability, had become wedded.

Perhaps the fairest judgment is that the 1961 experience was both unavoidable and necessary. For the leadership on all sides—Catholics, Protestants, NEA, tacticians in the administration and in Congress—and for supporters of school aid among the general public, the 1961 debacle was a chastening ordeal from which they gained both wisdom and humility. It shattered the locked-in positions and gave all parties room for maneuver in designing a school aid measure that could win, under a Protestant president, in 1965.

Education Becomes a National Responsibility   *(1963-65)*

By the end of 1962 the years of frustration had produced a pervasive pessimism. William V. Shannon wrote that "religious and philosophical antagonisms engendered by school questions are so bitter that a solution through normal . . . methods is no longer possible."[62] Congressional Quarterly concluded its review of the 1962 college aid struggle with the comment, "Several education aid backers said they felt that the entire subject was dead for the foreseeable future."[63] Yet, less than a year later, Lyndon Johnson was proclaiming that "this session of Congress will go down in history as the Education Congress of 1963."[64] And, by 1965, resistance to federal aid to education had been shattered and the Congress was preparing to pour more than $4 billion a year into the national education system at all levels from preschool classes to graduate school—more than 10 percent of all public expenditures for the purpose.

The sudden turnabout reflected, perhaps most of all, a simple fact: people *do* learn from experience. First, both sides of the religious controversy had learned. The NEA and its public school allies now knew that an all-or-nothing attitude would mean, for the public schools, nothing. Likewise, Catholic leaders now understood that an equal-treatment-or-nothing position would mean, for the Catholic schools, nothing. For each side the question was whether it preferred to maintain the purity of its ideological position or receive some tangible benefits for its schools. The Washington representatives of organizations on both sides were, with a few exceptions, cautiously on the side of accommodation: they were acclimated to the legislative world of practical compromise and, besides, they had a common need to produce results for their members. Accommodation was supported by public opinion polls, which showed that a majority of Americans no longer opposed aid to parochial schools.[65] Second, the tacticians had learned. The National Defense Education Act had shown that special-purpose aid, carefully designed, could be enacted at a time when general-purpose aid could not be. A special-purpose approach would make it possible for the tacticians to probe, jockey, negotiate, and compromise on a wide range of separable and lesser programs, and the antagonists could move quietly away from the irreconcilable positions they had assumed—and would be compelled to maintain—on general aid.

President Kennedy sent to Congress early in 1963 the widest range of programs he could assemble—two dozen in all, mostly in the form of special-purpose grants and loans. As a device to encourage educational organizations to work together for one another's programs—in other words, to hold the NEA in line on the college aid program—all of the proposals were embodied in a single omnibus bill. Public school aid was converted from "general" to "selective" aid, to be used in areas of greatest need in accordance with state plans, but it would still be limited to public schools and would still finance the teacher salary increases and classroom construction to which the President was committed. Kennedy asked for $1.5 billion for the purpose, to be spread over four years. Proposals for college construction followed the conference committee compromise of 1962—loans would be generally available but grants, except in the case of public community colleges, would be limited to facilities for training of scientists, engineers, mathematicians, and technicians, for libraries, and for graduate centers. Scholarships were abandoned, but the NDEA loan program would be expanded and new programs of insurance of private loans and part-time employment of college students would be instituted. With all these were combined the extension of other NDEA programs, an expansion and recasting of aid for vocational education, and new programs of aid for adult literacy training, expansion of university extension courses, and urban libraries.[66]

The Easier Measures Come First. The committees in their hearings tested the political winds on all the Kennedy proposals and made their choices. Breaking the omnibus bill into segments, they acted first on those that aroused least controversy. In June the House committee approved a vocational education bill combining some proposals of the administration with others from the American Vocational Association. Here the principle of federal aid was not in dispute—the federal government had been aiding vocational education for nearly half a century. The House Democrats had to beat back a Republican antisegregation amendment that they claimed would "kill the bill" (only twenty-three Democrats voted for the amendment, only six Republicans against it), but then the measure was easily passed, 378-21.[67]

Meanwhile, Edith Green's subcommittee, with jurisdiction over higher education, had carefully repeated the steps that had led to the easy passage of her college construction bill in January 1962. In collaboration with Peter Frelinghuysen of New Jersey, the ranking Republican, Mrs. Green again converted most of the President's proposed loan program to grants, without limitation to specific fields of instruction, and in this form the committee approved the bill. President Kennedy had made no secret of his acquiescence in the bill's transformation, but Frelinghuysen could not resist needling the chief executive. "Had our committee followed his advice," Frelinghuysen told the House, "the program . . . would be of little significance. . . . Apparently his advisers failed to read the testimony of experts before our committee."[68] A motion to limit the bill's benefits to public institutions was defeated, 136-62. The mood of the House had mellowed since the previous September. There was no scholarship issue this time. The NEA sent no telegrams, flew no representatives to Washington. Chastised both by its friends in Congress and by its own members—who, as one NEA official put it, "could not understand why their organization had defeated a school bill, *any* school bill"—the NEA in its 1962 convention officially softened its opposition to aid to private schools. In August of 1963 it simply looked the other way while a college bill with equal treatment for Catholic institutions passed the House handily, 287-113.[69]

The senate subcommittee on education approved both the vocational education and the college aid bills, but with important modifications. The vocational education fund authorization was increased, and an equalization feature introduced to give greater benefits to the poorer states. Two new programs, proposed by President Kennedy in a civil rights message received after the House committee had acted, were added—$50 million for part-time employment of high school youth, and an experimental plan for residential vocational schools. The vocational education program, thus revised, was incorporated in a bill that also extended the NDEA, with increased funds for student loans, and the program of aid for school districts serving large numbers of federal employees' children (referred to as the program for impacted areas).[70] The bill passed easily, 80-4.[71] The college construction bill was restored to essentially the administration version. Senator Morse, chairman of the Senate education subcommittee, had not planned to bring it to the floor at once, but Representative Delaney sent word from the House Rules Committee that the vocational education bill, with its all-public benefits, would not be allowed to go to a Senate-House conference until the college bill, containing its grants for private institutions, went with it. Accordingly, the latter bill was also passed, and with nearly equal ease, 60-19.

The conference committee settled the higher education issues quickly, in early November. It retained the Senate proviso that grants, except in the case of public community colleges, could be made only for facilities designed for instruction in particular subjects or for other specified purposes. But it dropped the requirement that the facilities *designed* for teaching of the approved subjects must also be *used* for them. Legislators quickly noticed, says Kliever, that "this made the Senate categorical approach meaningless" but it was "slurred over" in the conference report.[72]

The vocational education bill, however, was deadlocked on three changes the Senate had made in the House version: the equalization formula inserted to favor the poorer states and the two new programs—work-study and residential vocational schools—on which the House had held no hearings. The five House Republicans, joined by Mrs. Green to make a majority of the eleven House conferees, were adamant for the position of their chamber and Morse dared not yield on the equalization issue for fear of driving Senator Hill into his 1962 role of active opposition to the college bill.[73] The stalemate continued through November. President Johnson, in his first address to the Congress, on November 27, pleaded for action on the deadlocked bill. Then he personally entered the negotiations. Mrs. Green accepted a modified equalization scheme. She also accepted modified versions of the two new programs. The House Republican conferees announced they would carry their fight to the House floor. When the report was before the House, they moved for recommittal to eliminate the two new programs, described by Frelinghuysen as "novel, expensive, and quite possibly unwise." The new President, by a 193-180 vote, narrowly escaped his first defeat. Kliever, on the basis of his extensive interviewing, concluded that two factors made the difference: First, Phil Landrum, the Georgia Democrat who was the voice of southern conservatism on

the Education and Labor Committee, stuck with his northern Democratic colleagues and carried some southerners with him. Second, the bill carried as a hostage
the renewal of aid to federally impacted areas, which was the subject of pleas from
school superintendents throughout the country.

Neither bill proved troublesome in the Senate. On December 16 and 18, President Johnson happily signed the first two major pieces of legislation produced by
"the Education Congress of 1963."

Next year, the Congress completed work on aid to libraries and again renewed
the NDEA. In the latter bill it increased the authorization level for student loans to
$195 million by 1968, raised the number of graduate fellowships from 1,500 to
7,500 a year by 1967, extended aid for instructional equipment to include English,
reading, history, geography, and civics, and broadened various other programs—thus
illustrating the strategy of moving toward large-scale aid through gradual expansion
of special-purpose legislation.

Then Come the Harder Measures. There remained to be tackled the one element
of the Kennedy program that the committees had found too explosive to handle—
"selective" but large-scale aid for elementary and secondary schools. Chairman
Morse of the Senate education subcommittee saw little chance that the Kennedy
proposal of 1963—which limited aid to public schools—would fare any better in the
House of Representatives than had the Kennedy bill of 1961, and he and his aide
on the subcommittee staff, Charles Lee, began probing for a new approach. Openly
espousing the special-purpose strategy, they suggested as a new special purpose "the
education of children of needy families and children residing in areas of substantial
unemployment." The Congress had, after all, acknowledged a federal responsibility
for assistance to families on welfare and for aid to depressed areas. Assistance to
school districts "impacted" by federal activities was also long-established; would it
not be as logical to assist "poverty-impacted" districts? To make the logical relationship doubly clear—as well as to take advantage of the propulsive power of the
popular program for impacted areas—Morse proposed to enact his new program as
an amendment to the impacted areas legislation. His bill would authorize about
$218 million a year, to be distributed among school districts on the basis of unem-
ployment and welfare statistics.

By the time Morse introduced his bill, in February 1964, the President's decla-
ration of war on poverty provided still another context for the Morse approach. But
the administration was skeptical. Preoccupied with other legislative issues, HEW
neither endorsed the Morse bill nor devised an alternative. Finally, in July, Morse
called a hearing. Commissioner of Education Francis Keppel agreed that "the
broad, massive educational assault on poverty" required aid "on a larger scale and
scope" than was contemplated in the economic opportunity bill then pending. But
he found many technical flaws and administrative complications in Morse's bill and
asked time for further study. Morse could only castigate the administration,

through Keppel, for "stalling" and "dragging its heels."[74] But a few weeks later Keppel advised him, "The President wants us to tell you that we are for your bill. We are even going to expand it."[75]

Under the leadership of Assistant Secretary Wilbur Cohen, HEW staff had been "going over and over" the Morse bill and the questions it raised. Out of these discussions came a proposal for solution of the vexing religious issue. If the special purpose were the education of poor children, then could not the programs that would be financed be considered as benefits to children rather than aid to schools? If so, the courts would uphold extending the benefits to children attending church-related and other private schools—just as they had upheld publicly provided school lunches and bus service for children in private schools. President Kennedy might have been barred by his commitments from recommending such assistance to Catholic children, but President Johnson would not be. The HEW lawyers concluded that the proposed new programs for poor children could be classified as "child benefits." Keppel and his colleagues began exploratory talks with the NEA, the National Catholic Welfare Conference, and other groups, and even brought the NEA and the Catholics into communication. It became evident that the formula for accommodation might have been found.[76]

When Johnson sent his program for "full educational opportunity" to the Congress on January 12, 1965, it was clear that he had indeed expanded the Morse idea. Morse's $218 million (and Kennedy's $375 million) had become a round $1 billion a year, to be spent for "the special educational needs of educationally deprived children." The formula for distribution had been simplified; instead of welfare and unemployment statistics, the readily available census data on income would be used. The money would be distributed in proportion to the numbers of children in families with incomes under $2,000 a year. In addition, President Johnson proposed a series of measures, some old and some new—some of the latter having originated in a task force on education appointed by the President and headed by John W. Gardner, president of the Carnegie Corporation (and later to be named secretary of HEW). He asked for more aid for college construction, 140,000 scholarships a year, $100 million a year for aid for libraries, textbooks, and other instructional materials, another $100 million a year for a variety of new services to be provided centrally to supplement what individual schools could offer, funds for research and demonstration activities aimed at "educational reform," and aid to state departments of education to upgrade their capacity to administer the new and expanded federal programs.

Since the proposed aid to elementary and secondary schools was massive in amount, and since virtually all of the nation's school districts would benefit, the President's program was identified at once by all concerned as the old idea of general aid to education in a new form—a form carefully designed to circumvent previous constitutional barriers to benefits for parochial and other private school children. H. B. Sissel, speaking for the United Presbyterian Church, called the bill "a fantastically skillful breakthrough . . . in the stalemate which has been hung up on the church-state dilemma for so many years."[77] An opponent made the same point with a touch of bitterness; it offered "just enough aid to parochial schools to push away the veto of the Roman Catholic Church but not enough to drive away the support of the National Education Association. . . ."[78] And he was right. The official Catholic spokesman gave it qualified approval because "all children in need will benefit."[79] The NEA offered "whole-hearted support" and found no violation of the principle of separation of church and state.[80] The National Council of Churches on February 26 officially adopted the child-benefit theory, with carefully stated safeguards. The American Jewish Committee also endorsed it.[81] Some Protestant and Jewish groups maintained their opposition, but they represented fewer members. Organizations representing the preponderance of both Catholics and non-Catholics, as well as public school groups, had been either won over or neutralized until they could see exactly how the child-benefit theory was to be interpreted and applied as the legislation progressed.

Kelley and La Noue, in their authoritative review of the church-state issue as it developed during consideration of the bill, observe that the favorable response was influenced by three factors:

> For one thing, the great wave of public support for the President's message on education combined with Johnson's personal prestige and the overwhelming Democratic congressional majority made it difficult to criticize, let alone oppose, the bill. Second, in this ecumenical era discussion of the church-state aspects of the bill had to be undertaken with great restraint on all sides, since a considerable portion of both the secular and religious press regards exhibitions of religious rivalry and conflict as being in poor taste. Finally, although the major interest groups had been briefed about the general trends in the proposed legislation, the bill itself with all its novel provisions was not made public until ten days before the House hearings began. This was not nearly enough time for large national organizations to study the bill, to report to their constituencies, and to prepare careful commentary. The administration hoped (successfully as it turned out) to inhibit controversy by rushing the bill through.[82]

The Republican opposition saw that its main chance to defeat the bill lay in prying apart the new and extraordinary Catholic-Protestant-NEA coalition, whose members surely retained some measure of the old suspicion and hostility, by raising doubts as to how the child-benefit theory would work in practice—as to whether, on the one hand, the benefits would truly go to *all* children and, on the other, whether they would not in fact go to the private schools rather than to the pupils in those schools. The House committee corrected some ambiguities in the administration bill that raised these kinds of questions. For instance, where the original bill left open the possibility that title to equipment and materials, including textbooks and library materials, would pass to private schools, the committee incorporated an assurance that materials would remain in public ownership on "loan" to the private schools—even though the loans might be understood to be permanent.[83]

But the committee changes still left enough ambiguities for Republican exploitation on the House floor. On the opening day of debate, March 24, Representative Charles Goodell of New York sought to drive a wedge into the coalition on the question of whether, in order to provide benefits on an equal basis to all children, the public school authorities could send a teacher to teach in a private school. He pressed the bill's sponsor, Carl D. Perkins of Kentucky, for a "yes" or "no" answer. Democratic Representative B. F. Sisk of California, a Protestant, observed that if the answer were "yes" he would vote against the bill. Republican James J. Cahill of New Jersey, a Catholic, responded that if the answer were "no" he would vote against the bill. Goodell finally pushed Perkins into saying the answer was "no." Goodell then turned to Democrat Hugh L. Carey of Brooklyn, a Catholic subcommittee member,[84] to ask whether he agreed with Perkins. Carey replied that "we do not plan to put teachers in the private schools" but "they might be in the building." Goodell concluded that Carey's answer was "yes." Perkins corrected him: "There are special services as to which I would say 'yes,' but generally 'no.' " What was a "special service," Carey had explained earlier, "would be determined by pedagogy."[85] Later, Representative Frank Thompson, Jr., Democrat of New Jersey, drafted a statement designed to establish a clear legislative history that the services "must be special as distinguished from general educational assistance" and that the decision about the special services to be provided would be left to each local school district, operating under the constitution and laws of its state. Given this kind of "yes and no" answer, and with the controversy shifted to the communities, the coalition held. Both Sisk and Cahill—and the blocs, or potential blocs, for whom they had been speaking—voted for the bill. The final tally was 263-153. The landslide election of 1964 had foreordained the outcome: of the fifty-six freshman nonsouthern Democrats who voted, every one was recorded in favor of the bill.

In the Senate, debate centered upon the allocation formula, and numerous amendments were offered. But to avoid the hazards of another Senate-House conference, where so many education bills had foundered, the administration and the bill's managers had agreed to fight off all amendments, no matter what their merits, and Senator Morse, the bill's manager, had the votes to defeat every proposal. In response to the outraged cries of the Republicans that the Senate was becoming a "House of Lords" which could only delay but not amend legislation, he explained calmly that the bill could be amended next year if found defective. When the bill passed, only eighteen senators voted nay. The bill was signed two days later, in a Texas schoolhouse.

Many members of Congress saw the sun upon the horizon. Some hailed a sunrise. "We are finally at the threshold of a breakthrough," exulted Senator Ribicoff of Connecticut, the former HEW secretary. "Now we stand at the moment of beginning. . . . We have . . . finally put behind us the years of travail and controversy. We have opened ahead of us years of greatness and fulfillment."[86] "This is the precise moment in history for which we have waited," said Adam Clayton Powell. "Let us ring our bells of freedom and liberty throughout the land."[87] Wayne Morse was more matter-of-fact: "Let us face it. We are going into federal aid for elementary and secondary schools . . . through the back door."[88]

Others saw a setting sun. "We apparently have come to the end of the road so far as local control over our education in public facilities is concerned," said Howard Smith of Virginia. "I abhor that . . . but I think I see the handwriting on the wall. This is the day that the bureaucrats in the Education Department have looked forward to. . . ."[89] "Make no mistake about it," warned John Williams of Delaware. "This bill, which is a sham on its face, is merely the beginning. It contains within it the seeds of the first Federal education system which will be nurtured by its supporters in the years to come long after the current excuse of aiding the poverty stricken is forgotten. . . . The needy are being used as a wedge to open the floodgates, and you may be absolutely certain that the flood of Federal control is ready to sweep the land."[90]

The Congress still had a lone piece of unfinished business from the Kennedy twenty-four-point program of 1963—scholarships. President Johnson asked for 140,000 scholarships a year, averaging $500 each. This once highly inflammatory proposal was absorbed almost without notice into the new consensus—Republicans on the House committee accepted it with the single stipulation that a scholarship could not cover more than half of a student's need for financial aid. The President also proposed that the government insure $700 million in private student loans, with a proviso for federal subsidy of the interest rate—the 1959 Flemming approach to public school and college construction which the Democrats at that time had ridiculed as a "subsidy for bankers." These and other aids to colleges (for library materials and teaching, for general or "urban" extension and community service programs, and for assistance to smaller colleges) were approved in the House with only twenty-two dissenting votes.[91] In the Senate, only three votes were cast against a corresponding bill that included an additional innovation, a national teachers corps. The final bill also doubled the amount available for construction grants under the 1963 act, which the President had not requested, and removed the restrictions imposed at that time that the facilities must be designed for certain specified fields of instruction.

In one year, said President Johnson, Congress "did more for the wonderful cause of education in America than all the previous 176 regular sessions of Congress did, put together."[92]

Some Consequences. By the end of 1965 Senator Hill and former Commissioner of Education Brownell could look back upon their 1954 colloquy and agree that the question Brownell posed to the American people at that time had been decided by the people—the national "concern" for education had become, after a decade, a national "responsibility." The most important domain of traditionally exclusive state and local responsibility was now to be shared with Washington. The question would be, henceforth, not *whether* the national government should give aid but *how much* it should give, for what purposes—and with how much federal control. Already, in volume terms, the aid was substantial. By 1968, federal expenditures for education had multiplied more than ten-fold in a decade—from $375 million in 1958 to an estimated $4.2 billion.[93] The federal share of all expenditures for education by all levels of government had risen during the decade from less than 3 percent to about 10 percent. And it is safe to predict that the trend will not be reversed: federal assistance once given, accepted, and built into the ever-rising annual budgets of local school districts cannot later, as a practical matter, be withdrawn. The ease with which the combined political power of local school districts has defeated proposals by three presidents, of both parties, to reduce the funds for federally impacted areas testifies to that.

Yet the exigencies of politics had channeled the funds into a complex structure of special-purpose assistance which, a decade earlier, almost nobody would have recommended. Before the National Defense Education Act of 1958, and afterward as well, most advocates of federal aid for elementary and secondary education sought to deliver federal funds to the states and local school districts under the broadest definitions of purpose, with no—or almost no—strings attached. President Eisenhower had sought the funds for construction of buildings, the NEA and Kennedy to finance construction and raise teacher salaries. Ironically, with all the federal funds being poured into the nation's education in 1968, very little went for either of these purposes. One of the earliest advocates of federal aid, Senator Cooper of Kentucky, raised the basic question with regard to the neediest districts of his state: "Supplemental projects, however desirable, are not fundamental, it seems to me, and in many of these neglected areas should follow and build upon improvements made in the regular, basic educational program. . . . The needs of these schools . . . surely can not be met simply by superimposing special-purpose projects, important as they are, on a foundation fundamentally weak in facilities or staff." If the pressing needs were for classroom construction or higher teacher salaries, he suggested, that is where the federal funds should go.[94]

The backlog of school construction needs, which formed the heart of the argument for aid to education in the mid-1950's, has not appreciably diminished. The outmoded buildings in the urban slums that were in need of replacement then are now ten years older; few cities have made appreciable inroads on them.[95] The question of aid for the basic requirements of construction and teacher salaries must inevitably arise again. This will be particularly the case when and as a leveling off or reduction of military expenditures releases federal revenues for other purposes. To the extent that additional resources can be made available for elementary and secondary education, will the expansion of special programs—rather than an upgrading of established programs—be the best utilization of the funds?

The special-purpose approach also leads, inevitably, to a considerable measure of the very federal "control" of education that federal aid advocates have consistently disavowed. Under the Elementary and Secondary Education Act of 1965, it is true, authority for approval of the special programs planned by local districts is delegated to the states. The federal criteria are general enough—the programs must be designed for the "educationally disadvantaged" and they must extend to private school children in a form that will not constitute aid to the private schools themselves. But even though the federal government does not approve projects, its funds influence local school programs in directions chosen for the local boards of education by the federal government—and where is the boundary between influence and "control"?

It is perhaps significant that those who designed the Elementary and Secondary Education Act of 1965 have been among the principal critics of the quality of American education. John Gardner and Francis Keppel have not been among those who contended that, in the oft-repeated phrase of the early advocates of federal aid, "there is nothing wrong with American education that more money won't cure." The Gardner task force of 1964 devoted much of its discussion to the need for "innovation"—in other words, qualitative improvement. Even if the task force had not been compelled by the religious issue to adopt the special-purpose approach, it may be doubted whether its members would have been willing to propose general aid to the states without assurance that the aid would achieve certain priority objectives to be defined by the federal government. In his 1965 message President Johnson was specific about some objectives: to equalize educational opportunity for the disadvantaged, to improve libraries, to do more for the gifted and the slow learners, "to put the best educational equipment and ideas and innovations within the reach of all students."[96] Two paragraphs later he reasserted the familiar phrase, "federal assistance does not mean federal control"—but will "the best" always be left to state and local definition? And should it be? It is the national interest in education that justifies, in the first place, the expenditure of federal funds in aid to schools; how will the national interest be served unless the federal government defines what that interest is and then channels its funds in a way that is designed to serve it? Keppel has said that "we cannot any longer separate our local goals from our national goals" and "our approach ... must be unified ... by coordinated plans." How can approaches be unified, plans coordinated, and the national goals achieved without a central influence or "control"? Keppel further points out that the 1965 act requires reporting on what the federal money has been used for—and Congress and the President will expect "not just a fiscal accounting but an educational accounting."[97] If they are not satisfied with the state and local decisions reflected in those accounts, will they not make national decisions by statute the next time funds are authorized?

Ironically, the conservatives who opposed "federal control" most strongly could have minimized the federal influence by supporting measures like the Kelley bill or the Murray-Metcalf bill which offered aid with virtually no strings attached. But they chose instead to deny the need for federal aid of any kind, and so forfeited their opportunity to participate in deciding what form the aid would take. When it was ultimately provided, it was cast in a pattern least compatible with their principles.

The decisions of 1965, in any case, took the issue of federal "control" out of the realm of ideological debate and thrust it into the area of practical administration. Some measure of federal leadership, influence, and control is now with us. Federal money is now being used, and will continue to be used, as a lever to alter—qualitatively as well as quantitatively—the American educational scene. Federal "control" has been authorized by Congress—almost inadvertently, to be sure, under the pressure of other considerations, within very real practical limits, and in a rhetorical context of hostility to that objective, but nonetheless authorized. The meaning of the decision will be written in the processes of legislation and administration over the years as the product of national pressures and local resistance, of federal assertion and federal self-restraint—all as part of a new structure of federalism that is evolving, so far, without benefit of any enunciated and accepted theory.

FOOTNOTES

[1] *Public Papers of the Presidents, 1957,* p. 719.

[2] Address of Nov. 7, 1957, *ibid.,* p. 794.

[3] Address of Nov. 13, 1957, *ibid.,* p. 814.

[4] Letter to the editor, *Reporter,* July 23, 1959, p. 6.

[5] News conference, Nov. 10, 1954, *Public Papers of the Presidents, 1954,* p. 1040.

[6] President's Committee on Education Beyond the High School, *Second Report to the President* (July 1957), pp. 56-57.

[7] Harris Collingwood, *Engineering and Scientific Manpower in the United States, Western Europe, and Soviet Russia,* prepared for the Joint Committee on Atomic Energy, 84 Cong. 2 sess. (March 1956), p. v.

[8] Testimony of Clarence Mitchell, in *Science and Education for National Defense,* Hearings before the Senate Labor and Public Welfare Committee, 85 Cong. 2 sess. (March 5, 1958), pp. 878-79.

[9] Statement, undated, submitted in *Science and Education for National Defense,* Hearings, pp. 1351-52.

[10] *Cong. Record,* Vol. 104 (Aug. 13, 1958), p. 17290.

[11] *Ibid.* (Aug. 8, 1958), p. 16727.

[12] *Ibid.,* p. 16728.

[13] Statement of Sept. 2, 1958, *Public Papers of the Presidents, 1958,* p. 67, and *Waging Peace,* p. 243. James McCaskill, chief of the NEA legislative staff, offers evidence that the latter was Eisenhower's true view; while the NDEA bill was pending, he said, the President in a private conversation expressed himself against scholarships on the ground that "everyone should either work or pay his own way."

[14] The comparative figures used in this paragraph consider only the 294 members who were recorded on both votes.

[15]*Cong. Record,* Vol. 104 (Aug. 13, 1958), pp. 17331, 17330.

[16]Richardson letter, *Reporter,* p. 6.

[17]Quoted in *New York Times,* Jan. 22, 1959; reprinted in *Cong. Record,* Vol. 105 (March 2, 1959), p. 3123.

[18]Campaign speeches, *Public Papers of the Presidents, 1958,* pp. 760, 822, 758. See also Chap. 9, pp. 425-27, below.

[19]Stewart L. Udall, "Our Education Budget Also Needs Balancing," *Reporter,* June 25, 1959, pp. 23-25. Perhaps a more convincing expression of Eisenhower's withdrawal of support was his extemporaneous comment at his July 31, 1957, news conference, in reference to construction proposals (his own as well as the Kelley bill): "But I am getting to the point where I can't be too enthusiastic about something that I think is likely to fasten a sort of albatross, another one, around the neck of the Federal Government–I don't believe it should be done" (*Public Papers of the Presidents, 1957,* p. 576).

[20]The case against the bill is summed up in a speech by Democrat Lee Metcalf of Montana in the House on February 24; he called it "feeble and ineffectual," labeled it "deferred deficit financing," said sixteen states could not participate without constitutional amendments and others would require referenda, and argued that it would be no help to school districts–some or all of the districts in thirty-one states–that had reached their legal debt limits (*Cong. Record,* Vol. 104 [1958], pp. 2888-94). See also Munger and Fenno, *Federal Aid to Education,* pp. 89-90.

[21]Speech inserted in *Cong. Record,* Vol. 104 (July 3, 1958), pp. 13020-22.

[22]See, for example, comment by Representative John P. Saylor, Republican of Pennsylvania, on the mail he had received in support of the Metcalf bill (*ibid.,* Vol. 105 [Aug. 10, 1959]. p. 15408).

[23]See Munger and Fenno, *Federal Aid to Education,* pp. 117, 128, 130-31.

[24]*Federal Grants to States for Elementary and Secondary Schools,* Hearings before the Senate Labor and Public Welfare Committee, 86 Cong. 1 sess. (1959), p. 528. Cited by Munger and Fenno, *Federal Aid to Education,* p. 59.

[25]*Obstacle Course on Capitol Hill,* p. 162.

[26]Cooper, Clifford P. Case of New Jersey, and Jacob K. Javits of New York. Cooper and Javits reserved the right to offer a substitute embodying some features of the administration bill.

[27]Bendiner suggests that opposition by Speaker Sam Rayburn, of Texas, contributed to its death in the committee (*Obstacle Course on Capitol Hill,* p. 163).

[28]Statement of Nov. 29, 1959; inserted in *Cong. Record,* Vol. 106 (May 26, 1960), pp. 11286-88.

[29]And one Republican, Thomas E. Martin of Iowa.

[30]Democrat J. Allen Frear, Jr., of Delaware, an opponent of the amendment, voted for reconsideration, creating the tie vote that Nixon broke.

[31]*Cong. Record,* Vol. 106 (Feb. 3, 1960), p. 1945.

[32]*Ibid.,* pp. 1943-45. As it happened, the states and local governments did prove able to increase their expenditures for education by those amounts during the first half of the decade. The increase was $14.5 billion in the six years from 1960 to 1966 and the total reached $33.3 billion in the latter year (not adjusted for price changes); see *Economic Report of the President, February 1968,* p. 289.

[33]Because of parliamentary technicalities, the amendment was actually offered by Clark and is sometimes, like the earlier amendment, identified by his name.

[34]A complex procedural device for bypassing the Rules Committee, which had been used successfully to dislodge the area redevelopment legislation. See Chap. 3, p. 71.

[35]See Bendiner, *Obstacle Course on Capitol Hill,* p. 166, and Munger and Fenno, *Federal Aid to Education,* p. 134.

[36]Munger and Fenno, *Federal Aid to Education,* p. 162.

[37]Papers of Henry Roemer McPhee, Jr. (in Dwight D. Eisenhower Library, Abilene, Kan.).

[38]*Federal Aid to Education*, pp. 164-67.

[39]Bendiner, *Obstacle Course on Capitol Hill*, p. 171.

[40]See *The Speeches of Senator John F. Kennedy, Presidential Campaign of 1960*, S. Rept. 994, 87 Cong. 1 sess. (1961), Pt. I; quoted phrase is from his Los Angeles speech, Nov. 2, 1960 (p. 1235). Sorensen observes that in the campaign, as well as throughout his presidency, "he devoted more time and talks to this single topic than to any other domestic issue" (Theodore C. Sorensen, *Kennedy* [Harper & Row, 1965], p. 358).

[41]*The Joint Appearances of Senator John F. Kennedy and Vice President Richard M. Nixon, Presidential Campaign of 1960*, S. Rept. 994, 87 Cong. I sess. (1961), Pt. 3, pp. 84-85.

[42]Munger and Fenno, *Federal Aid to Education*, p. 183.

[43]Los Angeles speech, Nov. 2, 1960, *The Speeches of Senator John F. Kennedy*, S. Rept. 994, Pt. I, p. 1235.

[44]Speech of Sept. 12, 1960, *ibid.*, p. 208.

[45]Sorensen, *Kennedy*, p. 358.

[46]*Public Papers of the Presidents, 1961*, p. 109.

[47]Quoted by Hugh Douglas Price, "Race, Religion, and the Rules Committee: The Kennedy Aid-to-Education Bills," in Alan F. Westin (ed.), *The Uses of Power* (Harcourt, Brace & World, 1962), pp. 22-23; this section relies on his definitive case study of the 1961 aid-to-education struggle (pp. 1-71). The story is told in briefer style by Bendiner, *Obstacle Course on Capitol Hill*, pp. 180-89, and the chronology of events is recounted in *Congressional Quarterly Almanac, 1961*, pp. 215-46. The Price case study, abridged, is included in his article, "Schools, Scholarships, and Congressmen," in Alan F. Westin (ed.), *The Centers of Power* (Harcourt, Brace & World, 1964).

[48]Such an amendment had been offered to the school bill by Senator Wayne Morse, Democrat of Oregon, in 1960 but it was easily defeated. Significantly, Kennedy was the only Catholic senator recorded against it (he was paired). A similar amendment in the House was ruled "not germane" to a public school bill.

[49]*Federal Aid to Schools*, Hearings before the General Subcommittee on Education of the House Education and Labor Committee, 87 Cong. 1 sess. (March 16, 1961), pp. 392-95.

[50]News conference, March 8, 1961, *Public Papers of the Presidents, 1961*, p. 156.

[51]Sorensen, *Kennedy*, p. 360.

[52]"The Kennedy Aid-to-Education Bills," pp. 51-52.

[53]The committee had been "reformed" early in the year, after a torrid floor fight, by increasing the membership from twelve to fifteen and adding two administration Democrats— Carl Elliott of Alabama and B. F. Sisk of California—and one Republican; the administration could count on eight of the ten Democrats for support on most issues (see Price, *ibid.*, pp. 13-20; Bendiner, *Obstacle Course on Capitol Hill*, pp. 171-80). Also see Chap. 11, pp. 472-73.

[54]Bendiner, *Obstacle Course on Capitol Hill*, pp. 185-86.

[55]Sorensen says Delaney "concluded—and no doubt rightly—that once he agreed to the public school bill, the NDEA bill would be mutilated or killed" (*Kennedy*, p. 361). *Congressional Quarterly Almanac, 1961* (p. 214), notes that Elliott, Trimble, and Thornberry of the Rules Committee "reportedly would have voted to table the NDEA bill" and that, had they done so, the public school bill would not have survived. See also Munger and Fenno, *Federal Aid to Education*, p. 135.

[56]Bendiner, *Obstacle Course on Capitol Hill*, pp. 194-95.

[57]Munger and Fenno, *Federal Aid to Education*, p. 169.

[58]*Obstacle Course on Capitol Hill*, p. 199.

[59]*New York Times*, Sept. 1, 1961.

[60]"The Kennedy Aid-to-Education Bills," p. 69.

[61]*Kennedy*, p. 361.

[62]Quoted by Bendiner, *Obstacle Course on Capitol Hill*, p. 199.

[63]*Congressional Quarterly Almanac, 1962*, p. 238.

[64]Statement of Dec. 16, 1963, *Public Papers of the Presidents, 1963-64*, p. 57.

[65]Frank J. Munger emphasized the importance of the public opinion shift in "The Politics of Federal Aid to Education" (paper presented at the 1965 annual meeting of the American Political Science Association); he quotes the findings of the American Institute of Public Opinion that the proportion of adults supporting aid for parochial as well as public schools rose from 39 percent in 1961 to 55 percent in 1963 and 1965 (excluding those respondents–7, 8, and 8 percent, respectively, in the three polls–expressing no opinion). Conversely, Philip Meranto, *The Politics of Federal Aid to Education in 1965: A Study in Political Innovation* (Syracuse University Press, 1967), pp. 46-50, discounts the importance of the public opinion factor.

[66]Special Message on Education, Jan. 29, 1963, *Public Papers of the Presidents, 1963*, pp. 105-16.

[67]Douglas E. Kliever, *Vocational Education Act of 1963* (Washington: American Vocational Association, 1965). Kliever centers his attention on the vocational education bill but covers all education legislation enacted in 1963; this section relies upon his careful chronology.

[68]*Cong. Record*, Vol. 109 (Aug. 14, 1963), p. 14957.

[69]A factor in the softening of the opposition of public school organizations, as well as of Protestant church groups and the public generally, was undoubtedly the consistent position of President Kennedy against aid to parochial schools. As the country's first Catholic president consistently made clear that he was indeed independent of his church on public policy questions, concern aroused in the 1960 campaign regarding the breaching of church-state barriers died down. Munger, in his 1965 paper, observed that the President's staunch opposition to aid to parochial schools, by reassuring non-Catholics, may have contributed to a swing in public opinion which in turn made possible the passage, in 1965, of the kind of legislation Kennedy opposed ("The Politics of Federal Aid to Education").

[70]Public Laws 815 and 874, 81 Cong. 2 sess. (1950).

[71]Four senators, including Goldwater of Arizona, were paired against it.

[72]Kliever, *Vocational Education Act of 1963*, p. 54.

[73]*Ibid.*, pp. 57-59.

[74]*Expansion of Public Laws 815 and 874*, Hearings before the Subcommittee on Education of the Senate Labor and Public Welfare Committee, 88 Cong. 2 sess. (July 30, 1964), pp. 100-01, 96-97.

[75]Quoted by Morse in a speech before the American Personnel and Guidance Association in Washington, June 2, 1965.

[76]Meranto, *The Politics of Federal Aid to Education in 1965*, p. 70. Also Stephen K. Bailey, *The Office of Education and the Education Act of 1965* (published for the Inter-University Case Program by Bobbs-Merrill, 1966), p. 5.

[77]*Aid to Elementary and Secondary Education*, Hearings before the House Education and Labor Committee, 89 Cong. 1 sess. (Jan. 28, 1965), p. 784.

[78]Speech by Rabbi Maurice N. Eisendrath, Jan. 30, 1965, quoted by *Congressional Quarterly Weekly Report*, Feb. 5, 1965, p. 204.

[79]Testiomny of Monsignor Frederick G. Hochwalt, in *Aid to Elementary and Secondary Education*, Hearings, p. 804.

[80]Testimony of Robert E. McKay, chairman of the NEA legislative commission, in *ibid.* (Jan. 25, 1965), p. 235.

[81]Dean M. Kelley and George R. La Noue, "The Church-State Settlement in the Federal Aid to Education Act," in Donald A. Giannella (ed.), *Religion and the Public Order–1965*, Annual Review of the Institute of Church and State of the Villanova University School of Law (University of Chicago Press, 1966), p. 114.

[82]*Ibid.*, p. 119. In regard to the final point, the administration in its discussions with the key groups on the general outline of the bill had obtained a tacit agreement that they would emphasize their support of the measure as a whole and deemphasize their disagreement with particular provisions.

[83]*Ibid.*, pp. 129-30.

[84]Kelley and La Noue refer to Carey as the member "who speaks for parochial schools on the Committee" (*ibid.*, p. 124).

[85]*Cong. Record,* Vol. III (March 24, 1965), pp. 5747-48.

[86]*Ibid.* (April 8, 1965), pp. 7531-32.

[87]*Ibid.* (March 24, 1965), p. 5735.

[88]*Ibid.* (April 7, 1965), p. 7317.

[89]*Ibid.* (March 24, 1965), p. 5729.

[90]*Ibid.* (April 9, 1965), p. 7710.

[91]In 1966 a $2.9 billion expansion of college programs passed the House by a voice vote, with less than forty minutes of debate and no opposition at all (*New York Times* and *Washington Post,* May 3, 1966).

[92]Speech at San Marcos, Texas, before signing the Higher Education Act of 1965, Nov. 8, 1965, *Public Papers of the Presidents, 1965,* p. 1103.

[93]These figures, for fiscal years, include funds for activities classified under "education" in the functional tables of the federal budget, *The Budget of the United States Government, Fiscal Year 1969,* p. 540.

[94]*Cong. Record,* Vol. III (Aug. 10, 1965), p. 19114.

[95]The *Digest of Educational Statistics, 1965* (Office of Education), pp. 46-47, shows a total of 104,400 classrooms estimated by local officials to be needed to relieve overcrowding and another 309,200 in buildings built before 1920 or "combustible." Assuming that schools built before 1920 are obsolete, the total need is 413,600 classrooms—or more than the 340,000 originally estimated by HEW Secretary Hobby as the national shortage when the debate began in 1954.

[96]Message of Jan. 12, 1965, *Public Papers of the Presidents, 1965,* p. 26.

[97]Address to American Association of School Administrators, Atlantic City, Feb. 14, 1966.

THE OFFICE OF EDUCATION AND THE EDUCATION ACT OF 1965*

Stephen K. Bailey

Introduction

Probably the greatest landmark in the history of federal aid to education was the passage in April 1965 of the Elementary and Secondary Education Act (ESEA).[1] Although ESEA, like all important social legislation, was the product of a wide variety of intellectual, political, economic, and social forces, its effective genesis is found in the interaction of presidential, congressional, group interest, and bureaucratic forces in Washington. One of the important bureaucratic forces was the catalytic and innovative energy of the then Commissioner of the United States Office of Education, Francis Keppel. Whether Keppel's role is viewed as a self-conscious extension of his official position as an agency head in the federal bureaucracy or as a policy-making surrogate of the White House (and it was both of these), it illuminates the importance of federal agencies in the development of substantive legislation.

But policy initiation and the development of a policy consensus for legislative purposes was only one aspect of the U.S. Office of Education's relationship to ESEA. Major legislation may have a profound effect upon an agency's organization and administrative behavior. If legislation involves a major departure from tradition in intent and funding, it can serve to prod an agency into marked adjustments in internal organization and in external relations. To borrow language from modern systems analysis, a new "input" can have a dramatic effect upon "functional relations" within a system and upon the nature of the system's "output." This was certainly an apparent effect of the passage of ESEA upon the U.S. Office of Education (USOE).

Finally, a law must be administered. The effectuation of legislative intent by reducing general language to specific guidelines to be implemented by administrative discretion and sanctions is the root responsibility of executive agencies. This, too, is a creative activity. In a democratic ethos (possibly universally) the process is marked by a dialectical rather than a dictatorial process—by adjustments and feedbacks reflecting the interests and problems of those individuals and institutions ultimately affected by the new legislation. The detailed process is little

*Stephen K. Bailey, "The Office of Education and the Education Act," Inter-University Case Program #100. Copyright by IUCP and published for them by Bobbs-Merrill. Reprinted by permission of IUCP.

357

understood, but its general outlines are observable in the attempts of USOE to carry out the congressional mandates of ESEA.

For those proximately responsible for creating and implementing new laws, and for effecting relevant and derivative organizational and administrative adjustments, life is marked by a perverse law of rising hostility. Old habits, old relationships, old status patterns are inevitably disrupted. Public interests are often achieved at the expense of the personal interests of key innovators. Neither Frank Keppel nor his handpicked deputy, Henry Loomis, were with the Office of Education a year after the passage of ESEA. They had been consumed in the revolutions they had done so much to engineer.

In one sense, their role in social and institutional engineering is at the heart of the story that follows. But in a larger sense, this is a case study of a federal agency—an agency undergoing substantial stress as it attempted to relate to a new policy commitment of the federal government. A single case cannot provide a general theory of agency dynamics. On the other hand, it may suggest heuristic notions which ultimately can lead to a general theory of bureaucratic systems adjusting over time to substantial stress. The interaction of USOE and ESEA from 1964-1966 was in one sense a discrete slice of history. It seems probable, however, that these interactions have or will have their rough analogues in other bureaucratic systems reacting to external and internal forces of like intensity.

The U.S. Office of Education

The U.S. Office of Education (USOE) was established on March 2, 1867. Its legislative mandate was "to collect such statistics and facts as should show the condition and progress of education, to diffuse such information as shall aid the people of the United States in the establishment and maintenance of efficient school systems, and otherwise to promote the cause of education."[2]

For three-quarters of a century, in spite of programmatic accretions in such fields as the support of land-grant colleges, vocational education, and cooperation with New Deal agencies in carrying out educationally oriented relief programs, the USOE maintained relatively stable norms of institutional behavior and a low level of bureaucratic visibility in the executive branch of the federal government. From 1869 to 1939 it was a virtually autonomous agency within the Department of the Interior. Its chief functions were the gathering and dissemination of educational statistics, the preparation of reports, and the provision of consulting services in a number of different fields to state and local educational agencies. As late as 1950, USOE—which had been placed inside the Federal Security Agency by the Reorganization Plan of 1939, with consequent irritation to its officials and to coordination-seeking FSA officials[3]—had a total staff of just over 300 and a budget of only $40 million.

The fifteen-year period 1950-1965 was marked by drastically accelerating growth and change. In 1950 USOE was charged with administering a program of grants to school districts suffering from the impact of such federal installations as military bases and atomic energy plants. In 1953 the Eisenhower administration, following the recommendations of the First Hoover Commission, won congressional approval to convert the Federal Security Agency into the Department of Health, Education, and Welfare (HEW)—enchancing the visibility of USOE by the inclusion of the word Education in the title of the new department.

In 1954 the Cooperative Research Act was passed, giving USOE a new role of stimulating educational research through grants to colleges and universities. In 1956 President Eisenhower called a special White House Conference on Education, which illuminated the educational needs of the nation and pressed for added federal support of American education at all levels. Following the launching of the first Soviet satellite in 1957, Congress passed the National Defense Education Act, which mandated the USOE to distribute vast sums of money to American secondary and higher education to increase the production of scientific, engineering, and foreign language specialists.

By 1962 the USOE had grown to 1400 employees and an annual budget of $600 million. Even this tells only part of the story of the growth of the federal government's involvement in education. The USOE budget represented only a small fraction of the estimated total expenditures of the federal government for educational purposes.[4] In 1962, for example, the Department of Defense and the Veterans Administration together spent more on educational programs than USOE and the National Science Foundation combined, the latter two being the only federal agencies with a primary concern for education. In 1963, Congresswoman Edith Green, in a study of the Federal Government and Education reported that, all told, 42 departments, agencies, and bureaus of the government were involved in education to some degree. She listed nine agencies as conducting "major programs in education."[5]

Even though not *primus inter pares,* USOE by 1963 was becoming far more than a junior partner in this extraordinary federal commitment, and in 1963-1964 its position was further strengthened by the passage of the new Vocational Education Act and the Higher Education Facilities Act.

These swift developments were bound to have at least minor effects upon USOE's operating structure and sense of mission, and they served to establish tensions within USOE between older, tradition-minded personnel (mostly educational specialists linked to powerful professional associations on the outside) on the one hand, and, on the other, the younger generalists brought in to organize and implement USOE's new missions.

Throughout this period of rapid transformation, however, two important facts stand out. First, bureaucratic inertia and preoccupation inhibited radical and major adjustments of organization and staff to meet USOE's new responsibilities; second, attempts to develop legislation for various federal grants-in-aid *for elementary and secondary education* had been unavailing. In 1965 both of these logjams were broken. How they were broken illuminates the role of a federal agency in policy initiation and implementation and in precipitating a revolutionary and cathartic change in its own staff, structure, and behavior. To this process, and to its impact upon the fortunes of those responsible for effecting, we now turn.

The Politics of Policy Initiation

For almost a century bills had been introduced in Congress to tap the enormous tax base of the federal government to provide general support for public education. But no President had articulated the need for federal aid to education more eloquently or had given education a higher priority on his agenda of legislative proposals than John F. Kennedy.

Kennedy designated his education bill of 1961 "probably the most important piece of domestic legislation" of the year. In his general aid bill of that year, he asked for a three-year authorization of more than $2.4 billion to help the states construct elementary and secondary classrooms and boost teacher's salaries. In addition, Kennedy's educational requests included substantial loans to colleges and universities for the construction of dormitories, classroom, laboratories, and other academic facilities; a substantial federal scholarship program for prospective college students; support for educational television; aid for medical and dental education; aid for education of migrant workers and their children; and the establishment of a Federal Advisory Council on the Arts.

The following year, 1962, President Kennedy asked, in addition, for grants to improve the quality of teaching, a program to combat adult illiteracy, and special training for handicapped children.[6] All of the Kennedy recommendations emerged in whole or in part from the Office of Education, first under the leadership of Commissioner Sterling M. McMurrin and then under the leadership of Commissioner Frank Keppel. These commissioners and their staff advisers were, of course, supported by suggestions and assistance from educational associations and from education-minded legislators and their staffs.

Although Commissioner McMurrin was instrumental, during his eighteen-month incumbency, in developing general aid proposals for the President, USOE's policy role increased markedly in extent and sophistication with the appointment of Francis Keppel, former Dean of the Graduate School of Education at Harvard, as United States Commissioner of Education in 1962.

Quick, bright, energetic, politically inexperienced but sophisticated, Keppel had been Assistant Dean of Harvard's Graduate School of Education at the age of 23 and Dean at the age of 32. He was not a schoolmen's schoolman. He had been neither public school teacher nor superintendent. But he had a deep commitment to improving the quality of public education in America, and he (like President Kennedy upon Keppel's appointment) saw his role as Commissioner of Education largely in terms of achieving major legislative breakthroughs in the field of federal aid.

Although Kennedy lived to see a number of his categorical educational programs enacted by Congress, his general aid bills for elementary and secondary education were killed. In 1961 and again in 1963 the general aid bills died in such bruising combat as to lead careful observers to conclude that general federal aid to public education was probably impossible in the foreseeable future.[7]

'Red, Religion, and Race'

What killed the general aid bills in the early 1960's was simply a variation on a theme that had haunted exponents of federal aid over the decades. "Red, Religion, and Race" was the shorthand; "Red" standing for the fear of federal control of the educational system; "Religion" referring to the prickly issue of Church-State relations; and "Race" referring to the fear on the part of southern legislators that federal aid would be used as a club to enforce school integration. Minor issues were also present, particularly the question of what constituted equity in the distribution of federal funds among the several states. But the three "R's" produced the controlling and often unnatural congressional and pressure-group coalitions that defeated the Kennedy proposals.

The Kennedy years were nonetheless important. A series of bills were passed for the support of education and for various other categorical programs. More significant from the standpoint of our story, the Kennedy years left a fivefold legacy that was to have a determinative effect upon the future of federal aid to education: (1) Keppel as Commissioner of Education; (2) a general guilt complex (combined with a new legislative sophistication in getting categorical grants) on the part of the warring educational factions that had been bloodied in the process of blocking general aid to education; (3) an awakened national conscience over the issue of civil rights; (4) a shift in public opinion on the matter of federal aid to religious schools;[8] and (5) a liberalized Rules Committee in the House of Representatives.[9] An added fortuity was the succession of New York City's Adam Clayton Powell to the chairmanship of the House Committee on Education and Labor—replacing a southern conservative, Graham Barden.

How the confluence of these and other factors helped President Johnson to achieve dramatic breakthroughs first in civil rights and then in federal aid to education is a study in itself. The civil rights story particularly has been told in other places.[10] Suffice it to note here that Title IV of the Civil Rights Act of 1964 mandated the Office of Education to assist by advice and money in the desegregation of schools; Title VI created an injunction against federal grants to school districts and institutions of learning which practiced segregation. Not only did these titles move the Office of Education suddenly and massively into the hottest domestic political issue of our age; paradoxically, they removed, *de jure*, one of the most controversial issues from the legislative struggle for massive federal aid to education. While enormously complicating the administrative and political role of USOE, the Civil Rights Act of 1964 undercut one of the three traditional "R's" of opposition to federal assistance to elementary and secondary education.

President Johnson's Action

In the presidential campaign of 1964, Lyndon Johnson decided to make federal aid to education and the elimination of poverty his two central domestic issues. Ultimately, he saw the first as a condition of the second. He asked his writers, particularly Douglass Cater, to develop a series of speeches on these interrelated themes.

At the same time, under the urging of his then Director of the Bureau of the Budget, Kermit Gordon, the President established a series of task forces on various aspects of his Great Society Program. These task forces, held to secrecy and considerable anonymity, were to report to the President after the election on ways and means of accomplishing Great Society goals. Composed of able academics, private citizens, and government officials, the task forces met frequently during the late summer and early fall of 1964 and hammered out a series of legislative and administrative proposals.

The task force on education was chaired by John Gardner, who had made improvement of education the major philanthropic interest of the Carnegie Corporation, of which he was then president. Gardner had also written extensively and eloquently on various aspects of American education. Francis Keppel was a member *ex officio* of the Gardner task force. The task force recommendations which were submitted to the President in mid-November 1964 represented an amalgam of inputs from Gardner and other influential members of the study group. But these in turn had been substantially influenced by staff recommendations prepared within the Office of Education and transmitted to Gardner by Keppel.

Although the Gardner task force report was never made public, it is clear from conversations with task force members that the first draft of ESEA substantially reflected the task force's recommendations. But, as just noted, these reflected in large measure a series of policy decisions within the Office of Education. These internal policy decisions, in turn, had been refined in conversations and in memo exchanges between Keppel and the leadership of HEW (especially Under Secretary Wilbur Cohen). They had further been tested by Keppel in secret joint meetings with leaders of the National Education Association (the largest professional association of teachers and school administators in America) and the National Catholic Welfare Conference (the major voice of the Catholic church on educational and social policy in the United States), and in separate meetings with other powerful professional associations. They had been cleared by Keppel with key advisers in the White House (especially Douglass Cater, who played a major brokerage role of his own among Congress, the bureaucracy, and the educational associations) and in the Bureau of the Budget (William B. Cannon and Michael S. March). Finally, Keppel kept key senators and congressmen like Wayne Morse (Chairman of the Senate Sub-committee on Education), Lister Hill (Chairman of the Senate Sub-committee on Appropriations for Labor, Health, Education, and Welfare), Adam Clayton Powell (Chairman, House Committee on Education and Labor), Carl Perkins (Chairman, General Sub-committee on Education of the House Committee on Education and Labor), and John Fogarty (Chairman of the Sub-committee on Labor, Health, Education, and Welfare of the House Appropriations Committee) and their personal and committee staffs informed of the development of major policy lines, and, with strong and sometimes indispensable support from Cater in the White House, acted as a broker between most of these men and the Gardner task force.

In the dynamics of policy initiation and consent-building, it is difficult to identify effective cause. But in tracing the origins of the historic Elementary and Secondary Education Act of 1965, few inside observers and participants would question Keppel's seminal and pervasive influence. And back of Keppel in USOE were staff like Samuel Halperin (then Director, Office of Legislation), Francis Ianni (then Director, Division of Educational Research), and Peter Muirhead (then Director, Bureau of Higher Education), and others who prompted ideas, drafted supporting arguments, and fashioned legislative language. All in all, Keppel saw himself in a brokerage role—linking the White House (including the President and the Gardner task force) to the bureaucratic interests within USOE, and both of these to the Congress and to key group interests outside.

Keppel's success in this brokerage function was in part due (as he would be the first to admit) to broader influences at work in the society at large. Over a decade, the climate of opinion had been shaped by the illuminating and informed studies of James B. Conant; by the work of economists like Professor Theodore Schultz and Seymour Harris, who had shifted education from a "consumption function" to an "investment function"; by a host of more popular books, monographs, and articles which raised questions about Johnnie's ability to read or the effectiveness of education for the gifted child; by the sheer pressure of numbers on the American school systems; and, finally, by the educational implications of Soviet victories in space and weaponry.

In addition, the increased public awareness of the plight of the American Negro, and the anomaly of intractable pockets of urban and rural poverty in the midst of national prosperity, had set loose a series of questions, ideas, and pressures which deeply affected attitudes toward public education. All these factors intensified the guilt complex of both Catholic and public educational associations about the failure of the general aid bills during the Kennedy regime, inducing new thoughts, new attitudes, and a new readiness to cooperate in a search for a workable compromise over the Church-State issue. Certainly NEA's shift, from an insistence upon unrestricted general aid for public schools only, to an acceptance of massive categorical aid for the poor, with parochial schools sharing in the benefits, was one of the key factors in the new political climate.

A final key factor was the overwhelming election victory of President Johnson over Barry Goldwater in 1964 and the concurrent election to the House of some 80 liberal Democrats pledged to the enactment of federal aid to education. Johnson's priority concern with education and his superb legislative command of a sympathetic Congress infused with many new liberal Democratic members, were essential conditions for the passage of new federal aid legislation.

The Politics of Bill Drafting

This cursory review tells us little about the precise political issues that had to be negotiated by the Office of Education and its allies in developing the new educational policy.

The Elementary and Secondary Education Act of 1965 was something of a political *tour de force*. Its five basic titles reflected months of astute political innovation and bargaining. If "Race" had been knocked out of the way by the Civil Rights Act of 1964, "Red" (fear of federal control) and "Religion" had not. Each Title of ESEA represented a successful attempt to mollify fears about these two issues while accomplishing positive goals.

The positive goals were innovative and exciting: to focus federal attention on the children of poverty, those in greatest need of education, who were seldom getting it; to induce the rubbing of shoulders of educators and non-educators in the search for educational improvements; to create inducements for public and parochial schools to work together; to break down the "fortress school" concept so that schools would serve the larger community before and after hours and around the calendar; to promote research and experimentation in curriculum, method, and educational evaluation. But these positive goals were deeply linked to political reality—the need to develop interest group, bureaucratic, and congressional consent for a massive federal aid-to-education bill.

Title I

The heart of the bill was Title I, which began with a two-year extension of federal aid to impacted areas and then provided a formula of federal grants through the states to local school districts on the basis of indexes related to the number of school-age children who came from poor families.[11] Federal money, either under these basic grants or under special incentive grants, was to be spent on educational programs and facilities specifically designed to aid these educationally deprived children. Educationally deprived children in private schools would benefit from federal largess through locally designed programs of dual enrollment and through educational radio, television, and mobile educational services. (In order to avoid touchy constitutional issues, public school agencies were to retain title to all property acquired under the Act.)

In one fell swoop, Title I ducked an immediate fight with those Congressmen and Senators whose districts were already benefitting from "impacted area" aid;

avoided the symbolic dangers of "general aid" by establishing "poverty" as an educational category;[12] established a formula that would affect 95 percent of all counties in America, but that would particularly benefit central urban areas in the North and rural areas in the South (thereby cementing the two frequently warring factions of the Democratic Party in Congress); provided assistance to parochial school children; and stipulated a major role for state departments of education in administering the grants, thereby avoiding a contretemps with the powerful chief state school officers' lobby. And all of this was to be greased with a billion-dollar appropriation for the first year.

Titles II and III

Title II of ESEA, even more than Title I, must be looked upon as a major concession to Catholic educators. Title II authorized a five-year program of grants to states for the acquisition of school library resources, textbooks, and other printed instructional materials for use of children and teachers in public and private elementary and secondary schools. Allotments were to be made to each state simply on the basis of the number of children enrolled in public and private elementary and secondary schools.[13] Title II may also be viewed in part as a way of mollifying those states that felt themselves treated inequitably by the poverty formula in Title I.

ESEA's Title III made provision for "supplementary educational centers and services" with a grant formula that took into account both school age and total population estimates of each state compared to national totals for these categories. These supplementary centers and services might be built around a wide variety of activities: counselling, remedial instruction, vocational guidance, experimental pedagogy, the creative use of mass media, special courses in the creative arts, the development of "exemplary educational programs," etc. Title III was viewed by its drafters as the "cutting edge" of educational reform under the Act.

Although Title III required assurance that the planning of programs would involve the participation of state educational agencies (along with institutions of higher education; nonprofit private schools; and nonprofit private agencies, such as libraries, museums, musical and artistic organizations, and other educational and cultural resources), applications for grants were to be submitted directly from the local educational agency to the U.S. Commissioner of Education. If bypassing state educational agencies raised the hackles of the chief state school officers' association, it was deemed necessary by the authors of the act as the price of assuring creativity, flexibility, and inter-district and interstate cooperation in vital aspects of educational innovation. As in Titles I and II, private as well as public schools were to be beneficiaries of these experimental centers and services. Perhaps even more than Titles I and II, Catholic educators looked to Title III to upgrade the quality of education for parochial school children.

Titles IV and V

Title IV, for the support of educational research and dissemination projects, also bypassed the states. Contracts could be entered into directly by universities, colleges, and other public or private agencies, institutions, or individuals. An extension and modification of the Cooperative Research Act of 1954, Title IV was largely the brainchild of Francis Ianni and Ralph Flynt of USOE's staff and of Ralph Tyler, one of America's most renowned educators and a member of the Gardner Task Force.

In both Titles III and IV, if chief state school officers found their noses out of joint, a wide variety of local school agencies, universities, private enterprises, and individuals might be pleased by the chance to negotiate directly with USOE. These non-state interests had powerful political voices of their own. (According to one official who participated in the legislative struggle, university and industry interests actually did very little to support passage of these titles; perhaps the biggest push from non-state interests came from non-public educators.)

Title V provided modest funds for strengthening state departments of education. A favorite of Commissioner Keppel on intrinsic, philosophical grounds of "creative Federalism" and on the pragmatic assumption that no federal agency was capable of retailing educational grants as extensive and complicated as those under consideration, Title V had the political effect of mollifying the chief state school officers who were unhappy with Titles III and IV. Financial assistance to states was included as implementation money in other parts of the Act, but Title V was the final attempt to counter the charge of federal control—to assure governors, state departments of education, interested Congressmen and Senators, and local administrators and teachers that the federal government had no intention of usurping the traditional primacy of states and localities in formulating and controlling educational policy.

There was no evidence of archness or calculations to mislead in this symbolic deference to the states, but neither the provisions in earlier Titles for local or state initiative in applications for funds nor the grants in Title V for strengthening state departments of education quieted the fears of the unconvinced and the unconverted. How could more than one billion dollars of new federal money for elementary and secondary education *not* lead to increased federal control of the educational enterprise? Politically speaking, all that can be said is that these fears, like some other fears about aid to religious schools, were effectively countered, overcome, or temporarily subordinated by astute legislative craftsmanship and by untiring salesmanship—much of it originating in the U.S. Office of Education itself.

Passage in Three Months

The President submitted his education message and a bill draft at the beginning of the new Congress, on January 12, 1965. The President gave the bill unprecedented priority. The White House strategy seemed to be the mobilization of a massive congressional push before something could go wrong. With a few key changes, especially some involving the church-state issue, the bill sailed through the House Committee on Education and Labor, scraped over the shoals of a liberalized Rules Committee, and was passed by a whopping 263-153 roll call on March 26—barely two months after the start of committee consideration. In the Senate, thanks to the legislative shrewdness of Wayne Morse and supporting presidential artillery, the House bill was preserved intact. This maneuver precluded sending the bill to conference committee—a legislative stage which in the past had killed more than one aid to education proposal. On April 9, the bill was passed and sent to the President.

The seeming effortlessness of getting ESEA through Congress should not obscure the exhausting efforts of Keppel and Halperin, in USOE, and of Cater in the White House, in working with their congressional friends in building information and consent and in manipulating compromises so as to keep the bill from getting seriously hurt. Daily—when necessary, hourly—contacts between Keppel, Halperin, and Cater, on the one hand, and legislative leaders on the other, were maintained throughout the legislative struggle. Cater's role was especially important because strained relations between Keppel and certain key legislators like Adam Clayton Powell precluded simple bilateral bargaining and strategy making. Cater could get through when Keppel could not.

On April 11, outside the one-room schoolhouse at Stonewall, Texas, where he had first attended classes, the President signed Public Law, 89-10, with a comment that members of Congress who had supported the legislation would "be remembered in history as men and women who began a new day of greatness in American society."

The President also took this occasion to state that he had asked federal officials "to move immediately to prepare the Office of Education for the big job it would have to do, just as soon as the funds are appropriated," and that he would appoint a task force to assist the Secretary of Health, Education, and Welfare "in the next 60 days on organizational and personnel problems."[14]

The Politics of Internal Reorganization

With the passage of ESEA, USOE was faced with the realization that, as soon as appropriations were firm, it would be called upon to administer a vast and complicated new program—a program so large as to dwarf by comparison any single piece of legislation it had hitherto administered. Actually, Keppel had been aware of these probabilities and necessities much earlier. Months before, he had become convinced that a big legislative breakthrough was at hand. Having devoted his long days to legislative craftsmanship and to consent-building for the new proposal, however, Keppel had been unable to give concerted attention to problems of management, organization, or personnel within USOE itself. He was only aware that something had to be done to improve the structure and staff of the office if it were to carry extraordinary new burdens without chaos or collapse.

The Ancien Regime

Before Keppel, and well into his administration as Commissioner of Education, USOE was marked by a number of institutional characteristics that branded it an "old-line" bureau. These characteristics are easily summarized, for even before the Ink Committee studies in the spring of 1965, many of them had been identified over the years by a number of observers and task forces. [15]

(1) *Atomization and Specialization.* For decades, effective power in USOE was exercised by virtually autonomous units under the control of technical or professional specialists. The Office of the Commissioner was weak. The tenure of Commissioners was short—five incumbents in the single decade 1954-1964. During this same decade, office continuity was provided by a dedicated deputy commissioner, Wayne Reed, and by a number of venerable associate commissioners. However suited their leadership was to historically segmented operations and to the expectation of education's major professional associations, it was only in the most general sense supervisory. In a non-invidious sense, their "feudal baronies" were only marginally stronger than the "kingdom" of the Commissioner. Real power was lodged in the guilds of professional specialists who ran the operating sub-units of the major bureaus: library consultants; vocational education experts; reading and curricular specialists; experts on education of the handicapped; specialists in home economics, agricultural education, counselling and guidance—each with his special friends in Congress and appropriate professional colleagues at the regional, state, and local level. This meant, in effect, that there was no locus in the Office, and no machinery, for developing a national educational policy (the very phrase created shivers); no means of effecting intra-office communication; no generalist views to counteract and coordinate the views of specialists.

(2) *Superannuated Personnel and Personnel Systems.* In the years prior to the reorganization of 1965, the average age of new recruits to the Office had been over 50. Formal experience seemed a more valued criterion than either energy or imagination. Recruitment of able people was not helped by a very negatively oriented personnel management branch. Out of fairness, it must be pointed out that the operating bureaus contributed their share of sand to the personnel machinery. For example, they often waited until they had selected a person before asking that a job be established and classified for that person to fill. But even this doleful practice was testimony to the inability of the Personnel Management Branch to exercise appropriate managerial leadership within USOE. Top personnel officers controlled where they should have let loose; they relaxed where they should have been firm. There was no overall manpower planning for USOE, no system of career development, and no effective personnel evaluation system. (Like some schools without standards, *everybody* was "promoted" at the end of the year.)

(3) *Archaic Financial and Management Information Systems.* The system of financial and management accountability was almost totally decentralized, disparate, and ineffective. Finance officers and accountants were sprinkled like grains of pepper throughout the lower levels of the organization. The result was irritation rather than spice. Some financial records were kept on ledger sheets in longhand. A set of books in one division or branch was not comparable to a set in another division or branch. No one at the Commissioner's level had the financial or management information needed to make wise allocations of manpower and funds across the agency as a whole. The Office lacked, in the words of the Ink Committee, "a management reporting system adequate to keep top management currently informed on program status."[16]

(4) *An Unrationalized Bureau and Field Structure.* The bureau structure of USOE had 'growed' like Topsy. New legislative mandates were handled by sedimentary accretion to existing bureaucratic divisions. Prior to 1964, when the Bureau of Higher Education was established, the Office had been divided into three major operating bureaus: Educational Research and Development; International Education; and Educational Assistance Programs. The latter, particularly, became an undifferentiated catchall for any and every new grant-in-aid. As a bureau it had neither functional clarity nor clarity of focus by educational level. There was, in short, no organizing principle.

The Bureau of International Education faced another kind of issue: it was largely a service and brokerage agency for other federal departments (particularly State and the Agency for International Development). Furthermore, its volume of "business" was miniscule compared to the two other operating bureaus of the Office. For both these reasons it seemed to have no justification for being a separate operating bureau of USOE.

The Bureau of Educational Research and Development suffered from some of the same "catchall" problems as the Bureau of Educational Assistance. It also contained operating programs which could just as easily (and perhaps more logically) have been in the latter. Finally, the field offices of USOE were weak in staff, confused in purpose, and manned in large part by specialists who reported directly to sub-bureau units in Washington.

(5) *Anomie within the Executive Branch.* If USOE was plagued with internal problems of organization, management, and personnel, it also suffered from isolation and withdrawal from the rest of the executive branch. When Keppel became Commissioner, he found within the Office of Education (especially among career civil servants) an almost pathological suspicion of the Department of which it was an integral part: HEW. This mistrust went beyond the normal tensions between supervisory/coordinating and subordinates/coordinated agencies. It stemmed from a tradition of *de facto* USOE autonomy before transfer into HEW, and from the peculiar ethos of professional educators (the predominant career staff of USOE) that education should be isolated from politics. In the minds of these staff members, HEW, at the departmental level, was "politically" oriented, and should therefore be kept at arm's length.

Keppel spent months attempting to build bridges with the Department's Secretary and relevant assistant secretaries through his special cultivation of Assistant (later Under) Secretary Wilbur Cohen. For his part, Cohen had been of those who had recommended Keppel for the post of Commissioner. Cohen had hoped that Keppel would construct for USOE a new and healthy relationship with the top leadership of HEW. Keppel also spent time developing appropriate linkages with the White House staff and the Bureau of the Budget—both of which over the years had developed a most uncomplimentary view of the personnel and practices of USOE. What was still lacking, however, was any mechanism—formal or informal—for relating the work of USOE to the educational programs of the other departments and agencies of government. Combined, these non-USOE programs quite overshadowed the Office of Education in magnitude and in funding. This, in turn, contributed to the ingrownness and the sense of isolation of USOE itself.

(6) *Fear of the charge of Federal control.* Finally (and perhaps a basic cause of its other problems) the Office of Education operated under a restraining fear that someone might accuse it of trying to direct and dominate educational policy in the United States. This fear was less the product of timidity than the ingrained feeling, based on years of professional training and experience, that public education in American was a local matter. Whatever the dangers of federal control (and they exist), the historically and constitutionally conditioned reticence of USOE in this area had a crippling effect upon initiative and leadership. Reenforced in their modesty by state and local education offices, by educational professional associations, and by the long-held theology of "local control," USOE officials were afraid of their own shadows—except in those limited areas of professional specialization in which their advice was "sought."

The Controversial Deputy

This, then, was the old Office. This was the system that was to be so radically transformed by new political and administrative leadership and by the extraordinary turn in legislative fortunes in the biennium 1964-1965.

To deal with these difficulties and to start putting USOE into shape administering ESEA, Keppel felt the need for an executive officer, a deputy, who would have the insight and the toughness to remold the office—to transform it from a series of unconnected, comfortable, country stores into a modern supermarket. In March 1965, after months of trying, he finally attracted Henry Loomis away from his position as Director of the Voice of America. Loomis had had his training as a research physicist at Harvard and the University of California. After serving in the U.S. Navy in World War II, he had worked with the Atomic Energy Commission and had subsequently become Assistant to the President of the Massachusetts Institute of Technology, first under Dr. Karl Compton and then under Dr. James R. Killian, Jr. Prior to his appointment as

Director of the Voice of America, Loomis had served in important staff positions in the Department of Defense, the National Security Council, and the President's Office of Science and Technology (under Eisenhower). In 1965, he had won both a Rockefeller Public Service Award and a USIA Distinguished Service Award. Upon joining the Office of Education, Loomis began what was perhaps one of the most extraordinary, bruising, controversial, and effective administrative operations in the recent annals of the federal government.

He began under a heavy political cloud. Loomis was an Eisenhower Republican and continued all during his work under Democratic presidents to hang Eisenhower's (and only Eisenhower's) photograph on his office walls. His transfer from VOA to USOE was marred and nearly canceled by Johnsonian pique. Loomis' farewell address to his colleagues in VOA had insinuated that White House pressure to make VOA newscasts conform to U.S. State Department policies and interests had markedly increased under Johnson. Word of this farewell address, reported in one of the Washington newspapers, infuriated the President, who was already aware of Loomis' Republican sympathies as a result of protests the White House had received from the Democratic National Committee that Loomis had been uncooperative in buying and selling tickets for Democratic party dinners.

The weekend of his shift from the U.S. Information Agency to the Office of Education was suspenseful and agonizing to Civil Service Commission Chairman John W. Macy, Jr., HEW Secretary Celebrese, Commissioner Keppel, and Loomis' friends and admirers in the Executive Office of the President. It came down to the question of whether the White House was going to permit the Commissioner of Education to have a deputy of his own choice. Although the President finally gave in, Loomis' relationships with the White House were cool from then on. Keppel's adamant defense of Loomis, whom he admired for his demonstrated administrative abilities, in spite of his political loyalties and rigidities, unquestionably weakened Keppel's own rapport with the President.

This contretemps was to have at least one lingering effect upon the efficiency of USOE operations, for it led to a presidential insistence that all new super-grades for the Office (ultimately throughout the government) were to be personally cleared by Presidential Assistant Marvin Watson in the White House. In a hectic attempt to restaff the Office in late 1965 and early 1966, White House clearance added another hurdle to an already cumbersome process of personnel recruitment.

Loomis' initial difficulties were not entirely external and political. He had replaced Wayne Reed, a career civil servant, as Deputy. Reed was given a new position as Associate Commissioner for federal-state relations, and he accepted the shift philosophically and loyally. But the pain of status loss was nonetheless acute, and it was felt by all of Reed's friends and colleagues inside USOE and within the various professional associations and state and local educational agencies with whom Reed had worked comfortably and sympathetically over the years. Empathy for Reed was reenforced by fear. If Reed could be pushed aside, who would be next?

Finally, there was the issue of personality and background. Loomis (like Keppel), by speech, manner, and brains, was patently "Ivy League." Furthermore, Loomis' previous career had involved close association with the cream of American scientists and with the urbane polish of foreign affairs officers. Temperamentally a "no-nonsense" type, lacking Keppel's quick smile and light touch, Loomis entered his new post with a superb preparation for everything except a sympathetic understanding of the slow speech and sometimes muddled behavior of the "non-Ivy" types who peopled the halls and cubicles of USOE. He and his handpicked deputy, Walter Mylecraine (whom he had brought with him from the Voice of America), were accused of being rougher than necessary. To the traditional educational establishment, Loomis was alien, cold, domineering, and ruthless. This image was never dispelled; in fact, it was reenforced by the attitude and behavior of Walter Mylecraine, who had the unlovely responsibility of wielding the hatchets handed to him almost daily by his superior and appeared to many to enjoy this sadistic administrative activity.

This background makes even more impressive the results of Loomis' twelve-month tenure. With the unflagging support of the Commissioner, Loomis put the Office of Education through the wringer of almost total reorganization of structure and staff. USOE would never be the same.

The Ink Committee

Loomis took office on March 8, 1965. He was appalled by what he found. He was immediately convinced that only a thorough and complete reorganization of structure and staff would equip USOE to discharge its existing and prospective responsibilities with efficiency and dispatch. Some insiders, notably Russell Wood and Ralph Flynt, had long since developed notions of a desirable reorganization plan—particularly the desirability of a bureau structure based upon educational levels (elementary and secondary, higher education, and adult and vocational), and a staff office structure that would include a separate office for program planning and evaluation.

These notions made sense to Loomis as working hypotheses; the real problem, as he saw it, was political. If Keppel and Loomis were to conduct a mass reorganization by managerial fiat, the internal heat engendered might consume both of them. They recognized that existing bureaus, divisions, branches, and officials had powerful linkages to sub-units of Congress and to external professional groups. To take the full responsibility for dislodging existing patterns and relationships would be to construct a personal lightning rod that would attract all of the electricity of protest latent in disturbing the status quo. One law of survival in Washington was to distribute political heat as broadly as possible. On the other hand, if the responsibility were passed to the Secretary of

HEW and his administrative experts, traditional enmities between USOE and HEW might flare up again. Some thought was given to the possible use of private management consultants like McKinsey or Arthur B. Little, but Loomis was skeptical of their worth for the purposes at hand.

In the meantime, independently, President Johnson had decided that a full-scale review of USOE's administrative organization and procedures was imperative. With the President's full support, therefore, Keppel and Loomis reached an agreement with Douglass Cater in the White House that the President, on the occasion of signing ESEA, would appoint a special high-level task force from within the government but outside HEW. This would, in effect, pass the political burden of reorganization to the strong shoulders of the President and throw any adverse congressional or group interest reactions to reorganization into the complicated and forbidding arena of presidential relations.

The Chairman of the Civil Service Commission and White House aide on political executive recruitment, John Macy, recommended Dwight Ink, then Assistant General Manager of the Atomic Energy Commission, as chairman of the new task force. Two other members were appointed: Herbert Jasper from the Bureau of the Budget and Nicholas J. Oganovic (almost immediately replaced by Gilbert Schulkind) of the Civil Service Commission.

All these members were relieved of their normal responsibilities for the 60-day period, April 15-June 15, 1965. They took office space in USOE, conducted extensive interviews, read in-house documents, observed, appointed sub-units on financial management and personnel, and maintained close liaison with Loomis and Keppel.

The report was submitted to the President on June 15. Its major recommendations for structural reorganization closely followed the earlier notions of Ralph Flynt and Russell Wood. These called for a new four-pronged bureau structure: Elementary and Secondary Education; Adult and Vocational Education; Higher Education; and Research. The committee also recommended a new or revised collection of Staff Offices: Administration, Information, Legislation, Program Planning and Evaluation, Equal Educational Opportunities, and Disadvantaged and Handicapped. In addition, the report recommended two centers for auxiliary services: one for Contracts and Construction and one for Educational Statistics. Finally, it established or confirmed three new Associate Commissioners: one for International Education, one for Federal-State Relations, and one for Field Services. The last was to preside over a revitalized USOE field structure in the nine regional offices of HEW.

The task force report also called for a complete overhaul and centralization of financial and personnel management and (after prior agreement with BOB and the U.S. Civil Service Commission) recommended the establishment of 25 new super-grade (GS 16, 17, 18) positions to give new life, vitality, and status to the top management of the Office.

Rapid Reorganization

In order to preclude the formation of hostile counter-pressures inside and outside the Office, Loomis convinced Keppel that implementation of the task force report should be immediate and should be played very close to the chest. In consequence, less than two weeks after the submission of the report, the reorganization was effected. The speed of action, and the fact that the comprehensions of the plan made it shattering to all vested interests, produced a reaction of numbed, bewildered, bitter acquiesence. Vocational education, with an enormously powerful lobby behind it and dozens of friends on the Hill, had always enjoyed a special autonomy and influence within the Office. It was denied a separate bureau and faced the indignity of second billing in the title of the new bureau to which it was assigned. The Bureau of International Education was totally abolished. That a new Associate Commissioner was established for International Education was less a testament to a firm belief that the function belonged at that level in USOE than to the desire to retain the continuity of knowledge and the wisdom of venerable Ralph Flynt, who was being dislodged from the directorship of the Bureau of Educational Research and Development and deserved a high-status position until retirement. Of 36 traditional divisions of the Office of Education, only two did not suffer major changes in role or function. Of 25 old super-grade personnel, only eight were unchanged in status or responsibility. At lower levels, generalists superceded specialists throughout the entire USOE pecking order.

The anguish can only be imagined. The ensuing, if temporary, administrative chaos was shattering. For days and weeks, people could not find each other's offices—sometimes not even their own. Telephone extensions connected appropriate parties only by coincidence. A large number of key positions in the new order were vacant or were occupied by acting directors who were frequently demoralized by status loss. Those who could not live with the status loss resigned. And all of this came at a time of maximum workload. New guidelines, application forms, and procedures had to be developed for the various titles of ESEA. More serious, ambiguities in the enforcement of Title VI of the Civil Rights Act were—at the moment of reorganization—causing a deluge of letters, telegrams, phone calls, congressional threats, and visiting delegations.

That a total breakdown did not occur was a tribute to the dedication of countless professional employees, to the hard-driving efficiency and trouble-shooting of Loomis and Mylecraine, and to the tact of Keppel. Operating through a topside Executive Group, made up of all Associate and Assistant Commissioners, which had been created in March just after his appointment, Loomis had established an agency-wide communications system, a policy-clarifying system, and a system of rigorously enforced delegation which held the office together and held key officials accountable for getting specific tasks accomplished on time. The months of July through September, 1965, were painful—not to say traumatic—for the entire agency. But if they witnessed the wrecking of an old house, they also saw the creation of the foundations for a new one.

The new one had weaknesses of its own. Some aspects of centralization, as in the case of contracting services, provided an acute administrative bottleneck and had to be re-decentralized. The war against specialists threw out some "babies" with some "bath water," and this policy had to be modified in order to enable USOE to perform some of its historic and continuing functions of collecting statistics and facts to "show the conditions and progress of education." Furthermore, box shuffling is less important as an instrument to improve administrative rationality in some abstract sense than it is as a device for reshuffling and dislodging oldtimers and creating vacancies for needed new staff. Finally, reorganization is always tentative. USOE has not achieved its final shape. It never will. But in spite of these qualifications and conditions, the structural reorganization of 1965 was profound and effective.

New Tendencies

Following the categories used earlier to describe the "old-line bureau" characteristics of the Office, the post-reorganization characteristics, or at least tendencies, of USOE may be summed up as follows:

(1) *Centralization and Generalization.* The reorganization, supplemented by congressional assignments of policy discretions to the Commissioner, enormously increased the power of the Commissioner's Office and of the staff offices immediately responsible to him. Administrative services and control in such fields as financial management, personnel selection and evaluation, congressional relations,[17] program planning, and policy coordination were improved in quality, given new status, and centralized at the highest levels of the Office hierarchy. Even at lower levels, generalists replaced specialists in command positions and in the exercise of *de facto* power.

(2) *Younger Recruits and a New Personnel System.* Fresh faces took over the major direction of USOE at all levels. Twenty-five new super-grade slots and the determined effort of the Keppel (and now Howe) regime to hire young people from the Federal Service Entrance Examination and Junior Management Examination rosters, substantially lowered the age and increased the vitality index of new hirings. With the help of recruiting specialists loaned from the Civil Service Commission, the Office developed an impressive roster of potential executives— and hired a fair number of top-grade people. There was still a sizeable gap between hiring authorizations and personnel aboard, but the major problem lay beyond the Office's new personnel system: there was an absolute shortage of talent in the society at large of the kinds of people USOE needed to attract. Furthermore, there were more attractive jobs for able people in programs being

sponsored or aided by the Office of Education than there were within the Office itself—financially speaking and in terms of flexible conditions of work. But in spite of these difficulties, USOE now had a better manpower planning and recruitment system than it had had before the Ink Report. It also had enormously tightened its personnel evaluation system, and had begun a career development program.

(3) *Modern Financial and Management Information System.* Under the leadership of Norman Karsh, Assistant Commissioner for Administration, the USOE developed a flow of financial and management data that made it possible for the Commissioner to know what was being spent, by whom, how fast, and for what. (Karsh, who arrived on the scene in September 1965 with an express mandate from Loomis to "tidy the place up," recalls one call from Keppel late at night. Keppel had been asked by a congressman for the amount of money the federal government was spending on land-grant colleges and universities. The information was simply not available in useable form in USOE at that time. It is today.)

(4) *A More Rational Bureau and Field Structure.* The reorganization of the office into four new operating bureaus did not by any means solve all problems of jurisdiction and coordination. It did, however, even out the workload; it gave a more coherent rationale for the existence of each bureau; and it provided a critically useful opportunity to reshuffle and dislodge top-level staff. Field reorganization was still underway as of this writing. A pilot and "model" field office had been established in Atlanta, and a new, politically sophisticated, and able Associate Commissioner for Field Relations had been appointed in USOE, Washington. But most of this story is still ahead.

(5) and (6): *Anomie and Federal Control.* There is, as yet, little to report on the subjects of anomie and timidity. The creation by President Johnson of a Federal Inter-Agency Committee on Education, with the Assistant Secretary of HEW for Education (a new post created by John Gardner when he became Department Secretary in 1965) as its chairman, is still too recent to provide any encouragement that the problems of inter-agency program coordination have been solved—either in Washington or in the field. It is fair to say that the USOE's whopping new budgets, which have made it a highly visible part of the Washington scene, have provided new muscle and new morale in its dealings with other agencies.

Fear of the charge of federal control still haunts USOE, and this leads to the third major aspect of the politics of rapid growth.

The Politics of Policy Implementation

The passage of ESEA in April 1965, and the virtual assurance of congressional funding by late summer or early fall, faced USOE with complex problems of design, priority-setting, and consent-building. A new and largely uncharted frontier of federal, state, local, and private relationships lay before the agency. No two titles of the new Act could be handled together. Each had its own target, its own clientele, its own implied or explicit conditions. The behavior of the Office during the first months of designing and enforcing guidelines would be watched by state and local educators and by state and national professional associations for signs of "federal control." (Later, Congress might be expected to raise questions about the *lack* of adequate federal control.) The politics of Title VI of the Civil Rights Act were already heated. If recent legislation had given the Commissioner of Education a carrot, it had also given him a threatening stick. For all of these reasons, it was essential that the Office not create the impression of arbitrary governance in carrying out the mandates of ESEA.

Even before the bill was passed, the National Education Association requested USOE assistance in briefing key educational officials and teacher's groups on aspects and implications of the new legislation. Upon the President's signature, Keppel and Loomis took three immediate steps:

(1) They created a Planning Group, under the chairmanship of Russell Wood, to develop an overall schedule for implementing ESEA and to farm out work assignments and due dates for the development of regulations, guidelines, application forms, etc.

(2) They assigned Wayne Reed, by then Associate Commissioner for Federal-State relations, the responsibility for developing an Office of Education indoctrination program of traveling "information teams," and set the first two weeks of May as the target time for the first of a series of regional meetings with key educators and educational groups.

(3) They determined that top priority would be given to Title V (grants for strengthening state departments of education), and that the next priority would be given to implementing Titles I and II. Titles III and IV offered less time pressure and needed a longer period for policy gestation.

Over the ensuing weeks and months, these basic decisions were reflected in the activities and workloads of the office staff. The Planning Group made its initial assignments; questionnaires, guidelines, and regulations were drafted. These were, in turn, tested with leaders of the educational trade associations in Washington, and with regional and national meetings of chief state school officers, school superintendents, school boards, teachers' associations, and religious groups. These clientele reactions were fed back into the policy designs of USOE. Consequent modifications were made; new drafts were prepared. These, in turn, were cleared with the clientele groups. Formal regulations, guidelines, and application forms were finally issued. These were explained by USOE teams to the state departments of education, who, in turn, attempted to explain them to local educational agencies.

National and state professional associations like NEA, the American Association of School Administrators, the Association of Chief State School Officers, the American Council on Education, the National School Board Association, and the National Catholic Welfare Conference helped in the communication process—through journals, special bulletins, newsletters, and conferences. Educational suppliers, seeing a new billion-dollar market, prepared model applications and sent their best salesmen around the country to assist state and local officials in developing proposals for grants under the various titles.[19] Congressional offices received complaints, requests for information and interpretation, or calls for assistance in getting top officials in USOE to attend local conferences and workshops. These were referred to the Commissioner's Office or to USOE's legislative or information offices for answering, countering, or parrying.

In short, the process of policy refinement, communications, and compliance was one of multi-lateral—even kaleidoscopic—negotiating, bargaining, feedback, and compromise on both substantive and procedural matters. And this was not all. Vertical negotiations with Washington were criss-crossed with horizontal negotiations at the state and local levels. Local school districts were mandated by ESEA to make their peace with parochial schools, with other cultural agencies in the community, and with the educational programs run under the war on poverty conducted by the Office of Economic Opportunity.[20]

Following a recommendation of Dr. Conant, the states in early 1966 entered into preliminary discussions on the creation of an interstate educational compact designed to give state governments a more powerful role *vis-a-vis* the federal government in educational planning. Largely a product of the Governor's Conference, the new compact sets up tensions of its own between political and educational hierarchies at the state levels. But even in its early stages of formation, the compact has facilitated horizontal communications about educational matters among a number of states and regions. Many of these preliminary communications have revolved around problems of ESEA implementation and revision.

Thermidor: Keppel and Loomis Depart

Bureaucratic survival through accommodations to external pressures in the process of policy implementation is not the same thing, however, as personal survival. For the strains of these accommodations, and the trauma of internal reorganization, produced what observers of the French Revolution once called a "Thermidorean [counter] reaction."

A year after the passage of ESEA, neither Keppel nor Loomis was in the Office of Education. They left with neither a bang nor a whimper, but with self-analytical dignity. In the process of masterminding revolutionary legislative and administrative changes, they had inevitably used up reservoirs of goodwill—externally and internally. Internally, powerful old-timers had been shifted down, sideways, kicked upstairs, or induced to resign. They and their friends in Congress and in influential groups outside the government had been hurt or angered. Externally, special heat had been engendered by the attempted enforcement of Title VI of the Civil Rights Act of 1964. Southern reactions were particularly bitter, but they were not unique.

In September 1965 Keppel had had the temerity to hold up a grant for the Chicago school system on the issue of possible *de facto* segregation. Whether he deliberately avoided prior political clearance at the White House level, or thought it unnecessary, is still unclear. In any case, he ran smack into the buzz saw of big power politics. Mayor Daley, the plitical boss of Cook County, called the President; the President called Keppel on the carpet and told him to adjust this one fast. The President acted in part from his knowledge that the Attorney General had advised Keppel that Keppel's letter to Daley was legal unenforceable. The funds were released pending a further study and clarification of the racial policies of the Chicago school system, but Keppel refused to apologize publicly to the mayor, as Daley desired, and the Commissioner's currency with the President was not enhanced by the episode.

It is easy, of course, to make too much of this one event. The overall relationship of Keppel to the President had been one of mutual respect and support. Keppel was far too sophisticated and inner-directed to take offense at being strongly overruled on a political issue by the nation's chief executive, especially since Keppel's action had been legally questioned by the Attorney General. But symbolically the Chicago episode was important. It was a reminder to Keppel that a new face, unscarred by the external and internal battles of the years of revolution, was needed to consolidate gains, to win back traditional friends who had been hurt or alienated by the course of rapid change, to tidy up the battlefield. He convinced his old friend, now Secretary of HEW, John Gardner, of the wisdom of this course. The exit was graceful, via a brief tour as an Assistant Secretary in HEW with government-wide responsibilities for securing inter-departmental and inter-agency coordination in the field of education.

In January 1966 the new Commissioner of Education, Harold Howe II, was appointed. He had been handpicked by Gardner and Keppel, but he came with impeccable schoolmen's credentials. In background and personality, he represented a bridge between the new educational establishment and the old. Unlike either Keppel or Loomis, he had spent his mature years as a school superintendent. In temperament, he was a Newfoundland, compared to Keppel's Greyhound or Loomis' Belgian Police.

Loomis left in March, one year after he had arrived. His basic job, in his own eyes, had only begun. A sizable operation remained—especially in finding top-quality personnel for the unfilled slots in the Office T/O, and in creating an effective field organization. Basic managerial patterns had been set, new people hired, and a new organizational structure created. Yet the unfinished administrative agenda was still enormous. But internal and external political pressures were running at gale force. They blew him out the door. Lacking presidential confidence, and sensing increasing antipathies in Congress, among educational-professional associations, and within USOE itself, Loomis recognized that his future career would be more viable outside the federal government.

Conclusions

Many aspects of the politics of policy implementation remain untold in this brief summary. The day-to-day interaction with Congress and the President has only been hinted at, and nothing has been said about the hearings on the renewal and revision of the Act in the spring of 1966, or about the consequences of Adam Clayton Powell's early insistence that a Negro be hired to head at least one of the top bureaus in the reorganized USOE. (None had as of September 1966.)

The fact is that education has now become a large element in the congressional pork barrel. From now on, the problem for Presidents, faced with the costs of international conflict and the dangers of domestic inflation, will be less to induce congressional support for education than to keep congressional action within fiscal and budgetary bounds. Educational interests are far-flung; educators are frequently powerful public opinion formers; the costs of education are mounting; the support of education is increasingly safe and sure politically. Every senator and most congressmen have both elementary and secondary schools and the public or private institutions of higher education in their bailiwicks. There is no reason to believe that local protests against higher levies on property and sales taxes for education will diminish, or that states will move toward massively increased revenues for education with any great delight. The number of local, state, and university lobbies in Washington is mounting in almost direct proportion to the increase in federal spending for Great Society programs. At some critical point, what starts as presidential initiative becomes a self-generating congressional force. This happened long ago in the fields of health research and related health services. There are many who feel that this has already happened in key areas of defense hardware and federal paybills. It has most certainly happened in education. This strange reversal of roles on questions of fiscal prudence has received less attention by political science than it deserves. Department secretaries and agency heads who are dedicated to particular program areas are placed in the increasingly difficult role of supporting a parsimonious President against insistent congressional attempts to go beyond presidential requests in supporting the programs in question.

Nor has space permitted a full discussion of the politics of inter-agency adjustment and coordination in the process of policy implementation. In the case of USOE, the most difficult problems of intra- and inter-governmental program coordination have involved the Office of Economic Opportunity (especially Operation Headstart) and other agencies concerned with the war against poverty. But these are only the areas of *critical* overlap. Education is deeply involved in every aspect of human resource development. Few agencies of government at federal, state, and local levels are unrelated to human resource development. As social planning comes to equal physical planning as a key concern of government at all levels, USOE will find it increasingly necessary to devote substantial energy to problems of cooperative program planning and inter-governmental coordination. This, in turn, raises basic questions about the place of education in the macro-institutional structure of the federal government. Should the Office of Education become a cabinet department? A non-cabinet department within a Department of Defense-type structure in HEW? An independent agency subordinate to a National Board of Regents and one step removed from direct political control by either the President or Congress? Part of the politics of rapid growth is the emergence of questions of this type. And, of course, these questions raise even more basic questions about the impact of USOE upon traditional centers of educational policy-making in the nation.[21]

Finally, nothing has been said about the political tensions engendered by new information systems, and by Bureau of the Budget demands that defense-type systems of program planning and budgeting be developed throughout the government. USOE is struggling with these questions of policy implementation as this paper is being written. In retrospect, it will probably appear that the massive funding of education is a far easier exercise than the assessment and evaluation of the resulting programs. In establishing techniques of analysis and criteria of evaluation, USOE faces both a vertical and a horizontal problem. Vertically, the issue is how to establish an information system and a cost-benefit matrix which will relate the statistical and analytical habits and capabilities of 23,000 school districts in 50 different states to four operating bureaus within USOE, to the department-wide systems developed in the Office of the Secretary of HEW, and to the requirements of the Bureau of the Budget and the President. Horizontally, the question is how to set up evaluative indices which are acceptable to all the other federal agencies concerned with educational programs. And this assumes, of course, that the process of education is susceptible to scientific and quantitative, as opposed to judgmental and qualitative, assessment. It is no great task to prove that Johnny can or cannot read better with the passage of time and a chance of tutelage. But how does one establish a cost-benefit ratio for pure research? Can the quality and importance of aesthetic creativity and appreciation be assessed— no matter how elaborate the information systems and program planning and budgeting systems of wide, as well as detailed, applicability, how can the fundamental political questions of wise resource allocation be answered? The accounting aspects of the problem are simple compared to the conceptual problems inherent in applying cost-benefit analyses to soft services.

FOOTNOTES

[1] Public Law 89-10, 89th Cong., 1st Sess.

[2] *United States Government Organization Manual 1965-1966* (Washington: U.S. Government Printing Office, 1965), p. 254.

[3] For an example of these irritations, see Inter-University Case Program CPAC Case No. 16, *The Office of Education Library* by Corinne Silverman (Indianapolis: The Bobbs-Merrill Company, Inc.).

[4] What fraction depends upon whose statistics are used. Congresswoman Edith Green set the total federal expenditures for education in 1962 at $2.2 billion; HEW set it for that same year at more than $3.5 billion. Cf. U.S. House of Representatives, *The Federal Government and Education,* House Doc. No. 159, 88th Cong., 1st Sess. (Washington: U.S. Government Printing Office, 1963). p. 115; and U.S. Department of Health, Education, and Welfare, *Progress of Public Education in the United States of America 1963-1964* (Washington: U.S. Government Printing Office, 1964), p. 17.

[5] U.S. House of Representatives, *The Federal Government in Education, op. cit.,* p. 1, 115. The nine were Agriculture, AEC, Defense, NASA, NSF, NIH, PHS, USOE, and the Office of Vocational Rehabilitation.

[6] For a useful summary of the emerging interest of the federal government in education, see *Federal Role in Education* (Washington: Congressional Quarterly Service, 1965). An annotated summary of relevant laws appears in Michael Kursh, *The United States Office of Education* (Philadelphia and New York: Chilton Books, 1965), pp. 143-148.

[7] See, for example, Frank Munger and Richard T. Fenno, Jr., *National Politics and Federal Aid to Education* (Syracuse: Syracuse University Press, 19610; H. Douglas Price, "Race, Religion, and the Rules Committee: The Kennedy Aid to Education Bills," in Alan F. Westin, ed., *The Uses of Power* (New York: Harcourt, Brace, and World, Inc., 1961); and Robert Bendiner, *Obstacle Course on Capitol Hill* (New York: McGraw-Hill Book Co., 1964).

[8] See Frank Munger, "The Politics of Federal Aid to Education," a paper presented for delivery at the 1965 Annual Meeting of the American Political Science Association, Sheraton-Park Hotel, Washington, D.C., September 8-11, esp. pp. 9-12.

[9] In 1961, for fear the Rules Committee would block his legislative program, Kennedy sought and received the help of Speaker Sam Rayburn in enlarging and liberalizing the Rules Committee. But in the 1961 struggle, even the key liberals who were Catholic voted to bottle up the President's Education bill. In 1965, however, these same liberals voted with a slim majority to report out the Elementary and Secondary Education Act submitted by President Johnson.

[10] See especially Stephen K. Bailey, *The New Congress* (New York: St. Martin's Press, 1966), Ch. VI.

[11] "Poor" is described in terms of the number of families with an annual income below $2,000. A district qualified if at least 100 children came from such families, or if three per cent of the school-age population came from such families and more than ten children were involved. See Section 203, S.370, 89th Cong., 1st Sess.

[12] A year earlier, Senator Wayne Morse had recommended tieing educational aid to "poverty." Under Executive discipline, Keppel could not support the notion at that time, but the USOE staff was stimulated to pursue the implications of Morse's suggestion.

[13] During consideration in the House, in order to meet group interests and possible Constitutional objections to granting federal money to church-related schools, provision was made that local public school agencies would retain title to facilities and books provided to parochial schools under Titles I and II of the Act.

[14]Congressional Quarterly Serivce, *op cit.,* The Elementary and Secondary Education Act of 1965, p. 45.

[15]Note especially National Advisory Committee on Education, *Federal Relations to Education* (Washington: U.S. Government Printing Office, 1931); U.S. Advisory Committee on Education, *The Federal Government and Education* (Washington: U.S. Government Printing Office, 1938); U.S. Advisory Committee on Education, *Staff Study Number 2* (Washington: U.S. Government Printing Office, 1938-1939); U.S. National Resources Planning Board, *Research—A National Resource* (Washington: U.S. Government Printing Office, 1938-1941); Francis Chase, *Report on Administrative Survey of the U.S. Office of Education of the Federal Security Agency* (Chicago: Public Administration Service, 1950); U.S. Committee for the White House Conference on Education, *Report of the White House on Education* (Washington: U.S. Government Printing Office, 1955); and the U.S. Office of Education Committee on Mission and Organization, *A Federal Education Agency for the Future* (Washington: U.S. Government Printing Office, 1961). I have drawn particularly upon the classified reports of the White House Task Force on Education (the so-called Ink Committee), appointed by President Johnson on April 15, 1965. See below.

[16]Since the Ink Committee reports are still classified, I shall not identify precise references.

[17]An interesting example of the new centralization was the Congressional Correspondence Unit set up to handle mail from Capitol Hill. Instead of the 10-20 letters per month handled by the legislative staff in 1961, approximately 1,100 per month were processed by late 1965. Most of the increase resulted from widened congressional interest in USOE, although some of it was merely a drawing-in of mail previously scattered through 30 or 40 organizational units—all of which had formerly answered congressional mail in any manner they pleased without centralized policy direction

[18]John F. Hughes, Director of Program Operations for USOE's Bureau of Elementary and Secondary Education, warned state and local officals about the "assembly line" project mock-ups of educational suppliers. See U.S. Congress, *Hearings* Before the Subcommittee on Education of the Committee on Labor and Public Welfare, U.S. Senate, 89th Cong., 2d Sess., p. 1331.

[19]See Titles I and III, Public Law 89-10, 89th Congress, 1st Sess.

[20]For the impact of new federal programs upon the traditional role of local school boards in making educational policy, see Roald F. Campbell, "Federal Impact on School Board Decision-making," a paper prepared for the Cubberly Conference, Stanford, California, July 26-28, 1966.

ESEA—THE OFFICE OF EDUCATION ADMINISTERS A LAW*

Stephen K. Bailey and Edith K. Mosher

Program execution is at the very heart of the administrative process. An agency's top leaders may participate actively in program formulation, in legislative in-fighting, in making structural changes in the agency's organization; but these activities simply set the conditions and the framework within which the overwhelming majority of the agency's personnel fulfill their operating functions.

The carrying out of a new legislative mandate is rarely simple. Laws are neither self-explanatory nor self-executing in any detailed sense. And laws aimed at providing massive new services in a complex and pluralistic Federal system are particularly difficult to render operational. The process, in David Truman's phrase, of "finding a way of turning the controversial into the routine"[1] is itself far from routine. It involves creative acts of discretionary judgment; an endless interplay with affected clients in the development, interpretation, and modification of ground rules; an elaborate system of data gathering, analysis, and reporting for purposes of administrative and fiscal accountability as well as program execution; a constant sensitivity to demands by executive and legislative superiors, as well as by group interests and the press, for explanations of actions taken or contemplated; resiliency in dealing with the ambiguous functions of statutory or ad hoc advisory committees and panels; and an almost infinite capacity for adjusting to policy modifications imposed by political necessity or induced by administrative experience.

All this must occur within a general framework of predictability, consistency, and equity in the application of the law.

The actions of Federal officials are, of course, partly predictable. They are constrained by specific provisions of enabling and appropriations acts and by statements in congressional hearings, reports, and debates. Related statutes and precedents impose government-wide, standardized procedures for many of the administrative operations. Even when a statute leaves much to administrative discretion, the manner in which it will be executed may be anticipated from a knowledge of the relevant policy issues, the key political actors and interest groups, and the past performance of the agency—especially if its leaders took an active part in drafting and obtaining passage of the legislation.

*From *The Office of Education Administers a Law* by Edith K. Mosher and Stephen K. Bailey, Syracuse University Press, 1968, pp. 98-103; 109-119.

Probabilities, however, are not certainties. The accidents and dynamics of administration produce unique and unpredictable developments. When, as in the case of ESEA, a law unprecedented in scope has to be administered through State and local instrumentalities, on an impossible time schedule; by an understaffed agency in structural turmoil, beset by a deluge of complaints and demands for clarification of the legislation at hand, as well as cognate legislation already on the books; the wonder is not that mistakes are made—the wonder is that the law is implemented at all. Those who took delight in pointing out the inadequacies and deficiencies of USOE in carrying out ESEA during the first year of operations rarely stopped to examine the immensity of the task or the complexity of the context.

It is not surprising to find that the initial euphoric reaction of schoolmen to the passage of ESEA gave way, in many cases, to misunderstanding, confusion and disenchantment. Congressional consideration of ESEA had progressed so rapidly that few State and local school authorities understood the Act's specific provisions or its thrust toward certain basic educational changes. Schoolmen were dismayed to learn that ESEA was not "general aid." They were confused by the technicalities involved in eligibility; they were overwhelmed by the amount of paper-work required.

The general task of the USOE staff was to define the options available to the State educational agencies and/or the local educational agencies or other grantees, and to deal with the technical and political dilemmas posed by the statute in ways that would be likely to enlist the understanding, concurrence, and enthusiasm of these partner-clients. The matters to be considered were themselves likely to create controversy among the partners. For example: how could USOE be specific, even coercive, with regard to fiscal accounting, and at the same time be flexible and permissive in establishing criteria for local project design? How could project criteria be made universally applicable to school districts whose characteristics varied on every conceivable dimension, without stating criteria in terms either too vague or too detailed? What degree of uniformity in applying national standards should be expected or required from ESEA officials?

The implementation stage offered Federal officials their most important opportunity to exercise initiative and foresight in exploring policy alternatives, in ventilating controversies, and in testing strategies for obtaining a high degree of voluntary compliance with legislative intent. But implementation was fraught with dilemmas and uncertainties. The problems of implementation differed to some extent from title to title, but some tasks were common to all of the titles: hard and hectic staff work by program officials and legal talent within USOE and HEW, in the preparation of regulations and guidelines, questionnaires, and application and report forms; circuit riding by USOE staff, and both informal and formal "feedback" colloquies with professional associations and state and local educational officials in the paper planning and modification process; answering thousands of questions and requests for information coming directly by mail, telephone, or personal visitations—or indirectly through congressional or White House channels.

All involved, at some point, the cooperation and scrutiny of advisory councils, committees, and/or screening panels—ad hoc and statutory; and ultimately, a series of reviews by congressional subcommittees and by the less formal instruments of a free press and an inquiring academic and professional community.

What varied from title to title were the precise objectives and their attendant and peculiar administrative aspects; the locus of responsibility within USOE; the combination of agencies, public and private, charged with administering each title; the clientele; and the peculiar mix of what Gabriel Almond has called in another context "the attentive public."

In order to avoid undue repetition, major attention is given in this chapter to the implementation of one title only: Title I. Brief mention will be made of the other titles of ESEA and of the peculiar issues surrounding the implementation of Title VI of the Civil Rights Act of 1964. But Title I was by far the largest and most pervasive program under ESEA. The story of its implementation includes processes and problems which were in fact generic to ESEA as a whole.

Implementing Title I: The Setting

The scope of the task of administering Title I of ESEA was unprecedented. Subject to qualifying conditions for approvable projects, nearly 25,000 school districts in 54 States and territories were entitled to spend more than a billion dollars within 15 months, on a specifically targeted group: the educationally disadvantaged. For the initiation of the program to be smoothly integrated with preparations for the school year beginning in September, 1965, the tool-up period for school officials would have been, theoretically, the last three months of FY'65 (April—June) and the first quarter of FY'66, (July—September 1965). But monies for the Act were not even appropriated until September 23, 1965. To launch such an enormous undertaking would take at the very least a number of months. As a result, those responsible were beset not only by the inherent size and difficulties of tasks of implementation but also by mounting pressures to overcome a serious time-lag in putting the funds to work before the statutory deadlines for their expiration. The months spent in gearing up would bring the calendar closer and closer to the end of the fiscal year in which the money was to be spent.

These tight realities were further complicated by the fact that the enactment of Title I found educators, including those in USOE, in a poor state of readiness to move rapidly in carrying out its unfamiliar demands. To begin with, Title I was targeted to the very group of students for which traditional local school services had been least satisfactory. Although a few districts had had special programs to meet the needs of educationally disadvantaged children, these efforts had provided little certainty as to what activities were really effective. Furthermore, there was a widespread shortage of personnel qualified to plan and operate such projects. In fact, many districts entitled to Title I funds had no previous experience in carrying out federally-connected projects of any kind.

These general handicaps were substantial in themselves. However, as knowledge of the provisions of Title I became more widespread, it was apparent to local school administrators that other headaches were involved. The requirements that Title I projects be designed to meet the needs of educationally disadvantaged children, and be of appropriate size, scope, and quality, clearly implied that the services provided would have to be additional to, but not isolated from, the regular school offerings for such children. And the statutory emphasis on measuring the educational achievement of the beneficiaries of Title I projects appeared to lead in the direction of a national assessment of a school's effectiveness—a development long feared and resisted by school administrators throughout the country.

Hope, anxiety, uncertainty, inexperience, and fear at the local level comprised the intellectual and emotional setting within which USOE and SEA's had to implement much of the new experiment in national educational policy represented by Title I of ESEA.

ESEA Task Force Activities, April to June, 1965

Even though the reorganization of USOE was not to be completed before June 15, structural arrangements were made in mid-April to handle the initial tasks of implementing ESEA. The Executive Group set up a special Planning Group under the chairmanship of Russell Wood, then in the Office of Administration, later Acting Director of the Office of Program Planning and Evaluation. Task forces were organized for each of the ESEA titles, with staffs of 10 to 12 persons selected from throughout the agency for their competency in the various areas relevant to each title. In addition, three specialized subgroups were designated to work on services common to the implementation of all the titles: i.e., data sources and needs, form design, and fiscal requirements. The Executive Group assigned the highest priority to the preparations to launch Titles I and V—Title I because of its size and complexity; Title V because of the patent necessity of strengthening the administrative capacity of State educational agencies for their role in implementing new Federal programs including Titles I and II of ESEA.

The specific mission of the Title I Task Force was to develop regulations, guidelines, and the official forms required to administer the largest of the ESEA programs.

Other immediate USOE responsibilities for Title I were handled outside the task forces. For example, the National Center for Educational Statistics was made responsible for working with the Bureau of the Census and the Welfare Administration of HEW in bringing together the data required by the Title I formula. The appointment of the National Advisory Council, required by Section 212 of the Act, received top level attention in the Office of the Commissioner. During May, Associate Commissioner Reed, the former Deputy Commissioner, planned a series of regional meetings of leading school administrators, state and local, at which various high ranking officials of USOE explained the new legislation. As coordinator of the ESEA task forces, Wood periodically reported their problems and progress to the Executive Group, transmitted clarifications of policy decisions to the task forces, and saw to it that they held to specified deadlines.

Title I: A Summary of Sequence

The tasks of the Office of Education in implementing Title I may be grouped under the following classifications: (1) the development of standards and procedures for the funding and control of authorizations; (2) the construction of ground rules and guidelines for educational programming and project design; and (3) the preparation and analysis of reports and other informational and administrative data. These activities are logically sequential in the sense that funding-authorizations and program regulations are essential for subsequent official action, and reports must be based on some period of program execution. However, in the shaping of Title I, anticipatory and unofficial actions became important preludes to official decisions and rule-making. To illustrate, USOE officials held the first round of a series of regional meetings in May, 1965, to provide advance information to, and seek advice from, the educational community at a time when the preparation of official guidelines was just getting started. During the summer of 1965, official guidelines were actually drafted. In November, 1965 a number of USOE officials attended the annual conference of the Council of Chief State School Officers in Honolulu. This participation led shortly thereafter to some official changes in the Title I guidelines. The entire cycle of pre-clearance, official drafts, and post-clearance was reactivated on a small scale when Title I was amended in October, 1965 to include handicapped children in state-supported institutions.

Title I: Ground Rules for Educational Programming and Project Design[2]

Sections 205 and 206 of Title I dealt with program administration and set forth the respective responsibilities of the USOE, and SEA's, and the LEA's. These sections contain the statutory basis for altering the relationships among the three levels of government, for adding new dimensions to federally-funded school aid programs, and for USOE's unprecedented discretionary power in developing administrative ground rules. Specifically, the Commissioner of Education was authorized to establish criteria for State approval of LEA grant applications (Section 205 (a)) and to decide on the details necessary for approval of State applications to participate in the Title I program (Section 206 (a)). USOE officials were, in fact, charged with clarifying ambiguous legislative language relating to some of the most sensitive areas of school management. Just as the drafting of ESEA involved a delicate balance of intergovernmental interests, so the development of ground rules became a matter of vital concern to all the affected groups. Considerations of program administration and educational politics can scarcely be separated in the analysis of the rule-making task.

Development of Regulations and Guidelines

The official promulgation of *Regulations* and *Guidelines* for Title I was given highest priority as soon as the act was passed. From April to December, 1965, this task involved a painstaking process of intra-agency collaboration and of consultations with interested outsiders. A succession of draft documents was prepared. Although the two publications, *Regulations* and *Guidelines,* were interdependent in content and required the joint effort of lawyers and program specialists, they were technically distinct in regard to purpose and mode of preparation.

Under the Administrative Procedures Act of 1946, agency regulations are promulgated by the President and have the status of Federal law. They are the vehicle for specifying how a statute will be put into effect and may include any supplementary rules the statute instructs the agency to establish for this process. The statutory language is closely followed, although it may be amplified, and the sections of the law may be rearranged for greater clarity and for conformity to the government-wide codification scheme of the *Federal Register.* The drafting task calls for a legal counsel highly skilled in administrative law, aided by experienced program specialists. Their work may be somewhat simplified in the case of a statute like Title I of Public Law 89-10, which is technically an amendment to a previous law, because it is then possible to incorporate applicable definitions and other provisions verbatim from previously existing regulations. It is desirable to keep elaborations of policy or details of administrative procedures to a minimum in the Regulations, since a long process of official clearance is required to amend them in any particular.

Guidelines also express binding Federal policy in the sense that they must be completely consistent with the relevant statute and the regulations. But they are issued on the lesser authority of an agency head and may be amended at his discretion. They are a less legalistic and formal set of instructions, and responsibility for their preparation falls largely to program officials directly in charge of the administration of the law. These officials have considerable latitude in the kinds of content that will be included, such as operating standards, required procedures and forms, allowable deviations, hortatory and precautionary statements, etc. In general, Guidelines comprise relatively long-term directives in comparison with more ephemeral materials issued as ad hoc memoranda or as supplementary publications dealing with matters of specific moment.

Largely at the urging of the HEW legal advisors, the *Regulations* were restricted as closely as possible to statutory language and to the statement of concrete fiscal standards, such as those involved in making the sub-county fund allocations. Specific criteria for project approval and for detailed fiscal procedures, on the other hand, were reserved for the *Guidelines*. The *Regulations* were developed swiftly, and they were made ready for a first review by outsiders at all-day meetings of the Council of Chief State School Officers on June 24 and 25, 1965. During July and August subsequent drafts were reviewed by several of the interest groups concerned with the church-state issue, and the final version of the *Regulations* was distributed in typescript to the SEA's on August 26. Official publication of the *Regulations* in the *Federal Register* appeared on September 15.

In the meantime, agency personnel worked on the *Guidelines* and on a proposed project application form. A draft of the latter was also sent to the States on August 26.

A 76-page preliminary version of the *Guidelines* was first distributed and discussed at five regional meetings held between October 14 and 29. These conferences, dubbed "road shows," were first used in connection with the Higher Education Act of 1963. They involved the majority of the DPO professional staff and more than 500 State and local officials, including school administrators, finance officers, OEO field personnel, and a few representatives of private schools. This first draft of the *Guidelines* was vulnerable to criticism. It was long, discursive, and, in some ways, insensitive to State and local fears of "Federal control." The following is one example of tactless phrasing:

> Without these criteria [for ranking] the State educational agency has no basis to judge whether the local educational agency is fulfilling its obligation, and therefore, the State educational agency cannot approve the project applications without violating its assurance to the U.S. Commissioner of Education.[3]

While many State and local conferees found the meetings a useful and constructive experience, others used the opportunity to air various complaints not only to Federal officials but to the press and to members of Congress.

In early November, the Commissioner and a number of top USOE executives attended the CCSSO meeting in Honolulu. On that occasion the CCSSO adopted the following resolution:

> . . . We call upon the U.S. Commissioner of Education and all federal officials dealing with state departments of education to curtail federal discretion to that necessary under the laws. We believe state departments of education should assume full responsibility for their increasing functions. Federal administrative power of approval or disapproval should not be used to induce state departments to act or refrain from acting on matters not legally relevant to the matter under consideration for possible approval by the federal officials.[4]

Behind this verbiage lay numerous outspoken expressions of opposition to specific provisions of the Title I draft guidelines—expressions addressed to USOE officials in the conference sessions. In consequence, USOE acceded to a meeting in Washington on November 23, to permit a final review of the document by Chief State School Officers. Seventeen of the CSSO responded to the invitation to send representatives. Following the Washington meeting, the draft guidelines were again rewritten, and typewritten copies of the final version were sent to the States on December 3. With the exception of the targeting issue, which will be discussed below, few changes in substance were made in the final draft, but the document was considerably condensed and revised editorially, especially the sections on project design and evaluation which were placed after, instead of before, the section on fiscal administration—presumably in order to reduce their prominence.

Although the careful drafting and advance clearances of the *Regulations* and *Guidelines* produced documents which, in the main, were generally acceptable, the length of time required for this process caused a delay of several months before reasonably complete Federal ground rules were generally available to educators. An additional complication arose when several of the more aggressive SEA's followed a suggestion in a memorandum from Commissioner Keppel in July, 1965, that they prepare their own guidelines. When these were distributed before the USOE draft guidelines were completed, conflicts arose over differing SEA and Federal interpretations of project design requirements.

On the other hand, the time-consuming process of consultation served several useful, and probably indispensable, purposes in Title I implementation. It moderated the charges of arbitrary action by Federal officials; it increased understanding and acceptance of the new educational policies and objectives; and it garnered the benefits of experience which some of the front-running SEA's had gained in attempting to formulate draft guidelines of their own.

There was, however, one underlying tension which was imbedded in the very nature of the statute. Previous Federal aid to education (notably "impacted areas" and NDEA) had given wide discretion to LEA's and SEA's in devising local or State educational plans and programs.

Section 205 and 206 of ESEA Title I, on the other hand, gave most of the responsibility for detailed rule-making to the Federal government. This was perhaps the inevitable concomitant of a statute drawn in part to by-pass State restrictions on aid to church-related schools, and designed to serve the national interest in overcoming the pathologies of educational disadvantage in large cities whose interests had been systematically short-changed by rural-oriented SEA's. But the problems of Federal-State cooperation in attempting to fulfill the requirements of Sections 205 and 206 were neither fully anticipated nor well understood in advance. The "assurances from States" required in Section 206(a), for example, involved an application

"*. . . in such detail as the Commissioner* (U.S.) *deems necessary"* and
"*. . .* annual and *such other reports* to the Commissioner, *in such
form and containing such information* as may be necessary to enable
the Commissioner to perform *his* duties under this Title." (Emphasis
supplied.)

Because of the pressure of time and the need to move money out as quickly as
possible, the Commissioner permitted quite loose "assurances." The operating
effect of this section was, then, to allow States to qualify for funds *before*
providing USOE with staffing, organizational, or procedural commitments. But
combined with Section 205, which specifically moved the initiative for project
approval criteria to the Federal level, the loose construction of Section 206(a) by
the Commissioner prompted the States to busy themselves at the outset with the
task of computing sub-county allocations under the formula, rather than with
developing program instructions. When the Federal *Regulations* and *Guidelines*
were finally issued, most States simply reissued them as constituting the State's
own standards. A few States added various kinds of supplementary content, but
the Federal hand was clearly dominant. It should be remembered, however, that
USOE officials took extraordinary steps to insure State reactions to federally
established ground rules during the process of their construction. When USOE
officials consulted the State staffs, the overriding purpose was to find definitions
and procedures of the widest applicability and utility. Nonetheless, Federal
initiative was paramount.

To maintain influence in this new situation of diminished rule-making authority, the recourse of some SEA's was to work through an interest group structure.
Hence, the militancy of the CCSSO effort to reduce the discretionary authority
of Federal officials to a minimum. The militancy was largely ineffectual, however. Many of the SEA's welcomed USOE guidance; some felt that it did not go
far enough. They recognized that educators would lack guidance for making
consistent and uniform interpretations of the statutory purpose to benefit disadvantaged children, irrespective of locale, unless USOE provided operational mean-
ings for terms like "consistent," "sufficient," "show reasonable promise," and
"reasonably necessary" in Sections 205 and 206.

An example of the manner in which USOE proceeded to define the criteria
for project design is the low priority established for the use of Title I funds to
construct school facilities. The rationale for this federal policy was that the most
pressing needs of disadvantaged children could, and should, be met during FY'66
by educational and supplementary services in "operational" projects. The *Regulations* and the *Guidelines* both provided that a project application could not
cover construction of school facilities except in those exceptional cases in which
construction was demonstrated to be essential to a program or project. To the
SEA's and LEA's hungry for construction funds, the USOE priority for "operational" programs was viewed as a sorry example of Federal insensitivity to local

needs. To USOE staff, constraints upon using federal funds for facilities was simply a prudent way of insuring that ESEA would not become simply a general aid bill for school construction.

Some of these conflicts were in fact foreseen. When the administration bill was initially unveiled, congressional opponents of ESEA mounted an attack on the "unwarranted" expansion of authority given to the Commissioner of Education in connection with Title I. The following exchange occurred during the first day of hearings before the House General Subcommittee on Education in January, 1965:

> Mr. Goodell (Republican from New York) to HEW Secretary Celebrezze: Tell me about "basic criteria" . . . Can you tell me what "basic criteria"—not "control" but "criteria," you are going to impose on the States? . . .
>
> Secretary Celebrezze: We don't impose anything on the States.
>
> Mr. Goodell: They have to submit their plan in conformance to your criteria.
>
> Secretary Celebrezze: They can participate in a program or they don't have to. It is pretty well set out in the Act . . . It is in the law what the States might submit to the Secretary.
>
> Mr. Goodell: You are not telling me when you go to the States now after this law is passed, you are going to say, "Well, now there is the law, and you interpret it the way you want to." You are going to go to them with some specific criteria, if you will, basic criteria. I would like to know what they are . . . It is not what control or criteria you have written into this law, it is what you are going to do when you go there to the States and tell them what they can get money for. What kind of plans will qualify for money. And you won't impose it on them because if they don't want the Federal money, all right, but they all want it.
>
> Mr. Cohen (HEW Assistant Secretary): May I try to clarify one point that I think is related to this . . . I interpret "basic criteria" here as used to be in effect criteria defining what is in 1 to 6 (of Section 205) . . . Let me put it this way: I want to make this clear for the legislative history. "Basic criteria" doesn't mean here that the Commissioner may establish, just out of the blue, elements that he thinks the States have to comply with. "Basic criteria" here means definitions and explanations or guidelines, whatever you want to call them, of the terms and conditions that are specified here . . .
>
> Mr. Goodell: All right. You are going to define it. That means what programs are eligible for funds. You are saying to the State in effect, "This is which program is eligible and which isn't." You can

say it is criteria. I don't care about the term. I would like to know what you have in mind. How much discretion are you going to leave to the States and localities? . . .

Mr. Brademas (Democrat from Indiana): . . . I have the impression we are quarreling about something . . . we don't need to quarrel about. My point is that when we legislate we always talk about criteria.

Mr. Goodell: And that is where we get in trouble. When the Department starts imposing criteria, criteria nobody saw in the law. And it has always happened.[5]

The minority party members of the Senate Labor and Public Welfare Committee succeeded in having incorporated in the Committee report on ESEA a specific constraint on the authority of the Commissioner, as follows:

The minority pointed out that the language of the bill was ambiguous with respect to the authority of the Commissioner of Education under Title I to establish "basic criteria" beyond those stipulated in Section 205(a) to guide State educational agencies in determining whether a local school district's application for aid was satisfactory. The Senate report now acts to restrain the Commissioner from adding criteria beyond those written in the law.[6]

What is clear is that the first year of administering Title I of ESEA dramatized one of the most troublesome issues in Federal-State relations: how to dispense Federal monies for categorical national purposes without undercutting the traditional and decentralized responsibilities of State and local officials.

The Issue of "Targeting"

If the question of the use of funds for school construction dramatized the dilemma, the problem of "targeting" Title I funds (making sure that they were actually addressed to benefiting educationally disadvantaged children) illustrated, in the words of one commentator, how "delicate, difficult, tedious, and quarrelsome"[7] was the business of drawing up regulations and ground rules. During FY'66, "targeting" became a focal issue in the search for viable administrative compromises. USOE officials found themselves in the middle, accused on the one hand of being too liberal in ensuring local autonomy and, on the other, of exceeding their statutory authority.

To ensure that the Federal monies would not be thinly spread over the entire school population and for merely "more of the same" kinds of educational services, the legislative draftsmen of Title I had come up with the following wording for Section 205(a)(1):

. . . that payments under this title will be used for programs and projects . . . (A) which are designed to meet the special educational needs of educationally deprived children in school attendance areas having high concentrations of children from low-income families and (B) which are of sufficient size, scope, and quality to give reasonable promise of substantial progress toward meeting those needs. . . .

This language constituted a tangled skein of geographic, economic, educational, and institutional constraints, but its twin precepts were obvious: first, to reach the children in need; and second, to spend enough on each beneficiary to get results.

The first ground rules with regard to the selection of participants appear in the Title I *Regulations* of September 15, 1965:

The application by a local educational agency for a grant shall designate for each project the project area, which may include one or more school attendance areas with high concentrations of children from low-income families. The project area should, however, be sufficiently restricted in size in relation to the nature of the applicable project as to avoid jeopardizing its effectiveness in relation to the aims and objectives of the project . . . in no event may a school attendance area be designated as a project area if the degree of concentration of such children in the area is less than that of the school district as a whole. In exceptional circumstances, the whole of the school district may be designated as a project area. . . .[8]

The first LEA task in carrying out this rule would be to determine the target pupil pouplations, whether drawn from one or more school attendance areas; the next step would be to design projects of appropriate "size, scope, and quality" for particular children or groups of children from that population. The interdependent determinants were the degree of educational disadvantage of eligible participants, the kinds and costs of services considered most likely to promise progress in meeting their needs, and the amount of Title I funds available. The more children included in a project, or the lower the expenditure per child, the greater would be the dilution of the supplementary funding, and vice versa.

Federal officials were aware that monetary measures were not entirely satisfactory to indicate the quality of service offered to individual children, since there were many kinds of permissible projects which varied in cost factors. However, the administration had originally estimated that Title I projects would involve approximately 5.4 million children at a cost of about $200 each. This represented a rough professional judgment (based on the results of earlier compensatory programs) on the level of spending that would be required to make any substantial improvement in the educational achievement of the average disadvantaged child. It was also estimated that the incidence of "educational disadvantage" throughout the country was greater than that identified by the measures of hard-core poverty in the Title I formula and, further, that Title I funds could not provide all the services needed for target populations.

In an effort to provide the "saturation of services" for the most needy children, the Federal rule-makers included fairly specific rules in the draft of guidelines for the targeting process. The LEA's were to rank school attendance areas on the basis of the number of children from low-income families and then select their project areas in strict rank order of such concentrations. The SEA's were precluded from approving project applications which failed to state the explicit procedure by which project areas had been identified, ranked, and selected. The *Guidelines* also stated that the total LEA program, defined as the sum of its projects, should be designed to serve approximately the number of children that had been used to compute its eligibility for funds.

This effort of Federal officials to interpret the legislative intent of Section 205 (a)(1) had a mixed reception from school administrators. Many urged even more specific instructions from USOE concerning the design of projects that would be of appropriate size, scope, and quality. Others expressed a variety of concerns and complaints. For example, many local administrators objected to the formal ranking procedure for selecting project areas and to singling out some children for greatly increased benefits while excluding others of apparently equal need from any benefits. They argued for the long-standing equity principle that schools should make the same investment of funds in each student, perhaps because they could anticipate criticism in their own communities from parents of children excluded from Title I benefits. And, of course, equivalent expenditures are easier to compute.

While the first of the October "roadshows" was still in progress, Commissioner Keppel received numerous expressions of dissatisfaction with the draft *Guidelines* from educators and Congressmen. The Title I staff urged the retention of strict requirements for targeting on the grounds that these requirements would provide backing to school officials in resisting local pressures to dilute the federally-financed services. However, Keppel had become convinced (perhaps under interest-group and congressional pressure) that the mandatory provisions of both the September edition of the *Regulations* and the proposed *Guidelines* violated the commitment made to the Senate Labor and Public Welfare Committee not to add criteria for project design and approval beyond those in the statute. On basic philosophical grounds, Keppel was also unhappy about the degree of Federal authority and dictation written into the first draft of the *Regulations* and *Guidelines* by BESE. He insisted on the immediate elimination of the statement that LEA's should relate the number of Title I participants to the number of children upon which LEA eligibility had been based, and instructed the staff to develop more permissive statements concerning selection of beneficiaries and per capita concentration of funds.

Accordingly, in the revision of the draft *Guidelines* that followed the regional meetings of school administrators, the Honolulu conference of the CCSSO, and the meeting of State representatives in Washington in late November, 1965, Federal officials agreed to an all-out broadening of SEA and LEA discretion on the targeting issue. The final version of the *Guidelines* called for the ranking procedure to establish eligible project areas, but made its use contingent upon State approval. The extent of the concessions made to critics is well illustrated by the following amendment of Section 116.17 in the March, 1966, revision of the *Regulations:*

> ... A school attendance area for either elementary or secondary schools in which the percentage of children from low-income families is as high as the percentage of such children in the school district as a whole, or in which the number of children from low income families is as large as the average number of such children in the several school attendance areas in the school districts, may be designated as a project are. *Other areas with high concentrations of children from low-income families may be approved as project areas but only if the State agency determines that projects to meet the most pressing needs of educationally deprived children in areas of higher than average concentration have been approved and adequately funded.* (Italics supplied.)

One USOE official commented on the liberalization of the ground rules, "That is when we gave away the ball-game." However, the effect of the change is difficult to assess. The final FY'66 reports indicate that the number of children participating in Title I projects was 8.3 million with an average per capita expenditure of just under $120. This was a much higher coverage and lower per capita expenditure than had originally been contemplated.[9] And top USOE officials became satisfied that the majority of local school administrators identified target populations and project areas in accordance with congressional and USOE intent. Actually, many States adhered to the detailed ranking procedure for school attendance areas when it was no longer mandatory.

Whatever the final assessment of actual practice, the targeting issue proved that the course of negotiating ground rules, like the course of true love, never does run smooth.

FOOTNOTES

[1] See David Truman, *The Governmental Process* (New York: Knopf, 1960).

[2] The term "ground rules" refers both to the substance of program rules (whether issued as formal agency regulations or guidelines, supplementary memoranda, or other instructional formats), and to the procedural relationships established by federal officials to govern their negotiations in carrying out their rule-making tasks.

[3] Draft *Guidelines,* Title I, ESEA.

[4] Resolution VII, adopted at the Annual Business Meeting of the Council of Chief State School Officers, Honolulu, Hawaii, November 12, 1965. 11 pp. mimeo.

[5] *Hearings Before the General Subcommittee on Education, on Aid to Elementary and Secondary Education,* 89th Cong., 1st sess., House, 176-7.

[6] *Report No. 146,* 89th Cong., 1st sess., Senate, 84. In the same report (p. 9) HEW contended that it was unnecessary to include a specific constraint on the commissioner's authority to designate criteria.

[7]Elizabeth Brenner Drew, "Education's Billion Dollar Baby," *The Atlantic Monthly,* July, 1966, 39.

[8]*Code of Federal Regulations,* Title 45, Section 116.17(b).

[9]*Education USA,* National Education Association, April 3, 1967.

THE CASE FOR GENERAL AID*

U.S. Congressman Albert H. Quie

The time for seriously arguing the pros and cons of Federal aid to elementary and secondary schools has come—and gone. Federal financial assistance is here, and, what is more, it is likely to continue for the forseeable future. Education has been viewed traditionally by the American public as a legitimate and major responsibility of the State and local levels of government, but traditional views have, in a sense, been forced to yield to the realities of life—to the irrefutable fact that Federal aid to elementary and secondary education has been initiated and is continuing.

The theme, then, underlying much of the contemporary debate among educational and public policy-makers is this: are we (and should we) continue to move in a direction that is shifting educational decision-making away from its traditional base at the State and local levels and toward the Federal sphere? Phrasing the question in somewhat different terms: must the cost of attaining our national goal of equality and excellence of educational opportunity be at the expense of State and local autonomy, diversity and creativity?

To date, practically all Federal financial assistance in education has been in the form of categorical grants-in-aid. What this means is that the Federal government has identified certain phases of education deemed crucial to the national interests and has earmarked funds for programs designed to strengthen and improve these areas.

Narrow in scope, funded on a short-term basis, and requiring matching State funds as a prerequisite for supplementary Federal assistance, the categorical grant was initially conceived of as a mechanism that would apply the financial muscle of the Federal government to assist the States in meeting their obligations.

Through a liberal interpretation of what may be deemed in the best national interests, Federal authorities have, in rapid succession, identified phase after phase, and implemented program after program, with substantial dollar assistance. This identification process—with its subsequent investments of personnel and financial resources—is equivalent to the establishment of nationwide educational priorities. By staking its claim in a growing number of educational endeavors, the Federal government is assuming the role of the primary educational decision-maker. State and local educators have been virtually denied any meaningful voice in this dialogue. Rather, they have been presented with a *fait accompli* and must try to either satisfy their particular needs within this framework or opt not to receive needed Federal aid.

The categorical grant-in-aid has built-in deficiencies that place these "subordinate" partners at a further disadvantage. By virtue of their narrow dimensions, categorical grants can be awarded only for specific and limited purposes. State educational agencies and local school districts must attempt to accommodate a host of diverse community needs within these confining limitations. Absent is any degree of flexibility. Funds cannot be readily transferred to support needed and specially-designed or tailored programs that digress from within the bounds of the Federal grant program.

In addition, the categorical grants tend to fragment any overall or integrated educational program. Emphasis at the State and local levels shifts to those specific areas in which the Federal government has exhibited a genuine interest and a willingness to invest dollar aid. Planning is not only limited in breadth but also in time. Short-time planning follows in the wake of short-term authorizations of funding. Categorical grants are generally renewed and refunded on an annual basis. From one year to the next, State and local educators do not know whether or not funds will be available. And if funds are to be available, they do not know precisely how much they may expect to receive and when. Because no firm commitments can be made until the Congress has appropriated the requisite funds, planning tends to be sporadic and on a hit-or-miss basis. In a word, educators have no lead-time in planning. Long-term and intelligent planning gives way to "eleventh hour" efforts that fail to make optimum use of resources and to provide the best possible educational experiences.

In recent testimony before the House Education and Labor Committee with regard to proposed amendments to The Elementary and Secondary Education Act of 1965, educator after educator pleaded the case for sustained financial commitments that would pave the way for sound, long-term planning. Typical of the arguments heard were those voiced by Dr. Bernard Donovan, Superintendent of Schools for New York City, who expressed the funding-planning dilemma in these terms:

> There is need for a long-term funding of educational programs. It is difficult for a city to predicate a program upon an annual appropriation without the knowledge that that appropriation will be continued into a succeeding year.
>
> Almost every program involved in Federal legislation requires the appointment of personnel. It is impossible to employ personnel without a reasonable expectation of maintaining the appointment throughout more than the course of one year. Competent personnel are at a premium these days in school systems and it is impossible to attract such

personnel for Federal programs if they feel that their employment is simply on a year-to-year basis. Furthermore, the funding of Federal programs is tied inescapably to the funding of local programs. Good financial planning for school systems requires that sources of funds be known in advance so that effective planning can take place.

The administrative process that accompanies the categorical grant is an extremely cumbersome one. Those charged with the responsibility of implementing educational programs at the State and local levels must devote an inordinate amount of time to satisfying Federally-prescribed "guidelines." Applications for proposed projects must be drawn up and submitted to the appropriate Federal agencies and departments and must be followed by elaborate justifications, accountings and evaluations. The costs of this type of administrative procedure are high. The waste in terms of talent and in terms of taxpayers' dollars defies precise calculation on a nationwide basis.

Poorer and smaller State and local educational agencies just do not have the manpower to satisfy Federal paperwork requirements. Unable to surmount the bureaucratic barriers that confront them, they see Federal moneys awarded to larger and wealthier educational agencies and districts whose needs are not the most urgent and critical. Finally, the State "matching" requirements serve merely to broaden the gap that exists between the wealthy and the poor States.

Thus ironically, we find the Federal government contributing to make the "rich richer and the poor poorer." As long as this situation prevails, we shall fall short in realizing our national goal of affording equal and excellent educational opportunities to all.

An honest and thorough evaluation of the operations of the categorical grant leads to this conclusion: the great expectations originally held out for this mode of Federal financial assistance have not been met. We must, therefore, devise a more viable approach.

In what is commonly referred to as the "block grant," we have a most promising alternative. Moving in the direction of more general aid to education, the block grant appears to be a viable substitute and should alleviate the crippling deficiencies that have seen the categorical grant-in-aid bring chaos, confusion and centralized control into the field of education. Within broadly defined limits, established to guarantee that the legislative intent of the Congress is realized, the block grant would continue to return needed revenue to the State and local municipalities. It would, however, give these parties greater leeway in the application of these funds —leeway that would enable State and local educational authorities to adequately meet their diverse and pressing locally defined needs. State and local educators would again exercise their legitimate function of establishing a hierarchy of educational priorities on the basis of local community needs—a function that has been largely usurped by the Federal level of authority. This approach also envisions a longer-range authorization and appropriation of funds by Congress, thereby paving the way for long-term, comprehensive educational planning at the State and local levels.

This comprehensive plan or blueprint would then become the basis for a State plan which would, in turn, be submitted by the State educational agency to the Federal authorities for their approval. A single State agency would then be dealing directly with its counterpart at the Federal level. This would eliminate much of the administrative red tape and confusion that presently exists when more than 20,000 local school districts and 50 State departments of education attempt to work directly with the Federal agencies and departments.

On the other side of the coin, it would do away with the chaotic and ludicrous spectacle that finds the U.S. Office of Education attempting to process, evaluate, coordinate and approve or reject literally thousands of grant applications from eligible State and local agencies. The U.S. Office of Education simply cannot justify the majority of its actions solely on the basis of what is in the best interests of the local communities that are to be served. It is too aloof from these communities to fully understand and comprehend their specific needs.

By consolidating many small, separate grants into one lump sum award, by expanding the limits within which this money may be utilized, and by assuring the State and local educators who are at once responsive and responsible to the community to be served of a voice in setting forth educational priorities, the block grant concept should be a strong force working to revitalize the role these two levels play in planning.

Only by drawing upon the creative potential and the expertise of the three co-equal partners—Federal, State and local—can we fully develop our greatest national resource, our human resource.

THE CASE FOR CATEGORICAL AID*

U.S. Congressman John Brademas

In recent years Congress has enacted legislation to aid education in a wide variety of ways. The American people, acting through their elected President and Representatives in Congress, have determined to direct Federal funds to help meet critical national needs in education which are not being met effectively from local, state and private sources.

While general Federal aid to education—aid not targeted on critical needs—may be a desirable objective in the long run, I believe it imperative that we maintain for the present the prevailing pattern of categorical aid aimed at specific needs.

Let me here comment on a semantic difficulty in using the terms "general" and "categorical." General aid proponents have fostered the notion that, while categorical programs cover narrow areas of assistance encumbered with many restrictions, general aid offers flexibility free of red tape.

In practice no such clear distinction exists. Many Federal categorical programs incorporate fewer limitations and are nearly as broad as many state general support programs. The Elementary and Secondary Education Act (ESEA), for example, though directed at particular needs, is nevertheless extremely flexible in application and allows state and local authorities wide discretion.

State general aid programs, on the other hand, are often replete with detailed "strings" on curriculum, salaries, classroom size and number of teachers.

Moreover, Congress and the Administration even now are moving to broaden, consolidate and streamline existing categorical programs where appropriate. The Education Professions Development Act of 1967, for example, replaces a number of fragmented legislative authorities for training education personnel at every level with one comprehensive and flexible program.

A second semantic question touches on the allegation that the special purpose education programs passed by Congress in recent years must inevitably bring Federal control of our schools and universities.

Policy-making in education in the United States is so widely dispersed and deeply imbedded in American pluralism that effective control has never been—and never should be—concentrated in one institution or one level of government. Indeed, far from limiting the role of state and local education agencies, Federal aid

*This article appears by permission of and copyrighted by (1967) Visual Products Division, 3M Company, St. Paul, Minnesota. Permission also granted by Rep. John H. Brademas.

programs enacted in recent years have considerably enhanced their opportunities and responsibilities.

The ESEA in particular places initiative and heavy operating responsibility with the grassroots. Title I projects, involving grants to local school districts with concentrations of children from low income families, are drawn up entirely at the local level and approved by state education agencies. Title III programs, aimed at encouraging and supporting educational innovation, also place primary responsibility at the local level. Although the U.S. Office of Education must give final approval to project proposals, the school districts themselves conduct the projects.

Programs of Federal aid to elementary and secondary education, the level at which the greatest controversy arises, have simply not been shown to lead to Federal control of the curriculum, school teachers or educational policies. On the contrary, these Federal programs have served not to restrict but to expand the resources, options and effectiveness of local school agencies.

The specter of Federal domination of the schools through categorical aid has no foundation in fact. "Federal control of education," the shibboleth of those who have long opposed Federal aid altogether and of those who would now convert existing programs into block grants or generalized aid is simply not borne out by the objective record.

Having made these points, I want now to discuss specific reasons for my contention that for the time being it would be unsound and unwise to abandon the present categorical pattern in favor of block grants, as was proposed in some amendments to ESEA this year.

Supporters of such a shift to unrestricted general aid must come to grips with some thorny issues:

1. A renewal of strife over the church-state issue would pose an immediate dilemma. Controversies over this question contributed to the defeat of Federal school aid for many years. The ESEA broke this deadlock in 1965 with the provision that parochial school children could share in the benefits of a number of publicly operated programs authorized under the Act.

Yet the constitutions of over 30 states explicitly prohibit the use of any state funds for the support, direct or indirect, of church-related schools. Block federal grants to the states, to be distributed not on a categorical basis but at the discretion of state agencies, could therefore raise anew the issue of religion. The result could be to create widespread discord and vitiate the cooperative efforts between public and parochial schools that are now taking place under ESEA.

2. Not all states have the capacity to administer effectively a substantial infusion of block grants. Testimony before Congressional committees has shown that many state education agencies are not yet sufficiently equipped with staff and other resources to take on such a major administrative responsibility.

3. As important as personnel shortages and other administrative weaknesses in many states is the traditional unresponsiveness of state governments to the

overwhelming needs of urban school districts. Distribution formulas for state aid to local schools are typically weighted against the cities, thereby short-changing urban school children. By and large state education agencies have not been adequately attuned to the problems of education in our metropolitan areas.

We must not, of course, underestimate the needs of children outside the cities, but it is now clear that we must face up to the grave deficiencies of our inner city schools. The present pattern of distribution of ESEA funds is obviously more promising in this respect than would be a system of general aid channeled through the states.

Inequitable treatment of the cities in programs of state aid historically reflects the influence of rurally dominated state legislatures. And reapportionment of state legislatures will bring no sure remedy in this situation; in fact, the effect of reapportionment appears to be to strengthen the position of suburban interests rather than those of the inner cities. A Carnegie Corporation study in 1966 showed that suburbs received an average of $40 more per pupil in state school aid than the cities, and continued reapportionment is likely to widen this gap still further.

4. The question of school integration is still, 13 years after *Brown vs. the Board of Education of Topeka,* the most sensitive problem, North as well as South, in American elementary and secondary education. It is no secret that some members of Congress favor block grants to the states rather than categorical aid because they believe that state-directed programs offer a more promising refuge from the school desegregation guidelines than do current programs.

Although compliance with Title VI of the Civil Rights Act remains a condition of receiving Federal funds for a wide spectrum of programs, of which education is only one, there is surely little justification for arguing that turning Federal funds over to the states will make easier the effective implementation of either court decisions or legislative actions in resolving this difficult matter.

I should make clear that I am not unsympathetic to some form of general aid at a later date. Given the mounting cost of education and the limited tax resources of state and local governments, it may be essential for the federal government to underwrite the cost of the nation's educational system, providing a common floor of opportunity for every child in the country.

But general aid to the states will not be a sound proposition until the states demonstrate that they have the capacity and willingness to deal with today's critical educational problems. A White House Task Force on Education, in making a preliminary report this past summer, declared that unrestricted block grants are "an ultimately desirable—indeed necessary—objective." The report maintained, however, that this objective must be deferred until state legislatures and educational authorities have reordered their priorities.

If, moreover, general Federal aid to education does come about, it should be in addition to, not in place of, an effective program of categorical aid. General aid must not come at the expense of diverting resources from essential categorical programs aimed at problems that are national in scope.

Secretary of Health, Education and Welfare John Gardner has made clear that he favors continued concentration on programs "directed to targets selected by the elected representatives of the people in the Congress of the United States. They speak for the states and they judge the needs of the states against a background of national priorities.

"As long as Federal resources in the field of education are limited," Secretary Gardner maintains, "they should be used for the elimination of those educational programs which the Congress identifies as the greatest obstacles to the growth and development of our nation."

In the Elementary and Secondary Education Act and other Federal education measures, Congress has defined critical problems in education, and established the means by which Federal funds can be put where they are desperately needed. A hasty conversion to general aid would undercut these goals and slow down the progress made so far under ESEA and other programs.

As a nation, we can ill afford thus to reduce our national commitment to achieving both quality and equality of opportunity in education throughout America.